R. Rogers
1/73

Radar Observation of the Atmosphere

Louis J.
Battan

Radar
Observation
of the
Atmosphere

THE
UNIVERSITY
OF CHICAGO
PRESS
Chicago and
London

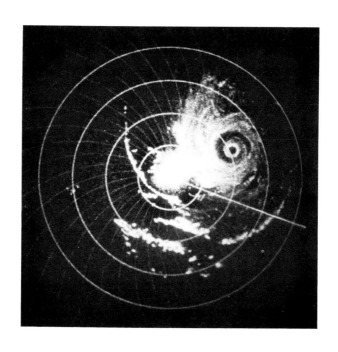

Contents

Preface

This book is an extensive revision of *Radar Meteorology*, which was published in 1959 by the University of Chicago Press. It was decided, because of the substantial new material, to adopt a new title. As before, the author has attempted, in a small volume, to review what is known about the use of microwave radar for observing atmospheric phenomena. This book is intended primarily for use by meteorologists, atmospheric scientists, and students who have had little training in electronics. At the same time, however, this material should be informative to a much broader spectrum of scientists and engineers.

Clearly microwave radar is only one of many available techniques for remote sensing of the atmosphere. The interested reader is referred to *Atmospheric Exploration by Remote Probes*, edited by Atlas (1969) and the April 1969 issue of the *Proceedings of The Institute of Electrical and Electronic Engineers*. Each of these publications contains a collection of papers dealing with a wide spectrum of observational methods. Two relatively new methods deserve particular mention. Over the last decade there has been significant progress in the use of radars which employ lasers as sources of electromagnetic radiation. Such instruments, known as lidars, were discussed in a survey article by Collis (1969). Starting in the late sixties, there has been remarkable progress in the development of Acoustical Echo Sounders. Such devices are sometimes called "acoustical radars" but this is not appropriate because the term radar implies the use of electromagnetic waves. The publications cited above contain articles on acoustical echo sounding. More recent work has been reported by Beran, Little and Willmarth (1971), Beran and Clifford (1972) and Hooke, Young and Beran (1972).

In the sixties considerable progress was made in the development of data reduction, analysis, and display techniques. Some thought was given to the inclusion of a chapter devoted entirely to such developments. In the end, it was decided to insert information on new techniques and instrumentation at appropriate places throughout the book when discussing the principles of observation, data analysis or interpretation.

ix

A great deal of information has been compressed into relatively few pages. Some readers may want to learn much more about certain topics. This can be done by examining the relevant references.

Louis J. Battan

1 Principles of Radar

Radar has been defined as "the art of detecting by means of radio echoes the presence of objects, determining their direction and range, recognizing their character and employing the data thus obtained." In radar meteorology the term "object" is construed to mean anything in the atmosphere which returns to a receiver a detectable amount of power. Thus, in the study of radar meteorology one must consider the reflections by raindrops, cloud droplets, ice particles, snowflakes, atmospheric nuclei, insects, birds, and regions of large index-of-refraction gradients. It is well to point out here that the source of the scattered power, regardless of its properties, may be called a "target."

Radar is based on the principle that an electromagnetic wave is propagated through space at the speed of light, 2.998×10^8 m/sec. The variation in this velocity in the atmosphere is small and predictable, if one knows the distribution of the index of refraction of the medium through which the wave is propagated. In most applications one can consider that the radar wave moves at the speed of light, taken to be 3×10^8 m/sec, and travels along straight lines. Thus, by means of an antenna producing a narrow beam in the manner of a searchlight beam, one can scan with the antenna until a reflection is obtained and determine the direction to the reflecting object. Also, by measuring the time interval between the transmission of the radio energy and the reception of the reflected signal, one can easily calculate the distance to the object.

For many purposes, a radar set can be considered to consist essentially of a transmitter, which produces power at the radar frequency; an antenna, which radiates the power and intercepts the reflected signals; a receiver, which detects, amplifies, and transforms the received signals into video form; and an indicator on which the returned signals can be displayed. The operation of a simple radar set is illustrated in figure 1.1. Most weather-radar sets employ a single antenna for both transmission and reception. An automatic switch is used to close off the receiver during the short interval when the transmitter is operating and protects the receiver from the tremendous pulse of transmitted power. For a detailed discussion of radar systems see Skolnik (1962).

1

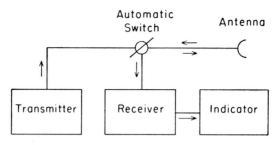

Fig. 1.1.   Block diagram of radar set

    With most radar sets, the frequency of operation is fixed, and, generally, the source of the microwaves is a special tube called a "magnetron." For the system to operate properly, the radar receiver must be tuned to the magnetron frequency.

    An important characteristic of a radar receiver is its so-called minimum detectable signal, i.e., the smallest signal which can be detected above the noise level. There are various schemes for detecting very weak signals. One of them involves long-period averaging, which acts to amplify a steady signal with respect to randomly varying noise signals. Another technique for increasing the sensitivity of a radar receiver is to use a maser preamplifier (Skolnik 1962). The term "maser" is an acronym for "microwave amplification of stimulated emission of radiation." In essence, it is a low-temperature, radio-frequency amplifier producing very small noise signals. Robbiani (1965) described a maser which increased a receiver sensitivity by a factor of about 18.

    Radar receivers usually are designed to have as low a minimum detectable signal as possible. In many receivers it is of the order of 10^{-13} w. On the other hand, the peak power transmitted is always quite high and may be of the order of 100 kw.

    Because of the large range of powers dealt with in radar systems, e.g., 10^{-13} to 10^6 w, it is common to express power in terms of decibels (dB). The difference in dB between power levels P_1 and P_0 is given as

$$p \text{ (dB)} = 10 \log_{10} \frac{P_1}{P_0}. \tag{1.1}$$

Note that the decibel measures a *difference* in power. It is usual in electronics work to take P_0 equal to a milliwatt, and hence p would be the power level of P_1 in decibels with respect to a milliwatt, designated as dBm. The minimum detectable signal of a receiver and the peak transmitted power might be -100 dBm and 90 dBm, respectively.

    The sensitivity of a radar receiver can be changed by means of the gain control. For any setting of the gain control, the range of signals which can be distinguished on a radarscope is usually small compared with the range of signals received from weather phenomena. If the receiver gain is adjusted so that weak signals are detected, strong ones may saturate the system and be cut off. The range of signal detection is called the "dynamic range" of the radar system. To increase the dynamic range, various schemes have been devised by which weak signals are amplified more than the strong ones.

A radar set such as the one blocked out in figure 1.1 is called a "noncoherent radar." In such equipment, no account is taken of the phase of the returning radar wave with respect to the phase of the transmitted wave. Most radar sets now in use for weather observations are of this type, and therefore noncoherent radars are sometimes called "conventional radars." As already noted, they supply information on the position of a target and its radar reflectivity. By means of special techniques to be described later, one may obtain limited information about the movements of aggregate targets such as raindrops.

A class of radar sets referred to as "coherent" or "Doppler" radars makes use of the Doppler principle. These instruments, in addition to obtaining the data collected by a noncoherent radar, also measure the velocity of the targets along the radar beam axis. Doppler radar sets will be discussed in some detail in chapter 8. At this point, it is adequate to note that the velocity measurements are made by noting the rate of change of the difference in phase between the outgoing and received signals. As a target moves, the phase changes at a rate proportional to the velocity of the target toward or away from the radar.

In most radar sets, the transmitted power is in the form of pulses of radio waves of short duration (e.g., 1 μsec). The frequency at which pulses are emitted is known as the "pulse-repetition frequency," PRF; a typical value is 1,000 per second. The maximum range of a radar set is specified by half the interval between pulses multiplied by the speed of light.

The frequency (f) of the radio waves used on weather-radar sets ranges from 1,500 to above 30,000 megahertz (MHz). Commonly, meteorologists describe radar sets in terms of wavelength, λ, rather than the frequency. Since these two parameters are related by $c = \lambda f$, the wavelength of the radar set can be calculated quite simply. It is common practice to divide the microwave spectrum into various bands, as shown in table 1.1.

In later chapters it will be shown that the hydrometeor-detection capabilities of a radar set are critically dependent on the wavelength. It may be stated here that, in general, the smaller the size of the particles, the shorter the wavelength required to detect the particles. For example, an S-band radar can generally detect rain but not cloud droplets, while a K-band radar will detect many clouds even though they are not yielding precipitation.

TABLE 1.1   Operating Frequencies of Weather Radar

Frequency (MHz)	Wavelength (Cm)	Band	Frequency (MHz)	Wavelength (Cm)	Band
30,000	1	K	3,000	10	S
10,000	3	X	1,500	20	L
6,000	5	C			

The precision of the measurements of azimuthal and elevation angles to a target is largely a function of the shape of the beam produced by the antenna. Obviously, the sharper the beam—i.e., the smaller the angular width—the better the resolution. Most weather-radar sets use symmetrical beams with widths of one to three degrees. Radar sets designed for measuring heights and vertical dimensions of small targets commonly have narrow vertical beams and wider horizontal beams; large search radars used for detecting aircraft generally have very wide vertical beams. The shape of the beam is governed by the shape and size of the antenna reflector and the wavelength of the radar set. Figure 1.2 illustrates the beam shapes produced by various types of antenna reflectors.

1.1 Radar Indicators

The type of indicator used in a weather radar depends on the information desired. Most indicators consist of a cathode-ray tube in which the beam of electrons is caused to scan across the tube, starting when the transmitter pulse is started and making a discernible indication on the tube when a signal is detected by the receiver. In conception, one of the most elementary indicators is the A-scope, or R-scope. It operates like the test oscilloscopes used in physics or electronics laboratories (fig. 1.3). The beam of electrons scans horizontally across the face of the tube at a fixed speed, and vertical deflections are produced when signals are received. The distance from the start of the sweep to the deflections gives the range of the target. It can be seen that the transmitted pulse also appears on the trace. This is produced by power which leaks through the automatic switch shown in figure 1.1. The magnitude of the deflections is a measure of the strength of the signal received. It is obvious that signals from many targets can be displayed on an A-scope at any one time. In weather radar the A-scope is generally used to identify the source of the backscattered energy, to assist in the tuning of the radar and to make quantitative measurements of returned power.

The most extensively used indicator on weather radars is the plan-position indicator, usually designated as PPI (fig. 1.4). As the name connotes, this display presents a plan view of the received signals on a

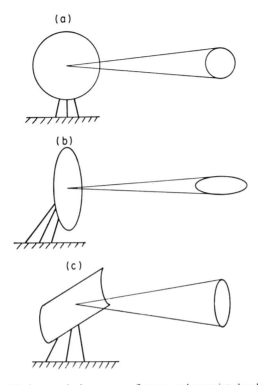

Fig. 1.2.   Various typical antenna reflectors and associated radar beams

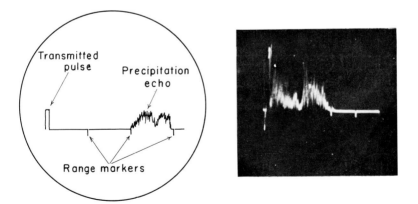

Fig. 1.3.   A- or R-scope. Photograph courtesy of P. Austin and U.S. Army Signal Research and Development Laboratory.

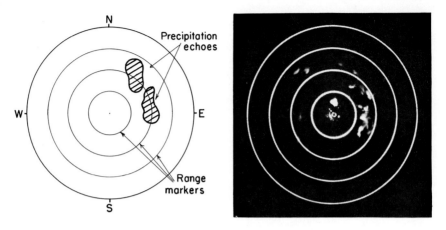

Fig. 1.4. Plan-position indicator (PPI)

polar coordinate system. It is used on radar sets with antennas which scan azimuthally. In this presentation, the electron beam scans at a fixed speed from the center of the oscilloscope to the outer edge, then returns rapidly to the center of the tube and scans outward again. The beam rotates around the scope in synchronism with the rotation of the antenna. From the PPI display one can immediately read the range and bearing to the target. The PPI scope is "intensity modulated." This means that the intensity of the bright spot corresponding to the returned signal depends on the strength of the returned signal. A strong "echo" on the scope represents a large amount of returned power. Radar sets with PPI presentations have great application for observations of severe storms and are widely used in weather stations.

Another common radar display is the range-height indicator, usually designated as RHI (fig. 1.5). This type of presentation is used with radar sets whose antennas scan vertically. In this scope the beam scans outward at a particular vertical angle, returns rapidly to the origin, and scans again at a different angle. The vertical angle of the beam is controlled by the vertical angle of the antenna. As can be seen in figure 1.5, the scope presents the position of the echo on a coordinate system with range as the abscissa and height as the ordinate. To make height determination easier, the vertical scale is usually exaggerated. Like the PPI scope, the RHI scope uses intensity modulation. It is therefore possible, in some measure, to note the strength of the returned signal by the brightness of the echo, provided the signal is not strong enough to saturate the receiving system. A height-finding radar is particularly useful in studies of cloud and precipitation growth and has been used extensively in cloud physics research.

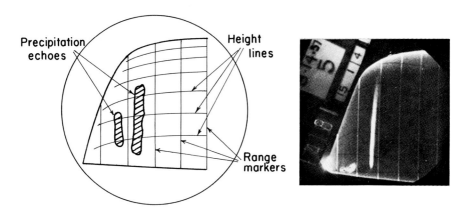

Fig. 1.5.   Range-height indicator (RHI)

It is frequently important to obtain a picture of the radar echo pattern at a fixed altitude above the ground. With azimuthally or vertically scanning radars, this cannot be obtained directly. One can, of course, take a series of PPI photographs at appropriate elevation angles or a series of RHI photographs at appropriate azimuth angles and manually reconstruct the echo pattern at any specific elevation. This was done by the Thunderstorm Project to obtain data on the three-dimensional characteristics of thunderstorm echoes (Byers and Braham 1949). However, this is a very tedious and time-consuming process.

The Stormy Weather Group at McGill University (Marshall 1957; East and Dore 1957) developed techniques for electronically synthesizing the echoes taken from PPI scans at progressively higher angles into a single picture showing intensity modulated signals at a constant altitude. Figure 1.6 shows how segments of the various scans are combined to give the constant-altitude display. The value of the data may be enhanced by modulating the echo intensity in terms of discrete shades of gray corresponding to known signal intensities. The name "constant-altitude plan-position indicator," or CAPPI, is given to this display.

Another technique for echo presentation developed at McGill University has been described by Zawadzki and Ballantyne (1970) and is called the Height-Azimuth-Range Position Indicator (HARPI). For any preselected, small-range increment, it displays echo intensity as a function of height and azimuth angle. The information is obtained by scanning continually in azimuth while the elevation angle of the beam is increased from 0 to 20 degrees at a rate of 1 degree per antenna revolution.

In the radar system used by Zawadzki and Ballantyne (1970) each rotation required 10 seconds. A range gate about 3 km long at a specific range and elevation angle produced an intensity-modulated echo display

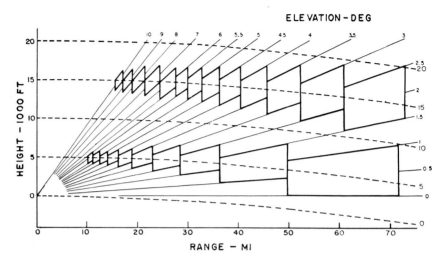

Fig. 1.6. Lines of constant altitude (*dashed*) corrected for the earth's curvature and normal refraction plotted against range. Diagram illustrates how a CAPPI is obtained. From Marshall (1957).

which depicted echo intensity in an altitude increment as a function of azimuth. As the elevation angle increased, the sampling gate obtained information at higher altitudes. By combining a series of horizontal scans, one obtains a height-azimuth display. If a number of range gates are employed, it is possible to obtain simultaneously a series of HARPI displays at a number of ranges. This indicator is of particular value in examining the three-dimensional structure of thunderstorm systems.

Many radar observations of clouds and precipitation have been made by fixing the antenna's position and allowing the weather phenomena to pass through the radar beam. When the antenna points vertically, the data may be displayed in the form of an intensity-modulated height-time

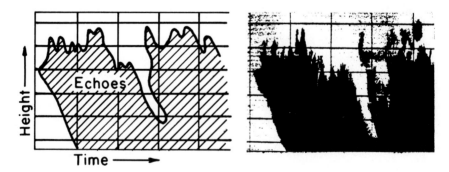

Fig. 1.7. Height-time indicator (HTI)

section, as shown in figure 1.7. Such a presentation, called an HTI, is obtained in the following way. The electron beam of an oscilloscope sweeps along the same line and is intensity modulated at altitudes where echoes are present. By means of a suitable camera, photographic film is pulled across the scope in a direction perpendicular to the trace.

The same type of recording system may be used with the antenna pointing horizontally. In this case, the display might be called "range-time indicator" (RTI), with the vertical axis of the display giving horizontal distance. A target approaching the radar would move diagonally toward zero range (r), and the slope of the echo would be $\Delta r/\Delta t$, the velocity of approach.

In recent years much use is being made of magnetic tape systems to record radar and subsidiary data. In more advanced facilities, the data are digitized before being recorded on tape. In this form they can be fed directly into electronic computers for analysis and interpretation.

In later sections of this book, other, more specialized types of radar indicators will be discussed.

2　Some Properties of Electromagnetic Waves

Since radar deals with the transmission, propagation, scattering, and reception of electromagnetic waves, it is appropriate to consider briefly some properties of such waves. An interested reader should consult a textbook on electromagnetic theory such as Jordan and Balmain (1968) for a more detailed consideration of the concepts involved. The basic equations used in studies of radio waves are the Maxwell equations defining the functional relationships between the electric and magnetic fields, which, when properly combined, compose an electromagnetic wave.

In the following paragraphs electric and magnetic fields are considered separately, and it is shown how they are combined in electromagnetic radiation.

2.1 Electric Field

An electric field exists in a region if an electric charge located in that region experiences a force of electrical origin. Since an electric charge experiences a force when it is brought into the vicinity of another electric charge or any other charged body, it is evident that any charged body creates an electric field.

The electric-field intensity, E, is a vector quantity having both a magnitude and a direction. By definition, the magnitude of the electric-field intensity at a point in the field is proportional to the force acting on a unit positive charge at that point. The direction of E is the direction of the force acting on a unit positive charge at that point.

It is frequently found convenient to represent an electric field by drawing lines of force, or flux lines, in the vicinity of a charged body (see fig. 2.1). These lines are usually designated by the vector D, called "electric displacement." If properly drawn and interpreted, they assist in understanding the properties of electric fields. In a region containing an electric field, the line of force at any point is parallel to the force which will act on a unit positive charge and, therefore, parallel to the direction of E, the electric-field intensity. The lines of force will originate on positively charged bodies and end on negatively charged bodies.

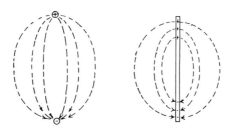

Fig. 2.1.   Examples of electric fields

The spacing of lines of force or flux lines is inversely related to the magnitude of **E**. By definition, the number of lines passing through a unit area perpendicular to the lines is equal to the magnitude of **D** and proportional to the magnitude of **E**. Conversely, the electric-field intensity is proportional to the number of lines passing through a perpendicular area, i.e., $\mathbf{D} = \epsilon_1 \mathbf{E}$, where ϵ_1 can be considered a proportionality constant and is called the "electric inductive capacity," or "permittivity," of the medium.

The magnitude of **E** is equal to the voltage gradient along the flux line. Thus the magnitude of the electric field can be determined by dividing the potential difference between two closely spaced points along a flux line by the length of the line between the points.

2.2 Magnetic Field

A magnetic field exists in a region when a moving electric charge experiences a force which cannot be attributed to an electrostatic force. It is found that the source of magnetic fields is the movement of electric charges in a conductor. The magnetic field produced by the ordinary bar magnet is thought to be caused by the spinning and revolving of the electrons of the atoms of the magnetized material. These moving electrons can be considered an electric current.

The force exerted by a magnetic field on an element of current **I** is a vector at right angles to the plane of **I** and a vector **B**; i.e., force = **I** $\times$ **B**. The vector **B** is designated the "magnetic induction" or "magnetic flux." For convenience, the magnetic field can be represented by lines of magnetic induction, **B**. It is shown experimentally that the lines of **B** are always parallel to the direction which would be assumed by a compass needle in the field. A basic property of magnetic flux lines is that they are always closed lines and surround the currents which produce them (fig. 2.2).

The lines of magnetic induction are everywhere parallel to the magnetic-field intensity, which is a vector designated by the symbol **H**. The magnitude of **H** is proportional to the number of flux lines passing through a unit

Fig. 2.2.   Example of a magnetic field

area perpendicular to the lines, i.e., $\mathbf{B} = \mu_1\mathbf{H}$, where μ_1 can be considered a proportionality constant and is called the "magnetic inductive capacity" of the medium.

The magnetic-field intensity $\mathbf{H}$ is also equal to the magnetomotive force per unit length of flux line in exactly the same way that the magnitude of $\mathbf{E}$ is equal to the electromotive force per unit length of electric flux line. The magnetomotive force is expressed in amperes, and the integral of the magnetomotive force over the entire length of any magnetic flux line inclosing a current $\mathbf{I}$ equals the current.

2.3 Radiation of Energy by a Radar Antenna

A radar antenna can be considered to consist of a thin cylindrical conductor whose total length is made equal to half the wavelength of the electromagnetic waves used by the radar. Such an antenna, called a "half-wave antenna," emits waves which are focused into a narrow beam by the antenna reflector. The antenna acts as a resonant system within which current, voltage, and distribution of charge oscillate at the frequency, f, of the electromagnetic waves involved. As shown in figure 2.2, the magnetic flux lines are circular in planes perpendicular to the antenna and concentric with it. The intensity of the magnetic field, i.e., the spacing of the lines, oscillates with the frequency, f, as the current oscillates at the same frequency.

The electric flux lines lie in the plane of the antenna and are symmetrical around it (fig. 2.1). The electric-field intensity also varies with a frequency f, and the flux lines are always perpendicular to the magnetic field.

To understand how the fields change with time, it is necessary to note the variations in current and voltage in the antenna (fig. 2.3). The current at any point on the antenna varies sinusoidally from a maximum positive to a maximum negative over the time corresponding to half a wavelength, i.e., $\frac{1}{2}c/f$. Over the same period the voltage difference measured between the center and the same point in the antenna goes from zero through a maximum and back to zero. The charge density, i.e., the charge per unit length at the same point on the antenna, varies with the same frequency and phase as the voltage difference. These oscillations of current and charge density are accompanied by oscillations in the electric and magnetic fields.

$$\sqrt{\mu_1}H = \sqrt{\epsilon_1}E .$$

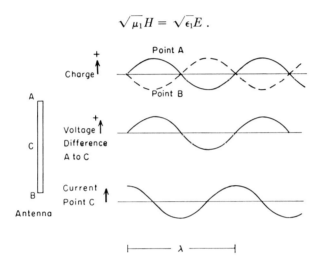

Fig. 2.3.   Time variations in charge, voltage, and current in a dipole antenna

It is known that the electric and magnetic fields represent stored energy which can be picked up by the same or a similar antenna. From the nature of the oscillations of the fields, it can be inferred that at the time of maximum current flow in the antenna all the energy is stored in the magnetic field; at the time of maximum voltage all the energy is stored in the electric field. At all other times the stored energy is partitioned between the electric and magnetic fields.

When the fields are caused to alternate rapidly, in addition to the stored energy (which is transferred from the magnetic to the electric field and back again), part of the energy is radiated, and a negligible amount is dissipated as heat in the antenna. The amount of energy radiated per cycle is smaller than the total amount stored in the fields, which are referred to as "induction fields." The strength of the induction fields decreases rapidly with distance from the antenna. Those parts of the magnetic and electric fields which are radiated—called the "radiation fields" —though smaller than the induction fields in the vicinity of the antenna, are much larger at a distance of several wavelengths from the antenna. The radiation fields can be propagated over long distances in all directions around a half-wave antenna.

As the flux lines are radiated outward, they "expand," so that the flux density following a particular point on a flux line varies inversely as the square of the distance from the antenna. Since the strength and direction of the fields produced by the antenna vary with a frequency f, the space distribution of the fields shows regular variations with a wavelength equal to λ.

It is important to note that the magnetic and electric fields remain perpendicular. The magnetic lines remain circular, concentric with the antenna and in planes perpendicular to it. Over every radial distance of half a wavelength they reverse direction. The electric flux lines lie in the plane of the antenna and also reverse in direction every half-wavelength. At any point in space the magnitudes of **E** and **H** vary sinusoidally and are perpendicular to each other; both are perpendicular to the direction of propagation, which is along a radius. In figure 2.4 the space variations in **E** and **H**, in a region close to the antenna, are shown at a particular time. At some distance from the antenna the phase relations of the fields change, and they become in phase with each other.

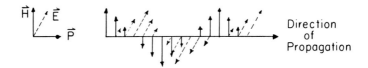

Fig. 2.4. Time variation in the electric- and magnetic-field components of an electromagnetic wave close to the antenna.

The following explanation is given for the physical mechanism for the propagation of flux lines through space. At every point, the time-varying magnetic field induces a voltage gradient in space. This voltage gradient is the electric field, which also varies with time and can be considered to be equivalent to a current, even though electric charge is not actually conducted. This "current" is called a "displacement current." It produces a magnetic field, as does a conduction current. In this way the varying magnetic field establishes a varying electric field, which in turn leads to the creation of a varying magnetic field. Each field periodically gives rise to the other, and neither can be propagated without the other.

Electromagnetic radiations can be obtained by other means than through the use of a half-wave dipole (see Skolnik 1962 for a discussion).

For example, microwaves propagate efficiently down the inside of a suitably designed metal pipe called a "waveguide." If the waveguide is open at an appropriate place, the electromagnetic power can radiate from it as such power does from a dipole.

An open-end waveguide or a dipole does not concentrate its radiation in a narrow beam. For this reason, they are used to irradiate antenna reflectors such as those shown in chapter 1. The reflectors focus the power in beams of the desired shape.

2.4 Polarization of Electromagnetic Waves

To specify the orientation of an electromagnetic wave in space, it is necessary to specify the orientation of one of the field vectors. Since the magnetic vector is always perpendicular to the electric vector, a knowledge of the orientation of the latter is sufficient to describe the orientation of the wave. The plane containing the electric field is conventionally referred to as the "plane of polarization"; it is also called the "plane of vibration." For example, when a half-wave antenna is placed so that it is horizontal, it will produce an electric field which is horizontal, and the emitted electromagnetic waves are said to be "horizontally polarized."

The polarization of a monochromatic electromagnetic wave can be determined by the values of the three parameters E_{xm}, E_{ym}, and δ, given by

$$E_x = E_{xm} \sin (2\pi ft),$$
$$E_y = E_{ym} \sin (2\pi ft + \delta),$$

(2.1)

where t is time, E_{xm} and E_{ym} are the amplitudes of the x and y components of the electric-field vector, and δ is the phase difference between the oscillations of E_x and E_y. Both E_x and E_y oscillate between values of zero and E_{xm} and E_{ym}, respectively. The value of δ measures the difference between the times that E_x and E_y reach either their maximum values or zero. Figure 2.5 illustrates the values of E_x and E_y in a left-handed coordinate system with the wave propagated in the z-direction.

When $E_{xm} \neq E_{ym}$ and $\delta = (n - 1)\pi$, with n any integer, the vector **E** will always make the same angle with the x-axis, while its magnitude oscillates between $|\mathbf{E}|$ and zero. In this case the wave is "linearly polarized."

When $E_{xm} = E_{ym}$ and $\delta = (2n - 1)\pi/2$, with n any integer, the values of E_x and E_y will vary between zero and E_{xm} and E_{ym}, respectively, with a phase difference of $\pi/2$; E_x will have maximum positive and negative values ($= E_{xm}$) when E_y is zero, and E_y will have maxima ($= E_{ym}$) when E_x is zero. Since the projection of **E** on the x-y plane is circular, the

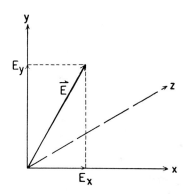

Fig. 2.5.   Electric vector in the *x-y* plane

electromagnetic wave is said to be circularly polarized. In such a circumstance, the electric vector rotates around the direction of propagation at a frequency f while maintaining constant amplitude.

When $E_{xm} \neq E_{ym}$ and $\delta = (2n - 1)\pi/2$, the electromagnetic wave is elliptically polarized because the projection of **E** on the *x-y* plane will have the form of an ellipse. Such a wave can be considered to be composed of two circularly polarized waves having different amplitudes and opposite directions of rotation.

Most radar sets now used in radar meteorology are linearly polarized. The plane of polarization is parallel to the orientation of the dipole or the short side of a rectangular waveguide if either of these types of antennas is employed.

In a later chapter, it will be shown that backscattered waves from nonspherical particles are polarized differently than the incident waves. This fact has been used in the study of the shape of precipitation particles in the free atmosphere.

3 Propagation of Electromagnetic Waves

For most purposes, the speed of propagation of an electromagnetic wave may be considered to be constant and equal to the speed of light in free space, 3×10^8 m/sec. However, for some problems one has to recognize that the atmosphere is significantly different from free space and that the observed air-mass properties are sufficiently variable to produce small changes in the speed of propagation. These small changes are important because they may lead to refraction of the radar ray and produce marked changes in the direction of propagation.

Using Maxwell's equations, one can show that in a homogeneous medium the velocity of a wave is given by

$$v = \frac{1}{\sqrt{\epsilon_1 \mu_1}}, \qquad (3.1)$$

where ϵ_1 is the permittivity of the medium and μ_1 is its magnetive inductive capacity. In free space the speed of the wave is equal to the speed of light and is given by

$$c = \frac{1}{\sqrt{\epsilon_0 \mu_0}}, \qquad (3.2)$$

where the zero subscript designates conditions in free space.

In the study of optics, it is common to define a term n, the index of refraction, as

$$n = \frac{c}{v}. \qquad (3.3)$$

Substituting for v and c, one obtains

$$n^2 = \epsilon \mu, \qquad (3.4)$$

where the dielectric constant of a medium $\epsilon = \epsilon_1/\epsilon_0$, and the magnetic permeability $\mu = \mu_1/\mu_0$. Since μ is approximately equal to unity in most media usually considered, it can be said that, for most practical cases,

$$n^2 = \epsilon. \qquad (3.5)$$

17

Since ϵ usually exceeds unity, the index of refraction does also, and the speed of propagation in most media is less than the speed of light in free space by a small but significant amount.

It should be noted that in its most general form the refractive index is a complex function,

$$m = n - ik, \tag{3.6}$$

where the real term, n, is the factor denoted in the equation $c = nv$. The term ik is equal to zero in a perfect dielectric and is associated with the absorption of the medium. At this point this term may be neglected, but in a later chapter dealing with the scattering by particles it will be found to be quite important.

Since the atmosphere is a nonhomogeneous medium with vertical variations in temperature, pressure, and humidity, one would expect vertical gradients of the index of refraction and, as a result, a bending of radio waves in the same manner as light rays passing from water to air. In some cases the gradients can be large enough to produce reflection of the waves.

In the study of refraction and reflection of radio waves, one can make use of ordinary ray theory if certain restrictions are met (see Bean and Dutton 1968):

1. The gradient of n must be small over a distance of one wavelength.

2. The amount by which individual rays converge over small distances relative to one wavelength must be small. This restriction prohibits the direct application of simple ray tracing when a ray touches a surface or passes through a focus. In a later section it is shown that, because of particular vertical distributions of the index of refraction, microwave energy may be trapped in a fairly shallow layer. The points where the rays are reflected from the upper or the lower surface of the layer are in regions where simple ray theory cannot be applied.

When the index of refraction changes very rapidly with height over a distance of one wavelength measured in the direction of propagation, partial reflection from the layer may occur. More will be said about this in a later chapter.

3.1 Meteorological Factors Determining the Index of Refraction

For *dry air*, the index of refraction, n, is given by

$$(n - 1)\ 10^6 = K_1 \frac{p}{T}, \tag{3.7}$$

where p is air pressure in millibars, T is temperature in degrees Kelvin, and K_1 is a constant which has a value of 77.6 (see Bean and Dutton

1968). By substitution from the equation of state, one obtains

$$(n - 1)\, 10^6 = K_1 R\rho = (\text{constant})\, \rho, \tag{3.8}$$

where R is the individual gas constant for air and ρ is the air density. For convenience, the term on the left side of equation (3.8) is often set equal to N, called the "radio refractivity," and units of $(n - 1)10^6$ are referred to as "N units."

In dry air the index of refraction has the same value over almost the entire range of the electromagnetic spectrum; it is the same for light and radio waves. However, when water vapor is added to the air, the value of N for the mixture becomes frequency dependent. It is well known that the water molecule is polar in nature and that the dipole moment of the molecule has a different response to different-frequency radio waves. With the extremely high frequencies of visible light, the water molecules are electronically polarized. With the lower frequencies of radar waves, the water molecules not only acquire electronic polarization but also reorient themselves rapidly enough to follow the electric-field changes. As a result, the index of refraction (and dielectric constant) of *water vapor* is greater for radio than for optical frequencies. For radio waves,

$$N = (n - 1)10^6 = \frac{K_3 e}{T^2} - \frac{K_2 e}{T}, \tag{3.9}$$

where e is the vapor pressure in millibars. For microwaves with wavelengths greater than 2 cm, K_1, K_2, and K_3 have values of approximately 77.6 °K/mb, 5.6 °K/mb, and 3.75×10^5 (°K)^2/mb, respectively (Bean and Dutton 1968).

Since the index of refraction is an additive quantity, the index of moist air can be calculated from

$$N = 77.6\,\frac{p}{T} - 5.6\,\frac{e}{T} + 3.75 \times 10^5\,\frac{e}{T^2}. \tag{3.10}$$

Carbon dioxide also contributes to N, but its contribution is less than 0.1 percent and can be neglected. At all atmospheric temperatures the second term of equation (3.10) will be much smaller than the others. Hence for all practical purposes equation (3.10) can be written

$$N = \frac{77.6}{T}\left(p + 4{,}810\,\frac{e}{T}\right). \tag{3.11}$$

Near sea level a typical value of n is about 1.0003 and $N = 300$.

Most statistics on the refractive index of the atmosphere have been obtained by calculations based on actual measurements of p, T, and e. Because most meteorological instruments, e.g., those on a radiosonde, have slow response (about 5–10 seconds), little information has been obtained on the small-scale variations of n. It also is evident that accurate determinations of n depend on accurate measurements of three meteorological quantities. It has been shown that, for $T = 15°$ C, $p = 1,013$ mb, and $e = 10.2$ mb (a relative humidity of 60 percent), errors in N are given by

$$\Delta N \approx -1.27\Delta T + 4.50\Delta e + 0.27\Delta p. \qquad (3.12)$$

Existing devices for measuring the vapor pressure in the free atmosphere are subject to large errors, particularly at low humidities. Bean and Dutton (1968) report that the standard deviation of refractivity obtainable from radiosonde data at an altitude of 1 km is approximately $2N$ units and that this quantity "appears to be the ultimate precision with which present conventional radiosonde sensors can yield the refractivity."

Radio refractive index can be measured directly by means of instruments called refractometers. Bean and Dutton (1968) give an excellent discussion of these devices. Microwave refractometers are based on the fact that the resonant frequency of a microwave cavity depends on the dimensions of the cavity and the refractive index of the enclosed medium. As outside air is passed through the cavity, the resonant frequency changes as the refractive index of the air changes.

A typical refractometer, such as the one first designed by Crain (1950), makes use of a closed reference cavity and an open one having identical dimensions through which the air is passed. The difference in resonant frequencies depends only on the n of the air. Crain's refractometer operated at 9,400 MHz (X-band), but other instruments have been designated to resonate at frequencies as low as 10 MHz. Changes in refractive index are given by the expression

$$\frac{\Delta f}{f} = -\Delta n = -10^{-6}\Delta N. \qquad (3.13)$$

Thus with the X-band refractometer, a one-N unit change of refractivity produces a 9.4-kHz change in frequency.

Microwave refractometers have been used on balloons and airplanes for probing the clear atmosphere and cloud systems. Unfortunately, the instruments are still fairly expensive and complicated and have not been used widely. Because of their very rapid response, depending essentially on the time required to replace the air inside the cavity, microwave refractometers offer a means of obtaining information on changes of N over distances of tens of centimeters.

Incidentally, microwave refractometers have been employed on certain experimental programs requiring a detailed knowledge of the water-vapor distribution in the atmosphere. This has been done because there has been no instrument for directly measuring humidity in the air accurately and rapidly. Since atmospheric pressure and temperature can be observed adequately, a knowledge of N, supplied by a refractometer, makes it possible to calculate the vapor pressure by means of equation (3.11).

3.2 Simple Refraction

Qualitatively, one can examine easily the consequence of atmospheric variations in n on the direction of propagation of radio waves. Since p and e decrease rapidly with height, while T decreases slowly with height, n decreases with altitude. In a standard atmosphere the vertical gradient of n is about $-4 \times 10^{-8}\ m^{-1}$. From equation (3.3) it follows that the velocity of the wave increases with height. As a result, the waves are bent downward. This becomes more obvious from a consideration of Snell's law:

$$\frac{n - \Delta n}{n} = \frac{\sin i}{\sin r} = \frac{V_i}{V_r},\qquad (3.14)$$

where i and r are the angles of incidence and refraction, respectively, both measured with respect to the normal. Since n decreases with altitude, we can consider the ray as moving from a layer of a particular n to a layer where the refractive index is $n - \Delta n$ (fig. 3.1). The result is that angle r is larger than angle i and the ray is bent downward. It is obvious that, if the beam were bent sufficiently, it could strike the ground beyond the line-of-sight horizon. As a matter of fact, there exists a distribution of $n(h)$ which could produce a ray curvature equal to the curvature of the earth, with, consequently, no "horizon."

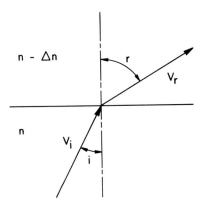

Fig. 3.1.   Variation in a ray path with a change of refractive index

3.3 Refraction in the Lower Troposphere

Appleton (1946) made an analysis of the curvature of a radio wave propagated through an atmosphere with an index of refraction varying with height. He considered a case in which the transmitter is at a height h_0 above the ground and sends out a ray at an angle ϕ_0 with the local horizontal plane (fig. 3.2). Hartree, Michel, and Nicolson (1946) showed

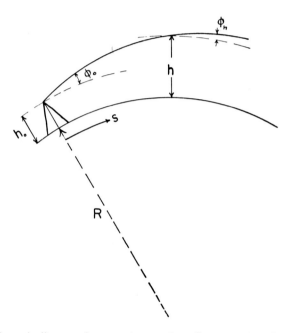

Fig. 3.2.   Schematic diagram of a ray path over a long distance (R is radius of the earth).

that, if dn/dh is small enough for ray theory to be applied, the exact differential equation for a ray in a spherically stratified atmosphere is

$$\frac{d^2h}{ds^2} - \left(\frac{2}{R+h} + \frac{1}{n}\frac{dn}{dh}\right)\left(\frac{dh}{ds}\right)^2 - \left(\frac{R+h}{R}\right)^2\left(\frac{1}{R+h} + \frac{1}{n}\frac{dn}{dh}\right) = 0. \quad (3.15)$$

Under practical conditions, the angles ϕ are very small, of the order of a few degrees, so that $(dh/ds)^2 \ll 1$. Also, n is very close to unity and can be considered unity with negligible error, and obviously $h \ll R$. With acceptable precision, equation (3.15) can therefore be reduced to

$$\frac{d^2h}{ds^2} = \frac{1}{R} + \frac{dn}{dh}, \quad (3.16)$$

which can be integrated to give

$$\left(\frac{dh}{ds}\right)^2 = 2 \int \left(\frac{1}{R} + \frac{dn}{dh}\right) dh + \text{constant.} \tag{3.17}$$

Since the angles ϕ are small, this equation can be written

$$\frac{\phi_h^2}{2} - \frac{\phi_0^2}{2} = \frac{h - h_0}{R} + n - n_0 \tag{3.18a}$$

$$= \left(\frac{h}{R} + n\right) - \left(\frac{h_0}{R} + n_o\right) \tag{3.18b}$$

$$= (M - M_0) \, 10^{-6}. \tag{3.18c}$$

The quantity $M = [h/R + (n - 1)] \, 10^6$ is called the "modified index of refraction" and is useful in the tracing of radio waves. It usually is expressed in "M units," and at sea level, is of the order of 300. It can be seen from equation (3.18) that, if one knows the vertical profile of M, it is possible to calculate the angle with the horizontal that the ray makes at any altitude.

3.4 Curvature of Ray Paths Relative to the Earth

If there were no atmosphere on the earth, or if n were constant, the radio-ray paths would suffer no bending and consequently would be straight lines. In this case the curvature of the rays relative to the earth's surface would be $1/R$. In the practical case of an existing atmosphere, the gradient of the index of refraction causes bending, and, as a result, the curvature differs from $1/R$. In the usual case, where the index of refraction decreases with height, the curvature is smaller than $1/R$. In fact, the curvature of a ray *relative to the earth* is given by

$$\frac{d\phi}{ds} = \frac{1}{R} + \frac{dn}{dh}. \tag{3.19}$$

It follows that, if dn/dh is negative and equal to $1/R$, the ray path will be concentric with the earth and travel around it without change of distance from it.

In studying the radiation pattern from an antenna, it is sometimes convenient to plot the ray paths as straight lines. In order to do this, it is appropriate to assume a fictitious earth with an effective radius equal to R', given by

$$\frac{1}{R'} = \frac{1}{R} + \frac{dn}{dh}, \tag{3.20}$$

from which

$$R' = \frac{R}{1 + R \ (dn/dh)}.$$ (3.21)

If the index of refraction is plotted for the standard atmosphere, the ray paths are nearly arcs of a circle (not concentric with the earth) over distances of normal radar detection. Since the standard vertical gradient of the index of refraction dn/dh is nearly linear and equal to about $-4 \times 10^{-8} \ m^{-1}$, the effective radius of the earth for propagation problems is about $\frac{4}{3}R$ (fig. 3.3). The value of the factor to be applied to R to obtain the effective radius of an earth over which the ray paths are straight lines depends on meteorological conditions but has a range of approximately 1.1–1.6.

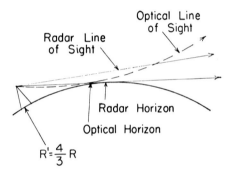

Fig. 3.3. Radar and optical lines of sight over an earth having an effective radius R' = $\frac{4}{3}R$.

If an antenna on the surface is pointing horizontally, the distance above a spherical earth of radius R' as a function of distance, s, along the earth can be shown to be approximately

$$h = \frac{1}{2} \frac{s^2}{R'}.$$ (3.22)

3.5 Nonstandard Refraction

When atmospheric temperature and humidity distributions deviate from the standard radio atmospheric conditions, the vertical gradient of the index of refraction will do likewise; as a result, the radio waves may deviate greatly from their normal or standard direction of propagation. In considering propagation of electromagnetic waves, it is convenient to think of propagation under standard refractive-index conditions as normal. When nonstandard index-of-refraction distributions prevail, "abnormal" or "anomalous" propagation occurs. For this reason, the differences between the standard and the actual refractive-index values are frequently considered rather than the actual values of M, and the ray paths are studied in terms of the curvature of the fictitious earth.

When abnormal downward bending occurs, it is called "superrefraction." The term "subrefraction" is applied when there is abnormal upward bending.

As was shown earlier, the ray paths can be traced by means of equation (3.18), which can be rewritten

$$\frac{\phi_h^2}{2} - \frac{\phi_0^2}{2} = (M_h - M_0)\, 10^{-6}, \tag{3.23}$$

where M_h and M_0 are the modified indices of refraction in M units at levels h and zero, respectively. Several specific cases of nonlinear dM/dh can be considered. In figure 3.4 are plotted three possible (M, h)

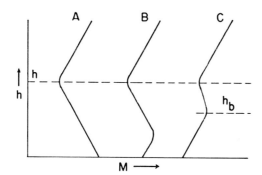

Fig. 3.4.   Three possible distributions of M which can lead to radar "ducts"

curves encountered in nature. In type A, below level h, M decreases with height. As a result, ϕ_h becomes smaller and smaller with increasing height, and the rays starting out at small angles are bent toward the earth. If sufficient bending occurs, the wave emitted from a ground station is said to be "trapped," and the region in which the energy is trapped is called a "duct." Within the duct the strength of the electromagnetic field is greater than it would be under standard conditions, and the duct acts as a guide and may direct the energy to long distances within a narrow layer near the earth's surface. From equation (3.23) one can calculate the maximum value of ϕ_0 at which trapping can occur, given a curve of $n = n(h)$. Bending toward the earth takes place when

ϕ_h equals zero:

$$(\phi_0)_{max} = [2 \, (M_0 - M_{min}) \, 10^{-6}]^{1/2}. \qquad (3.24)$$

If values of M_0 and M_{min} are taken as 355 and 350 M units at h equal to zero and 50 m, respectively, it is found that $(\phi_0)_{max}$ equals about 0.2°.

With a type B curve there is also a duct between the levels zero and h.

With a type C curve, radio waves emitted from a ground station may be bent upward between the ground and the level h_b. On the other hand, if a transmitter were placed at level h_b, the distribution of M would be similar to that of types A and B except that the origin of the system would have been displaced upward. In this case the duct would extend between altitudes h_b and h. Radar waves entering this duct at small angles will be partly confined inside and guided by the duct.

3.6 Meteorological Conditions Associated with Nonstandard Refraction

With the vertical distributions of temperature and vapor pressure as a function of pressure known, the vertical distribution of the refractive index can be calculated from equations already given. Figure 3.5 shows those meteorological conditions leading to the variations with height of the modified index of refraction which give rise to anomalous propagation.

Type A is probably the most common duct-producing situation and is usually brought about in one of three ways.

1. Nocturnal radiation, which occurs on clear nights, especially in the summer when the ground is moist, leads to a temperature inversion at the ground and a sharp decrease in moisture with height. It is found that these conditions frequently produce abnormal propagation, which becomes more pronounced as the temperature and humidity lapse rates become larger. Observations have shown, however, that when fog forms, propagation may return rapidly to normal.

2. When warm, dry air moves over cooler bodies of water, the air is cooled in the lowest layers, and at the same time moisture is added. In this way strong ducts of type A are produced. These conditions are frequently found over the Mediterranean Sea as air blows off the African continent. Extreme anomalous propagation has been experienced in this region. For example, there have been days when microwave radars have detected ground targets at ranges of 600–800 km even though the horizon was at perhaps 30 km. By the nature of the advection process, the resulting superrefraction can occur during either the day or the night and last for long periods of time. The duration would depend on the persistency of the flow patterns.

3. A more infrequent, but nonetheless important, source of ground ducts is the diverging downdraft under a thunderstorm. When the relatively cool air spreads out from the base of a storm, the result is a temperature inversion in the lowest few thousand feet. Because of the

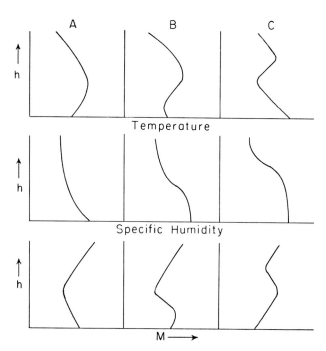

Fig. 3.5. Vertical distributions of temperature and specific humidity and associated vertical distributions of M.

evaporation of raindrops, the air has a high specific humidity, and the gradient is in the direction shown in figure 3.5 (*A* and *B*). As a result, a strong duct can be formed over a relatively small area in the vicinity of the thunderstorm. Since a thunderstorm is an instability phenomenon associated with strong vertical mixing, the stable low-level lapse rate is fairly short-lived, with a time duration of perhaps 30 minutes to 1 hour. It is important in radar storm detection, because radar observations are frequently of greatest utility during the time that thunderstorms are occurring in the vicinity. Figure 3.6 shows a photograph illustrating anomalous propagation associated with thunderstorms. From a careful surveillance of a radar screen, one can detect the establishment of anomalous propagation conditions by the sudden increase in the number and range of ground targets.

Ducts of type B are less frequent than those of type A. As can be seen from figure 3.5, they are sometimes associated with a low-level inversion through which the specific humidity decreases sharply. A situation such as this can be brought about in several ways.

1. A subsidence inversion close to the ground can lead to the proper conditions. This is especially true when the air close to the ground is initially quite moist.

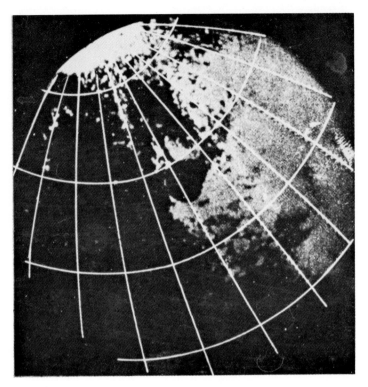

Fig. 3.6.   Photograph of a PPI scope showing the effects of a low-level duct formed by thunderstorms. Range markers are at 10-mile (about 16 km) intervals. Radar echoes from the ground (ground clutter) extend beyond 30 miles (about 48 km). The nearly circular area centered at 148° and 23 miles is a lake. From Coons (1947).

2. Type B ducts also can occur when warm, dry air is carried over a cool body of water by turbulent winds. The turbulence can cause the inversion to be lifted above the surface and result in a nearly adiabatic lapse rate in the low layers.

Ducts of types A and B are of most concern to radar meteorologists because most weather-radar sets are located at the ground. The antenna will frequently be pointed at small vertical angles, and the beam may undergo serious bending.

When the angle between the beam and the levels of constant refractive index is more than 1° or 2°, the amount of bending will be insufficient to keep the transmitted power inside the duct. For this reason, ducts of type C usually have little effect on the propagation from ground radars. Type-C ducts may be important, however, for airborne operations.

Ducts of type C are brought about by processes similar to those which produce ducts of type B except that the inversions of temperature and strong moisture gradients occur at higher levels.

4 Radar Detection of Spherical Particles

For many purposes it is important to know the size, composition, shape, and orientation of hydrometeors in the atmosphere. In this section, equations will be derived to express the power returned to a radar set by spherical particles composed entirely of ice or water and randomly distributed in space. In chapter 5, cases of partly melted ice spheres and nonspherical particles will be examined.

4.1 An Approximate Form of the Radar Equation

Let us consider a transmitter which radiates isotropically. The power will spread equally in all directions, and, at a range r, the power per unit area on the surface of a sphere of radius r is $P_t/4\pi r^2$, where P_t is the power during the brief period that the transmitter is operating. In practice, radar sets employ antennas which are highly directional, in order to concentrate the power into a narrow beam. The ratio of power per unit area along the axis of the radar beam to the isotropic value is a measure of the gain, G, of the antenna. It should be noted that, if the radar set uses one antenna for transmission and another for reception, the value of G would have to be replaced by G_t, the gain of the transmitting antenna.

If there is a target at range r with a cross-sectional area A_t, it will intercept an amount of power P_σ, given by

$$P_\sigma = \frac{P_t G A_t}{4\pi r^2}. \tag{4.1}$$

If it is assumed that the target does not absorb any power, but re-radiates it all isotropically, the power intercepted by the radar antenna, P_r, will be given by

$$P_r = \frac{P_t G A_t A_e}{(4\pi)^2 r^4}, \tag{4.2}$$

where A_e is the effective cross section of the antenna. It can also be written $A_e = \rho A_p$, when A_p is the apertural or cross-sectional area of the

29

antenna and ρ is the antenna efficiency whose value depends on the efficiency of the feed and the antenna illumination.

It was shown by Silver (1951) from theoretical considerations that $A_e = G\lambda^2/4\pi$. Also, when an antenna employs a circular, paraboloidal reflector the gain is given approximately by $G = 8\pi A_p/3\lambda^2$. Note that in this instance $A_e = \frac{2}{3}A_p$. By substituting for A_e and G in equation (4.2), one obtains

$$P_r = \frac{P_t G^2 \lambda^2 A_t}{(4\pi)^3 r^4} \approx \frac{P_t A_p^2 A_t}{9\pi\lambda^2 r^4}. \tag{4.3}$$

It was assumed earlier that the target had a cross section A_t and that it scattered isotropically. In practice, there are no targets—certainly no meteorological ones—which scatter isotropically. Nevertheless, it has been found convenient to introduce a function, σ, called the "backscattering cross section," which is defined as "the area intercepting that amount of power, which, if scattered isotropically, would return to the receiver an amount of power equal to that actually received." The function σ may also be defined as "the area which, when multiplied by the incident intensity, gives the total power radiated by an isotropic source which radiates the same power in the backward direction as the scatterer." This can be written

$$\sigma P_i = 4\pi r^2 S, \tag{4.4}$$

where P_i is the power per unit area incident on the target at a range r, and S is the backscattered power per unit area at the antenna.

For a single scatterer, equation (4.3) becomes

$$P_r = \frac{P_t G^2 \lambda^2 \sigma_i}{(4\pi)^3 r^4}. \tag{4.5}$$

This equation is perfectly general up to this point and can be applied whether the target be the moon, an airplane, or a raindrop. The problem for the meteorologist is to determine the form of σ_i for the meteorological elements he wishes to detect.

In equation (4.5) σ_i is given as the backscattering cross section of a single scatterer. In practice, the radar beam illuminates a large group of scatterers—e.g., raindrops—at the same time; the number is equal to that within a volume defined by the beam widths and pulse length of the radar set. In this case, it is necessary to consider the power reflected from a large number of drops. The backscattered signal voltage from a volume of randomly distributed scatterers is the sum of the signals scattered by each of the scatterers, with the phase of each signal taken into account. It has been found to vary from one reflected pulse to the next because of the movement of the particles with respect to one another. After a period of the order of 10^{-2} sec, a random array of scattering particles changes into an essentially independent one. If the received power is averaged over a large number of independent arrays, one can write

$$\bar{P}_r = \frac{P_t G^2 \lambda^2}{(4\pi)^3 r^4} \sum_{i=0}^{n} \sigma_i,$$ (4.6)

where the summation is carried out over the entire volume V_m from which power is scattered back to the receiver at any instant.

If the particles are uniformly distributed throughout V_m, the total backscattering cross section can be written as the backscattering per unit volume multiplied by V_m. The quantity V_m is given approximately by

$$V_m = \pi \left(r\frac{\theta}{2} \right) \left(r\frac{\phi}{2} \right) \frac{h}{2},$$ (4.7)

where θ and ϕ are the horizontal and vertical widths of the beam in radians.

It should be noted that, in calculating the volume illuminated, a depth of $h/2$ is used instead of h. This is done because the equations involved refer only to the scattered power which returns to the radar receiver at the same instant of time. The power backscattered by particles at a range $(r + h/2)$ from the front of the outgoing pulse of length h will arrive at the radar antenna at the same time as the power backscattered by particles at range r from the rear of the outgoing pulse of length h.

By substituting in equation (4.6), one obtains[1]

$$\bar{P}_r = \frac{P_t G^2 \lambda^2 \theta \phi h}{512 \pi^2 r^2} \sum_{\text{vol}} \sigma_i.$$ (4.8)

The factor $\sum_{\text{vol}} \sigma_i$ represents a summation of σ over a unit volume. It is called the "radar reflectivity," designated by the symbol η, and is commonly expressed in units of centimeters square per cubic meter or per centimeter.

It should be noted that in the derivation of equation (4.8) it was assumed that, across the radar beam between the half-power points, the transmitted power per unit area has the same value. Obviously, this is not the case. The transmitted power is maximum along the beam axis

1. There are various forms of the resulting equation (4.8). For example Marshall, Hitschfeld, and Gunn (1955) used

$$\bar{P}_r = \frac{P_t A_e h}{8\pi r^2} \sum_{\text{vol}} \sigma_i.$$

and decreases to half the maximum value at the angles corresponding
to half the beam widths (see chap. 9). When the factor G was introduced
into equation (4.1), the assumed constant value of transmitted power
was taken as the value along the beam axis. Clearly, the implicit assumptions about the character of the beam will lead to an overestimate of
the power backscattered to a radar set. The errors following from these
assumptions are examined in the next section.

4.2 A More Exact Form of the Radar Equation

When equations of the form of equation (4.8) were tested experimentally,
it was found that, when $\overline{P_r}$ was calculated for known values of $\Sigma\sigma_i$, the
average power was consistently too high. For a number of years an em-
pirical correction factor designated F was employed to compensate
for the observed discrepancy.

   In 1962, Probert-Jones succeeded, by a more rigorous derivation of
the radar equation, in explaining the discrepancy. He considered the
case of a paraboloidal antenna of circular cross section and assumed
that, within the main lobe, the power per unit area can be represented
by a Gaussian function. This is a satisfactory assumption in most cases.
He also took into account the fact that the so-called two-way power-
density pattern of an antenna is different from the one-way power-density
pattern. Probert-Jones showed that, when the entire beam is intercepted
by targets, and the properties of the beam pattern are taken into account,

$$\overline{P_r} = \frac{P_t G^2 \lambda^2 \theta \phi h}{512 \ (2 \ln 2) \pi^2 r^2} \sum_{\text{vol}} \sigma_i. \tag{4.9}$$

   In the derivation of this expression, Probert-Jones used the following
equation for the antenna gain, which can be shown to hold for a circular
paraboloid:

$$G = \frac{\pi^2 k^2}{\theta \phi}, \tag{4.10}$$

where k^2 is a nondimensional quantity depending on the fraction of
power from the antenna feed intercepted by the antenna reflector and
on the nonuniformity of illumination of the antenna. For circular antennas, k is close to unity and $\theta = \phi$. Earlier derivations of the radar
equations assumed that power per unit area across the solid angle between the antenna half-power points was uniform. Probert-Jones showed
that this is equivalent to stating that $G = 16/\theta\phi$. Thus, in earlier treatments of this problem, the gain was overestimated by a factor $16/\pi^2$,

which leads to a discrepancy in calculated $\overline{P_r}$ of 1.62 or 2.10 dB.

Probert-Jones also showed that, unless the derivation takes into account the equivalent cone for two-way transmission (i.e., the equivalent cone of received power), the equation for $\overline{P_r}$ will be in error by a factor $2 \ln 2$.[2] This leads to excesses in calculated $\overline{P_r}$ amounting to 1.39 or 1.42 dB.

As noted by Probert-Jones (1962), "Those radar equations that contain the gain explicitly, and in which a measured value is used, will give a received power $1\frac{1}{2}$ dB too great. The other equations will give a value $3\frac{1}{2}$ dB too great for the received power." Thus, in equations for $\overline{P_r}$ derived before about 1962, the correction factor F equals $(2 \ln 2)^{-1}$ or $\dfrac{\pi^2}{32 \ln 2}$, depending on whether a measured value of G has been used explicitly.

4.3 Fluctuating Echoes from Distributed Scatterers

A detailed examination of the radar echoes produced by precipitation shows rapid fluctuations of the signal strength. It changes from one pulse to the next perhaps a thousandth of a second later. Because of the persistence of the common oscilloscope, amounting to tenths of a second, the superimposed signals have a "grassy" appearance.

It has long been known that the echo fluctuations are caused by the movement, with respect to one another, of the randomly distributed particles within the radar volume being examined. As the particles move, the phases of the individual backscattered signals change and the summation of the signal contributions changes from one pulse to the next. A target composed of distributed targets which move with respect to one another is said to be *incoherent*. A solid object, such as a metal sphere, would be regarded as a *coherent* target.

In the equations derived in the last section, the scattering properties of the target were related to the average backscattered power $\overline{P_r}$. Only if this quantity is measured correctly will it be proportional to the sum of the backscattering cross sections of all the particles in the illuminated volume. The backscattered power in a single radar pulse depends not only on the backscattering cross sections of the scatterers but also on their relative positions.

The theory of fluctuating echoes from randomly distributed particles was developed by Marshall and Hitschfeld (1953) and Wallace (1953).

2. In this book the symbol $\ln X$ represents the natural logarithm of X. Logarithms to the base 10 will be written $\log X$.

They showed that the echo amplitude, A, and echo intensity, A^2, have the probability distributions

$$P(A)\ dA = \frac{2A}{\overline{A^2}}\, e^{-A^2/\overline{A^2}}\, dA, \tag{4.11}$$

$$P(A^2)\ dA^2 = \frac{1}{\overline{A^2}}\, e^{-A^2/\overline{A^2}}\, dA^2, \tag{4.12}$$

where, e.g., $P(A^2)\ dA^2$ is the probability of a value A^2 falling between A^2 and $A^2 + dA^2$. Equations (4.11) and (4.12) apply to populations of A and A^2 which are composed of independent samples of these variables. The quantity $\overline{A^2}$ is proportional to the average echo intensity and to $\overline{P_r}$. The averaging must be done over samples of A^2 sufficiently separated in time or space to have essentially zero correlation. As will be discussed in a later section, a period of the order of 10^{-2} second is required for the particles to shuffle from one array to another independent one. The averaging may also be carried out over intervals of range spaced at distances of $h/2$ because the distribution of particles would have essentially zero correlation over distances equal to or exceeding $h/2$.

Marshall and Hitschfeld also calculated the distribution of the average of k independent samples of A^2 and found that, when k exceeds about 10, the distributions are Gaussian. An extension of this analysis yielded information on the number of independent pulses over which the average would have to be computed in order to keep errors of $\overline{A^2}$ within certain limits (fig. 4.1). It was found that, if $A^2 (= P_r)$ were averaged over 25 independent samples, the measured $\overline{P_r}$ would be within ± 40 percent of the correct $\overline{P_r}$ 95 percent of the time. These discrepancies in power correspond to limits of -2.2 dB to $+ 1.5$ dB and are close to the experimental errors involved in the measurement of $\overline{P_r}$.

One procedure for increasing the dynamic range of a radar system is to employ a logarithmic receiver. Marshall and Hitschfeld (1953) derived an expression for the probability distribution of $\log A^2$. Kodaira (1960) extended the earlier work and calculated errors in the average power as a function of the number of independent pulses over which the average is taken.

4.4 Measuring P_r by Threshold Techniques

There are various ways to obtain $\overline{P_r}$. A common technique involves the electronic integration, over time, of signals from a particular volume in space. The average power can also be obtained by measuring the fraction of a large number of independent signals which cross a particular threshold of power. Marshall and Hitschfeld (1953) showed that the probability of A^2 equaling or exceeding the threshold C^2 equals e^{-C^2/A^2}. This

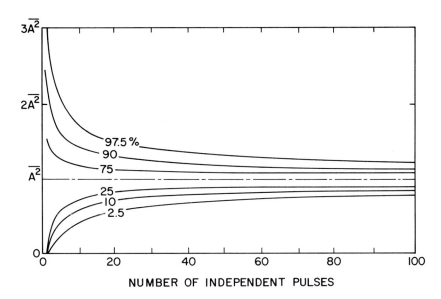

Fig. 4.1.   Number of independent values of A^2 needed to yield an estimated $\overline{A^2}$ having a value within predetermined limits of the true $\overline{A^2}$. The 90 percent curve, for instance, indicates that 90 percent of the averages of 50 independent values of signal intensity (A^2) may be expected to fall below $1.175\overline{A^2}$. From Marshall and Hitschfeld (1953).

expression is obtained by integrating equation (4.12) from C^2 to infinity. It also can be shown that

$$\frac{\bar{p}}{k} = e^{-C^2/\overline{A^2}}, \tag{4.13}$$

where $\bar{p}$ represents the mean of the number of samples of A^2 crossing the threshold C^2 out of k independent samples.

As would be expected, the accuracy with which the threshold-crossing technique can measure the true $\overline{A^2}$ depends on the level of C^2 and on the number of samples k. The optimum level of C^2, when $k \geqslant 50$, is between $1.2\overline{A^2}$ and $1.6\overline{A^2}$, corresponding to $\bar{p}/k$ between 0.2 and 0.3.

Atlas (1964) examined the implication of the foregoing discussion on the technique of measuring backscattered power by noting the echo threshold on a PPI or RHI scope. In this procedure the gain of the radar is adjusted until a precipitation echo is barely detected on the scope. Once this has been established, the amplitude of a signal from a microwave generator is adjusted until it also is barely detected on the same scope.

Atlas (1964) speculated that, at short ranges, only "one or two flashes out of some 50-odd independent samples which constitute the typical spot on the scope" will be adequate to make the echo barely discernible.

Equation (4.13) indicates that, if this were the case, the fraction $\overline{A^2}/C$ would be between about 0.25 and 0.3; hence, $\overline{A^2}$ would be about 5–6 dB below C^2.

The threshold level C^2 is obtained by introducing, into the radar system, signals of constant amplitude from a coherent source such as a signal generator. As a result, C^2 closely corresponds to the indicated power coming from the signal generator, and the calculated $\overline{A^2}$ would be some 5–6 dB greater than the true $\overline{A^2}$. Atlas (1964) noted that, as range increases, this discrepancy should decrease because the number of independent samples, k, per scope spot decreases linearly with range on a PPI scope. He noted that there were uncertainties in his analysis but made the important point that the use of threshold techniques employing unaveraged signals may lead to significant overestimates of the true average power.

Recently Marshall (1971) proposed a data-processing technique which does not suffer from the problem discussed by Atlas. Marshall's scheme examines the peak signal of k independent samples at 100 range positions along 600 radial lines on a PPI scope. Each dot appears as one of six shades of grey indicating target intensity. It was concluded that, with values of k between 7 and 75, the standard deviation of measured target intensity would be between 2 and 1 dB.

4.5 Backscattering by Small Spherical Water or Ice Spheres

Before examining the functional relationship of σ for spherical particles, it is appropriate to note qualitatively the process by which a drop scatters an intercepted radio wave. When a plane-polarized wave passes over a spherical drop, it induces oscillating electric and magnetic dipoles within the drop. Energy is taken from the incident field. Part of this energy is absorbed as heat by the drop, and part is reradiated as a scattered electromagnetic field having the same wavelength as the incident energy. At present, we shall be concerned with that part of the energy which is scattered.

A general theory describing the scattering of a plane wave by a sphere was first offered by Mie (1908) and has been studied by Stratton (1930), Kerr (1951), and many others. From the Mie theory, it has been shown that the backscattering cross section of a spherical drop is

$$\sigma = \frac{\pi a^2}{\alpha^2} \left| \sum_{n=1}^{\infty} (-1)^n (2n + 1)(a_n - b_n) \right|^2, \tag{4.14}$$

where a is the drop radius and $\alpha = 2\pi a/\lambda$. The quantities a_n and b_n are coefficients in the expression for the scattered field; the a_n terms refer to the scattering arising from the induced magnetic dipoles, quadrupoles, etc.; and the b_n terms refer to the electric dipoles, quadrupoles, etc. The letter n stands for the number of the terms in the expansions of a_n and b_n.

The quantities a_n and b_n can be expressed in terms of spherical Bessel functions and Hankel functions of the second kind with arguments α and m, the complex index of refraction;

$$m = n - ik,$$

where n is the ordinary refractive index and k is the absorption coefficient of the material involved. It should be noted that some authors express the complex index of refraction in the form $N = m - imk$.

Hand calculations of σ are laborious, but Ryde (1946) and Lowan (1949) calculated σ for spheres of α up to 1.25 times the wavelength. Electronic computers have made it simple to obtain the distribution of σ as a function of α and m, and several authors have published results of such analyses (Herman and Battan 1961, *a,b,c*; Herman, Browning, and Battan 1961; Battan, Browning, and Herman 1970*a*; Stephens 1961; Shifrin and Cherniak 1967*a,b*). Figure 4.2 shows calculations of the normalized backscattering cross section $(\sigma/\pi a^2)$ for water and ice spheres at $\lambda = 3.21$ cm. It is evident that, when α is very small, the backscattering cross section increases smoothly with α.

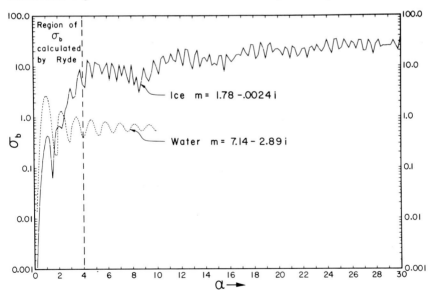

Fig. 4.2. Calculated values of the normalized backscattering cross section $(\sigma_b = \sigma/\pi a^2)$ for water and ice spheres. The water curve applies at a temperature of 0°C and a wavelength of 3.21 cm. The ice curve is valid for wavelengths from 1 to 10 cm. From Herman and Battan (1961*a*).

In a later section the backscattering from large spheres will be examined in some detail. At this point, consider those spheres with radii
much smaller than the radar wavelength or, in other words, those cases
where $\alpha << 1$. If terms containing higher than the fifth order of α are
neglected,

$$a_1 = -\frac{i}{45}(m^2 - 1)\alpha^5, \tag{4.15a}$$

$$b_1 = -\frac{2i}{3}\left(\frac{m^2 - 1}{m^2 + 2}\right)\alpha^3\left[1 + \frac{3}{5}\left(\frac{m^2 - 2}{m^2 + 2}\right)\alpha^2\right], \tag{4.15b}$$

$$b_2 = \frac{i}{15}\left(\frac{m^2 - 1}{2m^2 + 3}\right)\alpha^5. \tag{4.15c}$$

These terms can be used to obtain σ. Consider again that $\alpha << 1$.
Then only the first term of b_1, the electric dipole term, need be considered. Substitution in equation (4.14) yields the backscattering cross
section of a single particle,

$$\sigma_i = \frac{\lambda^2}{\pi}\alpha^6\left|\frac{m^2 - 1}{m^2 + 2}\right|^2 \tag{4.16a}$$

$$= \frac{\pi^5}{\lambda^4}|K|^2 D_i^6, \tag{4.16b}$$

where K is used to designate $(m^2 - 1)/(m^2 + 2)$ and D_i is the particle
diameter. Equation (4.16) also has been derived by assuming initially
that a sufficiently small drop will act as a dipole whose electric moment
is induced by the incident electric field. Because of its similarity to the
Rayleigh scattering formula, this equation is referred to as the "Rayleigh
approximation" of the backscattering cross section.

4.6 Complex Index of Refraction

For any given substance, the complex index of refraction, m, is a function
of λ and temperature. Table 4.1 gives values of n and k tabulated by Gunn
and East (1954). The quantities $|K|^2$ and $\text{Im}(-K)$ (the imaginary part
of $-K$), tabulated by the same investigators, are also listed. As will be
seen in a later chapter, the absorption of radar power depends on $\text{Im}(-K)$.
It is evident that, over the wavelength band most commonly used in
radar meteorology, 3–10 cm, and at temperatures between 0° C and
20° C, $|K|^2 = 0.93 \pm 0.004$. Hence for all purposes, when the scatterers
are known to be composed of water, $|K|^2$ can be taken to be 0.93.

The refractive index of an ice particle depends on its density. So-called
pure ice, i.e., ice not containing air, has a density of about 0.92 gm/cm³.
On the other hand a large snowflake made up of loosely bound ice crystals

TABLE 4.1   The Components of the Complex Index of Refraction,
                      $|K|^2$, and the Imaginary Part of $(-K)$ of Water as Functions
                      of Temperature and Wavelength

Quantity	Temperature (°C)	Wavelength (Cm)			
		10	3.21	1.24	0.62
n	20	8.88	8.14	6.15	4.44
	10	9.02	7.80	5.45	3.94
	0	8.99	7.14	4.75	3.45
	− 8	. . . .	6.48	4.15	3.10
κ	20	0.63	2.00	2.86	2.59
	10	0.90	2.44	2.90	2.37
	0	1.47	2.89	2.77	2.04
	− 8	. . . .	. . . .	2.55	1.77
$|K|^2$	20	0.928	0.9275	0.9193	0.8926
	10	0.9313	0.9282	0.9152	0.8726
	0	0.9340	0.9300	0.9055	0.8312
	− 8	. . . .	. . . .	0.8902	0.7921
$\mathrm{Im}(-K)$ . . .	20	0.00474	0.01883	0.0471	0.0915
	10	0.00688	0.0247	0.0615	0.1142
	0	0.01102	0.0335	0.0807	0.1441
	− 8	. . . .	. . . .	0.1036	0.1713

SOURCE: Gunn and East 1954.

has a very low density. In some cases its density may be no more than perhaps 0.05 gm/cm³. Cumming (1952) measured the dielectric constant of ice as a function of density. His data were employed by Gunn and East (1954) to obtain the data in table 4.2. It presents the components of the complex index of refraction for ice. Note that $n = 1.78$ at a density $\rho = 0.92$ gm/cm³, and $|K|^2 = 0.197$ at $\rho = 1$ gm/cm³. Both quantities are independent of temperature. The reason for giving $|K|^2$ at unit density needs some justification because ice always has a smaller density than that.

First of all it should be noted that measurements of precipitation rate at the ground, although commonly given in terms of millimeters per hour, refer to the rates of accumulation of water per unit of time. If the precipitation is in the form of snow, it is melted to give the appropriate rate of accumulation. Hence the precipitation rate is a measure of the rate of deposition of a given mass per unit of time.

Since the mass, M, of a spherical particle is given by $\frac{4}{3}\pi\rho a^3$, equation (4.16b) can be written

$$\sigma = \frac{36\pi^3}{\lambda^4}\frac{|K|^2}{\rho^2}M^2. \qquad (4.17)$$

TABLE 4.2   The Components of the Complex Index of Refraction,
$|K|^2$, and the Imaginary Part of $-K$ of Ice as Functions
of Temperature

Quantity	Temperature (°C)	Value
n	All temperatures when $\rho = 0.92$ gm/cm³	1.78
κ	0 −10 −20	2.4×10^{-3} 7.9×10^{-4} 5.5×10^{-4}
$|K|^2$	All temperatures when $\rho = 1$	0.197
$\mathrm{Im}(-K)$	0 −10 −20	9.6×10^{-4} 3.2×10^{-4} 2.2×10^{-4}

SOURCE: Gunn and East 1954.

According to Debye (1929), for a mixture of ice and air one can write

$$\frac{K}{\rho} M = \frac{K_i}{\rho_i} M_i + \frac{K_a}{\rho_a} M_a, \tag{4.18}$$

where the subscripts i and a refer to ice and air, respectively. Since the dielectric constant of air is very close to unity, K_a approaches zero and the second term may be neglected. Since $M \approx M_i$, it follows that K/ρ is nearly constant for ice-air mixtures. This conclusion is supported by the data published by Cumming (1952), which show that over a density range of 0.22–0.917 gm/cm³ the ratio K/ρ ranged from 0.50 to 0.46.

An ice particle with a mass M has a backscattering cross section proportional to the constant ratio $|K|^2/\rho^2$ and to M^2. If the density is taken to be 1.0 gm/cm³, σ will be proportional to $D_m{}^6$ where D_m is the diameter of the water sphere resulting from complete melting of the original ice particle.

4.7 Range of Rayleigh Backscattering

The question of the range of α over which the Rayleigh approximation may be used has been examined by various writers. Gunn and East (1954) published figure 4.3. It shows the variation of $\delta = \sigma_{\mathrm{Mie}}/\sigma_{\mathrm{Rayleigh}}$ as a function of α. Calculations are for water spheres at 18° C. As long as $D < 0.07\lambda$ (i.e., α is less than 0.22) over the range of wavelengths 0.9–10 cm, the Rayleigh value of σ will differ from the precise value of

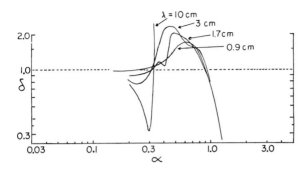

Fig. 4.3.   Ratio of Mie backscattering to Rayleigh backscattering by water spheres as a function of α. From Gunn and East (1954).

σ by no more than a factor of 0.75 corresponding to 1.5 dB. In all instances, the discrepancies will be such that σ_{Rayleigh} underestimates the true σ.

Ryde (1946) indicated that, for ice, the Rayleigh approximation for the backscattering cross section may be used for values of α up to 0.5 corresponding to $D < 0.16\lambda$.

It is evident from these results that, at wavelengths greater than 3 cm, precipitation containing drops no larger than 2 mm in diameter can be regarded as a Rayleigh backscatterer. Virtually all precipitation, except hail, can be so regarded at wavelengths of about 10 cm. It will be shown in a later section that dry snowflakes, regardless of size, may be treated as spheres of the same mass. Therefore, the comments about rain may also be applied to snow.

The preceding remarks were based on analyses of the radar cross sections of individual particles. Wexler and Atlas (1963) and Stephens (1964) considered the applicability of the Rayleigh approximation to a spectrum of raindrop sizes.

For many rains, the drop-size distribution is well represented by an empirical expression developed by Marshall and Palmer (1948),

$$N_D = N_0 e^{-\Lambda D}, \tag{4.19}$$

where N_D is the number of drops in a unit volume with diameters in the interval from D to $D + dD$; N_0 is a constant determined empirically to be 0.08 cm^{-4}; and $\Lambda = 41 R^{-0.21}$, where Λ is in units of (centimeters)$^{-1}$ and R, the rainfall rate, is in units of millimeters per hour.

Figure 4.4 shows Marshall-Palmer raindrop-size distributions for several rainfall rates. It is evident that, at small diameters, the exponential function does not fit the observations. For this reason, it is sometimes necessary to consider the Marshall-Palmer curves applicable at diameters

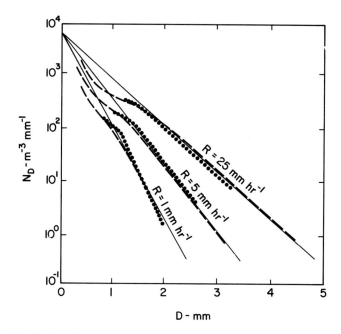

Fig. 4.4.   Distribution function (*solid straight lines*) compared with results of Laws and Parsons (*broken lines*) and Ottawa observations (*dotted lines*). From Marshall and Palmer (1948).

greater than 1–1.5 mm and to use some other expression at smaller diameters.

Wexler and Atlas (1963) employed Mie backscattering cross sections computed by Herman, Browning, and Battan (1961) and calculated $\Sigma\sigma$ for rainfall rates between 0.01 and 100 mm/hr. Wavelengths between 0.62 and 10 cm were considered. The analyses have shown that, at wavelengths between 3 and 10 cm, the Rayleigh approximation is valid for observing rain. As the wavelength falls below 3 cm, the discrepancies between Rayleigh and Mie cross sections increase, particularly at rainfall rates exceeding about 1 mm/hr.

4.8 P_r and the Backscattering from a Region of Spherical Particles

Knowing the backscattering cross section of individual spherical particles, one can calculate the total backscattering and make use of equation (4.9) to compute the average returned power.

Rayleigh scattering:

$$\overline{P}_r = \left(\frac{\pi^3 P_t G^2 \theta \phi h}{16 \times 64 \, \lambda^2 \ln 2} \right) \frac{|K|^2}{r^2} \sum_{vol} D_i^6 ; \qquad (4.20)$$

Mie scattering:

$$\bar{P}_r = \left(\frac{P_t G^2 \lambda^2 \theta \phi h}{\pi^2 \times 16 \times 64 \ln 2} \right) \frac{1}{r^2} \sum_{\text{vol}} \sigma_i. \qquad (4.21)$$

The quantity $\sum_{\text{vol}} D_i^6$ is commonly designated by the symbol Z. It is called the "reflectivity factor" to differentiate it from "the reflectivity" designated by η and equal to $\sum_{\text{vol}} \sigma_i$. When the particle-size distribution is given in terms of the number of drops, n_i, in discrete intervals of diameter, it is common to assume that all the particles in each interval have the same size and to write $Z = \sum n_i D_i^6$. Occasionally one sees $Z = N\bar{D}^6$. When this expression is employed, $\bar{D}$ refers to the mean sixth power of the particle diameters.

All the terms within the parentheses on the right-hand sides of equations (4.20) and (4.21) are fixed characteristics of the radar or are numerical constants. As noted earlier, at centimeter wavelengths, $|K|^2$ may be taken to be 0.93 and 0.20 for water and ice particles, respectively.

The r^{-2} relationship is valid when the entire beam is intercepted. If only a part of the beam is filled by scattering particles, the equation must be modified by a factor ψ, which is the fraction of the cross-sectional area of the beam intercepted by the region of scattering particles. In general, observations should be taken so that the beam-filling condition is fulfilled. This obviously is most easily accomplished when narrow beams are employed to observe weather phenomena at short ranges.

4.9 Effective Radar Reflectivity Factor

Equation (4.20) can be written

$$\bar{P}_r = \frac{C |K|^2 Z}{r^2}, \qquad (4.22)$$

where C is a constant depending on the characteristics of the radar set. If the scatterers are known to be raindrops which are small with respect to λ, measurements of $\bar{P}_r$ and r allow calculations of Z, which in turn gives $\sum D_i^6$ per unit volume. In many instances, the conditions for Rayleigh backscattering may not be fulfilled or it might not be possible to state whether they are fulfilled. In such instances, it would be more appropriate to write

$$\bar{P}_r = \frac{C |K|^2 Z_e}{r^2}, \qquad (4.23)$$

where Z_e is the "effective radar reflectivity factor." It can be calculated if $\bar{P}_r$ and r are known.

The quantity Z_e may be written in terms of the reflectivity

$$\eta = \frac{\pi^5}{\lambda^4} |K|^2 Z_e, \qquad (4.24)$$

which leads to

$$Z_e = \frac{\lambda^4 \eta}{\pi^5 |K|^2}. \qquad (4.25)$$

In calculating Z_e, the quantity $|K|^2$ conventionally is taken to be 0.93.

If each of the scatterers has a diameter D and a backscattering cross section σ, it can be shown that

$$Z_e = \frac{6 \lambda^4 \sigma M}{\pi^6 |K|^2 \rho D^3}, \qquad (4.26)$$

where M is the liquid-water content represented by particles with diameter D and density ρ. Atlas, Hardy, and Joss (1964) showed that $Z_e = 7.48 \times 10^3 \lambda^4 \sigma M / D^3$ for particles with density 0.9 g/cm³. The units of Z_e are millimeters to the sixth power per cubic meter when λ and D are in centimeters, σ in square centimeters and M in grams per cubic meter. This expression is useful for calculating the liquid-water contents required to give particular reflectivities at known wavelength, particle diameter, and backscattering cross section.

5 Backscattering by Melting Spheres and Nonspherical Particles

Chapter 4 dealt with the backscattering of plane-polarized radiation by spherical particles composed entirely of water or ice.

This chapter will examine the scattering by particles which are non-homogeneous and nonspherical. As would be expected, the functional forms of the scattering equations are quite involved, and as was done in the section on scattering by spheres, only the line of approach for setting up the pertinent equations and the final results of the analysis will be given. The reader interested in the details of the mathematical analysis is encouraged to consult the references.

5.1 Backscattering by Small, Melting Ice Spheres

Much of the precipitation reaching the ground originates as ice crystals, snowflakes, snow pellets, or hailstones. None of these hydrometeors can be called spheres in the strict sense, but some snow pellets and hailstones may be close to being spherical. Therefore, the analysis to be given here can be considered applicable, at least to some degree, to snow pellets and hailstones which melt as they fall through warm air. The equations also permit inferences about the scattering properties of non-spherical ice particles as they melt.

The first calculations of the radar cross sections of melting ice particles were made by Ryde (1946). He considered the scatterers to be small enough for the Rayleigh approximation to be applicable and assumed that during the melting process the particles consisted of a homogeneous mixture of ice and water. Under this assumption, he computed the dielectric constant of the mixture from the Debye (1929) equation

$$K \frac{(M_i + M_w)}{\rho} = K_i \frac{M_i}{\rho_i} + K_w \frac{M_w}{\rho_w}, \tag{5.1}$$

where the subscripts i and w refer to ice and water, respectively; M is the mass of the substances; and ρ is density.

This equation is strictly applicable only when the two substances in the mixture are nonabsorbers (Ditchburn 1958). In a later section of

45

Backscattering by Melting Spheres and Nonspherical
Particles

this chapter, this point will be examined in greater detail, but it should
be borne in mind that the validity of equation (5.1) is questionable when
the mixture contains water and ice.

Knowing the value of K and the particle size, one may calculate the
Rayleigh backscattering cross section by means of equation (4.16). The
results of such a procedure for a wavelength of 3 cm are plotted in figure
5.1. The ordinate is the ratio of the backscattering cross section of the
spherical particle to the cross section of the totally melted sphere. For
example, a homogeneous ice particle has a σ/σ_m equal to 0.215, the

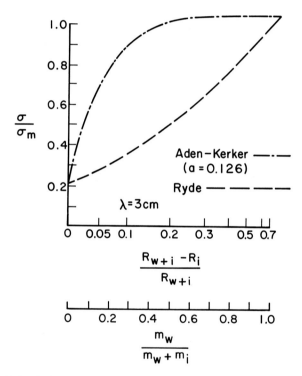

Fig. 5.1. Variation in backscattering of a melting ice sphere as a function of melted mass:
dashed curve, results of calculations from Ryde's theory, which assumes that the particle
consists of a homogeneous mixture of water and ice; *dot-dash curve*, a shell of water
surrounding an ice sphere. From Langleben and Gunn (1952).

ratio of 0.197 to 0.93. The abscissa has two labels; the fraction of melted
mass and the fraction of melted-particle radius. The assumption of a
homogeneous mixture of water and ice may be approached by wet snowflakes, but it would not apply to many frozen particles, such as snow
pellets and hail. Instead, one could reasonably expect these frozen

particles to develop skins of water whose average thickness would increase with time, until sufficient water accumulated to be shed as the particles moved through the air.

Kerker, Langleben, and Gunn (1951) and Langleben and Gunn (1952) studied the reflectivity of a melting spherical ice particle. Their results can be applied to those hydrometeors which are least likely to meet Ryde's assumption. Their approach was based on work by Aden and Kerker (1951), who developed an exact theory for the scattering by a particle composed of two concentric spheres with different indexes of refraction.

The Mie expression for the backscattering cross section, equation (4.14), is also applicable to scattering by melting spheres. The scattering amplitudes, a_n and b_n, are expressed in terms of spherical Bessel and Hankel functions of order n. The arguments of the functions are $m_1\alpha$, v, $m_2\alpha$, and m_2v, where m_1 and m_2 are the complex indices of refraction of ice and of water, respectively; $\alpha = 2\pi a_1/\lambda$, where a_1 is the radius of the ice sphere; $v = 2\pi a_0/\lambda$, where a_0 is the outer radius of the surrounding water shell.

As was the case with homogeneous spherical particles, by assuming that $\alpha << 1$, one may neglect terms higher than the first order in the expansion of a_n and b_n. Langleben and Gunn (1951) considered melting particles meeting this restriction and made calculations of σ. They considered special cases in which particle sizes and wavelengths yielded an $\alpha = 0.126$ (see table 5.1). Figure 5.1 shows the results of their calculations at a wavelength of 3 cm. The corresponding curve for 10 cm is very close to the one shown.

TABLE 5.1   Values of a, λ, and Corresponding Values of m in a Special Case ($\alpha = 0.126$)

Original Ice Particle Radius (Cm)	Wavelength (Cm)	m	
		Ice	Water
0.2	10	1.75	8.90
0.06	3	1.75	8.18–i 1.96
0.018	0.9	1.75	5.55–i 2.85

It is evident from this diagram that a thin coating of water results in a very large increase in the reflectivity of an ice sphere. For example, when one-tenth of the radius of an ice sphere of radius 0.2 cm melts, the backscattering of 3-cm radiation is approximately 90 percent of the value which would be backscattered by an all-water drop of the same radius. Clearly Ryde's treatment leads to a less rapid increase in reflectivity with increases in fractional melting than does the Aden-Kerker treatment. It seems reasonable to suppose that the most applicable approach depends on the type of particles involved. One might expect that ice particles of high density would start melting on the skin and develop a layer of water. Thus the Aden-Kerker theory would be applicable in the early stages of melting. At a late stage of melting of agglomerations of ice particles which originally had a high density, or during most of the melting of any large, low-density snowflakes, one might expect the concept of a mixture of water and ice to be more applicable. Unfortunately, little is known about the manner in which frozen hydrometeors melt. There is also considerable question about the validity of equation (5.1) when a highly absorbing substance such as water is part of the mixture.

5.2 Backscattering by Large, Melting Ice Spheres

The first measurements of the backscattering from large, melting ice spheres were made by Atlas et al. (1960). They suspended simulated hailstones from a balloon and observed them by means of radar sets operating at 3.3 cm and 4.67 cm. The ice spheres ranged in diameter from about 2 to 8 cm. It was found that the onset of melting was readily observed on a 3-cm radar as a sudden decrease in the backscattered signal. On the 4.67-cm radar the decrease of echo intensity generally was more gradual.

The decrease of backscattering cross section, σ, of large ice spheres (those with $D \geq 0.08\lambda$) as they become coated with water is to be expected from a consideration of the curves shown in figure 4.2. They do not indicate, however, the rate of change of σ as a function of the rate of melting or the quantity of water collected on the ice sphere. Atlas et al. (1960) reported that the maximum thickness of the water shell that could be maintained on a stationary melting ice sphere was 10^{-2} cm. Gerhardt et al. (1961) measured the backscattering from dry- and wet-ice pellets in the laboratory by means of an X-band continuous-wave radar. When particle diameters exceeded 3.5 mm there was close agreement between the measurements and Mie scattering theory.

Herman and Battan (1961b) extended the earlier work of Aden and Kerker (1951) and applied the complete Mie theory to the problem of large ice spheres surrounded by a shell of water. Calculations were made at wavelengths of 3.21, 4.67, and 10 cm. Spheres from 0.2 to 8.0 cm in diameter were examined. Their normalized backscattering cross sections were computed as the water shell increased from 10^{-8} cm to the point where the entire sphere was composed of water.

As was shown earlier (see fig. 5.1), when α is small, σ increases as an ice sphere melts. On the other hand, when α approaches or exceeds unity the variation of σ with water-shell thickness becomes erratic depending on sphere diameter and wavelength. This is illustrated in figure 5.2. In general, σ decreases as long as $\alpha > 1$, but between the ice cross section and the all-water cross section, σ sometimes exhibits some increases or decreases. In some instances the value of σ may extend beyond the range set by the all-water and all-ice sphere limits. Presumably, this result is caused by interference effects between the waves reflected from the front surface of the sphere, those reflected internally from the two water-ice interfaces and the back surface of the sphere, and waves on the surface of the sphere.

The thickness of the water shell needed to make an ice sphere act as though it were an all-water sphere depends on the wavelength. The thicknesses are 5×10^{-1} cm, 7×10^{-1} cm, and 1.0–2.0 cm at wavelengths of 3.21 cm, 4.67 cm, and 10.0 cm, respectively.

For the specific cases observed by Atlas et al. (1960) there was good agreement between the measurements and the calculations.

It is not possible to write a simple function relating σ to the fractional melting of large ice spheres as was done with small ice spheres. For a particular wavelength, sphere diameter, and thickness of water shell it is necessary to calculate σ from the complete scattering equations as was done by Herman and Battan (1961*b*). In their paper they presented curves for a wide range of conditions, and in many cases σ can be read directly off the curves. Unfortunately, unless calculations have been made for the specific sphere diameter of interest, it is not possible to extrapolate safely when water-shell thicknesses are greater than about 10^{-3} cm.

5.3 Backscattering from Spheres of "Spongy" Ice

It is known from the analysis of real and simulated hailstones that during so-called wet growth the stone is composed of a mixture of ice and water. List (1959) concluded that, in some instances, more than 50 percent of a hailstone mass could be liquid.

Battan and Herman (1962) calculated the backscattering cross section, at a wavelength of 3.21 cm, of "spongy"-ice spheres and solid-ice spheres coated with shells of spongy ice. The fraction of water contained in the spongy ice varied from zero to 1.0. Since there was no other better procedure, the dielectric constant of the mixture of water and ice was calculated by means of equation (5.1) as had been done by earlier investigators (Ryde 1946; Austin and Bemis 1950; and others). Nevertheless, Battan and Herman (1962) indicated reservations about the use of the Debye expression when one substance of the mixture is highly absorbing.

Figure 5.3 shows the normalized backscattering cross sections appropriate for ice spheres whose dielectric constants were obtained by means of equation (5.1). For convenience, they are called "spongy-ice spheres." As the percentage of water increases, the maxima in σ_b shifts toward smaller α. At the same time, the amplitude of the maxima diminishes.

Atlas, Hardy, and Joss (1964) examined the data in figure 5.3 and calculations of the backscattering by ice spheres with a shell of spongy ice and compared them with measurements of the backscattering by spheres of the latter type. Joss and List (1963) made such particles in a special hail tunnel and measured their radar cross sections at 5.05 cm. The spheres ranged in diameter from 2.0 to 2.4 cm, and the spongy-ice thicknesses ranged from 0.4 to 2 mm.

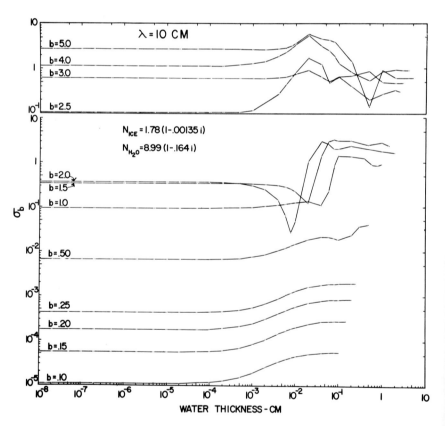

Fig. 5.2. Normalized backscattering cross sections, at wavelengths of 3.21 and 10 cm, of ice spheres coated with a layer of water. The quantity b is the overall sphere radius in centimeters, i.e., the ice-sphere radius plus the water-shell thickness. From Herman and Battan (1961b).

Figure 5.4 shows a comparison of the measured backscattering cross sections and computed cross sections. The ordinate shows cross sections in decibels with respect to the power which would be backscattered from all-water spheres. A mean value is taken for the sphere sizes involved. The ice line, also, is a mean, for spheres of diameter of about 2.0 cm. It is clear that there is excellent agreement between the "Herman and Battan" curve and the experimental results. Interestingly, the so-called Herman and Battan curve shown here corresponds to the backscattering from a solid-ice sphere having a *shell of water corresponding to the quantity of water contained in the spongy ice.* The measured backscattering did not correlate well with the values calculated by Battan and Herman (1962) in the case of a shell of spongy ice coating a solid-ice sphere. These results indicate that equation (5.1) does not give a good estimate of K when ice and water are mixed.

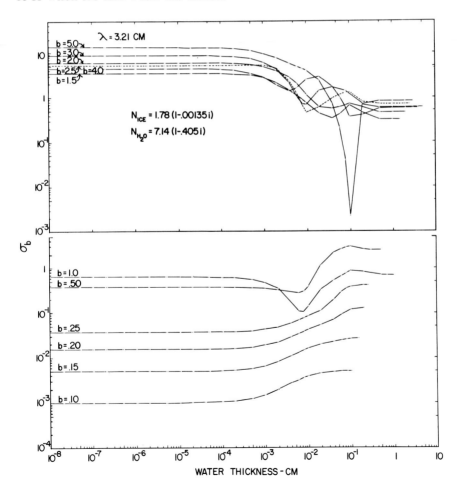

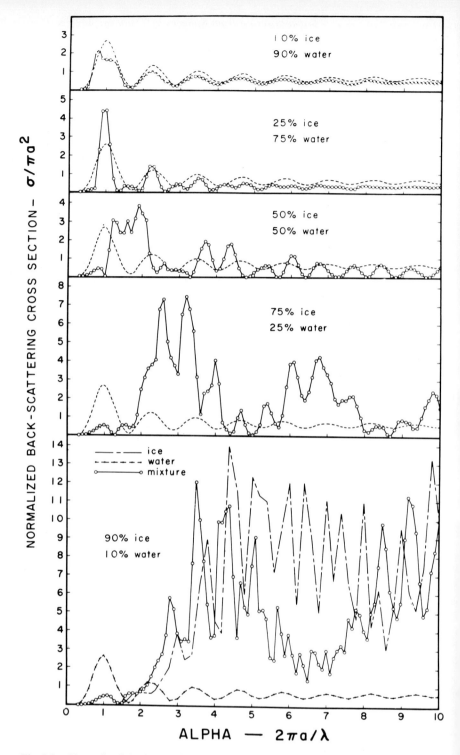

Fig. 5.3. Normalized backscattering cross sections of spongy ice spheres: *dot-dashed line,* solid ice; *dashed line,* all-water spheres. From Battan and Herman (1962).

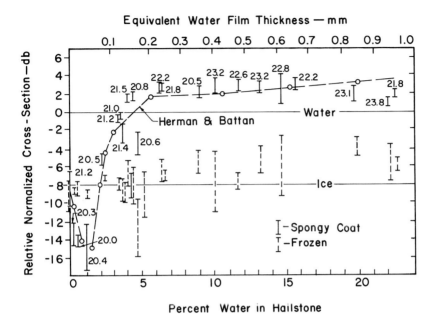

Fig. 5.4.   Measurements of the backscattering cross sections of ice spheres at 5.05 cm. The sphere diameters (in millimeters) are shown. They were composed of a solid ice core having shells of spongy ice ranging in thickness from 0.4 to 2.0 mm. *Solid vertical lines,* the range of backscattering as the stones were rotated; *dashed lines,* the backscattering after the stones froze entirely. From Atlas, Hardy, and Joss (1964).

Atlas, Hardy, and Joss (1964) used the data in figures 5.3 and 5.4 to argue that radar observations of hailstones can be explained in terms of spheres about 1 cm in diameter composed entirely of spongy ice or of solid ice cores coated with shells of spongy ice. This matter will be examined in greater detail in a later chapter.

5.4 Scattering by Small, Nonspherical Hydrometeors

Because many frozen hydrometeors are very markedly nonspherical, it is essential that some understanding be developed of their scattering properties. Theoretical work on the backscattering by small oblate and prolate spheroids was carried out by Atlas, Kerker, and Hitschfeld (1953); Labrum (1952); and Shupiatskii (1959). This work involved an approach similar to that used by Gans (1912), who developed a theory for the scattering of electromagnetic waves by ellipsoids which are small in relation to the wavelengths involved.

It is assumed that a plane-polarized wave which intercepts an ellipsoid can be considered to induce in the ellipsoid three orthogonal dipole moments, each of which is parallel to one of the axes. In deriving the

equation for the backscattering cross section of a small spherical particle, it also is assumed that a dipole moment is induced in the particle
and that, for a particle with $\alpha \ll \lambda$, higher multipole moments can be
neglected. A similar assumption is made for nonspherical particles;
however, it has not been possible to specify the critical value at which
a particle is too large for the assumption to be valid. This constitutes
one of the weak points of the theory.

   The manner in which an ellipsoid scatters a radar wave can be given
qualitatively if reference is made to figure 5.5. In this diagram, one con-
siders the special case of a prolate spheroid whose major axis (which
lies in the orientation plane) is in a vertical plane. A plane-polarized
wave in the plane defined by the plane of oscillation of the electric-field
vector and the direction of propagation intercepts the spheroid at any
arbitrary angle with the major axis x. In this example, the orientation

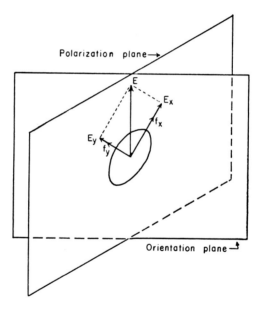

Fig. 5.5.   Schematic drawing of a nonspherical particle intercepting a plane-polarized wave.

and polarization planes are perpendicular. It is evident that in this case
the vector $\mathbf{E}$ has no component in the plane perpendicular to the orientation plane. In a more general case the ellipsoid would be oriented at
some angle relative to the vertical plane. This situation has not been
considered here because it complicates the description without giving
information which cannot be inferred from the special case presented.

   As can be seen, the incident electric-field vector lies along the line of intersection of the two planes. According to Gans, one can resolve **E** into two components along the axes of the ellipsoid. Each of the components of the electric field is then considered to act separately in the excitation of a dipole moment in the component direction. On the diagram the direction and relative magnitudes of the moments are shown as f_x and f_y.

According to the Gans theory, the magnitudes of the component dipole moments, which produce the radiation and backscattering, are proportional to the respective components of the incident **E** through a factor which depends on the shapes of the particles and their dielectric properties. Also, the dipole moments are directly proportional to the volume of the ellipsoid.

The following relationships have been found for the dipole moments f_x, f_y, and f_z, where x represents the axis of revolution, or a major axis, and y and z represent the symmetrical axes (note that the z moment is present only when the orientation plane and the polarization plane are not perpendicular, as is the case in fig. 5.5):

$$f_x = gE_x; \qquad f_y = g'E_y; \qquad f_z = g'E_z. \tag{5.2}$$

The value of the proportionality factor, g, is given by

$$g = m_0^2 \frac{V(m^2 - 1)}{4\pi + (m^2 - 1)P}, \tag{5.3}$$

where m and m_0 are the complex refractive indices of the particle and of the air, respectively; V is the volume of the particle; and P is a factor which depends on the shape of the particle. The quantity m_0 is close to one. In evaluating g', the value of P should be replaced by P', where

$$P' = 2\pi - \frac{P}{2}. \tag{5.4}$$

For a prolate spheroid,

$$P = 4\pi \frac{1 - e^2}{e^2} \left[\frac{1}{2e} \ln \left(\frac{1 + e}{1 - e} \right) - 1 \right], \tag{5.5a}$$

and for an oblate spheroid,

$$P = \frac{4\pi}{e^2} \left(1 - \sqrt{\frac{1 - e^2}{e^2}} \arcsin e \right) \tag{5.5b}$$

where e is the eccentricity, $(a^2 - b^2)/a^2$. The quantities a and b are the axes of the principal elliptical cross section.

When the eccentricity of the ellipsoid is close to 1.0, i.e., a long narrow prolate or a flat, platelike oblate spheroid, the values of P are equal to zero and 4π, respectively.

In the case of a sphere, $e = 0$ and $P = \frac{4}{3}\pi$, and substitution in equations
(5.3) and (5.2) yields

$$f = m_0^2 \left(\frac{m^2 - 1}{m^2 + 2}\right) a^3 E. \tag{5.6}$$

Various interesting features of equations (5.3) and (5.6) should be
noted. The dipole moments are directly proportional to V. Since the
scattered power is proportional to the square of the dipole moment,
equation (5.6) indicates that, for a sphere, the scattered power is proportional to the sixth power of the radius. This is in agreement with earlier
results.

The shape factor, P, affects the coefficient g only to the extent that the
dielectric constant (m^2) differs from unity. Since water has a dielectric
constant of about 80 (table 4.1), while ice has a value of about 3 (table
4.2), it is evident that shape effects are much more important in the case
of water particles.

Low-density ice has a value of m^2 close to unity. From equation (5.3)
it follows that, with low-density snowflakes, the shape effects would be
negligibly small, and the value of g would be proportional to its volume.
In terms of its microwave scattering properties, such snowflakes can be
regarded as spheres of the same volume.

Since the values of m^2 are essentially independent of λ for ice particles
but are largely dependent on λ for water particles, the values of g can
also be considered dependent on, or independent of, λ, depending on
whether the particle is composed of water or ice. Also, for water particles,
changes in λ become more important with increasing values of P.

When the index of refraction is complex, g and g' are generally complex, and, as a result, the oscillating dipole moments lag behind the
incident field in time. However, this effect is not usually important except at the short wavelengths, where the imaginary components become
large.

Equation (5.2) permits calculations of the scattering from a single
nonspherical particle if its size, shape, composition, and orientation
with respect to the electric vector are known. If N particles are excited,
the total scattered power will be N times the average amount scattered
by a single particle, where the average is taken over all possible orientations, sizes, and degrees of ellipticity.

Calculations of the backscattering by randomly oriented nonspherical
particles are shown in figure 5.6. The scattered field intensity is expressed
as a fraction of the amount which would be scattered by spheres of the
same volume. The ratio is referred to as the "normalized scatter intensity." Values have been calculated for water and ice oblate and prolate
spheroids with axial ratios ranging from 0.1 to 1.0 and for wavelengths
of 1.25, 3.2, and 10 cm. It is evident that nonspherical water particles

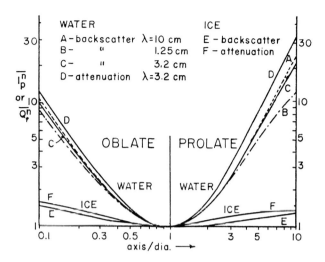

Fig. 5.6. Backscattering and attenuation from randomly oriented water and ice spheroids relative to water and ice spheres of equal volume as a function of the shapes of the particles. The attenuation curves will be discussed in chapter 6. From Atlas, Kerker, and Hitschfeld (1953).

can backscatter much more power than would be expected from spherical particles; e.g., with an axial ratio of 0.1, the normalized signal intensities are 10 and 25 for oblate and prolate spheroids, respectively. In general, large water droplets falling at their terminal velocities have oblate shapes, but they have fairly large axial ratios. They tend to oscillate and sometimes do reach axial ratios of perhaps a few tenths, but they remain this way for very short periods of time. The very small axial ratios of 0.1 or 0.2 might occur with partially melted ice particles. As was shown earlier in this chapter, a thin layer of water on a frozen particle can cause it to scatter almost the same amount as an all-water particle.

Figure 5.6 also presents normalized scattering intensities for randomly oriented oblate and prolate spheroids composed entirely of ice. Since the dielectric constant of ice is independent of wavelength, the plotted values are applicable for all values of λ from 1 to 10 cm. It can be seen that, even with axial ratios as low as 0.1, the normalized intensity is increased by less than a factor of 2. The calculations predict that, with low-density snow particles, it will be close to one, i.e., the scattering of spheroids will approximate the scattering of spheres of the same volumes.

The results presented in this section consider particles which are randomly oriented relative to the incident field. They always scatter more intensely than would spheres of equal volumes. When the particles are preferentially oriented, so that the major axes are parallel to the direction of polarization of the incident field, the scattered radiation intensity is greater than would occur from randomly oriented particles.

When the minor axes of the particles are parallel to the direction of polarization, the scattered radiation intensity is less than that from spheres of equal volumes. These effects are obviously greater for water drops than for ice particles and negligible for low-density snowflakes.

For aerodynamic reasons oblate particles tend to fall with flat faces oriented horizontally. As shown by Atlas, Kerker, and Hitschfeld (1953), the backscattering from such targets would depend on the polarization of the radar beam and on the angle of declination of the beam from the zenith.

5.5 Depolarization by Nonspherical Particles

Since the components of the backscattered field are proportional to the dipole moments involved, one can examine the polarization of the scattered wave by considering these orthogonal moments. If the transmitting antenna radiates a plane-polarized wave, it will detect only those fields polarized in the same plane. As a result, only a fraction of the returned power can possibly be received because f_x and f_y may have components in the plane *perpendicular* to the polarization plane (fig. 5.5). The sum of the components of the field scattered in the perpendicular plane is known as the "cross-polarized field component."

The total backscattered power is the sum of the parallel-polarized and cross-polarized components of the scattered power. It should be evident that, when the plane of polarization of the incident radiowave includes one of the axes of the ellipsoid, all the backscattered power will have the same polarization.

Depolarization is measured by the "depolarization ratio," which is the ratio of the power in the cross-polarized plane, P_c, to that in the parallel-polarized plane, P_p. Often it is stated in terms of decibels and is calculated from

$$D_p \text{ (dB)} = 10 \log \frac{P_c}{P_p}. \tag{5.7}$$

Figure 5.7 presents calculated depolarization ratios for randomly oriented water and ice spheroids. Water drops with axial ratios close to 0.1 lead to depolarization ratios of 10 and 30 percent for oblate and prolate spheroids, respectively. For ice particles, depolarization is small, about 3 percent at axial ratios of 0.1. This, of course, is a consequence of the low dielectric constant of ice. Theoretically, with low-density frozen particles, depolarization should be negligible.

The depolarization ratio is measured by means of two antennas designed to detect plane-polarized radiation. Normally, one antenna is used for transmission and reception, and another antenna detects the

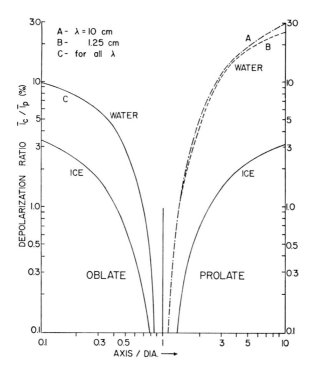

Fig. 5.7.   Depolarization ratios of randomly oriented water and ice spheroids. From Atlas Kerker, and Hitschfeld (1953).

cross-polarized signals. With randomly oriented spheroids, the depolarization ratio is less than 1.0, and D_p is negative. Typical values of D_p range from about −10 to −25 dB.

Another method for studying the shape of precipitation particles makes use of circular polarization. As indicated in section 2.4, a circularly polarized wave is one having an electric vector which is constant in amplitude but rotates, at the radar frequency, in a plane perpendicular to the path of propagation. When circularly polarized waves are scattered by a spherical particle, the backscattered signal is also circularly polarized but has an opposite direction of rotation from that of the transmitted signal. An antenna transmitting circularly polarized waves with one direction of rotation will accept only the waves with the same direction of rotation. Thus, backscattered power from a shower of perfectly spherical particles will not be detected if the transmitted wave is circularly polarized throughout the radar beam.

A procedure for employing a circularly polarized radar for studying particle shapes was discussed by Newell et al. (1955), Marshall and Gordon (1957), and Shupiatskii and Morgunov (1963). A single antenna

may be used for both transmission and reception as it alternately radiates
plane-polarized waves and circularly polarized waves. The ratio of the
backscattered powers $P_{circular}/P_{plane}$ is called the "cancellation ratio,"
and

$$\text{Cancellation} = 10 \log \frac{P_{circular}}{P_{plane}}. \qquad (5.8)$$

For randomly oriented scatterers, the cancellation ratio is less than unity,
and the depolarization is 3 dB greater than the cancellation.

As noted by Newell et al. (1955), a circularly polarized wave rarely
is circularly polarized throughout the beam. Usually it is circularly
polarized near the center of the beam but elliptically polarized off the
center. As a result spherical scatterers do not cause perfect cancellation.
The effects of the antenna on the cancellation can be computed and used
to correct measurements of cancellation. When the scattering particles
are very nonspherical, the antenna effects are small and can be ignored,
but as the particle shapes approach sphericity, corrections to the cancellation measurements become large. Furthermore, an antenna has a
"cancellation limit" which is the cancellation measured if the beam is
filled with spheres. The cancellation limit of the antenna used by Newell
et al. (1955) was −19 dB.

Some early measurements of the depolarization of microwaves by
precipitation were made by Browne and Robinson (1952) and Hunter
(1954). Wexler (1955) employed cross-polarization data to estimate the
nonsphericity of precipitation particles. With the scatterers assumed
to be spheroids, the effective axial ratios for oblate spheroids were 0.4
in snow, 0.5 in the melting region (bright band), and 0.75 in rain. The
corresponding cross-polarization ratios were −18 dB from snow, −15
dB from melting snow and ice particles, and −20 dB from rain. It should
be noted that the cross-polarization ratio in snow was quite large. This
is not in agreement with the predictions made by Atlas, Kerker, and
Hitschfeld (1953), who calculated that the ratio for snow particles of
density 0.05 gm/cm³ should be negligible.

Newell et al. (1955) measured cancellation ratios in snow, in the
melting layer, and in rain. As would be expected, the values extended
over a substantial range within each precipitation regime, but the distributions differed from one to the next. In snow, the melting layer,
and rain, the values were mostly in the ranges −19 to −13 dB, −16 to
−7 dB, and −19 to −12 dB, respectively. The distributions of the cancellation ratios in summer showers and winter precipitation were much
the same. The cancellation was not found to be a function of signal

intensity. It might have been supposed that the larger signal intensities would be associated with large drops having significant deformations from sphericity.

By means of their measurements, Newell et al. calculated axial ratios of ellipsoids corresponding to the observed cancellations. On the assumption that the particles were oblate ellipsoids, typical values of axial ratios in snow, the melting layer, and rain were 0.1, 0.4, and 0.7, respectively. Except for the first, these quantities are similar to those estimated by Wexler (1955) on the basis of cross-polarization measurements.

Excellent agreement was found by Newell (1958*a*) when he compared measured values of cancellation ratios with calculated values. Nonspherical frozen raindrops fell at the radar site. They were caught on black cloth and photographed. Computations revealed that the hydrometeors should have produced a cancellation ratio of about −7.0 dB. This ratio compared extremely well with the observed values found to be between −6.5 and −8.0 dB.

On the basis of flight tests during which a circularly polarized radar was used, Harrison and Post (1954) concluded that they could not distinguish hailstorms from other storms. On the other hand, Newell et al. (1955) found that two hailstorms gave large cancellation ratios.

More recently Barge (1970, 1972) employed an S-band radar to measure the depolarization caused by hail. The radar set transmitted circularly polarized signals and received two orthogonal circularly polarized signals. Equivalent radar reflectivities were computed for the so-called parallel and orthogonal components of the backscattered signals. The former is the component that would be received if the targets were spherical. The ratio of the parallel to orthogonal reflectivities is called the Circular Depolarization Ratio (CDR). It is not the same as the Cancellation Ratio (CR) defined by Newell et al. (1955) as the ratio of power received by a circularly polarized radar to the power received by a horizontally polarized radar. Nevertheless both ratios, CDR and CR, are sensitive to deviations of sphericity on the part of the scatterers.

The radar set was equipped with a so-called polarization diversity antenna and a signal processing system which allowed the simultaneous PPI display of signal reflectivity and of the CDR. In both displays, distinct shades of grey were used to indicate echo strength at 10–dB intervals of Z_e and 5–dB intervals of CDR.

Barge (1972) reported that combined observations of radar reflectivity and CDR provided a means of distinguishing hail of damaging size from rain and very small hail. Neither the Z_e nor the CDR taken alone were as effective in distinguishing hail as was the combination of the two quantities.

5.6 Backscattering by Large Spheroids

Gans's theory applies to particles which are small with respect to wave-length. As in the case of spheres, it would be expected that backscattering from large spheroids cannot be written as a simple function. Stevenson (1953) developed a theory for the scattering of a plane-polarized wave by an ellipsoid. Limited existing information on this subject has come from several experimental investigations.

Harper (1962) measured the backscatter from oblate spheroids composed of Plexiglass ($n = 1.61$), and Atlas and Wexler (1963) observed particles composed of ice and a plastic called "Stycast Hi k" ($n = 1.73$). These refractive indices are similar to the refractive index of ice ($n = 1.78$). Harper examined spheroids with major axes of 4.2 cm by means of equipment operating at a wavelength of 3.2 cm. Atlas and Wexler employed two wavelengths, 3.2 and 9.67 cm, and observed oblate particles having major axes between 0.127 and 3.81 cm. The smallest ones gave results consistent with Gans's theory.

In general, as the axial ratios of the large oblate spheroids increased, the values of the backscattering cross sections, σ, exhibited upward and downward excursions; they were sometimes smaller and sometimes greater than the radar cross sections of equivolume spheres. There were large differences in the curves from one particle size to the next. The results show that, as in the case of spheres in the Mie scattering region, it is not possible to offer a simple generalized function for σ in terms of the properties of the particle. The problem is further complicated for spheroids because the shapes, and hence the orientations, of the spheroids must be taken into account.

Hailstones are seldom spheres, and large stones sometimes deviate greatly from sphericity. Weickmann (1953) indicated that about 40 percent of the hailstones he observed were elliptical or "lens shaped." For certain purposes they may be regarded as oblate spheroids. Harper (1962) reported a storm in which 4–5 cm hailstones roughly resembled oblate spheroids having axial ratios of about 0.76. More recently Barge (1972) reported that of a total of 1,920 hailstones about 41, 21, 10, and 8 percent had shapes which were approximately oblate, conical, spherical, and prolate respectively. Notwithstanding these reports, it should be recognized that, although actual stones may be most appropriately "fitted" with spherical or oblate form, discrepancies in the shapes may be very important.

Atlas and Wexler (1963) found that for large laboratory oblate spheroids ($D/\lambda > 0.5$), the large-face cross sections tended "to follow the behavior indicated by geometric optics." One would expect the irregularities in the shapes of actual hailstones to have an important effect on their backscattering properties.

The absence of an acceptable theory from which detailed calculations can be made and the limited number of measurements make it impossible to generalize about the backscattering and depolarization by hailstones. This is particularly true for stones composed of mixtures of ice and water. Much research remains to be done on this subject.

6

Attenuation

In the derivation of the equations for the backscattered power in chapter 4, it was tacitly assumed that empty space existed between the radar and the target. No provision was made for attentuation, i.e., the loss of power as the transmitted pulse passes from the antenna to the target or as the reflected power returns to the antenna. In some circumstances, attenuation is so small that it can be neglected, but in others, it must be taken into account.

Attentuation is the reduction of intensity of the electromagnetic wave along its path and is defined by the equation

$$d\overline{P}_r = 2k_L\overline{P}_r dr,\qquad(6.1)$$

where $d\overline{P}_r$ is the incremental reduction of the backscattered power $\overline{P}_r$ caused by the absorption and scattering of the medium between the radar set and the target, r is the range, and k_L is the attenuation coefficient having dimensions (length)$^{-1}$. The factor 2 is necessary because the radar power traverses the same path twice. It is evident that k_L has the general form of the extinction coefficients used in optics.

When equation (6.1) is integrated over the range zero to r, one obtains

$$\overline{P}_r = \overline{P}_{r0}\, e^{-2\int_0^r k_L\, dr}\qquad(6.2)$$

where $\overline{P}_{r0}$ is the power which would have been received had there been no attenuation. This equation can also be written

$$10\log\frac{\overline{P}_r}{\overline{P}_{r0}} = -2\int_0^r k\, dr \qquad\text{or}\qquad \overline{P}_r = \overline{P}_{r0}\, 10^{-0.2\int_0^r k\, dr}\qquad(6.3)$$

In this form the reduction of $\overline{P}_r$ is expressed in decibels and the attenuation coefficient k, is expressed in decibels per length and is equal to $10\,(\log e)k_L$. One of the chief advantages of expressing attenuation in decibels is that losses by various causes can simply be added to give the total attenuation in decibels.

Since attenuation of microwaves can be caused by atmospheric gases, clouds, and precipitation, equation (6.3) can be written

$$10 \log \frac{\overline{P}_r}{P_{r_0}} = -2 \int_0^r (k_g + k_c + k_p)\, dr, \qquad (6.4)$$

where k_g, k_c, and k_p represent the attenuation (in decibels per unit of range one way) by gases, cloud, and precipitation, respectively.

The attenuation experienced by radar waves is a result of two effects: (1) absorption, and (2) scattering of power out of the beam. In general, gases act only as absorbers. As will be seen later in this chapter the same can be said of cloud droplets and small raindrops, but when large snow-flakes and raindrops are present, both scattering and absorption must be considered. At wavelengths greater than a few centimeters, attenuation by atmospheric gas is very small and usually can be ignored. On the other hand, cloud and rain attenuation has to be considered at wavelengths below the 10-cm band and can have serious effects in the 3- and 1-cm bands.

6.1 Attenuation by Atmospheric Gases

Although attenuation of microwaves by gaseous absorption can usually be neglected for radar sets operating at the longer wavelengths, it must be considered in certain radar problems involving wavelengths in the vicinity of 1 cm, especially when relatively large ranges are involved.

The only atmospheric gases which need be considered as absorbers are water vapor and oxygen. The theory of attenuation of electromagnetic waves by these gases was given by Van Vleck (1947 *a,b*) and has been discussed by various authors, notably Bean and Dutton (1968) and Gunn and East (1954). Each gas absorbs energy because the individual molecules behave like dipoles. Water vapor has a permanent electric dipole moment; oxygen has a permanent magnetic dipole moment. The incident electromagnetic wave passing over these molecules reacts with the molecules, causing them to oscillate and rotate in a variety of ways. According to quantum theory, each of the vibrational states is associated with a certain energy level. A certain amount of energy is needed to maintain the molecules at a new energy level, and this is given by hf, where h is Planck's constant and f is frequency. Thus it is visualized that the incident wave delivers to the gas molecules discrete amounts of energy (hf) during the transition from the lower- to the higher-energy level. When the molecule returns to the lower level, it reradiates the energy. However, the reradiation is random, and the reradiated energy does not add to the exciting wave. The net effect is an attenuation of the amplitude of the incident wave.

Most of the water-vapor absorption in the atmosphere is associated with the resonance band centered at a wavelength of 1.35 cm (22,235 MHz) and another group of lines centered near 0.2 cm. Oxygen absorption is mostly a result of a large number of narrow lines centered near 0.5 cm (60,000 MHz). Because of pressure-broadening effects, the lines tend to merge into one band. Figure 6.1 shows curves of attenuation in the atmosphere caused by oxygen and water vapor. The water-vapor

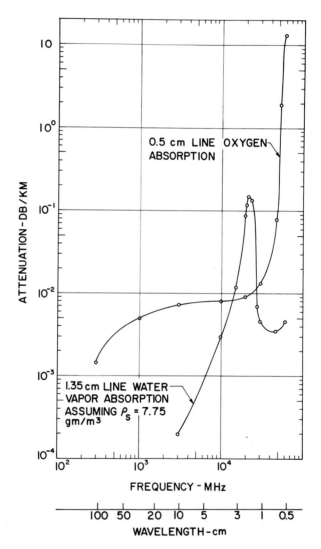

Fig. 6.1. Atmospheric absorption by the 1.35-cm line of water vapor for a mean absolute humidity of 7.75 g/m³ and by the 0.5-cm line of oxygen at a temperature of 20°C and a pressure of one atmosphere. After Bean and Dutton (1968).

absorption applies when the water-vapor density is 7.75 gm/m³, a mean value for Washington, D.C. Since the absorption is proportional to water-vapor density, the curve can be readily adjusted to other densities.

Bean and Dutton (1968) discussed the dependence of gaseous absorption on pressure and temperature. The reader interested in details should consult their work. Figure 6.1 allows certain generalizations. At wavelengths greater than 3 cm, gaseous attenuation is small and can be neglected unless long ranges are involved. Figure 6.1 indicates that, at a wavelength of 5 cm, attenuation amounts to about 0.008 dB/km, and the gaseous attenuation will reach 1 dB only with targets at ranges greater than about 62 km.

Radar sets operating in the K-band, particularly some of the early models having a frequency of 24,000 MHz (1.25 cm) are subject to very significant attenuation, particularly in humid atmospheres.

At millimeter wavelengths gaseous attenuation can be extremely large, exceeding 10 dB/km at 5 mm. For this reason they generally can be used only over very short ranges.

6.2 Attenuation by Hydrometeors

The attenuation of electromagnetic waves by hydrometeors in the atmosphere may result from both absorption and scattering, depending on the size, shape, and composition of the particles.

Mie scattering theory also leads to other cross sections besides the backscattering cross section. The scattering cross section, Q_s, is the area which, when multiplied by the incident intensity, gives the total power scattered by the particle; Q_a, the absorption cross section, is the area which, when multiplied by the incident intensity, gives the power dissipated as internal heat in the particle. The attenuation cross section, Q_t, is the area which, when multiplied by the incident power intensity, gives the total power taken from the incident radio wave. It is equal to the sum of Q_s and Q_a. For certain purposes it is convenient to employ normalized cross sections. They are obtained by dividing Q by the cross-sectional area of the particle.

When the particles are small with respect to the wavelength, i.e., $\alpha << 1$, we may obtain Rayleigh approximations of Q_s, Q_a, and Q_t.

$$Q_s = \frac{128}{3} \frac{\pi^5 a^6}{\lambda^4} \left| \frac{m^2 - 1}{m^2 + 2} \right|^2 , \tag{6.5}$$

$$Q_a = \frac{8\pi^2 a^3}{\lambda} \operatorname{Im} \left(-\frac{m^2 - 1}{m^2 + 2} \right), \tag{6.6}$$

$$Q_t = Q_a + Q_s. \tag{6.7}$$

The quantity Im is the imaginary part of $-(m^2 - 1)/(m^2 + 2)$. Values of Im $(-K)$ are given in tables 4.1 and 4.2.

The total attenuation by hydrometeors is equal to the summation of the attenuation by all the particles in the path traversed by the wave. The value of Q_t given in these equations applies to one spherical particle. To obtain the value over a unit distance, one can integrate the values of Q_t over all particles within a volume of unit cross section and unit distance. This will lead to

$$k_{(c+p)_L} = \Sigma Q_t. \tag{6.8}$$

The reduction of received power can then be expressed as

$$\overline{P_r} = \overline{P_{r_0}} \, e^{-2 \int (\Sigma Q_t) dr}. \tag{6.9}$$

If the value of the attenuation were to be expressed in terms of decibels per length of travel, then

$$k_{(c+p)} = \beta \sum_{\text{vol}} Q_t, \tag{6.10}$$

where β is a factor which depends on the units of length utilized in the problem. When Q_t is in units of square centimeters and the summation is made of over 1 m³, the attenuation in decibels per kilometer is given by

$$k_{(c+p)} = 0.4343 \sum_{\text{vol}} Q_t. \tag{6.11}$$

It is evident from the equations given above that $Q_s << Q_a$ for small particles having $\alpha << \lambda$, and therefore

$$k_{(c+p)} = 0.4343 \left[\frac{8\pi^2}{\lambda} (\sum_{\text{vol}} a^3) \, \mathrm{Im} \left(-\frac{m^2 - 1}{m^2 + 2} \right) \right]. \tag{6.12}$$

For large particles, both Q_a and Q_s must be taken into account:

$$k_{(c+p)} = 0.4343 \sum_{\text{vol}} (Q_a + Q_s). \tag{6.13}$$

As the particle size increases, the Rayleigh approximation becomes less valid, and it would be expected that equation (6.12) would give values of attenuation differing significantly from the true values. Gunn and East (1954) examined data calculated by F. T. Haddock for the special case of water at a temperature of 18° C. The ratios of Q_t (Mie) calculated from Mie theory (including terms of higher order than the first terms of a and b) to Q_t, calculated on the basis of the Rayleigh approximation, were plotted for values of α ranging from 0.03 to about 2.0. The results obtained for wavelengths 0.3–10 cm. are shown in figure 6.2.

It is obvious that the values of α over which the Rayleigh approximation can be used for attenuation computations is more limited than was the range for backscattering computations. The region where Q_t (Mie) is nearly equal to Q_t (Rayleigh) is known as the "Rayleigh region for

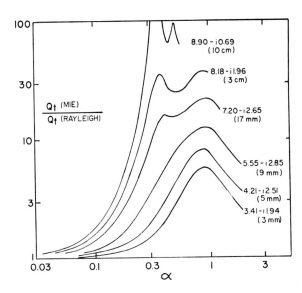

Fig. 6.2.   Ratio of Mie total scattering to Rayleigh total scattering by water spheres as a function of α. From Gunn and East (1954).

attenuation." Very small particles, such as typical cloud droplets, fall within this region. However, the large water drops associated with rain have values of α, at all wavelengths except 10 cm and greater, which result in large discrepancies between the Mie and the Rayleigh total absorption. For example, a drop 0.1 cm in diameter has values of α of about 0.03, 0.1, and 0.3 at wavelengths of 10, 3, and 1 cm, respectively. An examination of figure 6.2 shows that the values of α for wavelengths of 3 and 1 cm correspond to ratios Q_t (Mie)/Q_t (Rayleigh) of about 1.7 and 5. For this reason, the simplified equation (6.12) cannot be used for rain-attenuation calculations.

6.3 Attenuation by Clouds

Cloud droplets may be regarded as those water or ice particles with radii smaller than 100 μ. At radar frequencies, they fulfill the condition that $\alpha \ll 1$, and the attenuation may be calculated from equation (6.12). Generally, it is easier to estimate the liquid-water content of a cloud than its drop-size distribution. Reliable measurements of both parameters are scarce, but one can make reasonable estimates of the liquid-water content, M, from a knowledge of the vertical extent of the cloud and temperature of its base. Since $M = \frac{4}{3}\pi\rho\Sigma a^3$, where ρ is the density of the water or ice particles, the attenuation by clouds can be written as

$$k_c = \left[0.4343 \, \frac{6\pi}{\rho \lambda} \, \mathrm{Im} \left(-\frac{m^2 - 1}{m^2 + 2} \right) \right] M , \qquad (6.14)$$

$$k_c = K_1 M , \qquad (6.15)$$

where M is expressed in grams per cubic meter.

Values of the attenuation coefficient, K_1, by water and ice clouds were calculated by Gunn and East (1954) for various wavelengths at various temperatures and are given in table 6.1. Note that in table 4.2 the quantities $\mathrm{Im}\,(-K)$ are for ice particles considered to have a density of 1 gm/cm³.

TABLE 6.1   One-Way Attenuation Coefficient, K_1, in Clouds in DB/Km/Gm/M³

Temperature (°C)	Wavelength (Cm)			
	0.9	1.24	1.8	3.2
Water 20	0.647	0.311	0.128	0.0483
10	0.681	0.406	0.179	0.0630
Cloud 0	0.99	0.532	0.267	0.0858
− 8	1.25	0.684	0.34 (extrapolated)	0.112 (extrapolated)
Ice 0	8.74×10^{-3}	6.35×10^{-3}	4.36×10^{-3}	2.46×10^{-3}
Cloud −10	2.91×10^{-3}	2.11×10^{-3}	1.46×10^{-3}	8.19×10^{-4}
−20	$2.0\ \times10^{-3}$	1.45×10^{-3}	$1.0\ \times10^{-3}$	5.63×10^{-4}

SOURCE: Gunn and East 1954.

Several important facts are demonstrated by this table. The decrease in attenuation with increasing wavelength is evident. The values change by about an order of magnitude for a change of λ from 1 to 3 cm. At wavelengths in the 5- and 10-cm bands, cloud attenuation can be safely neglected. The data presented here also show that attenuation increases with decreasing temperature. These relations are a reflection of the dependence of the refractive index on both temperature and wavelength.

The effects of the different dielectric properties of water and ice are dramatically illustrated by the difference in attenuation. Ice clouds give attenuations about two orders of magnitude smaller than water clouds of the same water content. Obviously, the attenuation of microwaves by ice clouds can be disregarded for all practical purposes.

6.4 Attenuation by Rain

As already shown (see fig. 6.2), the Rayleigh approximation for attenuation is not generally applicable for raindrops except at the longer wavelengths. For drops with diameters smaller than perhaps 1 mm and a wavelength of 10 cm, the ratio Q_t (Mie)/Q_t (Rayleigh) is still fairly small, and equation (6.14) is applicable.

When observing rain by means of a radar operating at a wavelength shorter than 10 cm, one must calculate the value of the attenuation coefficient from the complete Mie equations for Q_t. In the general form, Q_t is a function of orders of the droplet radius greater than the third, and hence attenuation cannot be simply equated to the liquid-water content. In practice it has been found convenient to express rain attenuation as a function of the precipitation rate R.

The quantity R, commonly expressed in units of millimeters per hour, is a measure of the rate at which water reaches the ground. The contribution of an individual water or ice particle of mass M_i to the precipitation rate is given by

$$R_i = M_i (w_i - w_u), \tag{6.16}$$

where w_i is the terminal velocity of the drop and w_u is the updraft rate. In order to compute the precipitation rate from a unit volume of air, the value of R_i is integrated over all the drops in the volume. When all the particles have the same size, the precipitation rate can be written

$$R = \tfrac{4}{3} \pi \rho a^3 N (w - w_u), \tag{6.17}$$

where N represents the concentration of particles of density ρ. In the general case,

$$R = \tfrac{4}{3} \pi \rho \int_{a=0}^{\infty} N_a a^3 (w_a - w_u) \, da, \tag{6.18}$$

where w_a is a function of a, and $N_a da$ is the number of particles of radius between a and $a + da$ in a unit volume of air. These equations for R must be divided by the density of water, $\rho = 1.0$ gm/cm³, so that the units of precipitation will be in terms of length/time.

Ryde (1946) studied the attenuation of microwaves by rain and showed that the coefficient, k_p (in decibels per kilometer), could be expressed as a function of rain intensity R. Gunn and East (1954) and Hitschfeld and Bordan (1954) studied the same problem and proposed specific expressions having the form

$$k_p = K_2 R^\gamma, \tag{6.19}$$

where K_2 and γ are functions of wavelength. This equation can also be written

$$k_p = K' R, \tag{6.20}$$

where $K' = K_2 R^{\gamma-1}$ and usually is given in units of dB km⁻¹/mm hr⁻¹.

Wexler and Atlas (1963) used values of Q_t as a function of α calculated from the complete Mie equations by Herman, Browning, and Battan (1961) to compute attenuation as a function of rainfall rate. Raindrop-size spectra in precipitation from stratiform clouds were obtained from the Marshall-Palmer (M-P) distribution. See equation (4.19). A second set of raindrop spectra, called the modified Marshall-Palmer distribution, took into account the fact that, at diameters below 1.0–1.5 mm, depending on R, the drop-size spectra differ from the M-P curves. Raindrop spectra in shower-type precipitation from convective clouds were represented by measurements made in Florida by Mueller and Jones (1960). Knowing the distribution of raindrop size, one can compute ΣQ_t for any values of the wavelength and temperature. These quantities determine the appropriate dielectric constants.

Table 6.2, taken from Wexler and Atlas (1963), presents the quantity $K' = k_p/R$ as a function of wavelength at the indicated temperatures. Except at $\lambda = 3.2$ cm, where the differences between drop-size distributions may have been important, the discrepancies between the Gunn and East (1954) results and those in the other columns are largely attributable to the dissimilarities in temperatures (see table 4.2). Otherwise, the results are in fairly good agreement at each wavelength and do not appear to be sensitive to the precise form of the drop-size distribution. In general, the attenuation is nearly proportional to R. The largest deviation at 0°C is at 3.2 cm, where k_p is proportional to $R^{1.15}$.

The data in table 6.2 show that, at wavelengths of 10 cm, attenuation by rain is small and generally can be neglected. Even an extreme value of $R = 100$ mm/hr will produce attenuation less than 0.02 dB/km.

TABLE 6.2   One-Way Rain Attenuation K' (DB/Km/Mm/Hr)

Wavelength (Cm)	M-P (at 0°C)	Modified M-P (0°C)	Mueller-Jones (0°C)	Gunn and East (18°C)
0.62 . . .	0.50–0.37	0.52	0.66	. . . .
0.86 . . .	0.27	0.31	0.39	. . . .
1.24 . . .	$0.117R^{0.07}$	$0.13R^{0.07}$	0.18	$0.12R^{0.06}$
1.8	. . . .	. . . .	. . . . . .	$0.045R^{0.11}$
1.87 . . .	$0.0045R^{0.10}$	$0.050R^{0.10}$	0.065	. . . .
3.21 . . .	$0.011R^{0.15}$	$0.013R^{0.15}$	0.018	$0.0074R^{0.31}$
4.67 . . .	0.005–0.007*	0.0053	0.0058	. . . .
5.5	0.003–0.004*	0.0031	0.0033	. . . .
5.7	. . . .	. . . .	. . . . . .	$0.0022R^{0.17}$
10	0.0009–0.0007*	0.00082	0.00092	0.0003

SOURCE: Wexler and Atlas 1963.
*First value applies at 2 mm/hr, the second at 50 mm/hr, and there is a "smooth transition" between them.

As the wavelength decreases, however, k_p/R increases rapidly. At 3 cm, it is so large that attenuation must be taken into account when interpreting radar observations.

Medhurst (1965) summarized measurements of rain attenuation made by various investigators at wavelengths between 0.43 and 3.2 cm and compared them with values computed from the raindrop data of Laws and Parsons (1943). When the measurements are compared with the values computed from the Modified Marshall-Palmer curves given in table 6.2, there is reasonably good agreement at wavelengths of 3.2 and 0.62 cm. At $\lambda = 0.86$ cm, certain samples of measured attenuations are well correlated with calculated values, but in other cases the observed values exceeded the calculated ones. Measured attenuations of 1.25-cm radiation generally were larger than the calculated ones. The widespread scatter of measured attenuations can be ascribed to various factors, particularly the hard-to-measure spatial variations of R over the area of interest and the changes of drop-size spectra over space and time.

Boston (1970) calculated radar attenuation coefficients as a function of the rainfall reflectivity, η, ranging from 10^{-5} to 10^{2} cm^2/m^3 for various wavelengths from 0.5 to 10 cm. Marshall (1969) also called attention to the need, for some purposes, of expressing attenuation in terms of reflectivity. McCormick (1970) has derived several formulas of the form $k = cZ^{d}$, where the coefficients and exponents are wavelength dependent. If one assumes that $Z = 200R^{1.6}$ (see chap. 7) and makes use of expressions relating k to R such as those in table 6.2, the quantities c and d are easily obtained. This procedure was used to obtain the values of k_p for wavelengths of 3.21, 5.5, and 10.0 cm which are shown in table 6.3.

TABLE 6.3   Some Expressions of Attenuation by Rain Expressed in Terms of Z

Frequency (GHz)	Wavelength (Cm)	k_p (DB/Km)
15.0	2.0	$7.15 \times 10^{-4} \, Z^{0.725}$ *
9.3	3.21	$2.9 \times 10^{-4} \, Z^{0.72}$ †
8.0	3.75	$1.16 \times 10^{-4} \, Z^{0.806}$ *
5.5	5.5	$1.12 \times 10^{-4} \, Z^{0.62}$ †
3.0	10.0	$3.0 \times 10^{-5} \, Z^{0.62}$ †

* From McCormick 1970.
† Based on data in table 6.2 for Modified M-P distribution and $T = 0°$ C.

6.5 Attenuation by Snow

If snowflakes are composed of low-density ice and hence can be treated as spheres, and if the "sphere" diameters are small with respect to the wavelength, attenuation by snow can be calculated by means of equations (6.5), (6.6), and (6.7). Gunn and East (1954) used this approach and calculated k_s in dB/km in terms of the precipitation rate. As will be seen in chapter 7, empirical data show that, in at least some snowfalls, $Z = \Sigma D^6 = 2,000R^{2.0}$, where the units of Z are millimeters to the sixth power per cubic meter when R is in millimeters per hour of melted water.

At 0° C the attenuation in decibels per kilometer caused by scattering can be calculated by summing Q_s over a unit volume and substituting for $\Sigma a^6 = Z/64$ in equation (6.5) and employing equation (6.11) to yield

$$0.4343 \Sigma Q_s = 3.5 \times 10^{-2} \frac{R^2}{\lambda^4}, \tag{6.21}$$

where λ is in centimeters. It should be recalled that, for the units in the left-hand term to be decibels per kilometer, the units of Q_s must be square centimeters per cubic meter.

Attenuation by absorption can be calculated in terms of R by assuming that all the snowflakes are falling at the same speed, taken to be $w = 1$ m/sec. If it is further assumed that the precipitation particles are spherical in shape with densities of 1 g/cm³, then $\Sigma D^3 = 6R/\pi w$. Substitution of these quantities in equation (6.6) yields an expression for absorption losses at 0° C:

$$0.4343 \Sigma Q_a = 2.2 \times 10^{-3} \frac{R}{\lambda}. \tag{6.22}$$

The sum of equations (6.21) and (6.22) gives the attenuation coefficient for dry snow at 0° C,

$$k_s = 3.5 \times 10^{-2} \frac{R^2}{\lambda^4} + 2.2 \times 10^{-3} \frac{R}{\lambda}, \tag{6.23}$$

where R is in millimeters per hour and λ in centimeters. Table 6.4 lists attenuation coefficients at several wavelengths and snowfall intensities. It is evident that, at a wavelength of 10 cm, attenuation by dry snow can be safely neglected but that, at shorter wavelengths, it can be appreciable when r and R are large.

Where the hydrometeors are wet snowflakes, as is the case in the layer of air some 500 m thick just below the 0° C isotherm, the attenuation coefficients may be very much larger than those shown in table 6.4.

As shown in chapter 5, a thin coating of water can cause a small ice

TABLE 6.4   One-Way Attenuation Coefficients in DB/Km by Low-Density Snow at 0°C Calculated from Equation (6.23)

Wavelength (Cm)	Precipitation Rate—R (Mm/hr)		
	1	10	100
1.8	0.0046	0.344	33.5
3.2	0.0010	0.040	3.41
10.0	0.00022	0.0026	0.057

sphere to have a radar cross section nearly the same as that of an all-water sphere. Also, it was shown that small water ellipsoids may have scattering cross sections much greater than those of spheres of equivalent volume. Atlas, Kerker, and Hitschfeld (1953) calculated the attenuation cross sections of water and ice prolate and oblate spheroids. The results are shown in figure 5.6, where the Q_t of random arrays of ellipsoids of given axial ratios is compared with the Q_t of spheres having the same volume.

Snowflakes may be considered to be oblate spheroids of small axis-to-diameter ratios. In an extreme case, the ratio might be as low as 0.1. If such particles were composed of solid ice, the attenuation cross section would be only about 1.5 times larger than if the particles were spheres. On the other hand, if the ellipsoids were liquid, Q_t would be more than ten times greater than the Q_t of equivolume spheres.

If small ellipsoids were to behave in a manner similar to that of small spheres, a snowflake with a thin layer of water would attenuate nearly as much as an all-water ellipsoid. This would mean that, in the melting layer just below the $0°$ C isotherm, snowflake attenuation would be much greater than in the dry snow at higher altitudes. For example, at $\lambda = 3.2$ cm, if R were to remain constant, a comparison of tables 6.2 and 6.4 shows that attenuation when $R = 10$ mm/hr would be more than five times greater in the melting region. Furthermore, the shape effect illustrated in figure 5.6 might contribute another factor of about 10.

Also, it should be noted that the results in figure 5.6 apply to randomly oriented particles. Snowflakes tend to be preferentially oriented, with their long dimensions mostly horizontal. In such a circumstance a horizontally polarized radar looking nearly horizontally through the melting layer would suffer even greater attenuation than has already been indicated. A vertically polarized radar set would suffer less attenuation as a result of the nonsphericity of snowflakes.

6.6 Attenuation by Hail

Calculations of the attenuation cross sections of large water and ice spheres have been made by Battan and Herman (1962); Herman and Battan (1963); Battan, Browning, and Herman (1970a,b); and Battan (1971). Data by Herman, Browning, and Battan (1961) show that, for all-water spheres at $\lambda = 3.2$ cm, the normalized attenuation cross section, $\sigma_t \ (= Q_t/\pi a^2)$, increases monotonically to almost 3 and then slowly decreases to about 2.5 at $\alpha = 5$ (see fig. 6.3 from Atlas 1964). At $\alpha > 1$ the attenuation cross sections at 5.5 and 10 cm are within 5 percent of the values at 3.2 cm.

Figure 6.4 shows that the normalized attenuation cross sections σ_t

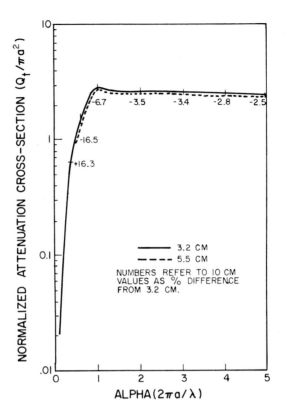

Fig. 6.3. Normalized attenuation cross sections of water spheres. From Atlas (1964).

of dry ice spheres vary much more than those of water spheres. At certain ice-sphere diameters (α between 2 and 3), σ_t is close to 5, about twice as large as that of water spheres, and it approaches 2 as α becomes very large.

Figure 6.5 presents the normalized attenuation cross sections of spheres composed of a mixture of water and ice. It should be recalled, as was noted earlier when backscattering cross sections were considered, that serious questions exist about the validity of the complex indices of refraction used to calculate the data shown. One should bear these reservations in mind in noting that the diagrams show how scattering and absorption contribute to the attenuation. When the spheres are 90 percent ice, most of the attenuation is caused by scattering. When the particles are only 10 percent ice, attenuation by absorption becomes quite important.

The oscillations of attenuation cross sections with increasing α can be seen to increase as the ice content of the ice spheres increases.

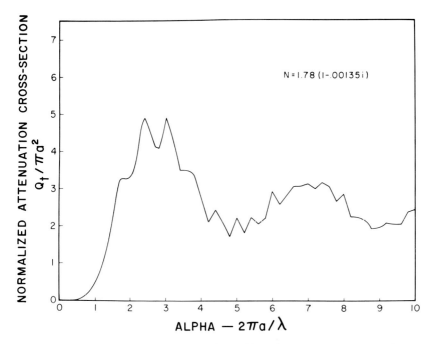

Fig. 6.4.   Normalized attenuation cross sections of ice spheres. From Herman and Battan (1963).

The normalized attenuation cross sections for wet-ice spheres as a function of overall sphere diameter are shown in figure 6.6. It may be recalled that in studies of the backscattering by ice spheres it was concluded that reasonable water coatings might be about 0.01 cm thick. It was also pointed out that solid-ice spheres coated with a layer of spongy ice appear to backscatter as if they were ice spheres surrounded by a layer of water whose overall mass was the same as that contained in the spongy ice. It might be surmised that equivalent water thicknesses exceeding 0.01 cm would correspond to the water in layers of spongy ice.

Figure 6.6 shows that, as long as the overall sphere diameter is less than about $\lambda/2$, water thicknesses of the order of 0.01–0.05 cm greatly increase the attenuation cross section.

It is evident from figures 6.4–6.6 that it is not possible to write a simple expression for the attenuation by ice spheres ranging in diameter from a few millimeters to a few centimeters. Of course, if the composition, refractive index, and the size distribution of ice spheres are known, it is possible to calculate ΣQ_t and hence the total attenuation. This procedure can be used to obtain an approximation of the attenuation caused by hailstones in the atmosphere. At the same time, it should be recognized

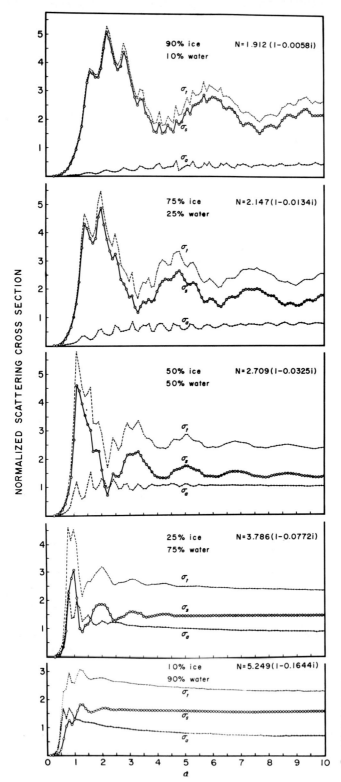

NORMALIZED SCATTERING CROSS SECTION

90% ice
10% water
N=1.912(1-0.0058i)
σ_t
σ_s
σ_a

75% ice
25% water
N=2.147(1-0.0134i)
σ_t
σ_s
σ_a

50% ice
50% water
N=2.709(1-0.0325i)
σ_t
σ_s
σ_a

25% ice
75% water
N=3.786(1-0.0772i)
σ_t
σ_s
σ_a

10% ice
90% water
N=5.249(1-0.1644i)
σ_t
σ_s
σ_a

a

Fig. 6.5. Normalized absorption, scattering, and attenuation cross sections of spongy ice spheres. From Battan and Herman (1962).

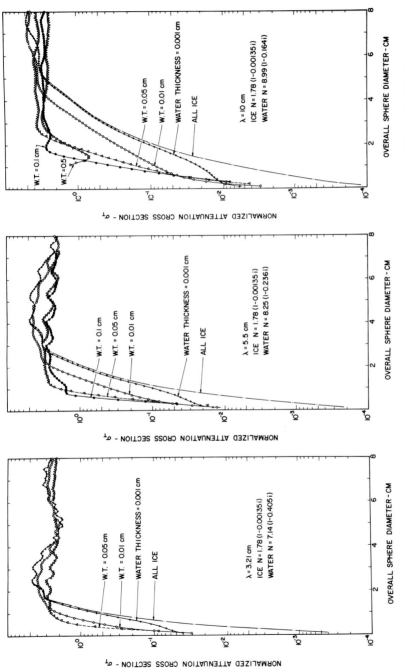

Fig. 6.6. Normalized attenuation cross sections of ice spheres coated with a uniform layer of water. Water-shell thicknesses (W.T.) are indicated. From Battan, Browning, and Herman (1970b).

that hailstones, unlike raindrops, may differ very greatly from a spherical shape. Also, uncertainties about their compositions and their complex indices of refraction introduce major uncertainties about the applicability of calculated attenuation coefficients.

Herman and Battan (1963) raised another question about the interpretation of ΣQ_t in terms of attenuation by dry ice spheres. Such particles scatter much of the incident power in the forward direction. This power is included in the calculated ΣQ_t, but it cannot be regarded as lost or attenuated power. If precise calculations of attenuation are needed and there is heavy hail, corrections can be made in the term ΣQ_t.

Notwithstanding the uncertainties, it is informative to examine the level of attenuation to be expected in a hail shower. According to Douglas (1964), some storms contain hail with a size distribution which, when normalized to a water content of 1 gm/m³, is given by

$$N_D = N_0\, e^{-3.09D} \tag{6.24}$$

in the range of D from zero to 4.0 cm. The quantity N_D, in units of per cubic meter per centimeter, is the number of hailstones with diameters between D and $D + \Delta D$, where $\Delta D = 0.32$ cm. The constant N_0 is equal to 31 m⁻³ cm⁻¹. Knowing N_D and Q_t as functions of D, and specifying the largest value of D, one can calculate the attenuation cross section as a function of maximum hailstone size, water-shell thickness, and wavelength. Such calculations were made by Battan (1971) and are shown in figure 6.7. These data show that, if typical hailstones can be approximated by ice spheres, they can produce appreciable attenuation, particularly when they become coated with water. Some representative

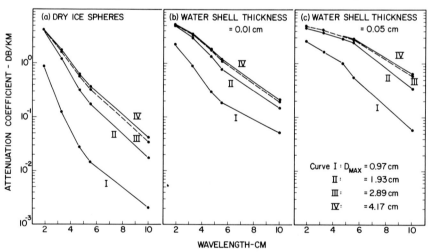

Fig. 6.7. Attenuation coefficient of a distribution of dry and water-coated ice spheres. From Battan (1971).

TABLE 6.5   One-Way Attenuation in DB/Km for Distributions of Spherical Hail Where $N_D = 31e^{-3.09D}$ and D_{max} Is as Shown

Distribution	D_{max} (Cm)	Water-Shell Thickness (Cm)											
		Wavelength 3.21 Cm				Wavelength 5.5 Cm				Wavelength 10.0 Cm			
		Dry	0.01	0.05	0.10	Dry	0.01	0.05	0.10	Dry	0.01	0.05	0.10
I	0.97	0.12	0.91	1.68	1.50	0.015	0.19	0.56	0.94	0.0020	0.051	0.058	0.080
II	1.93	1.21	3.01	3.72	3.49	0.18	0.79	2.48	2.30	0.017	0.15	0.34	0.89
III	2.89	1.66	3.46	4.03	3.79	0.33	1.12	2.82	2.60	0.034	0.19	0.60	1.18

SOURCE: Battan 1971.
NOTE: Appropriate for a distribution normalized to a liquid-water content of 1 g/m³.

quantities have been reproduced in table 6.5 to facilitate an evaluation of the quantities involved. It is evident that 3-cm waves can be severely attenuated with two-way attenuations over 8 dB/km in some circumstances illustrated in the table. Even at C-band wavelengths, large attenuations may occur.

The curves in figure 6.7 show that, in Douglas's exponential distribution, ice spheres exceeding about 2 cm in diameter contribute little to the attenuation. The reasons for this result are illustrated in figure 6.8. It shows the variation with sphere diameter, at two wavelengths, of Q_t, the attenuation cross section. Also depicted is the value of N_D as a function of D. The attenuation contributed by each interval of D is the product $N_D Q_t$ (in units of centimeters squared per cubic meter). It can be seen that, at diameters below about 0.5 cm, the quantity Q_t is so small that $N_D Q_t$ is also small. As D exceeds about 2 cm, the quantity N_D de-

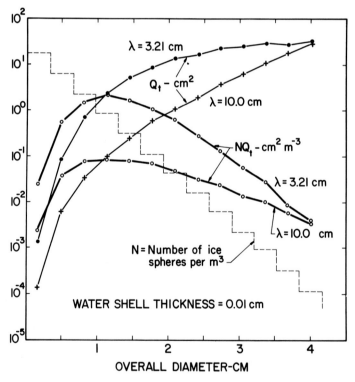

Fig. 6.8. *Heavy curve* NQ_t, contribution to the attenuation cross section by wet ice spheres of different sizes; *Curve* Q_t, attenuation cross section as a function of sphere diameter. From Battan (1971).

creases markedly while Q_t increases slowly, so that again N_DQ_t is small. Therefore, in the case of ice spheres coated with a water layer 0.01 cm thick, most of the attenuation of microwaves is by spheres with diameters between about 0.5 and 2 cm.

Incidentally, a similar analysis of the backscattering by wet-ice spheres shows somewhat similar results except that the upper limit of substantial contribution to Z_e is perhaps 2.5 cm.

The results in this section show that attenuation by wet hail can be appreciable. Uncertainties about the effects of deviations from sphericity on the part of actual hailstones and about their compositions introduce substantial uncertainties about the direct applicability of the quantities calculated by Battan and his associates on the assumption that the scatterers are wet-ice spheres. On the other hand, there were no better quantitative estimates in 1973. Clearly, it is essential to make measurements in the atmosphere of attenuation by hail. McCormick (1970) reported one set of measurements of attenuation by a storm having a Z_e exceeding 10^6 mm^6/m^3 and assumed to contain hail. At a frequency of 15 GHz ($\lambda = 2$ cm) he measured a maximum one-way attenuation of about 10 dB through a storm about 5–10 km in diameter. At the same time, by means of an expression relating attenuation to Z_e, he calculated a maximum attenuation of about 52 dB. The discrepancy could not be satisfactorily resolved. More observations are needed on occasions when data on the hailstone sizes are also obtained.

7 Use of Radar for Precipitation Measurements

It was shown earlier that, when precipitation particles are small with respect to the radar wavelength, the backscattered power is proportional to the radar reflectivity factor Z. Since empirical studies indicate a relation between Z and precipitation intensity, R, radar can be used for measuring rainfall. Some scientists have visualized that radar, which can observe precipitation over a very large area, ultimately will replace rain gauges. Others have taken the position that radar should complement rain gauges and that, when used together, they would provide significantly better information on the rainfall than can be obtained from a rain-gauge network alone.

Various studies have been made to test the validity of the equation relating backscattered power to rainfall intensity. Direct observations of rainfall have been compared with calculations made from simultaneous radar observations. In general the investigations have shown that properly calibrated radars can make reasonably accurate measurements of rainfall intensity and of accumulated rainfall over a small watershed.

7.1 Calculation of Radar Constant

Assume that a radar is observing rain and that the rain consists of spherical water drops small enough to permit the Rayleigh approximation to apply. If a 10-cm radar is used, all rains will meet this requirement. Also, under these conditions, attenuation can be neglected. The average power received by the radar when the entire beam is intercepted is given by

$$\bar{P}_r = \left(\frac{\pi^3}{1{,}024 \ln 2} \frac{P_t G^2 \theta \phi h}{\lambda^2} \right) \left| \frac{m^2 - 1}{m^2 + 2} \right|^2 \frac{Z}{r^2}. \tag{7.1}$$

For any particular radar set, the term inside the parentheses of equation (7.1) can be considered to be a constant for that radar. The value of P_t can vary with time, but over periods of a few hours, changes should be negligibly small. The Appendix presents values of the characteristics of a number of radar sets which have been used in weather work. Knowing the radar characteristics, one can calculate the radar constant. A

84

more precise procedure is to determine it empirically by making careful measurements of the power backscattered from a target of known cross section such as a metal sphere (see Atlas and Mossop 1960). Equation (7.1) reduces to

$$\bar{P}_r = \frac{C\,|K|^2 Z}{r^2}.\tag{7.2}$$

To use equation (7.2) for calculating precipitation rates, it is necessary to know the relation between Z and the precipitation rate, R.

7.2 Particle-Size Distributions in the Atmosphere

Observations of drop-size distributions as a function of precipitation intensity have been made in a variety of places and in various types of precipitation — widespread rain and snow from stratiform clouds, showery and orographic precipitation, etc. Because of the large variations observed in both time and space, the analyses of the data have been along statistical lines.

For a wide range of rain and snow conditions, one can write

$$N_D = N_0 e^{-\Lambda D},\tag{7.3}$$

where D is the drop diameter and $N_D dD$ is the number of drops per unit of air volume in the size range D to $D + dD$. When snow is involved, the value of D refers to the diameter of a sphere of water having the same mass as the original particle (Marshall and Palmer 1948; Atlas 1953; Gunn and Marshall 1958). In precipitation from stratiform clouds, N_0 has been found to be equal to 0.08 cm^{-4} for rain, when N_D is the number of drops per cubic centimeter per centimeter of size range. Sekhon and Srivastava (1970) have reported that, for snow, $N_0 = 0.025R^{-0.94}$ cm^{-4}, which compares with the quantity $0.038R^{-0.87}$ cm^{-4} reported by Gunn and Marshall (1958).

The parameter Λ depends on the rain intensity, and, when expressed in units of per millimeter,

$$\Lambda = 4.1R^{-0.21} \text{ (rain) (Gunn and Marshall 1958)},\tag{7.4a}$$

$$\Lambda = 2.29R^{-0.45} \text{ (snow) (Sekhon and Srivastava 1970)},\tag{7.4b}$$

where R is expressed in millimeters per hour.

When precipitation-size spectra are obtained by collecting the particles on a horizontal surface at the ground, it is necessary to correct for differing fall speeds in order to obtain particle concentrations in the free atmosphere. For example, if the sampling time were 1 sec, all drops with a fall speed of 10 m/sec in a 10-m column could be captured. In the case of drops with fall speeds of 1 m/sec, only those in a 1-m column would fall to the surface during the 1-second collection time. For any diameter D,

$$N_{D_i} = \frac{N_{D_0}}{A W_t \Delta t},$$ (7.5)

where N_{D_i} is the number of drops per unit volume, of diameter D and terminal velocity W_t, and N_{D_0} is the number of drops of diameter D collected on surface area A during time interval Δt.

When raindrops are involved, it is common to use the terminal-velocity data of Gunn and Kinzer (1949), which applies at sea level. At greater altitudes more precise data are given by Foote and DuToit (1969). Spilhaus (1948) showed that over the diameter range 1–4 mm the raindrop data of Laws (1941) yield

$$W_t = 1.42 \times 10^3 D^{\frac{1}{2}},$$ (7.6)

where D is in centimeters and W_t in centimeters per second.

For calculating the size spectra of aggregate snowflakes Gunn and Marshall (1958) used the expression

$$W_t = 2 \times 10^2 D^{0.31},$$ (7.7)

where the units are the same as in equation (7.6). Imai et al. (1955) employed a coefficient of 207.

Mueller and Jones (1960) reported that raindrops from convective clouds in Miami, Florida, exhibit a distinct frequency maximum at diameters of about 1.5 mm. Over the range of drop sizes smaller than those of maximum frequency, $\Lambda \; (= d \,(\ln N)/dD)$ averages about -4.3; over larger drop sizes Λ averages about 3.5.

It should be recognized that a distribution curve such as equation (7.3) is an empirical expression based on an accumulation of highly variable samples. Any small sample can vary substantially. Even large samples may do so. Geotis (1968) examined raindrop spectra in all types of rainfall over a two-year period. He found that, at diameters greater than 0.6 mm, the smallest drops he could measure, the drop concentration was exponentially distributed. Geotis reported that the coefficient in equation (7.3) varied with rainfall in an unsystematic manner.

It has been demonstrated that in the case of rain, Λ can be expressed in terms of the median-volume diameter. Equation (7.3) can be written

$$N_D = N_0 e^{-3.67 \; D/D_0},$$ (7.8)

according to Atlas (1964). The median-volume diameter, D_0, is defined as that drop diameter which divides the drop distribution in such a fashion that half water content is contained in drops greater than D_0.

Geotis (1968) also found that $\Lambda = -3.7D_0$ gave a good fit to the slope of the observed raindrop-distribution curve. He implied that D_0 would be a better indicator of the slope of the drop-size curves than R, but, as he noted, D_0 cannot be measured directly.

According to Donaldson (1955a), the drop-size distribution in drizzle is given by equation (7.8) if $N_0 = 70$ cm^{-4}.

There is little reliable data on hail distributions aloft, but according to Douglas (1964) the average spectrum of hailstones in Alberta, Canada, was

$$N_D = N_0^{-3.09D},\tag{7.9}$$

where N_0 (approximately 31) and N_D are in units of per cubic meter per centimeter. This average distribution curve was based on a total of 67 samples and involved the use of the following expression relating terminal velocity to hailstone diameter:

$$W_t = 16.2D^{\frac{1}{2}},\tag{7.10}$$

where W_t and D are in units of meters per second and centimeters, respectively.

An examination of individual hail samples reported by Douglas (1963 a,b) shows that there were large variations from the average. In many cases, the range of diameter was much smaller than would be indicated by equation (7.9).

As would be expected, the median-volume diameter is also related to the precipitation rate; however, there is fairly wide scatter, depending on the type of precipitation involved. The general form of the relation is

$$D_0 = b_1 R^{b_2}.\tag{7.11}$$

In rain, values of b_1 and b_2 reported in the literature have ranged from 0.30 to 1.32 and from 0.19 to 0.40, respectively. Representative values of b_1 and b_2 for rain (drizzle and "warm" orographic rains excepted) are 0.92 and 0.21, respectively, when D_0 is in millimeters. For snow, representative values of b_1 and b_2 are 0.14 and 0.48, respectively, when both D_0 and R refer to the water equivalents of the snow.

Similar types of statistical studies have been made of the relationship of liquid-water content, M, to precipitation rate. Equations for rain and snow, given in the literature, are the following:

Stratiform Rain: $M = 0.072R^{0.88}$
                       (Marshall and Palmer 1948),   (7.12a)

Thunderstorms
    Illinois: $M = 0.052R^{0.97}$
                       (Jones 1956),   (7.12b)
    India: $M = 0.070R^{0.83}$
                       (Sivaramakrishnan 1961),   (7.12c)

Snow aggregates: $M = 0.25R^{0.90}$
                          (Gunn and Marshall 1958),   (7.12d)
Hail: $M = 0.018R^{0.97}$
                          (Douglas 1964).   (7.12e)

In these equations, M is expressed as grams per cubic meter and R is in millimeters per hour. Equations (7.12a) and (7.12b) cannot be considered to be applicable in drizzles or rains from so-called warm orographic clouds such as those in tropical islands. These forms of precipitation are characterized by large numbers of small drops.

7.3 Relationship of Z to Liquid-Water Content and Precipitation Rate

Since the radar reflectivity factor $Z = \Sigma D^6$ and $M = (\pi/6)\rho\Sigma D^3$, if all the N particles in a unit volume were the same size, Z would be equal to $(36/\pi^2\rho^2 N)M^2$. Observations have shown that rain and snow particles are approximately exponentially distributed. Nevertheless, empirical studies demonstrate that Z is almost directly proportional to M^2. The following expressions have been reported in the literature:

Clouds: $Z = 4.8\times10^{-2}\ M^{2.0}$
                          (Atlas 1954),   (7.13a)
Precipitation
  particles in
  cumulus
  congestus: $Z = 3.8\times10^2\ M^{1.46}$
                          (Brown and Braham 1963),   (7.13b)
Snow aggregates: $Z = 3.8\times10^4\ M^{2.2}$
                          (Douglas 1964),   (7.13c)
Rain: $Z = 2.4\times10^4\ M^{1.82}$
                          (Douglas 1964),   (7.13d)
Hail
  Wet: $\lambda = 3.3$ cm, $Z_e = 8.0\times10^5\ M^{0.98}$ (7.13e)
  Wet: $\lambda = 10$ cm, $Z_e = 5.4\times10^6\ M^{1.21}$ ⎫   (7.13f)
  Dry: $\lambda = 3.3$ cm, $Z_e = 2.6\times10^5\ M^{1.03}$ ⎬ (Douglas 1964).   (7.13g)
  Dry: $\lambda = 10$ cm, $Z_e = 9.4\times10^5\ M^{1.12}$ ⎭   (7.13h)

In these equations the quantities M and Z are expressed in units of grams per cubic meter and millimeters to the sixth power per cubic meter, respectively. In hail, the large particle sizes make it necessary to consider the effective reflectivity factor. Also, as noted earlier, in the Mie scattering region Z_e depends on the refractive index and hence on the wavelength. Equations (7.13) indicate that, in dry and wet hail, the backscattered power should be nearly proportional to the liquid-water content.

In order to use radar for measuring rainfall intensity, most investigators have employed an empirical expression of the form

$$Z = A R^{b}. \tag{7.14}$$

Table 7.1 gives most of the results reported. As noted by Joss and Waldvogel (1969) and others, part of the variations may be ascribed to inadequate data for calculating the regression curve. Although the equations listed in the table differ markedly at small and large values of R, with the exception of curves for orographic rains, most of them do not differ greatly at rainfall intensities between about 20 and 200 mm/hr. This point is illustrated in figure 7.1, which shows the curves for the following equations, considered to be fairly typical for the indicated type of rain:

Stratiform rain:	$Z = 200R^{1.6}$	
	(Marshall and Palmer 1948),	(7.15a)
Orographic rain:	$Z = 31R^{1.71}$	
	(Blanchard 1953),	(7.15b)
Thunderstorm rain:	$Z = 486R^{1.37}$	
	(Jones 1956),	(7.15c)

where Z is in millimeters to the sixth power per cubic meter and R in millimeters per hour. Fujiwara (1965) analyzed data from many sources and offered different equations for continuous rain, rainshowers, and thunderstorms. Joss et al. (1970) presented still another set of Z–R equations for drizzle, widespread rain, and thunderstorms (see table 7.1).

Measurements of raindrop spectra have been made in nine localities mostly in the United States by means of a special camera devised by D. M. Jones of the Illinois State Water Survey. Reviews of the data have been reported by Cataneo and Stout (1968).

Cataneo (1969) proposed that the appropriate values of A and b can be adequately predicted by means of regression equations involving two variables: TD, the mean annual percentage of rain days which are thunderstorm days; RH, the mean annual relative humidity at a level 500 m above the ground. The equations are

$$A = 1.372 \,(\text{TD}) - 4.702 \,(\text{RH}) + 571, \tag{7.16}$$
$$b = -0.00444 \,(\text{RH}) + 1.776. \tag{7.17}$$

Cataneo used these empirical expressions based on the Z–R relation at nine localities to predict Z–R relations at five other places. The results were quite good. For values of R equal to 1, 5, and 10 mm/hr, the average differences between observed and predicted Z were 0.7, 1.5, and 1.6 dB, respectively. Notwithstanding the success in predictions, it appears that the good results may be somewhat fortuitous. The regression equations employ annual averages as variables and hence predict one

TABLE 7.1   Empirical Relations between Reflectivity Factor, $Z(Mm^6/M^3)$, and Precipitation Intensity, $R(Mm/Hr)$

Equation	Reference	Location	Remarks
$320R^{1.44}$	Wexler, R. (1947)	Washington, D.C.	8 rain intensities, each a mean of about 10 storms of same intensity
$214R^{1.58}$	Wexler (1948)	Washington, D.C.	98 storms—original data
$224R^{1.54}$		Ynyslas, Great Britain	5 rainstorms
$630R^{1.45}$		Shoeburyness, England	4 rainstorms
$208R^{1.53}$		Hawaii	50 storms, orographic rain
$190R^{1.72}$	Marshall, Langille, and Palmer (1947)	Various locations	Various types of rain
$220R^{1.60}$	Marshall and Palmer (1948)	Various locations	Various types of rain
$295R^{1.612}$	Hood (1950)	Canada	270 samples, 7 rainstorms; light rain 1–3 mm/hr; heavy thunderstorms 50 mm/hr
$180R^{1.55}$	Boucher (1951)	Cambridge, Mass.	63 rain samples, widespread rain both uniform and variable; showers and thunderstorms
$127R^{2.87}$	Higgs (1952)	Australia	Showers, 8 months of observation
$16.6R^{1.55}$	Blanchard (1953)	Hawaii	Orographic rain within cloud
$31R^{1.71}$			Orographic rain at cloud base
$290R^{1.41}$			Nonorographic rain—thunderstorms
$396R^{1.35}$	Jones (1955)	Central Illinois	1,270 1-minute observations—all rains
$486R^{1.37}$			560 1-minute observations—thunderstorms
$380R^{1.24}$			330 1-minute observations—rain showers
$313R^{1.25}$			380 1-minute observations—continuous rain
$150R^{1.54}$			
$257R^{1.55}$	Litvinov (1956)	Mount El'brus, USSR	Rain (melted granular snow and strongly granulated particles), 344 spectra, 6 rains
$398R^{1.47}$			Rain (melted snow of average granulation), 367 spectra, 7 rains
			Rain (melted non-granulated snow), 140 spectra, 4 rains
$162R^{1.16}$	Atlas and Chmela (1957)	Lexington, Mass.	Stratiform rains, 16 April 1954
$215R^{1.34}$			Stratiform rains, 23 April 1954
$350R^{1.42}$			Stratiform rains, 27 April 1954
$310R^{1.34}$			Stratiform rains, 28 April 1954

Relation	Reference	Location	Remarks
$220R^{1.54}$	Sal'man (1957)	Near Leningrad, USSR	Showers and steady rain
$303R^{1.7}$	Shupiatskii (1957)	Near Moscow, USSR	Various types of rain, $R < 7$ mm/hr
$405R^{1.49}$			Various types of rain, $7 < R < 60$ mm/hr
$289R^{1.59}$			Various types of rain, $R > 60$ mm/hr
$109R^{1.64}$	Ramana Murty and Gupta (1959)	Kandia, India	Orographic, Monsoon rains
$342R^{1.42}$		Delhi, India	Nonorographic, Monsoon rains
$700R^{1.6}$	Imai (1960)	Tokyo, Japan	One day, probably warm rain
$300R^{1.6}$			One day continuous rain
$200R^{1.5}$			Air mass showers
$200R^{1.5}$			Prewarm frontal rain
$219R^{1.41}$	Sivaramakrishnan (1961)	Poona, India	Thunderstorms
$67.6R^{1.94}$			Steady rains
$66.5R^{1.92}$			Warm rains
$204R^{1.70}$	Muchnik (1961)	Kiev, USSR	Showers and steady rains
$205R^{1.48}$			Continuous rain
$300R^{1.37}$	Fujiwara (1965)	Mostly Miami, Florida	Rainshowers
$450R^{1.46}$			Thunderstorms
$184R^{1.28}$		Various locations	
$278R^{1.30}$		Entebbe, Uganda	
$240R^{1.30}$		Lwire, Congo	
$176R^{1.18}$		Palma	
$151R^{1.36}$	Diem (1966)	Barza, Italy	
$179R^{1.25}$		Karlsruhe, Germany	Spring
$227R^{1.31}$		Karlsruhe, Germany	Summer
$178R^{1.25}$		Karlsruhe, Germany	Fall
$150R^{1.23}$		Karlsruhe, Germany	Winter
$137R^{1.36}$		Axel Heiberg Land	
$330R^{1.41}$	Gorelik et al. (1967)	Chernozem (near Moscow)	About 10 days, 20,000 samples on filter paper, all types of rain
$298R^{1.46}$		Vashnevo (5 km away)	
$520R^{1.81}$	Foote (1966)	Tucson, Arizona	32 showers and thunderstorms on mountain peak. 2,500 meters
$730R^{1.55}$	Doumoulin and Cogombles (1966)	France	Measured on 12 March 1964
$255R^{1.45}$		France	Measured on 4 September 1964
$426R^{1.50}$		France	107 drop-size distributions

TABLE 7.1   (continued)

Equation	Reference	Location	Remarks
$286R^{1.43}$	Mueller and Sims (1966)	Miami, Florida	
$221R^{1.32}$		Majuro, Marshall Islands	
$301R^{1.64}$		Corvallis, Oregon	
$311R^{1.44}$		Bogar, Indonesia	
$267R^{1.54}$		Woody Island, Alaska	
$230R^{1.40}$	Stout and Mueller (1968)	Franklin, North Carolina	
$372R^{1.47}$		Champaign, Illinois	
$593R^{1.61}$		Flagstaff, Arizona	
$256R^{1.41}$		Island Beach, N.J.	
$140R^{1.5}$	Joss et al. (1970)	Locarno-Monti, Switzerland	Drizzle
$250R^{1.5}$			Widespread rain
$500R^{1.5}$			Thunderstorm rain

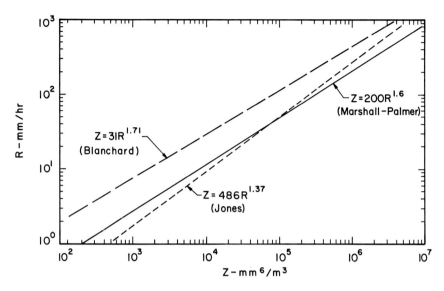

Fig. 7.1.   Plots of various *Z-R* relationships

Z–R for any locality. In fact, at any one place the character of the rainfall can vary widely.

In a region with a high thunderstorm frequency, the prediction scheme
could be successful in estimating the *Z–R* in thunderstorm rains but
might be a distinct failure in widespread rains from nimbostratus clouds.
This point was made by Stout and Mueller (1968). They asserted that
the major differences in *Z–R* relationships are primarily associated with
differences in geographic locality, but they maintained that at one locality "different types of rain or different synoptic conditions" could
lead to differences in rainfall amounting to 150 percent. Attempts were
made to relate empirically the quantities *A* and *b* in equation (7.14) to
such parameters as rainfall type, thermodynamic stability, and synoptic
classification. Wilson (1966a) found that the *Z–R* relationship in Oklahoma thunderstorms sometimes differed appreciably from one storm to
the next.

It appears that, by taking into account the climatological character
of the region and by further classifying the situation in terms of the
characteristics of the weather system, it should be possible to select a
Z–R relationship which is more accurate than one of those listed among
equations (7.15). Joss et al. (1970) proposed that the characteristics
of the echoes could be used to identify the character of the rain. This
information would allow the selection of an appropriate *Z–R* equation.
If this is done automatically by means of a computer it should be possible
to increase the accuracy of radar measurements of rainfall.

In evaluating the uncertainties in the Z–R equation, one should recognize that present techniques for measuring the average backscattered power are also subject to error. Stout and Mueller (1968) estimate that "under ideal conditions of careful calibration with a noise source" the accuracy may be somewhat better than ±3 dB. Such an uncertainty is of the same order of magnitude as that introduced by uncertainties in the Z–R relationship. They further state that modern signal processing techniques can reduce the error in $\bar{P}_r$ to ±1.5 dB. To fully utilize such precision, it is necessary to use some rational schemes for selecting a Z–R relationship.

In the past it has been common when other information has been lacking to use $Z = 200R^{1.6}$ for all rains. The data on hand show that this procedure is no longer appropriate. Equations (7.15) allow the choice of a Z–R relationship for three classes of rain. The articles already cited indicate that it should be possible to develop a procedure for predicting a most appropriate Z–R relationship.

The Z–R expressions in table 7.1 and in equations (7.15) were obtained by measuring raindrop spectra. Rainfall intensity was either calculated from the raindrop data or observed directly. Radar reflectivity factor Z was obtained by computing ΣD^6 in a unit volume. This implies that the expression is valid only when the radar wavelength is much longer than the diameter of the largest drops.

When this is not the case, it is necessary to replace Z with Z_e, the effective radar reflectivity factor (eq. [4.25]). The relationship of Z_e to R can be obtained by direct measurements of $\bar{P}_r$ and R. Stout and Mueller (1968) summarize the work of various investigators. Beriuliev et al. (1966) found A and b of 340 and 1.5, respectively, quantities which are in fair agreement with those measured directly. On the other hand, the determinations of A by Doherty (1963), Wilson (1966a), and Aoyagi (1964) generally yielded lower values of A than those shown in table 7.1. It should be recognized that there are a number of distinct difficulties in obtaining Z_e versus R directly. For example $\bar{P}_r$ corresponds to the backscattering from a volume above the ground, while R is measured at the ground. The scattering volume has a much larger horizontal area than that sampled by rain gauges.

Caton (1964) measured R by means of a rain gauge at the same time that a vertically pointing 3-cm pulsed-Doppler radar set was used to determine raindrop spectrum (this technique will be discussed in chap. 8). This analysis yielded $Z = 240R^{1.3}$, which changed very little between the cloud base and the melting level. By means of the same procedure Gorelik et al. (1967) calculated an average expression $Z = 263R^{1.30}$.

The Z_e-R relationships for specific drop-size distributions and wavelengths were calculated by Wexler and Atlas (1963) from Mie backscattering cross sections published by Herman, Browning, and Battan

(1961). The results of the analysis are shown in table 7.2. The quantities in the table can be compared with $Z = 296R^{1.47}$, which is the result obtained by direct integration of the Marshall-Palmer distribution for Rayleigh scattering. At wavelengths below 3.2 cm, the discrepancies between Z and Z_e are quite large, but such wavelengths are seldom used to measure radar reflectivity because, as was shown in chapter 6, they are heavily attenuated by rain.

TABLE 7.2 Z_e-R Relations Calculated Assuming Mie Scattering

Wavelength (Cm)	R Interval (Mm/Hr)	M-P (0°C)	Z_e (Mm⁶/M³) Gunn and East (18C)	Mueller and Jones (0°C)
0.62	0–5	$240R^{1.1}$	. . . .	$450R$
	5–20	$345R^{0.9}$	. . . .	. . . .
	20–100	$540R^{0.75}$	. . . .	. . . .
0.86	0–5	$350R^{1.32}$	. . . .	$950R$
	5–20	$450R^{1.15}$	. . . .	. . . .
	20–100	$780R^{0.95}$	. . . .	. . . .
1.24	0–5	$356R^{1.5}$	. . . .	$1280R$
	5–20	$460R^{1.35}$	. . . .	. . . .
	20–100	$820R^{1.15}$	. . . .	. . . .
1.87	0–20	$330R^{1.54}$	. . . .	$1150R$
	20–50	$500R^{1.4}$	. . . .	. . . .
	50–100	$750R^{1.3}$	. . . .	. . . .
3.21	. . . .	$275R^{1.55}$	$310R^{1.56}$	$890R$
4.67	. . . .	$280R^{1.45}$	. . . .	$860R$
5.5	. . . .	$280R^{1.45}$	. . . .	$860R$
5.7	. . . .		$210R^{1.6}$	. . . .
10	. . . .	$295R^{1.45}$	$210R^{1.6}$	$810R$

SOURCE: Wexler and Atlas 1963.

There have been few measurements of the radar reflectivity of snow as a function of the precipitation intensity. One reason is that it is more difficult to obtain accurate particle-size distributions and precipitation rates.

On the basis of the published results (see table 7.3) an appropriate expression appears to be

$$Z = 2,000 \, R^2, \tag{7.18}$$

where Z and R are in the usual units and R refers to the precipitation rates when the snow is melted. Carlson and Marshall (1972) concluded, from an analysis of observations of a snowstorm, that the exponent 2.0 was generally satisfactory, but there was ". . . some evidence that a slightly higher value might have been a little better."

TABLE 7.3   *Z-R* Relations for Snow.

Equation	Reference	Source of Data	Location	Remarks
$600R^{1.8}$ $2150R^{1.8}$	Imai et al. (1955)	Same	Japan	Snowflakes, 20 minutes on one day Mostly aggregate snowflakes, about 1 hr 40 min
$2000R^{2.0}$	Gunn and Marshall (1958)	Same	Montreal, Canada	Aggregate snowflakes, 10 days
$1780R^{2.21}$	Sekhon and Srivastava (1970)	Various	Japan and Canada	Reanalyzed data of Imai et al. (1955), Magono (1957), Gunn and Marshall (1958), and Ohtake (1968)

It should be noted from a comparison of equations (7.15a) and (7.18) that, when the precipitation rate exceeds about 0.16 mm/hr, the value of Z is greater for snow than for rain.

Since snowflakes fall slowly (about 1 m/sec), while raindrops fall five to ten times faster, the concentration of snowflakes must be larger than that of raindrops in order to yield the same R. Also, the heavier the rainfall rate and the larger the raindrops, the greater the difference $(Z_{snow} - Z_{rain})$.

7.4 Comparison of Calculated and Observed Values of Precipitation Intensity

Knowing the relationship between the reflectivity factor, Z, and the precipitation rate, R, one can write

$$\bar{P}_r = \frac{C_1 R^b}{r^2}, \tag{7.19}$$

where $C_1 = C|K|^2 A$; the quantity C is the calibration constant in equation (7.2).

With this simple formula, tests can be made to compare the calculated and measured values of R. This is done by measuring the scattered power from the raindrops falling into one or more rain gauges at a known range, r. The radar beam is pointed as low over the gauges as is practicable. Obviously, a sensitive, fast-responding recording gauge is needed in order to permit meaningful measurements of rain intensity. In all rains there are some time variations in intensity, and in convective showers very rapid changes may occur over a period of the order of 1 minute.

The value of $\bar{P}_r$ is measured by comparing the magnitude of the radar echo received from the rain scatterers with the magnitude of a known signal. The known signal may be obtained by observing the backscattering from a metal sphere at a known range (Atlas and Mossop 1960). More commonly, the known signal is produced by a high-quality microwave signal generator or radar test set adjusted to produce a pulse at the radar frequency.

The simplest technique for observing the known signal and the precipitation echo makes use of an A-scope or R-scope (fig. 1.3). The vertical scale can be calibrated by introducing, from the signal generator, pulses with magnitudes covering the range of received signals. In this way it can be established that a known displacement corresponds to a received power, P_r. Some of the early quantitative work with weather radar made use of the A-scope comparison techniques, but this procedure has the disadvantage that, because the radar echo typically has a very irregular appearance and is constantly fluctuating, it is difficult to obtain a precise value of the time-averaged P_r. By means of this procedure, however, it was established many years ago by Atlas (1948) and Bunting and Latour (1951) that precipitation rates calculated from the radar equation were significantly correlated with the actual observed precipitation.

Hooper and Kippax (1950b), using the technique of matching the amplitude of the echo and a calibrated signal on the same scope, made comparisons of the measured return power and the power calculated from measured rain and snow intensities. They reported good agreement at wavelengths of 9.1, 3.2, and 1.25 cm. Austin and Williams (1951) pointed out that Hooper and Kippax actually calculated the "average peak signal" rather than the average signal required by the theory. A limited number of measurements showed that the difference between the two averages was about 5–7 dB.

Another procedure used to test the validity of the radar-rainfall equation employs the PPI scope (fig. 1.4). The settings of the radar controls are fixed at constant values, and a signal generator is used to determine the smallest magnitude of the returned power needed to give a detectable echo. Once this is established, the boundary of the echo is judged to correspond to the threshold $\bar{P}_r$. If the echo covers only a small interval of range, a line of constant $\bar{P}_r$ would correspond to a line of constant R.

By changing the gain setting of the radar receiver, one can change the threshold of rain intensity. In this way, it is possible to obtain a series of so-called isoecho contours, i.e., lines of equal echo intensity, which correspond to isohyets when range variations are small.

One of the chief difficulties with this scheme is that an echo threshold determined by means of a signal of constant amplitude (i.e., the test signal) differs from a threshold determined by a highly fluctuating signal. This idea was discussed in section 4.4, where it was noted that at small ranges discrepancies of several decibels might occur. Notwithstanding this difficulty, various schemes have been developed by means of which quantitative precipitation measurements are made from the echo distribution on a PPI. There are obvious advantages in any technique which can yield the distribution of $\bar{P}_r$ and hence R over an area many tens of kilometers in radius.

The change of gain setting can be done manually or automatically, or, as was first done by Atlas (1947), one can use a receiver capable of discriminating between returned signals of two or more different intensity levels. With two intensity levels, the signal from the heaviest rain can be inverted electronically so that it will "cut a hole" in the echo produced by the lighter rain.

This process can be repeated with alternating regions of light and dark with the boundary of each corresponding to a measured $\bar{P}_r$ threshold (fig. 7.2). The lines of constant $\bar{P}_r$ are sometimes called "isoecho contours."

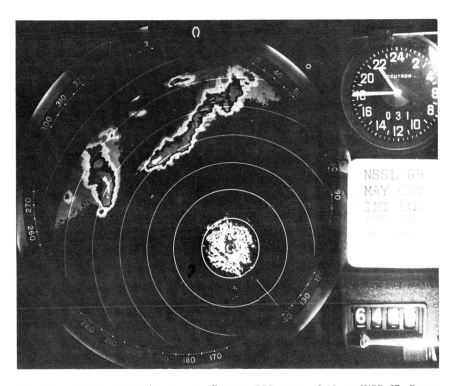

Fig. 7.2. Isoecho contouring on an off-center PPI scope of 10-cm WSR-57. Range markers at intervals of 20 nautical miles (37 km). Courtesy of National Severe Storms Laboratory, Norman, Oklahoma.

Scientists at McGill University have developed various procedures whereby echo-intensity distributions on a PPI are displayed by various discrete shades of grey. The most recent procedure was discussed by Marshall (1971).

Several devices have been developed to produce high-quality displays of isoecho contours. Kodaira (1961) developed techniques for integrating the backscattered signals, normalizing them for range, correcting them for attenuation, and displaying echo contours corresponding to specific rainfall rates. Wein and Gunn (1964) discussed a scheme devised at McGill University for producing an intensity-contoured PPI display. The staff at the National Severe Storms Laboratory has developed a 10-cm radar system which presents PPI isoecho-contoured signals at 10-dB intervals. A summary of their equipment was given by Wilk et al. (1967).

In recent years attention has been given to methods for measuring $\bar{P}_r$ in incremental areas and for displaying signal intensities in digitized form. More will be said about these techniques in a later section.

As already noted, Stout and Mueller (1968) estimated that, under ideal conditions with careful calibration, measurements of $\bar{P}_r$ can be made with an accuracy of about ±3 dB. For greater precision, either analogue or digital integrators may be used.

Austin and Williams (1951) employed a "pulse integrator" to obtain an accurate measure of the average backscattered power. This device obtains an average of the signal voltage, $\bar{A}$, received from a large enough sample of pulses to give a good measure of the true mean. By squaring this value, one obtains $(\bar{A})^2$, a quantity approximately equal to $\bar{P}_r$. The correct $\bar{P}_r = \bar{A^2}$. It can be shown by solving for $\bar{A}$ by means of equation (4.11), however, that the pulse-integrator measurement is only about 1 dB below the value of $\bar{P}_r$ that one would obtain if $\bar{A_2}$ were measured directly.

Probert-Jones (1962) summarized the results of various evaluations of the radar-rainfall equation. He found that earlier investigators had used an inexact form of the various equation. After correcting for various discrepancies as well as other errors found in the original analyses, Probert-Jones found that the differences between $\bar{P}_r$ calculated by means of the radar equation and the measured $\bar{P}_r$ were small. Table 7.4 shows that for seven projects the average difference was 1.4 dB. This would correspond to a rainfall discrepancy of 18 percent if $Z = AR^{1.6}$.

Since the analysis of Probert-Jones (1962), a number of additional tests have been made of the value of radar for measuring rainfall rate and have had results similar to those reported by earlier investigators. The small overall difference of 1.4 dB given in table 7.4, is the average of seven averages. Individual measurements at a single time and place could be very much larger.

TABLE 7.4   Average Differences between Calculated $(\bar{P}_{r_c})$ and Measured $(\bar{P}_{r_m})$ Power Backscattered by Rain

Author	Radar Wavelength (Cm)	$\bar{P}_{r_c} - \bar{P}_{r_m}$ (DB)
Hooper and Kippax (1950b)	3.2	1.5
Atlas (1948)	3	1
Hood (1950)	10	1.5
Hood (1950)	3	2
Austin and Williams (1951).	10	3.5
Roberts (1959)	3	1.5
Roberts (1959)	0.8	−0.5
Langille and Thain (1951)*	3	0.5
Average	. . . .	1.4

SOURCE: Probert-Jones 1962.

*This project measured backscattering from snow rather than rain.

Joss et al. (1970) compared measured rainfall rates with those calculated from observations obtained by means of a vertically pointing 4.67-cm radar. They found good agreement between measured and calculated daily rainfalls; the standard deviation was 28 percent when only days with more than 10 mm of rain were involved. By employing different $Z–R$ relations for drizzle, showers, and thunderstorm rains the standard deviation was reduced to 13 percent.

As the range on an azimuthally scanning radar increases, the accuracy of the radar-measured rainfall rate decreases, partly because the beam gets progressively higher above the ground. Wilson (1964) found that when the 10-cm WSR-57 was used the discrepancies between hourly rainfalls measured by rain gauge and radar increased slightly as ranges increased beyond 75 km, but they increased greatly beyond 110 km. Carlson and Marshall (1972) concluded that small elevation-angle errors can introduce significant errors in the radar measurements of snowfall. On the other hand, Joss et al. (1970), observing along the zenith, found that "the height at which the radar reflectivity factor is measured is of no consequence to the determination of the amount of rainfall, as long as it is measured below the melting level."

It has been recognized that the errors of rainfall measurements decrease as the averages are extended over time and space (e.g., Muchnik, Markovich, and Volynetz 1966). The measurement of precipitation over an area will be discussed in a later section. Before doing so, it is appropriate to examine the consequences of attenuation, which have so far been neglected.

7.5 Rain-Intensity Measurements at Attenuating Wavelengths

The measurement of rain at attenuating wavelengths has been studied by Atlas and Banks (1951), Hitschfeld and Bordan (1954), and others. It has been shown that, with radar sets operating at wavelengths below 10 cm, rain attenuation can amount to a substantial reduction in backscattered power.

When attenuation is taken into account the power received by a radar is given by

$$\bar{P_r} = \frac{C\,|K|^2 Z}{r^2}\,(10)^{-0.2\int_0^r k\,dr}. \tag{7.20}$$

As noted in chapter 6, attenuation by gases usually can be neglected, and equation (7.20) can be written

$$10\log\bar{P_r} = 10\log\frac{C\,|K|^2 Z}{r^2} - 2\int_0^r (K_1 M + K_2 R^\gamma)\,dr, \tag{7.21}$$

where K_1 is in decibels per gram per cubic meter per kilometer and (K_2R^{γ}) is in decibels per kilometer (see tables 6.1 and 6.2).

Using the relations $Z = 200R^{1.6}$ and $\overline{P}_r = (C/r^2)\,200R^{1.6}$, one obtains

$$10 \log \overline{P}_r = 16 \log R - 20 \log R$$

$$-2 \int_0^r (K_1M + K_2R^{\gamma})\,dr + 10 \log C_1, \qquad (7.22)$$

where $C_1 = 200\,|K|^2$.

Atlas and Banks (1951) made use of this equation to study the effects of attenuation in causing deformation of the echoes from rain showers having circular cross sections. They expressed $\overline{P}_r$ in terms of a fixed minimum detectable power, $P_{\min}$, and defined a term

$$y_{\min} = 10 \log \frac{\overline{P}_r}{P_{\min}} = 16 \log R - 20 \log r$$

$$-2 \int_0^r (K_1M + K_2R^{\gamma})\,dr + 10 \log C_2, \quad (7.23)$$

which expresses the received power in decibels above a fixed power level, $P_{\min}$. Note that, in so doing, the value of the constant on the right side of the equation is changed to C_2. Atlas and Banks found that, with radar sets operating at 3 cm, attenuation could result in very serious deformation of echo shapes.

Hitschfeld and Bordan (1954) solved equation (7.22) to obtain an expression for the rain intensity R in terms of the other parameters:

$$R = \frac{r^{B/A}\,e^{y/A}}{\left[(1/a)^{\gamma} - (\gamma C/A) \int_0^r r^{B\gamma/A}\,e^{y\gamma/A}\,dr \right]^{1/\gamma}}, \qquad (7.24)$$

where $A = 6.944$, $B = 8.680$, $C = 2K_2$, $y = 10 \log \overline{P_{ra}} + 2 \int_0^r K_1M\,dr$, and $(1/a)^{\gamma}$ is the integration constant. The quantity a may be regarded as the calibration constant of the radar. If the rain intensity, R_1, is known at range r_1 and y is known between $r = 0$ and r_1, then

$$\left(\frac{1}{a} \right)^{\gamma} = \frac{r_1^{B\gamma/A}\,e^{y_1\gamma/A}}{(R_1)^{\gamma}} + \frac{\gamma C}{A} \int_0^{r_1} r^{B\gamma/A}\,e^{y\gamma/A}\,dr. \qquad (7.25)$$

According to Hitschfeld and Bordan (1954), "The quantity a can be interpreted as the minimum detectable value of the rainfall at range one mile, when the received power has the minimum value that can be received, and when the attenuation due to intervening rain is zero or negligible."

It should be noted in equation (7.24) that, at nonattenuating wave-lengths, $C = 0$, and thus the denominator is a constant, and any errors in the term a have the same effect, regardless of the value of R. In this case circular showers will appear as circular echoes, and deformations such as those calculated by Atlas and Banks will not occur.

From an error analysis, Hitschfeld and Bordan concluded that quanti-tative measurements of rainfall with a radar set at an attenuating wave-length are subject to considerable error unless the performance of the radar set is known with great accuracy. They expressed the opinion that "the requisite precision is probably not usually possible, and hence radars using attenuating wavelengths are not generally recommended for quantitative rain measurements." They showed that in many cases accepting $\bar{P}_r$ without making attenuation corrections may lead to smaller errors than when attempts are made to take attenuation into account. A relatively small error in a, in cases where attenuation is large, can lead to extremely large errors in rainfall. It was shown, however, that if a radar set at an attenuating wavelength is to be used for quantitative rainfall measurements, it should be calibrated accurately against a rain gauge deep in the storm, where the attenuation is appreciable. When the value of a is determined in this way, equation (7.24) can give satisfactory values of the rainfall rate at points between the radar set and the calibra-tion gauge.

It is evident that, for quantitative rainfall measurements, radar sets operating at nonattenuating wavelengths, preferably about 10 cm, should be used whenever possible.

7.6 Estimation of R from Attenuation Measurements

In the preceding section, it was shown that rainfall attenuation can cause large errors when R is calculated from measured $\bar{P}_r$. It has been proposed that R could be determined by measuring attenuation. Collis (1964) conducted tests by means of a radar set operating at a wavelength of 0.87 cm. Fixed targets of known cross sections were observed during rainy and dry days. In the analysis, measured attenuation rates in dB/km were compared with 5-minute mean rainfall rates on a number of dates. Results were disappointing, but it was speculated that more success would have been achieved had a 3-cm radar been employed. At this wave-length the raindrops would be mostly Rayleigh scatterers, and a more consistent relationship between attenuation and rainfall rate would be expected.

Juillerat and Godard (1963) also compared attenuation of 0.86-cm waves with rainfall rates. They employed a 3.4-km path length and observed rain intensities below 4 mm/hr. The radar-computed rainfalls and those observed by eight rain gauges differed by less than 25 percent when cumulative amounts in five rains were considered. When 15-minute accumulations were examined, the differences were much greater.

If a single radar is used, known targets must be employed to indicate attenuation between the radar and the target. Another technique employs two radar sets, one at a nonattenuating wavelength (e.g., 10 cm) and another at a wavelength which is strongly attenuated (e.g., 1.8 cm). Simultaneous measurements would yield attenuation along the path and allow calculations of rainfall rate along the path. Atlas (1954) first proposed this scheme for measuring the liquid-water content, and it was reexamined recently by Eccles and Mueller (1971), who suggested the use of radars operating at 3 and 10 cm. Abshaev (1968) also proposed that liquid-water content could be measured by means of simultaneous observations at wavelengths of 10 and 3.2 cm.

Cartmill (1963) and Rogers and Wexler (1963) developed the theory for using a dual-wavelength technique for measuring rainfall rates. Cartmill used wavelengths of 10 cm and 5.6 cm, while Rogers and Wexler employed wavelengths of 1.82 cm and 0.86 cm. The last two authors tested their scheme over short path lengths in shower precipitation and obtained discouraging results. To obtain the rainfall distribution it is necessary to measure the radial gradient of echo intensity. The variable nature of shower precipitation makes it difficult to make accurate measurements by means of two radar sets. Sulakvelidze and Dadali (1968) also proposed that precipitation be measured by means of a multiwavelength radar system.

7.7 Measurement of Rainfall Over an Area

The preceding sections dealt with procedures for measuring the rainfall rate R. For certain problems such as the effect of rain on soil erosion, the short-period rainfall intensity is an important factor. In most instances, however, the summation of R over space and time is the crucial quantity of interest. A farmer is concerned with the total precipitation over his cultivated area during the total period of the storm. The hydrologist needs to know the amount of rainfall over a watershed during a given period of time, because, having such information, he can apply appropriate techniques for predicting stream and river flows.

In practice the total amount of water which has fallen over any area during a particular time period is inferred from scattered measurements by rain gauges. The spacings between the gauges may be anywhere from 10 to 50 km or more. During periods of widespread rain, such as occur with stable types of cloud systems, the variability of rainfall over small distances is not very great. Although so-called continuous rain has centers of heavy rain, the variations in space are not so extreme as those usually observed in convective rains. If only rain-gauge data are available, one easily can be misled about the total amount of rain over an area produced by thunderstorms. Observations by means of closely spaced gauges have shown that, over distances of a few kilometers, strong gradients of precipitation are common. Shortly after World War II it was recognized that radar was capable of observing the location and areal extent of thunderstorms and that, at the very least, qualitative radar observations used in conjunction with rain-gauge measurements would make it possible to draw isohyets more accurately. In recent years, increasing attention has been given to the development of radar systems for quantitative precipitation measurements over an area (Kessler 1968).

One of the earliest attempts to use radar for obtaining direct measurements of rain falling over a small area was made by Byers et al. (1948). Rainfall observations collected by gauges at 1-mile intervals in a small area were compared with a time summation of the area or volume of the radar echoes over the same area.

Various investigators have used photographic integration of the echoes on a PPI scope to estimate the precipitation over an area (Rockney 1954; Hiser, Senn, and Conover 1958; Tarble 1960; Leber, Merritt, and Robertson 1961; and others). The scheme examined by Hiser, Senn, and Conover is the following: After the radar set was properly warmed up and adjusted, the shutter of a camera containing slow film was opened and allowed to stay open for several hours. In this way the equivalent of several thousand separate scans of a PPI scope was superimposed. By means of a densitometer, measurements were made of the film density at points over existing rain gauges. The film density is related to $\bar{P}_r$. From these data, the radar was calibrated for each day (fig. 7.3). It was then possible to measure the film density at points where no rain gauges existed and infer the total rainfall. With a radar set operating at 10 or 5 cm. and rain of light or moderate intensity, attenuation could be neglected without introducing serious errors. This procedure has some technical difficulties—mainly because of the necessity that the radar calibration remain constant during the period of integration, the restrictions introduced by the film, and the requirement for precise densitometer measurements—but it has the advantages of being relatively simple in principle and of not involving expensive or complicated electronic equipment.

Tarble (1960) and Leber, Merritt, and Robertson (1961) did not keep the camera shutter open for the entire period of interest. They employed Polaroid cameras and made multiple exposures. Tarble generally made one exposure every 5 minutes for a 1-hour period. In slow, steady rain

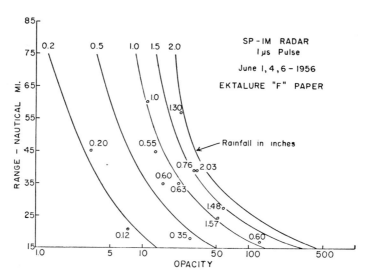

Fig. 7.3.   Typical calibration of radar system and long time-exposure film for the purpose of measuring total rainfall. From Hiser, Senn, and Conover (1958).

one exposure every 10 minutes for a total of 3 hours was found more suitable. This procedure allows the weather observer to change the operation of the radar between exposures. For example, if he wishes to increase the elevation angle to examine echo tops, he can do so without ruining the integrating film plate.

Leber, Merritt, and Robertson (1961) used ten exposures per hour and integrated the hourly rainfall amounts to yield 24-hour isohyetals during a heavy rainstorm. They used another PPI scope to supply quantitative echo intensities from which precipitation was calculated assuming $Z = 200R^{1.6}$. When these data were analyzed in conjunction with the once-hourly multiple exposures, the integrated 24-hour rainfall pattern was in excellent agreement with results given later by an analysis of rain-gauge data. Of course, the radar data also gave much more detail.

For the most part, the techniques already described are empirical in nature, in that they compare echo intensity and rainfall directly and establish a relation between them by means of statistical procedures. A number of investigators have devised schemes for measuring the $\bar{P}_r$ in incremental areas over a region of interest and then calculating R for each incremental area. If this is done at regular intervals, e.g., every 10 minutes, the distribution of R can be integrated in space and time to yield total precipitation over the region.

The first system of this kind was devised by Austin and Richardson (1952). They used a special pulse integrator to take an average of the power received by the S-band SCR-615B from precipitation over an area defined by a range depth of 16.1 km and an azimuthal sector of 10 degrees. Observations were made in the range intervals 19.3–99.5 km. At smaller ranges, ground clutter introduced errors; at ranges longer than 100 km, the beam extended high above the ground. Clearly, the area over which P_r was averaged increased with range. The pattern of rainfall yielded by the radar measurements was compared with isohyetal patterns based on rain-gauge observations. In general, the agreement was encouraging. Unfortunately, the rain gauges were too widely spaced to permit a good test of the radar system. Some areas exceeding 40 km in diameter were without a gauge.

Another electronic device for measuring the rainfall over an area was described by Farnsworth and Mueller (1953). They called it an "area integrator" because it was designed to measure the area of echo over a fixed region. The video signal from the precipitation echo over the region operated a gating circuit, which allowed pulses from an oscillator to pass to a counter. Each count indicated that an incremental area contained an echo.

To obtain echo information which could be related to precipitation, a calibrated radar set was used with receiver gain stepping. On the first step the PPI scope presented echoes corresponding to the lightest rain, and an oscillator at frequency f was used to supply the pulses. After one scan of the antenna, the receiver gain was reduced by a fixed amount corresponding to a known reduction of the threshold of detectable power. On this step, heavier rain had to be present in order to give a detectable echo. To allow straightforward counting of pulses, the oscillator frequency was simultaneously changed to a value $f + \Delta f$, where the increase in frequency corresponded to the increase in rainfall rate needed for detection. The stepping-down of receiver gain and the increasing of oscillator frequency were continued until the gain became so low that no echo was received. When the cycle was completed, a counter gave the total number of pulses, each of which, in principle, corresponded to a certain rainfall rate over a certain area. If this unit rate were known, multiplication with the counter number would yield the total rainfall in unit time over the area involved.

The original model of the area integrator suffered several drawbacks. One of the most serious was that, as the electron beam swept radially, a range pulse at a long range represented a larger area than a pulse at a short range. This difficulty presumably could be corrected by building an oscillator whose frequency increased with range so that each pulse represented the same incremental area.

Tests were made of the abilities of the area integrator to measure the echo area. They were encouraging, but the absence of reports to the contrary suggests that this device did not do a satisfactory job of rainfall measurement.

A number of investigators have developed schemes in which the PPI presentation is divided into rectangular or square incremental areas, and the value of $\overline{P_r}$, and hence R, is calculated for each area. The simplest procedure is a manual scheme sometimes called the "tick method." A transparent overlay, divided into squares perhaps 10×10 km, is put over a PPI scope. The receiver sensitivity is set so that the threshold of detection corresponds to a known rainfall rate (approximately). A "tick" mark is put in each square containing an echo. This is often done by tracing the echo outline on the overlay. Then the gain setting of the radar is changed to correspond to a heavier rainfall and the process is repeated. This procedure leads to a pattern of isohyets which can be integrated in space. By repeating the procedure, time integration becomes possible.

For some years, work has been in progress to adopt modern data-processing techniques to automate the procedure just outlined (Kessler and Russo 1963; Schaffner 1963; Atlas et al. 1963; Kodaira 1961, 1963; McCallister, Teaque, and Vicroy 1966; Wilk et al. 1967; and others).

A so-called storage tube has been employed to act as a memory for a PPI or RHI presentation (Schaffner 1963; Kodaira 1963). It is an electronic device having a screen on which charges may be stored. The charge at each point depends on the quantity deposited by an electron beam. When the screen is scanned again by an electron beam, the output charge depends on the stored charge. The readout procedure can be repeated several thousand times without destroying the stored pattern of charge.

If a PPI echo pattern is impressed on a storage tube, various procedures may be employed to read out the echo intensities in incremental areas (e.g., 10×10 km), convert the signal strength to digital form, compute radar reflectivity factor Z, or calculate precipitation rate. The information so obtained can be coded according to position and put on punch cards, punched tape, magnetic tape, or any other recording medium. It can then be transmitted to other locations via radio, telephone or teletype.

The average power in an incremental area may be read off directly and retained in the memory unit of a computer. In the "Storm Radar Data Processor" (STRADAP) described by Atlas et al. (1963) and Bradley et al. (1964), measurements are made of the backscattered power in area intervals given by 1 degree of azimuth and 1.85 km (1 nautical mile) in range as the antenna scans in azimuth and steps in 1- to 2-degree increments of elevation angle. This procedure required 3.6 minutes when the radar set AN/CPS-9 was employed. The STRADAP logic examines the data and "selects the maximum of the numerous elemental arc measurements of average power in each 5 by 5 nautical mile square and stores a 3-bit binary word in a rectangular coordinate memory system of magnetic cores," according to Atlas et al. (1963). The STRADAP system can supply digitized printouts of log Z_e at prescribed altitudes, commonly at about 3-km intervals up to 12 km. It also may give the pattern of maximum echo heights. A scheme similar to STRADAP has been developed at the Main Geophysical Observatory in Leningrad (Sal'man, Gashina, and Divinskaya 1968; Petrushevskii et al. 1968).

A method for data reduction developed by the National Severe Storms Laboratory (NSSL) has been adapted to the WSR-57, a 10-cm radar (Lhermitte and Kessler 1965; Wilk et al. 1967; Wilk and Kessler 1970; Sirmans, Watts, and Horwedel 1970). The video signals from logarithmic amplifiers are fed into circuits which simultaneously integrate the backscattered signals in 200-range intervals, each 1.2 km in depth. The signals pass to an integrator quantizer. It compares the amplitude of each video signal with particular signal amplitudes. Twenty discrete amplitude levels are employed. The output of this system is displayed on a PPI scope as contours of echo power designated by varying shades of gray (see fig. 7.2). In normal operations at the National Severe Storms Laboratory, the PPI scope displays three shades of gray at 10-dB intervals, but more may be included.

The output of the NSSL integrator also is fed to an analogue-to-digital converter whose output is recorded on magnetic tape. The logic circuits are designed to yield radar reflectivity factor Z, in terms of azimuth and range increments. The magnetic tape records log Z rounded to the lower whole integer for incremental areas defined by 2 degrees of azimuth and 2.6 km in range. The quantized echo data can be converted by a computer to any suitable coordinate system. Figure 7.4 shows a PPI display and the distribution of log Z presented on a cartesian coordinate system.

McCallister, Teaque, and Vicroy (1966) described tests in which digitized values of echo intensity over a known grid were used to calculate rainfall over a watershed. The data were supplied by a WSR-57 at the Greater Southwest Airport near Fort Worth, Texas, operated by NSSL and equipped with the circuitry for yielding values of log Z in rectangular areas 6.2×10.3 km (i.e., an area of about 64 km^2) over a total range of 185 km. The digitized echo intensities were transmitted by teletype and by facsimile to a computer center where calculations were made of rainfall rate R as a function of position by means of the expression $Z = 200R^{1.6}$. It was found that when the rainfall over an area was integrated, about 90 percent of the rain was contributed by echoes in which log $Z > 3$, i.e., $R > 3$ mm/hr, approximately.

Echo-intensity distributions over the entire area were obtained at

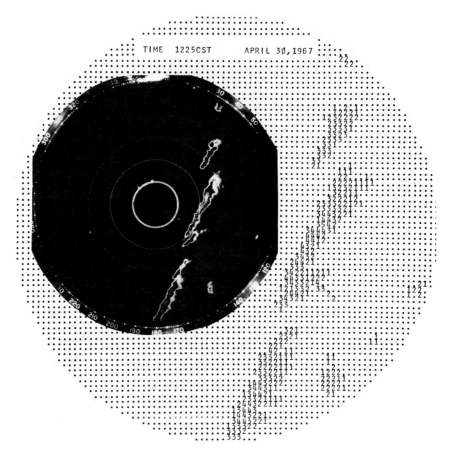

Fig. 7.4. Simultaneous display of isoecho contours on a PPI scope (range-marker interval = 20 nautical miles = 37.1 km) of the 10-cm radar WSR-57 and of digitized echo intensity measurements in terms of log Z. Each number gives the echo power from an incremental area about 2.6 km on a side. From Wilk et al. (1967).

30-minute intervals. Once the computer contained these data, a program was written to smooth the observations by extrapolating the movement of echoes.

Radar data were transmitted from the radar set to the Fort Worth River Forecast Center, where rainfall quantities were computed and compared with rain-gauge observations as well as runoff. Excellent agreement was found between the radar and gauge rainfall amounts and distributions.

The scheme just discussed ultimately will be extended to include other radar sets and one or more data-collection centers to gather and assemble the digitized data. Figure 7.5 shows a composite map displaying data from four radar stations. For this system to reach its full potential, all radar sets must be carefully calibrated and maintained. When it comes into being, it will be possible, on a current-time basis, to obtain far better information on precipitation over the nonmountainous areas than is currently supplied by rain-gauge networks.

J. W. Wilson (1970) employed data collected by means of the NSSL, WSR-57 radar to show that the accuracy of area rainfall measurements can be improved when a rain gauge in the area is used to calibrate the radar. He estimated that, over an area of 2,600 km^2, at least four uniformly spaced rain gauges would be required to yield the same accuracy of rainfall measurement as could be achieved by a radar calibrated with one gauge near the center of the same area.

Collis (1963) reported a procedure for using radar to obtain rainfall amounts at a large number of fixed locations surrounding the radar. At each of 141 address points, which in a typical operation might be spaced 20–30 km apart, quantized echo intensities were numerically integrated. In the prototype, the signal intensities at 12-minute intervals were assessed in six classes as follows: 2.5, 7.6, 15.2, 30.4, 61.0, 103 mm/hr. Electromechanical counters set in a map, at positions corresponding to each address, displayed accumulated precipitation. This equipment, in a sense, supplied a network of "radar rain gauges" which gave a continuous, essentially up-to-the-minute record of accrued rainfall at each "gauge" station.

Tests showed that Collis's Radar Rainfall Integrator measured light, widespread rainfall with fair accuracy. As expected, the device appeared to underestimate heavy convective rainfall. The typical spacing of the address points was too large to adequately sample thunderstorms whose typical diameters would be less than 10 km. An inherent disadvantage of this scheme is that it ignores a great deal of information, i.e., the radar data between the address points. Nevertheless, the system is relatively inexpensive, and one can imagine that it might have some applications.

In closing this chapter on the measurement of precipitation by means of radar, it is necessary to note that the techniques described tacitly assume that the radar beam is fairly narrow (less than perhaps 3 degrees) and is directed at a low elevation angle (close to zero degrees). As the radar beam is elevated, the distance over which rainfall estimates are valid decreases because ever higher regions of the atmosphere are sampled as the range increases.

In mountainous regions, where there are large and important watersheds, a single radar can observe only a small area. At present, if radar

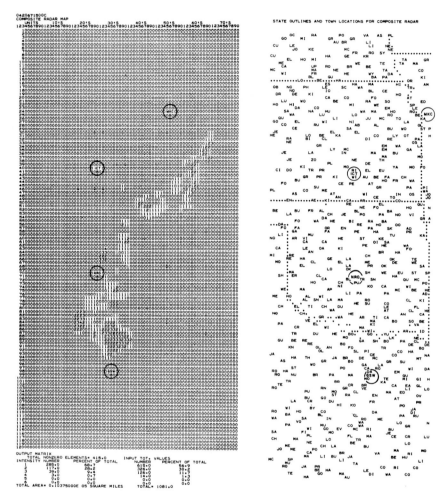

Fig. 7.5. *a (left)*, a composite map showing radar data collected at four sites (marked by circles) in midwestern United States, 1500 CST, 20 April 1967. Integers greater than zero are ten times the average logarithm of the reflectivity factor in areas 5 × 5 nautical miles (about 9.3 × 9.3 km). In areas where overlapping radar data disagree, the highest arithmetic mean is given by the computer. The map dimensions are 400 by 600 nautical miles (about 740 by 1,110 km). The map is stretched vertically because the printer listed ten columns but only eight rows per inch. The map was produced in delayed time but suggests the great potential value of a data-collecting and data-processing system disseminating rainfall and storm data on an operational basis automatically. *b (right)*, a geographical strip 300 miles (550 km) wide (part of the area illustrated in [*a*]) including portions of the states of Texas, Oklahoma, Kansas, Nebraska, and Missouri. Radar sites are shown by circles, and the letters refer to town sites which would be served automatically by a computer-linked data-processing system. The map is stretched vertically as in (*a*). From Kessler (1968).

were to be used to measure precipitation, it would be necessary to employ a number of sets at different elevations. Even by so doing there would still be difficulties in discriminating precipitation echoes from ground echoes. Most studies described in this chapter were carried out over fairly flat areas. It is important that more attention be given to the measurement of rain and snow over mountainous terrain. Perhaps new techniques—possibly involving Doppler radar—can be devised to deal with this important problem.

8

Pulsed-Doppler Radar

Most meteorological radars are noncoherent and are used to observe the location and pattern of echoes and to measure the intensity of the backscattered signals. The radars also can detect the pulse-to-pulse change in signal strength. As was noted earlier, this information can yield estimates of the relative motion of the scatterers. For many purposes, it is useful to know the velocity of the scatterers with respect to a fixed point on the ground. A noncoherent radar cannot give such information except in a few special circumstances.

The velocity of scatterers in the free atmosphere can be obtained by means of coherent radars. The name "Doppler radar" has been given to the class of radar sets which measures the shift in microwave frequency caused by moving targets. Brantley and Barczys (1957) first reported the use of a continuous-wave Doppler radar to observe a weather phenomenon. In subsequent years there has been rapid development of pulsed-Doppler radar systems and of techniques for interpreting the data they yield. Review articles have been written by Atlas (1964) and Lhermitte (1966b, 1969a).

8.1 The Doppler Shift Frequency

Assume that a target is at a range r from a radar set operating at a frequency f_0 (corresponding to a wavelength λ). The total distance traversed by a very narrow pulse in going to the target and back to the antenna obviously is $2r$. Measured in terms of the wavelength, the distance amounts to $2r/\lambda$ or, in radians, $(2r/\lambda)2\pi = 4\pi r/\lambda$. If the electromagnetic wave emitted by the antenna has a phase ϕ_0, the phase after it returns will be

$$\phi = \phi_0 + \frac{4\pi r}{\lambda}. \tag{8.1}$$

The change of phase as a function of time, e.g., from one pulse to the next, is

$$\frac{d\phi}{dt} = \frac{4\pi}{\lambda} \frac{dr}{dt}. \tag{8.2}$$

114

If the target at range r is moving along the radar beam axis, the target velocity $V = dr/dt$. The quantity $d\phi/dt$ is the angular frequency, ω, which equals $2\pi f$. Substitution in equation (8.2) gives

$$f = \frac{2V}{\lambda}, \tag{8.3}$$

where f is the Doppler shift frequency and V is the radial velocity of the target. It is also called the "Doppler velocity." Table 8.1 displays the quantity f as a function of V and λ. It is evident that, for all meteorological targets, f is in the audio range. These frequency shifts are extremely small in comparison with the carrier frequencies corresponding to the indicated wavelengths. Nevertheless, by means of various procedures it is possible to readily detect the Doppler shift frequencies.

TABLE 8.1   Doppler Shift Frequencies in Hertz for Various Radar Wavelengths and Target Velocities

V (M/Sec)	Wavelength (Cm)			
	1.8	3.2	5.5	10.0
0.1	11	6	4	2
1.0	111	62	36	20
10.0	1,111	625	364	200
100.0	11,111	6,250	3,636	2,000

8.2 A Pulsed-Doppler Radar

If the radar were observing a single, small water drop of diameter D moving at a radial velocity V, a pulsed-Doppler radar would detect a signal of intensity proportional to D^6 and a single Doppler shift frequency, f. It would do this by detecting the change of phase from one pulse to the next. The way this is done can be illustrated by means of the block diagram of one type of pulsed-Doppler radar shown in figure 8.1 (for details, see Skolnik 1962).

As in any pulsed radar, the transmitter produces a signal having a frequency f_0 (e.g., 9,245 MHz) and lasting for a brief period τ (e.g., 0.25 μsec). Most of the power passes through the duplexer to the antenna and is radiated as an electromagnetic wave. A small amount of the signal from the transmitter goes into a so-called locking mixer where it is mixed with a signal from a very stable local oscillator called the STALO. The signal out of the locking mixer has an intermediate frequency (e.g., 30 MHz), which passes on to the coherent oscillator. This device, commonly called a COHO, oscillates at the intermediate frequency while maintaining the phase of the transmitted radar wave.

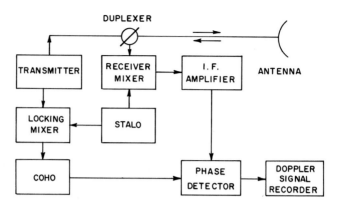

Fig. 8.1.   Block diagram of a pulsed-Doppler radar

When a backscattered signal is received at the antenna, it is mixed with the signal from the STALO to produce an intermediate frequency (IF) having the phase properties of the reflected electromagnetic wave. After amplification, the receiver IF signal is compared with the IF signal from the COHO by means of a phase detector which measures the difference in phase ϕ_1 between the two signals. The next pulse yields a phase ϕ_2, and the difference from pulse to pulse yields $\Delta\phi/\Delta t$ and f, the Doppler shift frequency.

It is clear that, in order to measure a frequency f, it is necessary to obtain measurements of ϕ at a frequency of at least $2f$. For example, if the wave were a pure sine wave of frequency f, and observations were made at the same frequency, they would all have the same amplitude. Sampling at a rate $2f$ would reveal alternating high and low values of the signal and reveal the existence of frequency f.

Since the rate at which pulses are transmitted in a radar set is the pulse-repetition frequency, the PRF, the maximum Doppler shift frequency which can be detected is given by

$$f_{max} = \frac{PRF}{2}. \qquad (8.4)$$

This corresponds to a maximum Doppler velocity of

$$V_{max} = (PRF)\frac{\lambda}{4}. \qquad (8.5)$$

Therefore, if a 3.25-cm radar set has a PRF = 4,000/sec, the largest Doppler shift frequency and velocity it can measure are 2,000 Hz and 32.5 m/sec, respectively. The maximum velocity is proportional to both PRF and λ; hence if it is desired to unambiguously measure high velocities, it is desirable to use long wavelengths and high PRFs. For example, at $\lambda = 10$ cm and PRF = 8,000 m/sec, $V_{max} = 200$ m/sec.

If a target is moving at such a high speed that the change of phase from pulse to pulse exceeds 2π—i.e., the target moves a distance exceeding one wavelength—the Doppler radar does not give an unambiguous measure of f or V. See Atlas (1964).

Since the maximum Doppler frequency and velocity are proportional to the PRF, it also follows that they are uniquely related to the maximum unambiguous range, r_{max}. It is given simply by $r_{max} = \frac{1}{2}(c/\text{PRF})$, where c is the speed of propagation of an electromagnetic range. Substitution in equations (8.4) and (8.5) yields

$$f_{max} = \frac{1}{4}\frac{c}{r_{max}} \tag{8.6a}$$

and

$$V_{max} = \frac{\lambda}{8}\frac{c}{r_{max}}. \tag{8.6b}$$

If a Doppler radar operated at 10 cm and V_{max} were 200 m/sec, the maximum unambiguous range would be only 18.7 km. It is clear that, if conventional Doppler techniques are employed, it is necessary to compromise between V_{max} and r_{max} if the former is to be measured unambiguously.

8.3 Doppler Frequency and Fluctuation Frequency

As already noted, a single target—a raindrop, e.g.—moving with a velocity V toward a coherent radar will produce a Doppler frequency given by equation (8.3). If the target consists of a spectrum of drop sizes a_i, each with velocity V_i along the radar beam axis, a Doppler radar detects a spectrum of Doppler shift frequencies. Before considering the properties of such a spectrum, it is instructive to examine the contribution of each scatterer to the backscattered signal.[1] Such an exercise will show how the Doppler shift frequencies are related to a quantity called the signal fluctuation frequency, F. It is the rate of fluctuation of the signal strength from a particular volume of distributed scatterers. The time or space averages discussed in chapter 4 for obtaining $\overline{P}_r$ were designed to average out these signal fluctuations.

It can be shown that the electric field backscattered from a distribution of point targets such as raindrops is given by

$$A\,(t) = R\,\left[\delta_i\,(t)\,e^{-i\,\omega_0 t}\right], \tag{8.7}$$

1. The discussion in this section follows Atlas's (1964) treatment of the same subject.

where R designates the real part of the complex-valued function having an amplitude $\delta(t)$, and $\omega_0 = 2\pi f_0$ is the angular frequency corresponding to the carrier frequency of the radar, f_0 (see Born and Wolf 1959). In this treatment, the phase is taken to be zero at time zero. This assumption simplifies the discussion without loss of generality.

If the radar were observing a single raindrop moving at velocity V_1 and producing a Doppler shift frequency f_1, and if the amplitude of the signal from the raindrop were δ_1 (a constant), the complex-valued amplitude would be given by $\delta_1(t) = \delta_1 e^{-i\omega_1 t}$. The backscattered field from this drop would be

$$A(t) = R\left[\delta_1 e^{-i\omega_1 t} e^{-i\omega_0 t}\right]$$
$$= \delta_1 \cos 2\pi (f_0 + f_1)t. \tag{8.8}$$

A radar set measures the quantity $A(t)$, and, if its variation with time is obtained, the Doppler frequency f_1 can be deduced. A noncoherent radar set measures the signal power P_r. It is proportional to $A^2(t)$ averaged over one or more cycles of the carrier frequency, f_0. Omitting the proportionality constant for simplicity, one can write the quantity P_r as the product of $\delta(t)$ with its complex conjugate; i.e.,

$$P_r = \left(\delta_1 e^{-i\omega_1 t}\right)\left(\delta_1 e^{i\omega_1 t}\right) = \delta_1^2. \tag{8.9}$$

As expected, the backscattered power from a single drop is constant regardless of its velocity.

Two raindrops producing backscattered amplitudes δ_1 and δ_2 and having radial velocities V_1 and V_2 will produce Doppler velocities f_1 and f_2, respectively. The complex backscattered electric field will be the sum of the fields from each of the raindrops; i.e.,

$$\delta(t) = \delta_1 e^{-i\omega_1 t} + \delta_2 e^{-i\omega_2 t}. \tag{8.10}$$

Substitution in equation (8.7) yields the varying backscattered field which can be measured by a Doppler radar,

$$A(t) = \delta_1 \cos (\omega_0 + \omega_1)t + \delta_2 \cos (\omega_0 + \omega_2)t. \tag{8.11}$$

Averaging $A(t)$ over one cycle of f_0 gives the signal power

$$P_r = \delta_1^2 + \delta_2^2 + 2 \delta_1 \delta_2 \cos (\omega_2 - \omega_1)t. \tag{8.12}$$

It is seen that the backscattered signal can be considered to consist of a constant amount $\delta_1^2 + \delta_2^2$ plus a varying amount $2\delta_1 \delta_2 \cos (\omega_2 - \omega_1)t$. When equation (8.12) is averaged over one cycle of the angular frequency $\psi = \omega_2 - \omega_1$, one obtains $\overline{P_r}$, which is a constant.

The quantity ψ can be written

$$\psi = 2\pi F = 2\pi (f_2 - f_1), \tag{8.13}$$

where the symbol F is defined as the frequency of the signal fluctuation. It measures the fluctuation of echo power observed on any radar set. In the special case of two targets, $F = f_2 - f_1$, or, in words, the fluctuation frequency is the difference between the Doppler frequencies of the two targets.

As was noted in chapter 4, the signal fluctuations depend on the motion of the scatterers with respect to one another. This point is verified by equation (8.13) for two scatterers. If they were moving at the same velocity, V_1, and hence at zero velocity with respect to one another, $f_1 = f_2$ and $F = 0$. As a result the signal strength would be constant.

The treatment discussed in this section can be extended to a very large number of scatterers. Lhermitte (1960a) has shown that

$$P_r = \sum_i \delta_i^2 + 2 \sum_{ij} \delta_i \delta_j \left[\cos (\psi_{ij} t)\right]. \qquad (8.14)$$

The first term on the right is the sum of the contributions to the back-scattered signals by each of the targets and is a constant. When P_r is averaged over time, the last term on the right goes to zero and $\overline{P}_r$ can be related to the sum of the backscattering contributions by all the scatterers in the illuminated volume.

The fluctuations of P_r with time, observed on a noncoherent radar, is composed of contributions of all the fluctuations $F_{ij} = f_i - f_j$. It is evident, therefore, that the Doppler-frequency spectrum and the signal-fluctuations spectrum are closely related.

8.4 The Doppler Spectrum

As already noted, the signal given by equation (8.14), which is back-scattered by an ensemble of moving targets, contains information about their radar cross sections and radial velocities. By means of a suitable data-processing scheme, it is possible to extract the backscattered power as a function of Doppler shift frequency. Such a function, usually designated as $S(f)$, is called the *Doppler spectrum*. The power in each frequency interval Δf can be equated to the $\Sigma \eta$, i.e., the summation of the radar reflectivity of the particles moving at velocities corresponding to Δf. By means of the relation $f = 2V/\lambda$, the quantity $S(f)$ can be written as $S(V)$. Figure 8.2 shows typical spectra for rain and snow.

The total average power received by a radar set is given by

$$\overline{P}_r = \int_{-\infty}^{\infty} S(f)\, df = \int_{-\infty}^{\infty} S(V)\, dV, \qquad (8.15)$$

where $S(f)\, df$ and $S(V)\, dV$ are the powers in the intervals of Doppler frequency and velocity, $S(f)\, df$ and $S(V)\, dV$, respectively.

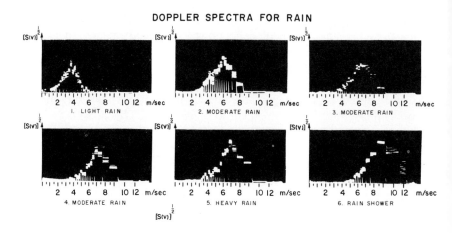

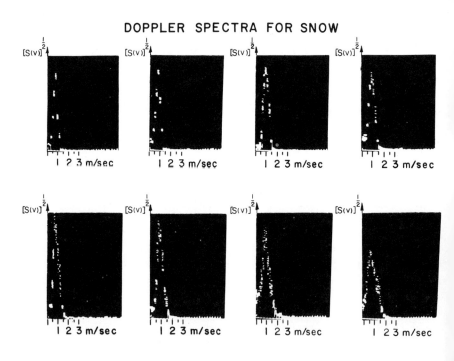

Fig. 8.2. *a*, Doppler spectra of rain where the ordinate is proportional to signal voltage. The quantity $S(V)$ in equation (8.15) is proportional to the square of the signal voltage. *b*, Doppler spectra of snow. Same coordinates as in (*a*). Courtesy of R. M. Lhermitte and D. Atlas, Air Force Cambridge Research Laboratories.

If, in each velocity interval dV, there are $N(V)$ targets, each of which backscatters an amount of power represented by p, equation (8.15) can be written

$$\bar{P_r} = \int_{-\infty}^{\infty} N(V)p(V) \, dV. \qquad (8.16)$$

For certain applications it is desirable to know the relative power in each velocity interval. It can be obtained by means of the expression

$$\frac{N(V)p(V) \, dV}{\int_{-\infty}^{\infty} N(V)p(V) \, dV}. \qquad (8.17)$$

If this operation is performed for every velocity interval, one obtains the *normalized Doppler spectrum*.

Given a time-varying signal called the coherent video, represented analytically by equation (8.14), one may employ various schemes for obtaining the Doppler spectrum.

Lhermitte (1963*a*), Rogers (1963), and Atlas (1964) discussed how the Doppler spectrum can be derived from the autocorrelation function. Blackman and Tukey (1958) developed methods for calculating the signal-power density spectrum of a time-varying function. They were used by Battan and Theiss (1966). The coherent-video signals, recorded on magnetic tape, were digitized and fed to a computer which calculated the Doppler spectra. Very useful fast Fourier transform algorithms were developed by Cooley and Tukey (1965). They allow the calculation of 10–20 spectra per second, a rate compatible with the data-collection speed. These techniques have been employed by Lhermitte (1969*b*; 1970).

Doppler spectra can also be obtained by means of electronic spectrum analyzers. Such schemes have been used by Boyenval (1960), Battan (1963*a*), Caton (1963), Rogers (1963), Groginsky (1966), and others. A variety of such devices have been employed. In a simple one, the Doppler signals are recorded on magnetic tape and then passed repeatedly through one or more filters whose central frequencies and characteristics are known. In more complicated systems, radar data may be collected at 10 or more ranges, by means of fixed gates, and fed to a number of narrow-band filters centered at the various frequencies of interest. The output of each filter is integrated for periods of from 0.6 to 3 seconds. After integration the signals can be depicted either in analogue form on a scope or chart (fig. 8.3) or digitized and recorded in that form (Groginsky 1966).

To obtain the Doppler spectrum of a typical precipitation target, it is

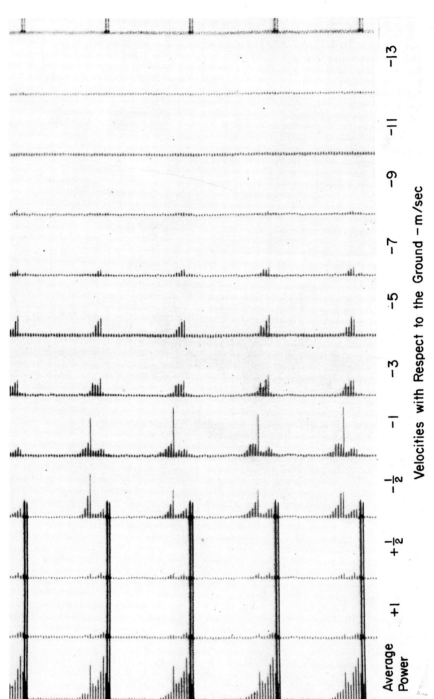

Fig. 8.3.   Facsimile recording of Doppler spectra as a function of altitude in the case of steady winter precipitation. In each velocity channel the power is proportional to the square of the length of the line representing the signal. In this diagram negative velocities designate downward motions. The height distribution is obtained by a range gate which steps from zero to 4,600 m in 152-m intervals and repeats the sequence every 20 seconds. Note that above the pronounced strong echo at an altitude of 1,070 m, virtually all the power was backscattered by particles falling

necessary to examine the backscattered power from a particular volume of scatterers for a finite period of time (of the order of a second). It can be shown that, the longer the record, the more precise the estimated Doppler spectrum, provided that the time series is stationary (Blackman and Tukey 1958). In most weather targets, the character of the back-scatterers in a particular radar volume does not undergo much change in periods of the order of a few seconds, but it would not be safe to assume stationarity for periods approaching a minute if a thunderstorm were being observed.

In some Doppler radars, the antenna is fixed and a narrow gate moves from zero range to maximum range in a series of steps. The length of time that the gate spends at each range is called the "dwell time" and is the length of the record from which the Doppler spectrum is obtained. In other radar sets, as already noted, a series of gates are fixed at particular ranges. This allows the simultaneous collection of Doppler spectra at many ranges. In certain radar systems, the range gates are fixed while the antenna slowly rotates in azimuth. In later parts of this chapter, it will be seen how these schemes have been used to observe various atmospheric phenomena.

8.5 The Spread of the Doppler Spectrum

The spread of the Doppler spectrum depends on a variety of factors:

1. The spread of terminal velocities of the scatterers. In the case of rain, this is equivalent to saying that the greater the range of drop sizes the greater the spread of the Doppler spectrum. This effect is most pronounced when the radar beam is pointed vertically. As the elevation angle, α, is reduced, the component of the fall velocity decreases in proportion to $\sin \alpha$.

2. The turbulence spectrum of the air. Small raindrops and ice particles respond rapidly to changes in air velocity and will faithfully exhibit the turbulent air motions. Large raindrops and ice particles, particularly hail, will not respond readily to small-scale turbulence.

3. Shear of the air motion across the radar beam. When the beam is pointed horizontally, vertical shear of the wind will be most important.

4. Uniform air motions across a radar beam having a finite width. If a wide beam is employed and targets are carried across it perpendicular to the beam axis, for example, the targets at the edge of the beam will be producing greater $\Delta\phi/\Delta t$, and higher Doppler velocities, than the targets close to the beam axis because of the spherical configuration of the surface of equal phase ϕ.

The spread of the Doppler spectrum can be measured in a number of ways. One can obtain the total spread by taking the difference between the positive and negative velocity bounds (see fig. 8.4). To do this, it is necessary to identify the Doppler frequencies (or velocities) at which the signal strength just exceeds the noise level.

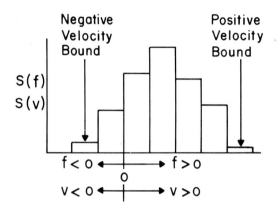

Fig. 8.4. A schematic drawing of a Doppler spectrum showing power as a function of Doppler velocity. When scatterers move downward they produce positive Doppler shift frequencies and velocities.

A more convenient measure of the spread of the Doppler spectrum is its variance, σ_V^2. Typical precipitation distributions produce spectra which approach a Gaussian character, as is shown in figure 8.4. Sometimes there are deviations with more than one maximum. Nevertheless, the variance is an appropriate indicator of the spread of a Doppler spectrum. To calculate it, one must first obtain the *mean Doppler velocity*. It is given by

$$\bar{V} = \frac{\int_{-\infty}^{\infty} V S(V) \, dV}{\int_{-\infty}^{\infty} S(V) \, dV}. \tag{8.18}$$

This expression gives a mean velocity wherein each measured velocity is weighted according to the quantity of power backscattered by targets moving at that velocity. Knowing the drop-size distribution and having an expression of the velocity of the particles as a function of their diameters, one could calculate $\bar{V}$ in still air by substituting a reflectivity variable for $S(V) \, dV$. If Rayleigh scattering were involved, one could substitute $N(D)D^6 dD$.

The variance σ_V^2 of the Doppler spectrum can be obtained from

$$\sigma_V^2 = \frac{\int_{-\infty}^{\infty} (V - \bar{V})^2 S(V) \, dV}{\int_{-\infty}^{\infty} S(V) \, dV}. \tag{8.19}$$

As in the calculation of $\bar{V}$, the results are independent of the expression used to measure backscattered power — $S(V)\ dV$ can be in watts or be expressed in terms of radar reflectivity η, radar cross section σ, or reflectivity factor Z. Table 8.2 shows typical values of $\sigma_V{}^2$ for various types of hydrometeors.

TABLE 8.2 Variance of Doppler Velocity Spectrum for Particular Types of Precipitation Particles Falling in Still Air, when Antenna Beam is Pointed Vertically

Type	Variance		Sources
Snow	0.04–0.25 m²/sec²*		Hitschfeld and Dennis (1956); Lhermitte (1962); Rogers and Tripp (1964)
Melting snow	0.5 m²/sec²*		Lhermitte (1963*b*)
Rain	0.7–1.0 m²/sec²*		Lhermitte (1962, 1963*b*)
Hail (ice spheres)($\lambda = 3.2$ cm†)			Boston and Rogers (1969); Donaldson and Wexler (1969); Battan and Theiss (1968)
Max. Diam.	Dry	Wet	
2 cm	8 m²/sec²	19 m²/sec²	
4 cm	24 m²/sec²	19 m²/sec²	

*These quantities apply near sea level.
†Variance in case of hail is very sensitive to λ when maximum diameters exceed about 2 cm.

Hitschfeld and Dennis (1956) showed that the total variance $\sigma_V{}^2$ can be written as the sum of the variances produced by the four factors listed above. The effects of uniform motion of scatterers across the radar beam can be significant if the winds are strong and the beam is not narrow. If it is close to 1 degree in width, however, this effect can be disregarded.

The effects of wind shear also depend on the beam width. They have been analyzed by Lhermitte (1963*b*); Sloss and Atlas (1968); and Atlas, Srivastava, and Sloss (1969). These analyses indicate that the contribution of the cross-beam wind shear to the Doppler-spectrum variance is negligibly small providing beam widths close to 1 degree are employed. As the beam approaches 2 degrees and larger, the measured variance becomes significant at ranges greater than some tens of kilometers.

If a radar beam is pointing upward and has a width of about 1 degree, the variance of the Doppler spectrum will depend on the spread of the components of the target terminal velocities and the turbulence in the scattering volume. If the first of these effects can be determined independently, measurements of $\sigma_V{}^2$ can be used to infer the turbulence characteristics of the air. On the other hand, if the effects of turbulence are small, the Doppler spectrum yields information about the particle-size spectrum.

As will be noted later in this chapter, there are still disagreements over the degree to which the Doppler spectrum is spread by turbulence.

8.6 Signal Fluctuations

The fluctuations of the pulse-to-pulse video signals yield information about the turbulence in the scattering volume. As indicated earlier, the spectrum of F is related to the spectrum of f. Hitschfeld and Dennis (1956), Lhermitte (1963a), Rogers (1963), and others have examined the properties of the signal fluctuations. One item of particular interest is the so-called time to independence. It is a measure of the time, τ, required for the correlation between the amplitude of the video signal at time $t + \tau$ to be independent of the signal amplitude at time t. Theoretical studies assuming a Gaussian fluctuation spectrum have led to the expression (Atlas 1964)

$$\tau_{0.01} = 1.71 \, \lambda \times 10^{-3} \text{ sec,} \qquad (8.20)$$

where $\tau_{0.01}$ is the time required for the autocorrelation function to fall to 0.01 and λ, the radar wavelength, is in centimeters. This equation was derived for a Doppler spectrum having a $\sigma_V = 1$ m/sec. The quantity $\tau_{0.01}$ is inversely proportional to σ_V.

By means of signal fluctuation measurements Rogers (1957) reported $\sigma_V = 0.6$ m/sec as a common value. If this quantity were used, equation (8.20) would become $\tau_{0.01} = 2.8\lambda \times 10^{-3}$, where λ is in centimeters. At wavelengths of 10, 3.2, and 1.25 cm, $\tau_{0.01}$ would equal 28, 9.0, and 3.5 msec, respectively. The last two values are in good agreement with experimental results. Bartnoff, Paulsen, and Atlas (1952) measured a time for independence of 4 msec at a wavelength of 1.25 cm. Fleisher (1953) and Stone and Fleisher (1956) reported times between 10 and 100 msec at a wavelength of 3.2 cm.

Knowing the time required for independence, one can satisfactorily specify the averaging time needed to obtain an adequate measure of $\bar{P}_r$ when the radar is viewing the same scattering volume. It should be at least $10\tau_{0.01}$. Therefore, at 10 and 3.2 cm, the averaging times should be at least 3×10^{-1} and 9×10^{-2} sec, respectively.

The signal-fluctuation spectrum can be measured by recording the pulse-by-pulse backscattered power and then making a power-spectrum analysis of the record. As already noted, the resulting fluctuation spectrum, $S(F)$, would be a measure of the relative motion of the scatterers and hence of the turbulence in the scattering volume. A simple technique for arriving at similar information involves the measurement of the number of times in a given sampling period that the signal strength exceeds a particular threshold level. Such a technique is the basis for an instrument developed by Rutkowski and Fleisher (1955) called the R-meter. The relation between the output of the R-meter and the variance of the Doppler spectrum have been discussed by Rutkowski and Fleisher (1955), Lhermitte (1963a), and Rogers (1963).

Rogers (1963) showed that the expected rate, L, at which the radar signal crosses its average value in either direction (up or down) depends on the type of receiver used in the radar. If a linear detector is employed, i.e., a receiver which measures the signal voltage A, (eq. [4.11]),

$$L = 2\pi e^{-\pi/4} \sigma_f. \tag{8.21a}$$

Therefore,

$$L = 4\pi e^{-\pi/4} \frac{\sigma_V}{\lambda} = 5.74 \frac{\sigma_V}{\lambda}, \tag{8.21b}$$

since the standard deviation of Doppler frequency σ_V and the standard deviation of Doppler velocity are related by $\sigma_f = 2\sigma_V/\lambda$.

If the radar set uses a square-law detector and hence measures a quantity proportional to A^2 (eq. [4.12]),

$$L = \frac{4\sqrt{\pi}}{e} \sigma_f, \tag{8.22a}$$

and, therefore,

$$L = \frac{8\sqrt{\pi}}{e} \frac{\sigma_V}{\lambda} = 5.22 \frac{\sigma_V}{\lambda}. \tag{8.22b}$$

As Rogers (1963) noted, as a receiver varies between linear and square law, the rate L at which the average signal level is crossed varies only about 10 percent. Therefore, small variations of the power law of the receiver are of minor importance when an R-meter is used to measure the variance of the Doppler spectrum.

Lhermitte (1963a) examined the rate of positive crossings ($L/2$) of the signal voltage, A, above the level of $\bar{A}$ in terms of the fluctuation rate (F) of the signal. He found that

$$\frac{L}{2} = (\overline{F^2})^{\frac{1}{2}}. \tag{8.23}$$

Lhermitte (1963a) compared the curve represented by equation (8.23) with experimental data and obtained good agreement. It is evident that the variance of the Doppler spectrum of distributed targets can be obtained from an incoherent radar by means of an R-meter or any other device which can measure the rate at which video signals cross a prescribed threshold.

It should be noted that, according to theoretical analyses by Bechtel and Prinsen (1967), instabilities in the carrier frequency of an incoherent radar can lead to large errors in R-meter estimates of the standard deviation of the Doppler spectrum. Lob (1968) carried out a theoretical study of the effects of receiver noise on the R-meter.

8.7 Measurement of Turbulence

Table 8.2 gives ranges of Doppler-spectrum variances when precipitation particles are falling in still air. The quantities obviously depend on the distributions of the radar cross sections and fall velocities of the scatterers. Observed values of the variances commonly exceed the values given in table 8.2 because of the effects of turbulent air motions. Hitschfeld and Dennis (1956) demonstrated that

$$\sigma_V{}^2 = \sigma_{V_t}{}^2 + \sigma_{V_p}{}^2, \tag{8.24}$$

where $\sigma_{V_t}{}^2$ and $\sigma_{V_p}{}^2$ are the contributions to the variance by turbulence and the fall speeds of the particles, respectively. If a wide radar beam is employed, the effects of wind shear and uniform motions across the beam would contribute to the variance and two more terms would be added to equation (8.24).

By measuring $\sigma_V{}^2$ and estimating $\sigma_{V_p}{}^2$, one can obtain the turbulence energy in the atmosphere. Rogers and Camnitz (1962) showed theoretically how Doppler radar observations could be used to obtain the radial component of atmospheric turbulence, and Rogers and Tripp (1964) made observations of the Doppler velocity and variance of snow. By assuming that $\sigma_{V_p}{}^2$ for snow was between zero and 0.25 m²/sec², they calculated the variance of turbulent air motions. They found that root-mean-square turbulent velocities were between 0.4 and 2 m/sec with most of them below 1 m/sec. It also was found that about three-quarters of the energy is usually in wavelengths shorter than 100 m.

At the Central Aerological Observatory in Moscow, there has been considerable work on the measurement of turbulence in terms of the properties of the radar-signal fluctuation and Doppler-frequency spectra (Gorelik, Kostarev, and Chernikov 1958, 1962; Gorelik and Mel'nichuk 1966; Gorelik and Smirnova 1961; and Gorelik 1965, 1968). These analyses have led to techniques for calculating such quantities as root-mean-square velocity fluctuations and the eddy dissipation rate in various types of clouds as well as in a cloudless sky.

Lhermitte (1968b), Sweeney (1970), D. A. Wilson (1970), and Børresen (1971) measured the character of turbulent air motions by means of Doppler radar observations of snow.

By dispersing "chaff," i.e., large numbers of very light metallic dipoles, turbulence can be measured in a cloudless atmosphere (Lhermitte

1969*a,b*; Chernikov et al. 1969; Gorelik and Tolstykh 1970). The technique of tracking chaff to obtain wind information is discussed in section 11.4.

Recognizing that, at present, airborne weather radars do not have Doppler capability, Atlas and Srivastava (1971) showed that, by measuring the fluctuation spectrum of the echo signals from two volumes by means of a noncoherent radar, it is possible to infer turbulence in the atmosphere.

8.8 Measuring Updraft Velocities

A pulsed-Doppler radar with its antenna pointed vertically supplies observations allowing inferences of the vertical velocity of air in convective clouds. Several schemes for doing this have been reported.

Probert-Jones and Harper (1961) were the first to show that the pattern of vertical air motion could be obtained. They recorded observations of the Doppler spectrum at height intervals of 150 m. At all levels above the 0°C isotherm they assumed that ice crystals or snowflakes were present in detectable concentrations. Hence, they took the negative end (upward velocity) of the Doppler spectrum as an estimate of the velocity of the ice particles with respect to the ground. By adding 1 m/sec, to account for the terminal velocity of particles, they obtained a measure of the vertical air velocity.

In order to estimate air speeds below 0°C, Probert-Jones and Harper made two assumptions: (1) that vertical air speed is continuous through the melting layer, and (2) "that there will be little change in the terminal velocity of the largest drops in their fall to the ground" from the bottom of the melting layer.

On the basis of these assumptions it was inferred that changes in the maximum downward Doppler velocities as a function of height could be attributed to changes in air velocity. This procedure was used to estimate air speed in the rain regions.

Battan (1964) and Battan and Theiss (1966) extended the technique of Probert-Jones and Harper. They assumed that in most parts of a shower there are particles with fall speeds of about 1 m/sec. Above the 0°C level they might be frozen; below it, small raindrops would be the scatterers. Hence, through the entire depth of a precipitating column, the negative velocity bound (maximum upward) of the Doppler spectrum plus 1 m/sec was taken to be the vertical air velocity. Atlas (1964) pointed out that this scheme was likely to be in error at the forward edge of a shower where raindrop sorting commonly occurs (Gunn and Marshall 1955).

Clearly, the validity of employing the negative bound of the Doppler spectrum depends on a number of crucial factors. It is necessary that slow-falling scattering particles be present, that they be detectable, and that it be possible to identify them as particles whose terminal speeds can be estimated reasonably well.

When a broad spectrum of particle sizes exists, as it commonly does, it may be assumed safely that the particle diameters will range from those too small to be detected to those quite easily detectable. Distribution curves such as those proposed by Marshall and Palmer (1948) would satisfy this description.

When a broad raindrop spectrum is present, the precision with which air motion may be inferred depends on the minimum size of the drops detected. Typical X-band radar sets, such as those employed in the studies already mentioned, are capable of detecting drops with diameters of perhaps 200–300 μ. Note that the maximum range involved is usually less than 10 km. One can reasonably take the terminal velocities of the detectable drops to be no more than about 1 m/sec.

There is one obvious drawback in the technique based on identification of the tails of the Doppler spectra. It is inherent in any scheme involving detection of a threshold, and it comes about because of difficulties in discriminating signal from noise. This is particularly true when a power spectrum is derived from a record of finite length. A certain degree of arbitrariness is involved in the selection of the threshold level.

Another difficulty encountered when using the bounds of the spectrum arises because of uncertainties about the role of turbulence. In early work it was assumed that its effect on the Doppler spectrum was small. Atlas (1964) noted that, on the basis of turbulence measurements by means of the R-meter by Rogers (1957), Doppler-spectrum broadening might be as large as 0.5 m/sec. Donaldson (1967) and Donaldson and Wexler (1969) concluded that it could be considerably larger. This matter will be examined in later parts of this section.

Certain pulsed-Doppler radars measure the mean Doppler velocity, $\bar{V}$, and the radar reflectivity factor Z as a function of height. Rogers (1964) proposed a procedure for estimating the vertical air velocities from measurements of $\bar{V}$ and the radar reflectivity factor Z made by means of a zenith pointing radar. Incidentally, if one wishes to measure only the median Doppler velocity this can be obtained without knowing the Doppler spectrum (see Pilié, Jiusto and Rogers, 1963).

Rogers (1964) made several assumptions in his analysis: (1) that the raindrops are spheres and are small with respect to the radar wavelength, hence that Rayleigh scattering prevails, and therefore $Z = \int ND^6 \, dD$; (2) that the sizes of the backscattering particles are exponentially distributed in the manner described by Marshall and Palmer (1948), i.e.,

$N_D = N_0 e^{-\Lambda D}$; (3) that the terminal velocity, W_t, and the particle diameter are uniquely related according to an expression derived by Spilhaus (1948), i.e., $W_t = KD^{\frac{1}{2}}$. For raindrops smaller than about 5 mm in diameter, the Spilhaus equation gives good results. At larger diameters the deviations between actual terminal speeds and those given by the equation increase rapidly.

Starting from these given conditions, Rogers derived an expression for a quantity W_0, which is the mean Doppler velocity in still air of the raindrops which would produce the observed Z. By substituting the given conditions in

$$W_0 = \frac{\int_0^\infty W_t N(D) D^6 \, dD}{\int_0^\infty N(D) D^6 \, dD}, \qquad (8.25)$$

one obtains the equation

$$W_0 = 3.8 Z^{0.072}, \qquad (8.26)$$

where W_0 is in meters per second and Z is in millimeters to the sixth power per cubic meter. The coefficient K relating terminal velocity was taken as 1,420 cm$^{\frac{1}{2}}$/sec (Spilhaus 1948), and it was assumed that $Z = 213 R^{1.56}$.

The *downdraft* velocity W_a is given by the expression

$$W_a = \bar{V} - W_0, \qquad (8.27)$$

where $\bar{V}$ is measured positively downward. For example, if $\bar{V} = -9$ m/sec, corresponding to an upward motion causing a negative Doppler shift frequency, and $W_0 = +5$ m/sec, $W_a = -14$ m/sec and is an updraft of this speed.

Sometimes confusion arises in discussions of the sign of Doppler velocities. A target moving toward the radar, i.e., one moving downward when the antenna is zenith pointing, will produce a positive shift in Doppler frequency. In other words, if the radar transmits a frequency f_0, a downward-moving target returns a wave with frequency $f_0 + 2V/\lambda$. In meteorology, it is conventional to consider vertical velocity positive when the air is moving upward, and for this reason positive Doppler shift frequencies on a zenith-pointing radar have been equated with negative velocities by some authors. In this book the practice used by most radar meteorologists is followed; namely, *a positive Doppler velocity is one where the target is moving toward the radar.* Raindrops moving downward will be said to produce a positive Doppler velocity corresponding to a Doppler shift frequency in the positive direction.

Rogers recognized that his assumptions introduced uncertainties in this method but stated that, when raindrops are the scatterers, it should give updraft estimates to within about 1 m/sec. He proposed that, in snow, comparable accuracy could be obtained by assuming that the particles (and hence W_0) have terminal velocities of 1 m/sec. Aoyagi (1969) estimated that when $Z = 200R^{1.6}$ is used, the mean Doppler velocity (W_0) can be measured to an accuracy of within ± 1.5 m/sec. He also calculated W_0 versus Z for several Z–R relations and compared the results with measurements close to the ground. He found good agreement.

From an analysis of Doppler-radar observation in a thunderstorm, Sekhon and Srivastava (1971) calculated raindrop spectra in a thunderstorm and found

$$N_D = N_0 e^{-\Lambda D}, \tag{8.28a}$$

$$\Lambda = 38R^{-0.14}, \tag{8.28b}$$

$$N_0 = 0.07R^{0.37}, \tag{8.28c}$$

where N_D and N_0 are in units per centimeter to the fourth power and Λ in units per centimeter. By means of these expressions, they derived a formula for the mean Doppler velocity such a distribution would produce in still air and obtained

$$W_0 = 4.3Z^{0.052}, \tag{8.29}$$

where W_0 is in meters per second and Z in millimeters to the sixth power per cubic meter.

Joss and Waldvogel (1970) measured raindrop-size distributions at the ground at one-minute intervals. Seven storms, representing various types of rainfall in three different countries, were analyzed. This investigation yielded the equation

$$W_0 = 2.6Z^{0.107}, \tag{8.30}$$

which is considered to be valid in the reflectivity range from 10 to 2×10^5 mm^6/m^3.

Table 8.3 shows values of W_0 calculated by means of the three expressions given above. It is evident that, over the indicated range of Z, the three equations gave values of W_0 which are in good agreement. These results show that the scheme, first proposed by Rogers (1964), for obtaining updraft velocity in a rain storm should yield values to within about 1 m/sec provided the raindrop sizes are exponentially distributed. It is not clear, at this time, how good the Rogers technique is in the case of a hailstorm or when rain and hail coexist.

Rogers's procedure was used by several other investigators (Atlas 1966; Donaldson, Armstrong, and Atlas 1966; Easterbrook 1967;

TABLE 8.3 W_0 versus Z Calculated from the Equation of Rogers (eq. [8.26]), Sekhon and Srivastava (eq. [8.29]), and Joss and Waldvogel (eq. [8.30])

Z (Mm⁶/m³)	W_0 (M/Sec)		
	Eq. (8.26)	Eq. (8.29)	Eq. (8.30)
10^1	4.5	4.9	3.6
10^2	5.3	5.5	4.6
10^3	6.3	6.2	5.9
10^4	7.4	7.0	7.6
10^5	8.7	7.9	9.7

Donaldson and Wexler 1968; Donaldson 1967). In the last paper it was argued that, because of turbulence broadening of the Doppler spectrum, Rogers's method may be superior to methods based on the bounds of the Doppler spectrum.

Gorelik and Logunov (1968) suggested that improved estimates of vertical air motions could be made if measurements of raindrop sizes at the ground were obtained at the same time Doppler-radar data were collected. They speculated that, with such information, accuracies of 0.2–0.3 m/sec were attainable. Wiley et al. (1970) did have simultaneous-drop spectra and Doppler data and made measurements of air motion in widespread rain. Velocities ranged between about −2 and +2 m/sec. They estimated that under favorable conditions they could measure vertical air speeds to within 0.25 m/sec.

There have been few comparisons of the techniques of inferring up-draft speeds. Battan and Theiss (1970a) published an analysis of the draft speeds in a small thunderstorm. The field of vertical motions was obtained by means of Rogers's technique and by means of the Battan-Theiss technique which involves taking the negative tail of the velocity spectrum and adding one meter per second. In this discussion the symbols W_R and W_{BT} will be used to designate the two estimates of draft speeds.

The storm occurred on 7 August 1967 near Vail, Arizona, where the elevation is 1,050 m. As the thunderstorm passed overhead, it produced a brief shower of fairly heavy rain. During the period 1425 to 1440 MST, 3.0 mm of rain was measured by a recording rain gauge near the radar. Almost all of it fell before 1430 MST.

The Doppler data were obtained by means of a vertically pointing 3.2-cm radar with a 1.3-degree beam. A narrow gate obtained Doppler information at altitude intervals of 152 m. The gate-dwell time at each altitude was 0.67 second. A period of 54 seconds was required for the gate to travel to an altitude of about 12 km and repeat the cycle. Doppler spectra at each altitude were obtained by means of a pair of crystal-controlled filters of width 5 Hz (3 dB down). The filters were centered at frequencies corresponding to 0.5, 1.5, 2.5, 3.5, etc., m/sec, and the analogue Doppler recordings on magnetic tape (one recording positive, the other negative Doppler shifts) were run through the filters a sufficient number of times to yield spectra extending from -19.5 to $+19.5$ m/sec. The filter outputs were in digital form.

The digitized spectra were fed into a computer which yielded the following information: average backscattered power in decibels with respect to a milliwatt normalized to an altitude of 1,600 m and Z_e; mean Doppler velocity, $\bar{V}$, and the variance of the Doppler spectrum; the Doppler spectrum where the power was calculated for each velocity interval of 1 m/sec; the calculated value of W_0 and the downdraft velocity $W_R = \bar{V} - W_0$.

The negative bound of the Doppler spectrum was taken as the velocity at the midpoint between the channel containing zero signal and the adjacent channel containing a signal exceeding the noise. This procedure made the selection of the upper bound an objective one.

Figure 8.5 shows vertical profiles of W_R and W_{BT} as well as the spread of Doppler velocity. The ends of the Doppler spectra indicated by the crosses and horizontal lines have been shifted 1 m/sec in the negative direction.

Table 8.4 shows a tabulation of $W_{BT} - W_R$ as a function of the range of Doppler velocity at altitudes below 4.2 km, i.e., at altitudes where the precipitation was mostly, if not entirely, in the form of raindrops. Since Rogers's formula is strictly applicable only when the radar scatterers are raindrops, the data in the table should give a measure of the comparability of the two techniques involved.

The distribution of $W_{BT} - W_R$ has a distinct maximum in the interval zero to 0.9 m/sec, the mean value is 0.6 m/sec, and the standard deviation is 1.2 m/sec. In obtaining W_{BT}, the upward velocity given by the negative bound of the Doppler spectrum was increased 1 m/sec on the assumption that the smallest drops which could be detected would be about 300 μ in diameter and would have terminal speeds of 1 m/sec. If it had been assumed that the smallest detectable drops had diameters of about 130 μ and terminal velocities of 0.4 m/sec, the average of $W_{BT} - W_R$ would have been zero. This result leads one to wonder if, at the short ranges involved, the Doppler radar used in this investigation could have been detecting such small particles. At a range of 2 km, there must be about 10^5 m^{-3} water drops with diameters of 130 μ in order for a backscattered signal of 10^{-12} w to be produced. This concentration appears to be unreasonably large.

Table 8.4 also shows that the larger the spread of Doppler velocity, the greater $W_{BT} - W_R$. This relationship also stands out in figure 8.5.

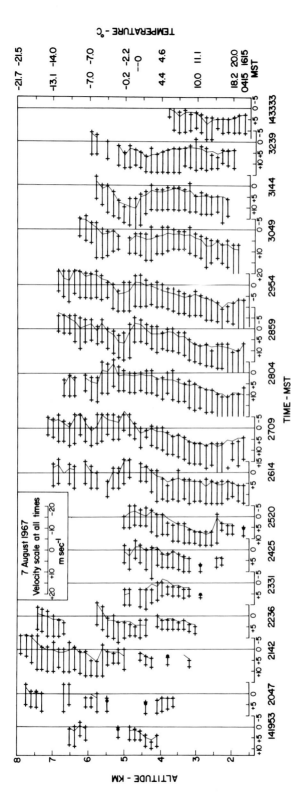

Fig. 8.5. Vertical profile of Doppler velocity: *crosses connected by horizontal lines, the spread of the Doppler spectrum (in every case the spectrum has been shifted 1 m/sec in the negative direction); dots or solid light line near the negative tails of the Doppler spectra, updraft velocities (W_R) calculated by means of Rogers's formula.* From Battan and Theiss (1970a).

TABLE 8.4   Tabulation of $W_{BT} - W_R$ as a Function of the Range of Doppler Velocity, ΔV, at Levels below 4.2 km, i.e., in the Rain

ΔV (M/Sec)	$W_{BT} - W_R$								Total
	−2.1 to −3.0	−1.1 to −2.0	−0.1 to −1.0	0 to 0.9	1.0 to 1.9	2.0 to 2.9	3.0 to 3.9	4.0 to 4.9	
1–2	. . . .	. . . .	1	. . . .	. . . .	. . . .	. . . .	. . . .	1
3–4	1	. . . .	16	7	. . . .	. . . .	. . . .	. . . .	24
5–6	1	3	7	10	. . . .	. . . .	. . . .	. . . .	21
7–8	. . . .	6	5	23	5	. . . .	. . . .	. . . .	39
9–10	. . . .	. . . .	9	27	25	3	2	. . . .	66
11–12	. . . .	1	. . . .	4	5	2	4	. . . .	16
13–14	. . . .	. . . .	. . . .	1	1	1	3	2	8
Total	2	10	38	72	36	6	9	2	175

SOURCE: Battan and Theiss 1970a.

See, for example, the observations at 3.5 km and 142614 MST, at about 3.7 km and 142804 MST, and at about 3.2 km and 143049 MST and 143144 MST. In most instances, when $W_{BT} - W_R$ was large, the negative tail of the Doppler spectrum showed evidence of having been spread toward a larger negative velocity. The Doppler velocity corresponding to the positive tail generally varied smoothly from the values at altitudes above and below the level of high $W_{BT} - W_R$. The larger drops corresponding to the positive tail would respond more slowly to air-velocity changes than the smaller drops producing the negative tail, but even large raindrops reach terminal velocities over a fall of perhaps 10 or 20 m. These results imply that the turbulence spreading of the Doppler spectrum in this storm was relatively small in general.

Figure 8.6 shows the cumulative distribution of σ_V^2 measured in the thunderstorm depicted in figure 8.5. Also shown is the distribution of the variance in a storm producing large hail and the variance observed when the radar antenna was pointed horizontally through a rain shower. In this case, the effects of particle-fall speed should have been quite small, and turbulence and shear effects must have accounted for the variance values, which were usually below 1 m²/sec² but which exceeded 4 m²/sec² about 5 percent of the time. The observed variance in the 7 August storm was somewhat larger than that observed on 25 August 1969, but the difference can be accounted for, at least in significant part, by the effects of particles falling through the vertically pointing beam. The hailstorm on 10 August 1966 yielded hailstones exceeding 2 cm in diameter and exhibited values of σ_V^2 greater than about 10 m²/sec² in about 10 percent of the observations.

The data on the variance measured when the antenna was pointing

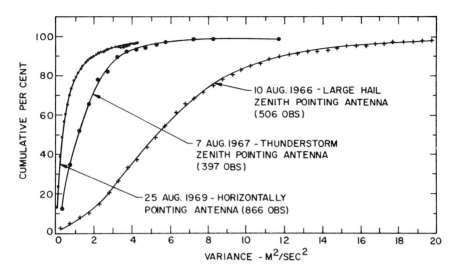

Fig. 8.6. Variances of Doppler spectra observed by means of 3.2-cm Doppler radar at the University of Arizona. From Battan and Theiss (1971*b*).

horizontally support the view expressed by Donaldson and Wexler (1969) that sometimes turbulence or wind-shear effects may substantially increase the variance of the Doppler spectrum. Although most of the time the tails of the spectra will be spread less than perhaps 1 m/sec, sometimes they may be spread much more.

The data contained in figure 8.5 were used to construct diagrams showing the vertical air velocity as a function of height and time as the thunderstorm passed overhead. Figure 8.7*a* and 8.7*b* shows the patterns of W_{BT} and W_R, respectively. The similarities of the patterns of up- and downdrafts are obvious. This thunderstorm shows features characteristic of others reported in the literature. The updrafts are generally observed in the upper part of the cloud, while downdrafts are observed in the lower part of the cloud. In part, this is explained by the fact that the radar sets cannot detect cloud droplets which would be expected to be ascending throughout most of the convective cloud in its early stages of growth.

Unusually strong downdrafts were measured in the lowest 2 km of the atmosphere. Speeds greater than 10 m/sec occurred below 2.5 km MSL. The terrain was at an elevation of 1,050 m. Near the ground at the radar site, the winds were strong. At 1429 MST it was observed that the rain was making an angle of less than 30 degrees with respect to the ground and was blowing from the southwest.

Figure 8.7 illustrates another feature of thunderstorms emphasized by Battan and Theiss (1970*a*), namely, the highly variable nature of the

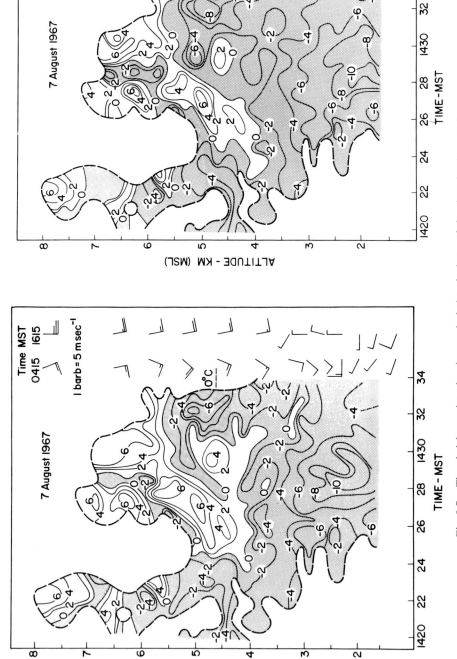

Fig. 8.7. Time-height section showing vertical air velocity: *a* (*left*), given by the negative tail of the Doppler spectrum plus 1 m/sec (W_{BT}); *b* (*right*), given by Rogers's formula (W_R).

field of vertical motion. It is evident that in this storm the concept of a jetlike updraft is not realistic. Instead there are eddies having characteristic sizes of 500–1,000 m. Airplane flights through the upper parts of large thunderstorms also show this character in the horizontal field of vertical motion (Sinclair 1968). Easterbrook (1967) used radar data to observe the fields of air motion in convective clouds and showed large variability over heights of several kilometers, but he averaged out what he called "more or less random small scale irregularities." It appears that such averaging may mask an essential feature of convective clouds.

8.9 Measurement of the Size Distribution of Scatterers

When the antenna of a narrow-beamed Doppler radar is pointing vertically, the terminal velocity of a scatterer, W_t, will be given by

$$W_t = V - W_a, \tag{8.31}$$

where V is its Doppler velocity and W_a is the downdraft velocity.

The Doppler spectrum gives the quantity of power $p(V)dV$ scattered by particles with Doppler velocities between V_i and $V_i + dV_i$. If the air motion is negligibly small, i.e., a few centimeters per second, one can write $W_t = V$. If W_a is not negligible, but is known, W_t is obtained by means of equation (8.31). In either circumstance, it is possible to express the Doppler spectrum in the form of the backscattered power as a function of W_t.

Consider the simple case of steady rain falling through air having a negligible vertical velocity. Assume also that the raindrop diameters are much smaller than the wavelength and hence that the backscattered power is proportional to $\int ND^6 \, dD$. The backscattered power in any small interval of terminal velocity W_t, produced by drops having diameter D, is given by

$$p(W_t)dW_t = k \, N(D)D^6 \, dD, \tag{8.32}$$

where $N(D) \, dD$ is the number of raindrops per unit volume in the terminal velocity interval dW_t. The constant k depends on the properties of the radar and the range and the dielectric properties of the raindrops. It can be obtained from equation (4.20). Since all the quantities in equation (8.32) except $N(D) \, dD$ are known, this quantity can be calculated in a straightforward manner. Such a computation would yield the number of raindrops per unit volume in a size interval ΔD centered at diameter D (see fig. 8.8).

This procedure for calculating raindrop-size distributions has been employed by a number of investigators (Boyenval 1960; Lhermitte

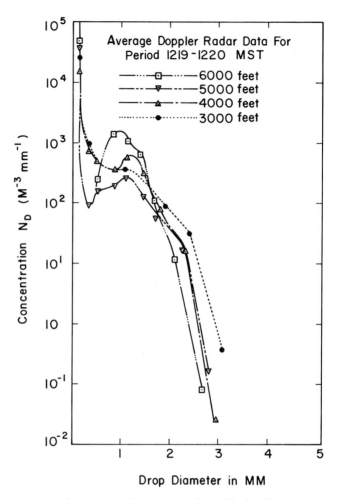

Fig. 8.8.   Average drop-size distributions at various altitudes. From du Toit (1967).

1960*b, c*; Rogers and Pilié 1962; Wilson 1963; Caton 1964, 1966; Rogers and Jiusto 1966; du Toit 1967; Gorelik et al. 1967). Most analyses have dealt with meteorological situations where vertical air motions were small and the precipitation was light and steady. Figure 8.3 shows pulsed-Doppler radar observations of such a case. Each horizontal line is proportional to the backscattered signal voltage (the square root of the backscattered power) produced by particles falling at approximately the indicated velocities. Snow aggregates above about 1,070 m were falling at speeds of 0.5–1 m/sec. The 0°C isotherm was about 1,000 m above the ground. The melting snowflakes had a high radar cross section and a small fall velocity. These points are illustrated by the sharp spike which shows the height of the "bright band." It will be discussed in more detail in chapter 10.

Below the bright band, raindrops were present, and it is evident that they had fall velocities ranging from 0.5 to about 9 m/sec. Most of the received power was being backscattered by raindrops having speeds between about 2 and 6 m/sec.

Figure 8.3 shows that a pulsed-Doppler radar can yield great detail about the raindrop-size distribution in space and time. In this illustration the height spacing of the Doppler spectra is 152 m. The heavy double lines representing the start of a new series of vertical steps are at 20-second intervals. If a number of range gates are used simultaneously, the detail of observation will be correspondingly increased.

The scheme just outlined is effective for measuring the size distribution of raindrops for a number of reasons: (1) the scatterers are composed of water whose temperature can be reasonably approximated, therefore allowing accurate estimates of the refractive index; (2) raindrops are nearly spherical and are small, and therefore Rayleigh scattering theory can be employed; and (3) the relation between raindrop diameter and terminal velocity is known, and the slope of the W_t versus the D curve is fairly steep. Near sea level one can write $W_t = 1,420D^{\frac{1}{2}}$ over the range of D from 0.05 to 0.5 cm (Spilhaus 1948). When D is expressed in centimeters, W_t is in units of centimeters per second. At upper levels the data of Foote and du Toit (1969) should be employed (see fig. 8.9).

The compositions and hence the refractive indices of snow crystals and snow aggregates often are unknown. Also, the range of terminal velocities is small in relation to the range of particle size (see eq. [7.7]). At present it is not possible to infer much about the size of snowflakes from an examination of Doppler-radar observations.

Hailstones may have a variety of shapes ranging from a spherical shape to an amorphous mass of ice with protruding spikes (Weickmann 1953; Barge 1972). The stones may be composed of dry ice, wet ice, spongy ice, or a combination of two or more of these substances. The fall speed of a hailstone depends on its shape, size, and density and the properties of the environment. These factors would indicate that, except in special circumstances, it might not be possible to infer hailstone-size distributions. Nevertheless, because of the importance of devising a scheme for the indirect detection of hailstones in the free atmosphere, the utility of Doppler radar for this purpose must be thoroughly investigated.

If it is assumed that hailstones are spheres of known density and drag

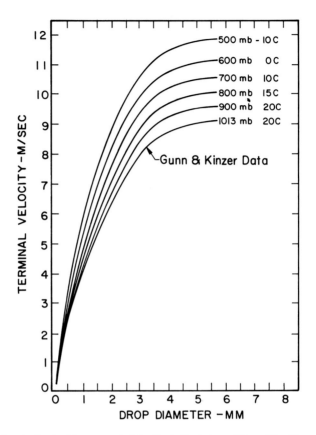

Fig. 8.9.   Terminal velocities computed for the indicated conditions. The Gunn and Kinzer (1949) curve is also shown. From Foote and du Toit (1969).

coefficient, it is possible to calculate their terminal velocities as a function of diameter (Macklin and Ludlam 1961). In his analysis of hailstone-size distributions Douglas (1964) used $W_t = 16.2D^{\frac{1}{2}}$, where V is in meters per second when D is in centimeters.

By means of techniques discussed in the preceding section, it is possible· to infer the vertical air motions and hence express the Doppler spectrum in terms of terminal velocity W_t and D.

The backscattered power in any interval of W_t would depend on the backscattering cross section, σ, of the particles having the observed W_t. Clearly, the quantity σ depends on the composition of the ice spheres. This point is illustrated in figure 8.10. The curves show that, when hailstone diameters are less than about 2.4 cm, the differences in backscattering cross sections of spheres of the indicated compositions are within a factor of 10. If nothing is known about the composition of the

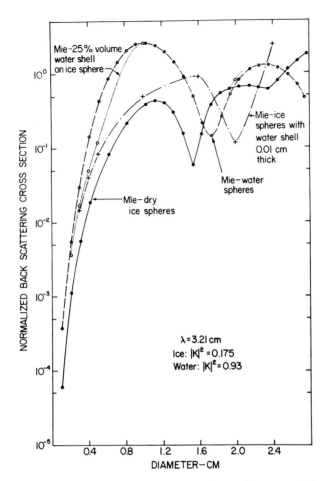

Fig. 8.10. Normalized backscattering cross sections for various types of ice and water spheres. From Battan and Theiss (1968).

hailstones and one takes an average value of σ_b for each D, the errors on this account would generally be less than a factor of 5.

After estimating σ as a function of D, one can write

$$p(W_t)dW_t = k' \, N(D) \, \sigma(D)dD, \qquad (8.33)$$

where $N(D) \, dD$ is the number of ice spheres per unit volume in the terminal velocity interval dW_t and $\sigma(D)$ is the backscattering cross section of particles having diameter D (and velocity W_t).

Battan and Theiss (1968, 1971a) employed this procedure to calculate the size distribution of ice particles in the free atmosphere. In both

analyses the slopes of the calculated distribution curves were substantially greater than the slope of the Douglas (1964) hail-distribution curve.
This point is illustrated in figure 8.11. Two Doppler spectra produced
by scatterers 610 m above the radar were averaged to calculate the
curves. At the time of the Doppler-radar observations, hailstones having diameters as large as 2.5 cm were falling on the radar. To obtain the
dashed curve it was necessary to assume that the particles were nonspherical and falling in accordance with a speed relationship given by
Lhermitte (1971). At the same time, backscattering was assumed to be

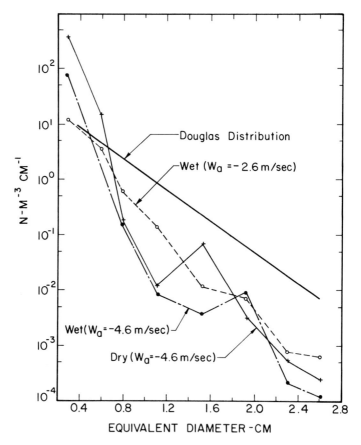

Fig. 8.11. Spectra of dry and wet ice particles calculated from a measured Doppler spectrum for two downdraft speeds. The value of −4.6 m/sec was obtained by employing
equation (8.27). The pronounced maxima at diameters of 1.5 and 1.9 cm correspond to
minima in the backscattering curves. By shifting the spectra 2 m/sec, the peak in the "wet"
curve is reduced. It was assumed that the terminal velocity of the ice particles was given
by a curve for nonspherical hail published by Lhermitte (1971). From Battan and Theiss
(1971a).

occurring from spheres, an assumption whose validity is questionable. Clearly the procedure of calculating hail-size spectra from Doppler spectra is quite complicated and needs further investigation.

If an observer is interested primarily in qualitative information about the presence of hail, a Doppler radar can often give unambiguous answers. As shown in figure 8.9, the maximum terminal speeds of large raindrops range from about 9 to 12 m/sec between sea level and the 500-mb height, respectively. If Doppler-radar observations show particles falling at higher terminal speeds it can be inferred that large ice particles are present. Also, the higher the speeds above the limits shown in figure 8.9, the greater the hailstones are likely to be.

If the effects of turbulence on the Doppler spectrum are small, and the negative tail of the Doppler spectrum is attributed to particles having terminal speeds of about 1 m/sec or less, the spread of the Doppler spectrum is a measure of the terminal speed of the fastest-falling particles. For example, if the negative tail of the Doppler spectrum is at -5 m/sec and the positive tail is at 9 m/sec, the terminal velocity of the fastest-falling particle would be about 15 m/sec.

Figure 8.12 shows the height-time distribution of the spread of the Doppler spectrum in the same thunderstorm whose updraft field is shown in figure 8.7. If the conditions noted above were met, the data represent the terminal velocities of the fastest-falling particles at the indicated heights and time. It is likely that there was hail aloft at about 1430 MST.

As discussed earlier, it was noted that a more common measure of the spread of the Doppler spectrum is the variance σ_v^2. Wexler (1967), Battan and Theiss (1968, 1971a), Donaldson and Wexler (1969), and Boston and Rogers (1969) examined the mean Doppler velocity and variance of hailstone distributions. In general, these investigators assumed that hailstones follow an exponential size distribution and calculated $\bar{V}$ (*in still air*) and σ_v^2 as a function of maximum diameter and wavelength. Boston and Rogers (1969) concluded that by means of a dual-wavelength Doppler-radar system it should be possible to distinguish hail. One of the two wavelengths should be short enough that Rayleigh scattering does not prevail, but not so short that attenuation would be overwhelming. The analysis by Battan and Theiss (1971a) tended to confirm the value of σ_v^2 as a hailstone-size indicator, but the relation of $\bar{V}$ and maximum hailstone size apparently was obscured by strong vertical motions of the air.

8.10 Measurement of Wind Speed

Although the rawinsonde is an excellent device for measuring the wind velocity, it has a number of disadvantages. For example, it is difficult to

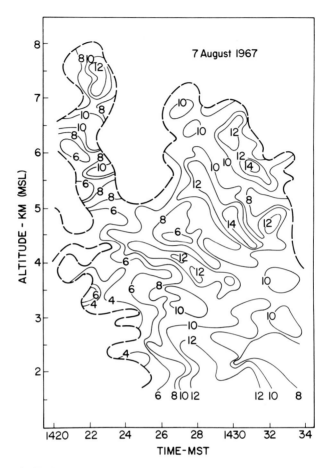

Fig. 8.12.   Distribution of the spread of Doppler velocity (m/sec). From Battan and Theiss (1970*a*).

launch the balloon when the winds are strong and gusty. More important is the fact that a rawinsonde or any other technique involving the tracking of a rapidly rising or falling target gives essentially a one-dimensional height distribution of wind velocity. If the pattern of wind at one altitude is required, it is necessary to release a number of rawinsonde transmitters (or rawin targets when radar tracking is employed).

Various studies have been made of how a radar set may be employed to measure wind-velocity distribution. Noncoherent radars have been used to track small echoes, which are assumed to move with the wind. This procedure was investigated by Byers and Braham (1949), Ligda and Mayhew (1954), Jordan (1960), Fujita and Black (1970), and others. Winds obtained in this way sometimes have been called "spawinds."

Although of some value, the technique of tracking weather echoes suffers from the inability to take into account the changes with time of the size and shape of the echo and from the fact that the volume of scatterers giving the echo moves with a velocity which is a weighted average of the velocities at various altitudes.

Wind velocities in the atmosphere also can be measured by means of radar tracking of chaff. This technique is discussed in chapter 11.

Starting with Probert-Jones (1960), a number of investigators developed schemes for employing Doppler radar for wind-velocity measurement. If there are scatterers in the atmosphere, a Doppler radar will measure their instantaneous velocities along the direction of the beam. With only one radar, it is possible to obtain wind velocity only in certain particular meteorological circumstances. It has been found, however, that they occur often enough to make a single Doppler radar a useful wind-measuring device. If two, or preferably three, radars are used simultaneously to scan the same region of scatterers, three-dimensional air-flow patterns can be obtained. More will be said about such a system in later paragraphs.

Lhermitte and Atlas (1961) proposed a wind-measuring method which is very useful when a Doppler radar is surrounded by scatterers having uniform motion. The technique, called Velocity-Azimuth-Display (commonly written VAD), employs an azimuthally scanning beam at an intermediate elevation angle, perhaps 45 degrees.

The Doppler velocity measured at height h, when the antenna is pointing at an elevation angle α, depends on the fall velocity of the particles, V_f, and on the wind velocity V_h (see fig. 8.13). If β is the azimuth angle of the antenna with respect to the upwind direction, the Doppler velocity V is given by

$$V = V_h \cos \alpha \cos \beta + V_f \sin \alpha. \tag{8.34}$$

The quantity V is actually a spectrum of Doppler velocities having a variance which depends on the variances of V_h and V_f. They are a measure of the spread of particle-fall velocities and turbulent air motions. When VAD is used in practice, the mean Doppler velocity $\bar{V}$ is taken to represent the best estimate of the effects of particle and wind speeds.

When the radar beam is pointed upwind, $\bar{V}$ has a direction toward the radar. When the beam extends downwind, $\bar{V}$ may be toward or away from the radar set depending on the relative magnitudes of the components of V_h and V_f.

If the wind velocity and the particle-fall velocities are uniform over the region being observed, the mean Doppler velocity will vary sinusoidally, with maxima and minima occurring when the beam azimuth

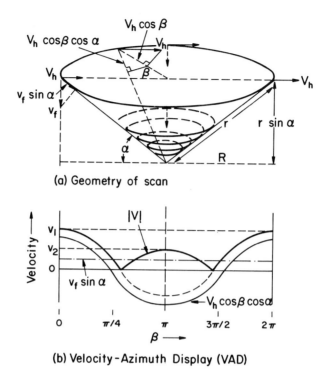

(a) Geometry of scan

(b) Velocity-Azimuth Display (VAD)

Fig. 8.13. *a,* Geometry of scan for wind measurements by VAD technique; *b,* wind and fall speeds make up VAD pattern indicated by $|V|$ when folding occurs. From Atlas (1964); After Lhermitte and Atlas 1961.

passes the upwind ($\beta = 0$) and downwind ($\beta = \pi$) directions, respectively (fig. 8.14). When

$$\beta = 0, \ \bar{V}_1 = V_f \sin \alpha + V_h \cos \alpha,$$

and when

$$\beta = \pi, \ \bar{V}_2 = V_f \sin \alpha - V_h \cos \alpha.$$

These equations can be solved to yield the wind speed at height h:

$$V_h = \frac{\bar{V}_1 - \bar{V}_2}{2 \cos \alpha}. \tag{8.35}$$

Wind direction is obtained by noting the azimuth angle of maxima and minima in the VAD pattern. The particle-fall speed is given by

$$V_f = \frac{\bar{V}_1 + \bar{V}_2}{2 \sin \alpha}. \tag{8.36}$$

From this discussion it should be evident that it is not necessary to make observations around the entire 360 degrees of azimuth as shown

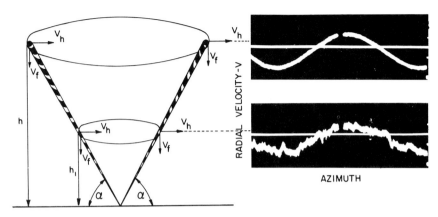

Fig. 8.14. Velocity azimuth display with examples of actual results. From Lhermitte (1969*a*).

in figure 8.14. Observations at a number of points would allow the fitting of a family of curves.

The VAD supplies more information than just the wind velocity and fall speeds of the scatterers. The width of the scope trace depends on the variance of the Doppler spectrum. The broadening of the trace shows an increase in the variance of either V_f or V_h, or of both. Irregularities in the wind field or of particle-fall velocities around the radar lead to irregularities in the patterns of the VAD output. The lower trace in figure 8.14 shows not only the broadening of the trace as a result of increased variance but also irregularities of the trace. In comparison, the upper trace shows uniform air and particle motions around the radar.

Certain Doppler radars display only $|\bar{V}|$, i.e., the magnitude of the velocity $\bar{V}$. When this is the case, the negative portion of the VAD display is "folded" over as indicated in figure 8.13. The quantities indicated as V_1 and V_2 represent the values of Doppler velocity at $\beta = 0$ and π, respectively, but it should be noted that V_2 also appears as a positive velocity.

The altitude for which V_h is applicable is given by $h = r \sin \alpha$. By moving the sampling gate or changing the elevation angle, winds can be observed at all altitudes where there are enough backscattering particles to give a VAD pattern.

According to Lhermitte and Atlas (1961), wind speeds are measurable to better than ±0.5 m/sec and wind direction to within a few degrees. These estimates may be valid on occasions when the winds and particle-fall speeds are uniform over the sampling area. Note that, if $\alpha = 45°$ and $h = 4$ km, the area scanned by the beam rotating in azimuth would have a diameter of about 8 km.

When precipitation is mostly from convective clouds, it would be expected that, over distances of the order of 8 km, there would be large variations of V_f, the vertical velocities of the particles. They could exceed 10–20 m/sec. There also could be substantial variations of V_h. For these reasons, wind observations by means of VAD could be in error by many meters per second.

When the wind velocity along a circle surrounding the radar is not constant, convergence or divergence may be occurring. Caton (1963), recognizing this idea, devised a scheme whereby the wind components around a VAD sampling circle of radius R are used to yield the horizontal divergence, $\text{div}_2\ V$. It can be shown that

$$\text{div}_2\ V = \frac{1}{\pi R} \int_0^{2\pi} V_h \cos \beta\ d\beta. \tag{8.37}$$

If equation (8.34) is integrated around the sampling circle at a fixed elevation angle α and range r, one obtains

$$\int_0^{2\pi} \bar{V}\ d\beta = \cos \alpha \int_0^{2\pi} V_h \cos \beta\ d\beta + \sin \alpha \int_0^{2\pi} V_f d\beta. \tag{8.38}$$

Integrating the last term on the assumption that V_f is constant and substituting in equation (8.37) yields

$$\text{div}_2\ V = \frac{1}{\pi R \cos \alpha} \int_0^{2\pi} \bar{V}\ d\beta - \frac{2\ V_f \tan \alpha}{R}. \tag{8.39}$$

This expression can yield accurate estimates of divergence when the elevation angle is small and when the fall speeds of the particles are uniform around the radar and accurately known. For example, it is useful when the backscatterers are snowflakes. As noted by Lhermitte (1969a), if $\alpha = 10°$ and $r = 15.4$ km ($R = 15$ km), a change in estimate of 0.5 m/sec in V_f will modify the calculated $\text{div}_2\ V$ by 2×10^{-5} sec^{-1}.

Caton (1963) and Harrold (1966) employed a procedure similar to the one just described to measure horizontal divergence between the altitudes of 1.2 and 3.3 km on one day. Caton reported values ranging from -1.2×10^{-5} to 43.1×10^{-5} sec^{-1}. In the same article Caton reported wind measurement aloft made by means of a procedure similar to, but slightly different from, the VAD technique of Lhermitte and Atlas (1961).

The VAD technique was further extended by Browning and Wexler (1968), who showed that in certain situations a single pulsed-Doppler radar could yield not only wind velocity and divergence but also such kinematic properties of the wind field as deformation and the orientation of the axis of dilation.

Børresen (1971) demonstrated how the variability of the VAD pattern may be used to map qualitatively the turbulent regions in a snowstorm. He found that turbulent regions were strongly oriented and associated with regions of pronounced vertical wind shear.

A rapid method for obtaining the profile of wind was proposed by Lhermitte (1962). It employs a Doppler radar whose beam rotates slowly in azimuth while the sampling gate moves continuously toward greater range (and altitude). In a series of measurements made on 24 February 1962, he maintained the elevation angle, α, at 30° while the range gate moved from zero to 12.2 km, corresponding to an altitude change from zero to 6.1 km. This required 6 minutes, during which time the radar beam completed 60 rotations, each at a successively higher altitude. During each rotation, the radar yielded VAD data averaged over an altitude interval determined by the altitude change of the range gate and the size of the sampling volume. The latter quantity depends on the beam width and increases with range. In Lhermitte's operations, the averaging altitude ranged from about 100 m at altitudes near 1 km to about 250 m at altitudes near 4 km.

Instead of using a spectrum analyzer to obtain patterns such as those shown on the VAD picture in figure 8.14, Lhermitte (1962) employed a frequency meter which measured the frequency with which the radar signal crossed a prescribed level and yielded $(\overline{V^2})^{\frac{1}{2}}$. Under assumed conditions of $\alpha = 30°$ and a total signal variance of 9 m²/sec², $(\overline{V^2})^{\frac{1}{2}}$ is only 2 percent, or 0.3 m/sec, greater than the correct mean Doppler velocity $\overline{V}$. Such conditions apply even in heavy rain.

The output of the frequency meter was always a positive frequency. As a result, the VAD pattern would be a folded one, as shown in figure 8.13. Lhermitte recorded the data in the form shown in figure 8.15. As the sampling gate rotated and moved to higher altitude, it produced a velocity exhibiting two maxima and two minima for each rotation. The two maxima in the folded pattern have been connected with lines. The average of the two maxima, drawn as a smooth line, is the vertical profile of $V_h \cos \alpha$, i.e., the wind speed multiplied by the cosine of the elevation angle (see equation [8.35] and recall that in the folded pattern the sign of V_z is reversed). In this example $V_h \cos \alpha = 0.87\ \overline{V}_h$. The average refers to the altitude layer scanned during one complete cycle of the rotating range gate.

When a folded pattern is involved, the sign of V_2 in equation (8.36) is reversed, and half the difference between the two velocity maxima gives $\overline{V}_f \sin \alpha$ and yields the average particle-fall velocity.

Lhermitte (1966*a,c*) employed the VAD technique just outlined to obtain the structure of the wind field in a snowstorm and to obtain detailed cross sections of the low-level jet stream over central Oklahoma

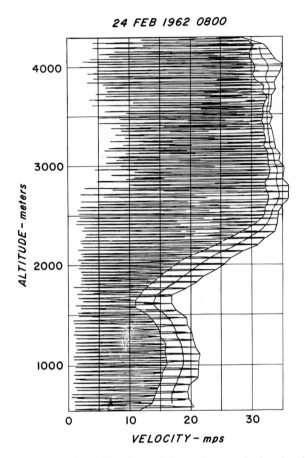

Fig. 8.15. Observed records of Doppler radial speed versus both azimuth and height on 24 February 1962. From Lhermitte (1962).

(see fig. 8.16). In the latter investigation the motions of clear-air targets were observed. Browning and Atlas (1966) also measured horizontal wind motion by tracking clear-air dot-angel echoes. As will be seen in chapter 12, such echoes are commonly caused by the backscattering of single insects.

The VAD technique was extended almost to its limit by Donaldson (1970b), who observed the winds in an anvil cloud by scanning the antenna in azimuth while its elevation angle was as high as 80°. He expressed the view that this procedure could detect significant temporal and spatial changes in the wind, but that estimates of divergence were not trustworthy when the elevation angle exceeded about 60°.

As noted by Peace, Brown, and Camnitz (1969), the VAD scheme is

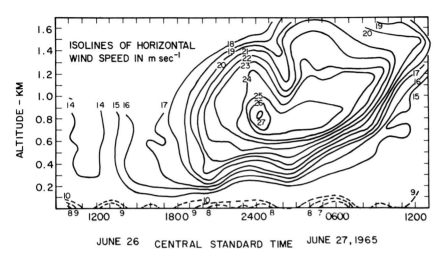

Fig. 8.16.   Altitude-time presentation of isocontours of horizontal mean wind speed near Norman, Oklahoma. From Lhermitte (1966*a*).

limited in its application because it requires nearly uniform backscatterers in most directions around the radar and because it yields wind data only in the vicinity of the radar. In the case of widely scattered convective clouds, the VAD technique is of doubtful value. Peace, Brown, and Camnitz proposed a procedure for measuring the horizontal motion field in individual convective storms by means of a single pulsed-Doppler radar. Their scheme involves the crucial assumption that the horizontal, mesoscale wind field in convective storms is "quasi-steady." They stated, "By making repeated azimuth scans through a moving convective cell for a 5–10 min period (during which time changes in the velocity field should be negligible) velocity changes due to changing viewing angles can be measured. In this way Doppler velocity measurements usually contain enough information about two orthogonal components of air motion to permit reconstruction of the two-dimensional horizontal wind field within the cell."

Peace, Brown, and Camnitz (1969) derived the mathematical expressions required to apply their procedure. The horizontal wind field of a thunderstorm echo measured by means of the single Doppler-radar scheme was compared with results obtained when two Doppler radars viewed the same storm (Peace and Brown 1968). Good agreement was reported. More tests are needed before the Peace, Brown, and Camnitz techniques can be said to be demonstrably effective. The requirement for a nearly steady horizontal motion field (with respect to a moving reference frame) for a period of 5–10 minutes appears to be a very restrictive one. Observations of the updraft distribution in thunderstorms show large variations over periods of a few minutes. As shown by Kraus (1970), low-level wind patterns in a thunderstorm are highly variable over small distances. It might be expected that there would be appreciable changes in horizontal winds over periods of a few minutes. Until more measurements are made, a judgment on this question has to be reserved.

8.11 Simultaneous Observations with More than One Doppler Radar

Since a Doppler radar can only measure radial velocities, a single radar is limited in its measurement of air motions and particle sizes. As shown by Browning et al. (1968), a great deal can be learned about a cloud when a zenith-pointing Doppler radar is accompanied by another Doppler radar some 20 km away.

In some circumstances, two Doppler radars operating simultaneously may yield accurate observations of the horizontal wind field in regions remote from the radars. Pilié, Jiusto and Rogers (1963), Lhermitte (1968a, 1969a) and Armijo (1969) discussed various aspects of this problem.

Assume that two radars some 10–60 km apart are observing the same volume in space and are measuring the mean Doppler velocities V and $\overline{V}_2$. These quantities may be related to the wind speed V_h in the following way:

$$\overline{V}_1 = V_h \cos \alpha_1 \cos \delta + (W_t + W_a) \sin \alpha_1, \tag{8.40}$$

$$\overline{V}_2 = V_h \cos (\beta_2 - \beta_1 + \delta) \cos \alpha_2 + (W_t + W_a) \sin \alpha_2, \tag{8.41}$$

where α_1 and α_2 are the elevation angles and β_1 and β_2 are the azimuth angles, measured from north of the two radar sets. The quantity δ is the azimuth angle between the wind-direction vector and β_1. The term $W_t + W_a = V_f$ is the motion of the particles with respect to the ground, i.e., the terminal velocity W_t plus the vertical air velocity W_a. If the elevation angle is less than 5 or 10 degrees, $(W_t + W_a) \sin \alpha \approx 0$. As long as the storm is not exactly between the radars, i.e., as long as $\beta_2 \neq \beta_1 + 2\pi$, one can solve for the wind speed and direction:

$$V_h = \frac{1}{\sin (\beta_2 - \beta_1)} \left[\frac{\overline{V}_1^2}{\cos^2 \alpha_1} + \frac{\overline{V}_1^2}{\cos^2 \alpha_2} - \frac{2 \overline{V}_1 \overline{V}_2 \cos (\beta_2 - \beta_1)}{\cos \alpha_1 \cos \alpha_2} \right]^{\frac{1}{2}}; \tag{8.42}$$

$$\tan \delta = - \frac{1}{\sin (\beta_2 - \beta_1)} \left[\frac{\overline{V}_2 \cos \alpha_1}{\overline{V}_1 \cos \alpha_2} - \cos (\beta_2 - \beta_1) \right]. \tag{8.43}$$

Lhermitte (1970) has reported observation of the low-level horizontal field of motion in a convective storm. He employed two X-Band pulsed-Doppler radars separated by a distance of 15 km. His analysis yielded very detailed wind observations at various altitudes between 250 and

1,500 m (see fig. 8.17). From the wind data, calculations were made of the patterns of streamlines, convergence, and updrafts. Lhermitte's article shows that two Doppler radars can supply a great deal of information about the circulation in convective clouds. As he notes, however, unless there is independent information about particle-fall speeds, the two-radar technique is restricted to measurements at small elevation angles (less than 10°) and hence at low elevations. Lhermitte noted that Rogers's (1964) formula relating Z to the mean terminal velocity of scattering raindrops offers one possibility of extending the capability of the two-radar technique to higher altitudes.

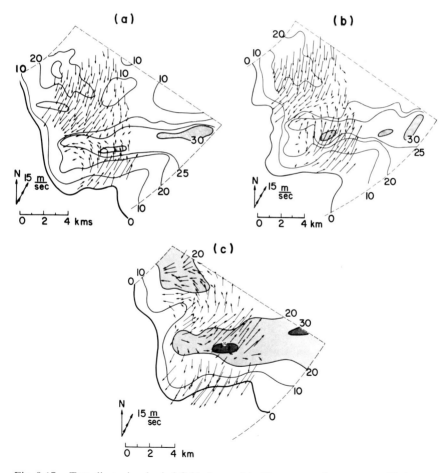

Fig. 8.17. Two-dimensional wind field observed inside a convective storm on 29 August 1969 at 1414 MST as derived from dual-Doppler radar data. Data are presented at different mean altitudes: *a*, 250 m; *b*, 500 m; *c*, 1,500 m. Storm reflectivity, 10 log Z, is also shown. From Lhermitte (1970).

A dual-Doppler technique was also employed by Brown and Peace (1968) to measure the wind-velocity distribution in convective storms.

Lhermitte (1968a, 1969a) carried the multiple-Doppler radar procedure to its logical conclusion; namely, he proposed that by employing three radar sets simultaneously it should be possible to measure the x, y, z distribution of the u, v, and w components of the wind in a convective storm. If the subscripts 1, 2, and 3 designate the radars and if each examines the same volume in space,

$$\overline{V_1} = V_h \cos (\beta_1 - \beta_0) \cos \alpha_1 + V_f \sin \alpha_1, \tag{8.44}$$

$$\overline{V_2} = V_h \cos (\beta_2 - \beta_0) \cos \alpha_2 + V_f \sin \alpha_2, \tag{8.45}$$

$$\overline{V_3} = V_h \cos (\beta_3 - \beta_0) \cos \alpha_3 + V_f \sin \alpha_3, \tag{8.46}$$

where β_0 is the azimuth angle of the wind-velocity vector, and the other symbols have the same meaning as in equation (8.41). These three simultaneous equations give the radial velocities from three different directions at any point, x, y, z. They allow the calculation of the horizontal wind velocity and the quantity V_f equaling $W_t + W_a$. As in earlier sections of this chapter, the symbol W_a is used to designate the vertical component of air velocity. It can be estimated from the continuity equation

$$\frac{\delta W_a}{\delta z} = - \left(\frac{\delta u}{\delta x} + \frac{\delta v}{\delta y} \right), \tag{8.47}$$

where the horizontal divergence is calculated from the measured horizontal-wind field, and suitable boundary conditions on W_a are assumed. Once W_a is known, one can infer W_t as a function of x, y, z.

To employ the triple-Doppler scheme on a practical basis, it is necessary to have a suitable computer to process the data. It is not considered practical to systematically scan a storm by maintaining the intersection of three radar beams as the common volume moves through the x, y, z coordinate system. Instead, it would be more efficient for each radar to use a large number of sampling gates appropriately spaced in range. The Doppler data from each radar could be stored, and the composite velocity field synthesized after the storm has been completely scanned in azimuth and elevation by each radar. Interpolation techniques would have to be introduced to take into account changes occurring between the beginning and ending of each radar's scanning operation.

The task of processing the Doppler observations and calculating the distribution of air and particle velocities can be handled by a large, modern, high-speed computer. There is considerable doubt that, at this time, the data processing can be done at the same speed as the observations are acquired. The Doppler measurements can be recorded on magnetic tape for analysis after the storm has ended.

As noted by Lhermitte (1968*a*) the triple-Doppler procedure is a complex and sophisticated one. On the other hand it represents a unique method for measuring three-dimensional air and particle motions in clouds. For this reason the procedure needs to be exploited.

8.12 Plan Shear Indicator (PSI)

The so-called Plan Shear Indicator (PSI) is a technique devised by Armstrong and Donaldson (1969) for displaying on a PPI scope regions of strong wind shear or regions where there is a large spread of the Doppler spectrum. The PSI employs a so-called Coherent Memory Filter (CMF) to make coarse but "real-time" Doppler spectral analyses over the entire range of the radar (Chimera 1960; Atlas 1963; Groginsky 1965).

The CMF is a device for obtaining approximate Doppler spectra simultaneously at many ranges. The CMF employed by Armstrong and Donaldson (1969) yielded spectra at 192 ranges spaced at intervals of 855 m (5.7 μsec in time) and hence covered a total radar range of 164 km. In simple terms the CMF compares the frequency shift from pulse to pulse of a target at range r with a known scanning frequency. The system senses and integrates signals when the Doppler shift frequency corresponds to a known scanning frequency. The signals from a series of 20 radar pulses are so integrated at each of the 192 range intervals.

If the antenna of the Doppler radar is fixed and the output of the CMF is examined on an A-scope display, one obtains a series of Doppler spectra wherever there are targets (see fig. 8.18). The spread of the spectrum depends on the velocity distribution of the targets. A moving coherent target such as a metal sphere will give a very narrow spectrum. As noted earlier in this chapter, precipitation targets will give spectral widths depending on the character of the precipitation and air motions.

The position of the Doppler spectrum depends on the velocities involved. In the equipment described by Armstrong and Donaldson (1969), the spectrum is shifted in range in proportion to the radial velocity of the target. For example, a fixed target with zero radial velocity is centered at its true range at the beginning of the range time interval. In figure 8.18 such a case is illustrated at the start of the second range interval, which extends from 11.4 to 17.1 μsec. With increasing mean Doppler velocity, the Doppler spectrum is shifted outward by greater amounts from its true range.

As noted by Armstrong and Donaldson (1969) and Groginsky (1965), the maximum unambiguous velocity, V_{max}, measured by the CMF, is $\lambda/2(\mathrm{PRF})^{-1}$, which is twice the value obtained by more conventional

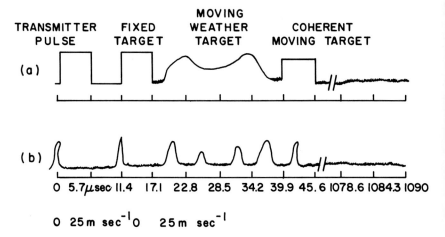

Fig. 8.18.   *a*, Typical A-scope display of radar video; *b*, corresponding display of Coherent Memory Filter output video. Note the velocity interval of 0–25 m/sec every 5.7 μsec. Fixed targets appear at zero velocity, while the appearance of moving targets in the velocity interval depends upon their radial-velocity components. From Armstrong and Donaldson (1969).

spectral-analysis systems (eq. [8.5]). In the CMF whose output is depicted in figure 8.18, $\lambda = 5.45$ cm and $(\text{PRF})^{-1} = 1,090$ μsec; therefore, $V_{\max} = 25$ m/sec. A point target at range r moving at 20 m/sec will appear on the scope at a range $r + (20/25)(855$ m).

In general, the indicated range r_n is given by

$$r_n = \frac{c\tau}{2}\left(n - \frac{V_n}{V_{\max}}\right),\tag{8.48}$$

where c is the speed of the radar wave, τ is the radar-pulse duration, n denotes the number of range elements between the radar and the target and is an integer between one and $(\text{PRF} \times \tau)^{-1}$, and V_n is the indicated radial velocity. The shift in range of an echo composed of a target moving at velocity V_n is shown in figure 8.19. In this analysis a target velocity was considered positive if it were directed away from the radar. Therefore, targets moving toward the radar appear at a range r_n, which is greater than the true range. Targets moving away from the radar appear at less than the true range.

Since the quantity $V_n/V_{\max}$ in equation (8.48) usually is less than one, while n is much larger than one, the incremental displacement of the indicated range is very small compared with the target range $(nc\tau/2)$. For this reason target velocity cannot be read accurately off the scope. On the other hand, changes in radial velocity are easily detectable on a

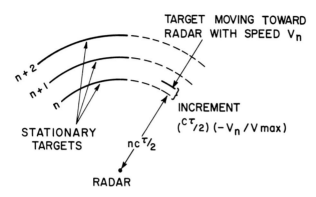

Fig. 8.19. *Left*, PSI display for stationary targets; *right*, PSI display for a moving target. The moving target is located at the same distance from the radar as the nearest stationary target but is displaced from it on the PSI display by an increment which depends on its velocity. From Armstrong and Donaldson (1969).

plan-shear indicator (PSI), i.e., a PPI displaying information from a Coherent-Memory Filter.

If the radial velocities of the targets are constant, the PSI presents a number of circular, evenly spaced arcs in all regions where the targets backscatter detectable power. If there is radial shear of target motion — e.g., motion increasing with range — the spacing between the arcs would change. If there is tangential shear of target motion — i.e., if the radial velocity increases along a line perpendicular to the radar beam — the radius of the arc will vary with azimuth. For example, if a vortex exists, the changes in velocity in azimuth and range would lead to wavy patterns in the PSI display (Donaldson 1970*a*). Such an example is shown in figure 8.20.

As noted earlier, the width of the arc depends in part on the spread of the Doppler spectrum. When the antenna is pointing at a low elevation angle and the spacings between the PSI arcs are small, it can be reasoned that turbulence and other variance-increasing processes are present. Donaldson and Wexler (1969) have related the spread of the Doppler spectrum to hazardous flying conditions. This PSI technique displaying precipitation-velocity patterns is a very useful one because it combines a great deal of data in an easily interpretable fashion.

8.13 Specialized Doppler Radars

On 10 June 1958 Smith and Holmes (1961) detected a tornado on a 3-cm continuous-wave (CW) Doppler radar. The equipment measured substantial power at velocities up to 92 m/sec. Such a radar has essentially

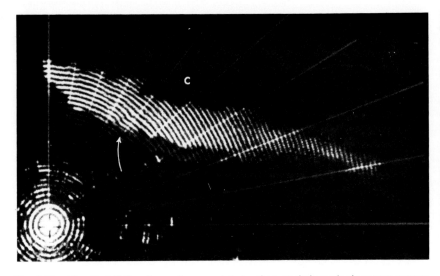

Fig. 8.20.   Detail of PSI pattern. Arrow points to characteristic cyclonic vortex pattern. The end of the arrow is at a range of about 20 km. From Armstrong and Donaldson (1969).

no velocity-measuring limitation, but it supplies no information about the range to the target. Brown et al. (1971), using an X-band pulsed-Doppler radar with a maximum unambiguous velocity of ±34 m/sec, observed an intense cyclonic vortex associated with a radar hook echo in Oklahoma.

It appears to be within the present state of technology to design and build a pulsed-Doppler radar for tornado detection. It would need to detect high velocities (up to 100 m/sec or more), to have sufficiently fine spatial resolution to locate a tornado, and to have appropriate data-processing and display equipment to allow immediate and easily interpretable velocity and intensity information. Various authors have discussed this idea (e.g., Smith and Holmes 1961; Atlas 1963; Lhermitte and Kessler 1964).

Ground-based Doppler radars suffer from their limited mobility even when they are installed in a truck or trailer. A downward-pointing *airborne* pulsed-Doppler radar could have many important applications. For example, it could be flown over the tops of violent storms and used to map the fields of air and particle velocity. It would be of particular value in observing hurricanes, severe hailstorms, and thunderstorms associated with tornadoes. Even when a multiple Doppler-radar system is employed, the opportunities for observing tornadic storms will be few.

The idea of an airborne pulsed-Doppler radar for observing meteorological targets was first pursued by D. Atlas in 1962; at that time, he was associated with the Air Force Cambridge Research Laboratories near Boston, Massachusetts. Because of various logistical and technical problems, a successful airborne Doppler radar was not constructed. Lhermitte (1969*a*) observed that "it is now feasible to consider that an airborne pulse Doppler radar can be developed at reasonable cost with acceptable chance of success." Subsequently Lhermitte (1971) published an analysis of how an airborne pulsed-Doppler radar could be employed to obtain information on air motions and hydrometeor sizes. He made a detailed study of the procedures of the data collection and analysis to be used when the radar beam is pointed downward. Also, he briefly considered the use of a fixed beam, pointing horizontally in a direction perpendicular to the flight path. An airborne Doppler radar could yield very useful data on the structure of precipitating systems and would be of particular value in the investigation of violent thunderstorms and hurricanes. One may look forward to such a radar in the seventies.

9

Distortion of Echoes Resulting from Finite Pulse Length and Beam Widths

Radar has been widely used to measure the size, shape, and location of targets in the atmosphere. Of particular interest have been such items as the horizontal and vertical extents of thunderstorms and other weather phenomena. When making such measurements it is essential to realize that the resulting echo may differ substantially from the region of targets which produced it. In chapter 6 it was shown that, as a result of attenuation, circular rain showers can appear as markedly noncircular echoes. In this chapter it will be seen that the finite pulse lengths and beam widths may also lead to echo distortions.

The smallest distance between two targets which can be measured is called the resolution of a radar. For example, if two airplanes are 150 m apart and they can just barely be recognized as two echoes rather than one echo, the resolution of the radar is said to be 150 m. The smaller the pulse length and the beam widths of a radar, the smaller the resolution.

9.1 Pulse-Length Effects

A radar transmits a pulse whose duration is τ and which is composed of a train of waves at the radar frequency of length h given by τc. If the traveling pulse encounters a single small scatterer at a range r, the back-scattering begins when the front edge of the pulse passes over the particle and ends when the rear edge passes over it. As a result, the scattered pulse also has a length h as it returns to the radar set.

When the particle is at range r, the total distance traveled by the pulse is $2r$. Radarscopes are designed to present the range to the target r rather than the round-trip distance. As a result, the returned pulse, of length h, appears on the scope with a length of $h/2$. It is evident that, if the special single particle under consideration were capable of returning a detectable signal, the range depth of the echo would be in error by a distance of $h/2$. The actual range of the particle is given by the front edge of the returned echo. It should be clear that the range indicated on a scope can never be smaller than the actual range.

162

Some range distortion of the echo also occurs when a radar observes a region of scattering particles. If the actual range depth is d, the scattered signal train has a length $2d + h$, and, if the particle sizes are large enough that the signal strength is detectable over the entire returned-signal train, the echo has a length $d + h/2$. The indicated range of the front of the echo corresponds to the actual range of the front of the region of scattering particles (fig. 9.1, a). If the particle sizes are those normally encountered, one would expect the magnitude of the returned signal to increase as the outgoing pulse of length h enters the scattering region and to decrease as it leaves the scattering region, so that the profile of scattered power would appear as shown in figure 9.1, b. In order for an echo to be detected, the radar receiver requires power above a certain threshold. For this reason, the indicated range to the front of the echo may also be in error, but it cannot exceed the true range by more than $h/2$.

Since the horizontal dimensions of weather echoes are generally large compared with the pulse length, the problem just discussed is usually not serious. In certain special problems, however, such as the study of echoes from shallow layers, or of so-called dot angles (see chap. 12), the effects of the finite pulse length may be significant, especially when long pulse lengths are used. They must also be considered when tracking small targets having high reflectivity, such as airplanes, rawin reflectors, or "chaff," an assemblage of metallic dipoles dispersed from an airplane or a rocket (see chap. 11).

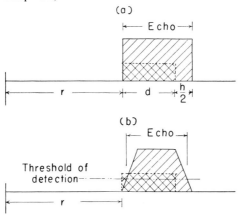

Fig. 9.1. Effects of pulse length on the range and on the radial dimensions of an echo. The *cross-hatched area* represents the region of scattering particles. The *hatched area* in (a) represents the power distribution in a hypothetical case in which all the particles are highly efficient backscatterers. Diagram (b) depicts more realistic conditions. The radar would detect an echo only when the indicated threshold was exceeded.

9.2 Beam-Width Effects of the Major Lobe

The distortion and range errors resulting from finite pulse lengths are
the same regardless of the range, because the length of the transmitted
pulse does not change with range. It is obvious, however, that the cross
section of a radar beam increases with increasing range. As a result,
one can expect the echo-distortion effects produced by the finite beam
width to increase with range. To evaluate them it is necessary to know
the power distribution in the beam.

Many weather-radar sets make use of an antenna consisting essentially of a point source (e.g., a dipole) at the focal point of a parabolic
reflector. The power is reflected from the surface and directed along
lines parallel to the axis of the parabola. In the imaginary plane across
the open face of the parabola, all the radiation is in phase. In calculating
the shape of the beam, one may consider each incremental area in this
imaginary plane to be radiating independently. The interference of the
waves from each of these "radiators" creates a concentration of energy
into a beam along the parabola's axis, which is known as the "major
lobe." Smaller, secondary lobes are usually found with their central
axes directed at various angles with the parabola's axis (fig. 9.2). The
actual shape of the lobes depends on the shape and size of the antenna,
the wavelength involved, and the type of "feed" used as a source. When
the reflector is a paraboloid with the source at its focus, the shape of the
beam may be considered symmetrical.

It has been standard practice to define the beam width as twice the
angle between the direction of maximum power and the direction at which
the power is half the maximum value. This latter direction specifies the
so-called half-power point. In some radar applications only the power
in the major lobe is considered because the minor lobes represent relatively small amounts of power. The summation of the power within the
solid angle defined by the half-power points is about 80 percent of the

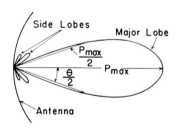

Fig. 9.2.   Schematic cross section of radar beam from a parabolic antenna reflector. Note
that the angles are much larger than in a real radar beam (see fig. 9.4 for realistic angles).

total power. The assumption that all the transmitted power is contained within the half-power points leads, therefore, to an error of about 1 dB. On the other hand, when a target has a high reflectivity, even the low-level power from the side lobes may lead to sufficient backscattered power to give an echo. In such cases, as will be shown later in this chapter, large echo distortions may result.

The beam pattern produced by a circular antenna has been discussed by Silver (1951) and Probert-Jones (1962). It can be shown that the antenna gain G is given by

$$G = \frac{\pi^2 k^2}{\theta \phi},\tag{9.1}$$

where θ and ϕ are the horizontal and vertical beam widths to the half-power points and k^2 depends on the properties of the antenna and equals $\alpha \beta f^2(\beta)$ (α is the fraction of the total power from the feed intercepted by the antenna reflector, and β is a factor dependent on the degree of uniformity of the antenna's illumination). For a so-called perfect, circular paraboloid antenna, $\alpha = \beta = 1$ and $f^2(\beta) = 1.04$. For practical antennas of circular cross section, α equals 0.8–0.9 and $\beta f^2(\beta)$ is about 1.2. Therefore, for circular dishes, one can take $k^2 = 1$.

Probert-Jones (1962) shows that

$$\theta \phi = f^2(\beta) \frac{\lambda^2}{d^2},\tag{9.2}$$

where d is the antenna diameter and $f^2(\beta)$ in a practical antenna is given by Silver (1951) to be about 1.6. If the antenna is circular and uniformly illuminated, the major lobe will be symmetrical, and the half-power beam width will be proportional to λ/d.

A great deal of work with weather radar has been done by means of height-finding radar sets, i.e., radar sets which scan in the vertical plane. These radar sets sometimes have narrow vertical beams and wider (but still narrow) horizontal beams. For example, the World War II radar set AN/TPS-10 has a major lobe $\theta = 2.0°$ and $\phi = 0.7°$. As one would expect from equation (9.1) (which can be used to estimate beam widths even though the antenna is not a paraboloid), the AN/TPS-10 has an antenna whose vertical dimension is about three times larger than its horizontal dimension.

Now consider the effects of the finite beam width on the shape of the echoes in cases when the side lobes are neglected.

When the antenna of a radar set scans azimuthally, the sweep on a PPI scope appears as a narrow line pointing in the direction of the axis of the radar beam. As the center of the beam approaches a small target such as an airplane, ever increasing amounts of power are scattered back to the antenna. When the backscattered power reaches a detectable level, an echo appears on the scope. As long as the returned power exceeds this level, the echo will continue to be received. Usually, the threshold of detection will be exceeded over a finite portion of the beam. As a result, on a PPI scope the echo from an airplane appears as an arc whose dimensions greatly exceed those of the airplane. The wider the beam, the greater the possible distortion. The echo elongation increases with range up to a certain point, then decreases rapidly when the back-scattered power becomes too small, because of the r^{-4} effect, to give any echo at all. Fortunately, the size of an airplane is known to be small, and the distortion by the beam is the same as the beam approaches and moves away. Thus the bearing to the airplane is indicated by the center of the echo and can be read accurately off a scope.

The effects of the finite beam width on some precipitation regions are similar to those in the case of an airplane; for several reasons, however, one cannot simply eliminate the detection error, as was done for the airplane. The problem is complicated by the fact that the distribution of particle sizes in the precipitation areas and hence the reflectivity are not known. As a result, it often is not possible to calculate what part of the beam will contain sufficient power to give a detectable echo. When the raindrops have a high reflectivity, as is the case with active thunderstorms, one might expect an echo to be received before the beam axis enters the rain. As a result, the dimensions of the echo perpendicular to the beam would be exaggerated.

When the precipitation is very light, as indicated by very weak echoes, the error may be in the other direction. It is possible that the entire beam may have to be intercepted before a detectable echo is received. In this case the echo will appear to be too small.

9.3 Effects of Side Lobes

It should be noted that up to this point the effects of side lobes have been neglected. For the measurement of precipitation rates, this is usually permissible. However, when targets have high reflectivities or are located at small ranges, the side lobes may produce serious echo distortions. Sometimes radar sets detect reflections of power in the side lobes from nearby buildings. Vertically scanning radar sets may indicate targets "below the ground" because, when the axis of the antenna is directed at a negative angle, the side lobes are close to the horizon and detectable power may be reflected from strong targets at small ranges. Vertically scanning airborne radar sets at low altitudes sometimes receive detectable signals by surface scattering of power in the side lobes (fig. 9.3).

The effects of the side lobes on the vertical extent of radar echoes have been examined by Aoyagi (1963), Probert-Jones (1963), Donaldson and Tear (1963), and Donaldson (1964). The radiation pattern of a circular

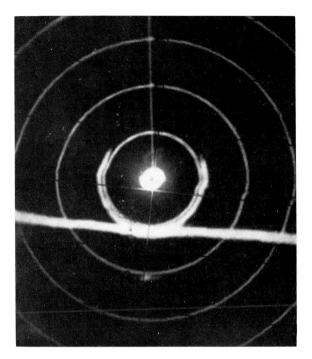

Fig. 9.3. Scope of an airborne vertically scanning AN/APQ-13 radar set showing circular arcs caused by backscattering of power in the side lobes. The airplane was at an altitude of about 1,900 m (6,200 feet) above sea level (a nearly horizontal line, since the airplane was flying over the ocean). Range markers are at intervals of about 1.8 km (1 nautical mile).

antenna can be assumed to be composed of a main lobe and a series of symmetrical side lobes. The distribution of power in each side lobe with respect to the power in the main lobe is given by the expression

$$10 \log \frac{G_\phi}{G_m} = -3 \left(\frac{\phi - \phi_m}{\phi_0} \right)^2, \qquad (9.3)$$

where G_m is the gain along the axis of the main lobe at angle ϕ_m and ϕ_0 is the angle at which the gain falls to one-half of G_m. A model antenna pattern is given in table 9.1 and sketched in figure 9.4. In the latter, the two-way gain function is displayed for an antenna with $\phi_0 = 0.5°$. It

TABLE 9.1   Model Antenna Beam

	Power Relative to Main Lobe	Half-Power Angular Radius	Angular Distance from Main Lobe
Main lobe	0 dB	ϕ_0	0
Side lobe 1 . . .	−20 dB	$\phi_0/2$	4_{ϕ_0}
Side lobe 2 . . .	−27 dB	$\phi_0/2$	6_{ϕ_0}
Side lobe 3 . . .	−30 dB	$\phi_0/2$	8_{ϕ_0}

SOURCE: Donaldson 1964.

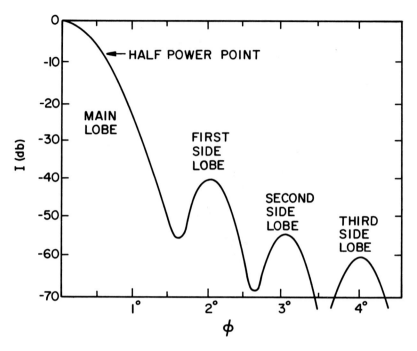

Fig. 9.4.   Two-way gain function of model antenna beam having half-power beam width
of 0.5 degree. This is a good approximation for the AN/CPS-9. From Donaldson (1964).

shows, for example, that at an angle of 2° from the beam axis, the back-scattered power from a small target would be 40 dB less than it would be if the target were on the beam axis.

The backscattered power is proportional to G^2, and the two-way radiation pattern of the antenna can be obtained by summing the contributions by each lobe of the beam pattern. The contribution by the *main lobe* is obtained from equation (9.3) and is given by

$$\left(\frac{G_\phi}{G_m}\right)^2 = 10^{-0.6(\phi/\phi_0)^2}. \tag{9.4}$$

Substituting the appropriate quantities for the main lobe and the first three side lobes from table 9.1 in equation (9.3) and summing them yields

$$I = (G_\phi/G_m)^2 = 10^{-0.6(\phi/\phi_0)^2} + 10^{-4} \times 10^{-2.4(\phi-4\phi_0)^2/\phi_0^2}$$

$$+ 4 \times 10^{-6} \times 10^{-2.4(\phi-6\phi_0)^2/\phi_0^2} \tag{9.5}$$

$$+ 10^{-6} \times 10^{-2.4(\phi-8\phi_0)^2/\phi_0^2}.$$

Side lobes greater than the third can be assumed to contribute no power.

Knowing the two-way radiation pattern and the reflectivity factor, Z, of the target, one can calculate the reflectivity factor Z_m. This is the quantity which would be measured. If Z is specified as a function of height, y, in an x-y plane perpendicular to the beam, and if the beam-width dimension in the x direction, at range r, is small with respect to the diameter of a storm, the vertical distribution of Z_m can be computed from the expression

$$Z_m = \frac{\int \int Z I \, dx \, dy}{\int \int I \, dx \, dy}, \qquad (9.6)$$

where I is the projection of the circular radiation pattern given by equation (9.5) on the x-y plane at range r. Donaldson (1964) assumed the various height distributions of Z shown in figure 9.5 and calculated Z_m as a function of range. These model profiles were selected to approximate average distributions of Z in convective clouds. They were based on the results of earlier investigations by Donaldson (1961).

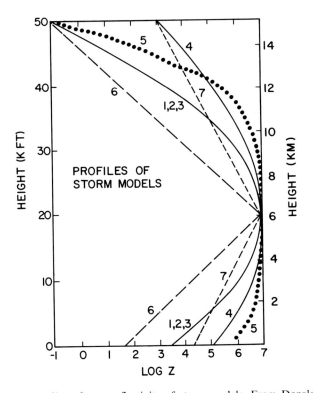

Fig. 9.5.   Height profiles of core reflectivity of storm models. From Donaldson (1964).

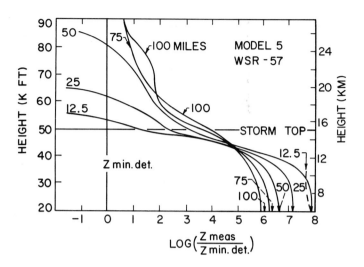

Fig. 9.6. Measured reflectivity profiles of storm models at various ranges, distorted by 2-degree half-power beamwidth of WSR-57 radar (refer to fig. 9.5 for the undistorted profile of this model 5 storm). The abscissa expresses the ratio of measured reflectivity to minimum detectable reflectivity. From Donaldson (1964).

Figure 9.6 illustrates the results of calculations of model 5, representing an extremely severe storm of a maximum reflectivity $Z = 10^7$ mm^6/m^3 and extending to a height of 50,000 ft (15.2 km). The quantity $\log Z_m/Z_{min}$ at various ranges is plotted as a function of height when Z_{min} is the minimum detectable level at the indicated range. The data plotted in figure 9.6 apply to the WSR-57 (see Appendix), a radar with a main beam lobe which is 2 degrees wide at the half-power points ($\phi_0 = 1°$). The same results would apply to observations by the AN/CPS-9 (see Appendix) having a 1-degree beam but at ranges twice as large as those shown on the diagram. Donaldson took the values of Z_{min} to be $10^{-3}r^2$ and $10^{-4}r^2$, respectively, for the WSR-57 and the AN/CPS-9, where Z is in millimeters to the sixth power per cubic meter and r in nautical miles.

The curves in figure 9.6 clearly illustrate that, in a very severe thunderstorm with a reflectivity profile such as the one depicted, the measured echo top may exceed the actual storm top by many kilometers. Probert-Jones (1963), who also studied this problem, reached the same conclusion. The results show that, when intense storms are being observed, vertical distortions increase with range. In the case of weak echoes, the radar may underestimate the vertical extent of the storm.

It is evident that, when a vertically scanning radar is employed to measure the top of thunderstorm echoes, large errors may occur in some circumstances. Fortunately, certain steps can be taken to reduce the possible discrepancies. It is evident that, if the power from the first side lobe is negligible, the maximum height error will be about $r\phi_0$. The power in the first side lobe can be neglected as long as Z_m is less than 40 dB above Z_{min} (see table 9.1). This is equivalent to saying that, if the main beam is pointing over the echo top and the cloud is illuminated only by the first and higher side lobes, no echo will be seen unless the back-scattered power corresponds to a $Z \geq Z_{min}$. If Z_{min} of the radar is set according to the gain of the main beam, the actual Z of the cloud ob-served by the side lobes must be 40 dB greater than Z_{min} to give an echo. Therefore, the effects of the side lobes can be eliminated by reducing the gain of the radar receiver by 40 dB below the optimum. An examina-tion of figure 9.6 shows that if the effective Z_{min} were 40 dB below the Z_{min} used to make the calculations (i.e., log $(Z/Z_{min}) = 4$) the observed echo tops would all be below the actual storm tops but that all discrep-ancies would be smaller than 5,000 ft (1.52 km).

The steeper the gradient of Z at the echo top, the smaller the dis-crepancies. When the gradient is small, as in model 6 (fig. 9.5), the observed echo tops would be far below the actual storm tops. According to Donaldson (1964), when the gain is 40 dB below the optimum, the echo tops can be about 5 km below the storm tops.

Clearly the interpretation of observations of vertical extents of thunder-storms must be done with caution. If quantitative measurements of back-scattered power are available, it is possible, with the characteristics of the antenna known, to be more confident about the inferences of storm-top heights. Without such analyses, it is important to bear in mind that errors in the measurement of storm tops may amount to many kilometers.

Donaldson (1961*b*) also analyzed the effects of a finite beam width in the reflectivity distribution in two thunderstorms. As would be ex-pected, the wider the beam, the smoother the echo patterns.

9.4 Other Factors Distorting Echoes

Before leaving the subject of echo distributions, it is appropriate to note again that, as shown first by Atlas and Banks (1951) and discussed in chapter 6, attenuation can cause echoes to look very different from the showers which produced them. This effect depends on the degree of attenuation and hence on wavelength. By employing longer waves (e.g., 10 cm) this effect can be minimized.

Occasionally one sees PPI echoes which have the appearance of stretched-out ellipses whose major axes extend along radials. Such echoes, which usually are seen at short ranges, may be the result of backscattering from precipitation at ranges greater than the so-called maximum range, r_m, of the radar. The quantity r_m clearly is determined by the PRF of the radar. The time between pulses is $(PRF)^{-1}$, and $r_m =$ $\frac{1}{2}(C/PRF)$. If a strong target is present at a greater range than r_m, its backscattered signal from pulse n_i will not arrive at the radar until after pulse n_{i+1} already has been transmitted. Since each pulse triggers a new sweep of the scope, the returned signal from the target at range r will appear at range $r - r_m$. The angular dimensions $(\Delta\theta)$ of the echo will be maintained, but since it appears on the scope at a range much smaller than r, its linear width $(r - r_m)\Delta\theta$ will be greatly reduced. If the target were a circular shower at range r, its echo would approximate an ellipse at range $r - r_m$. Such echoes are called "second sweep echoes." They usually are easily recognized by their shapes and orientations.

10 Use of Radar in Cloud Physics Research

Cloud physics may be regarded as that branch of the atmospheric sciences dealing with the study of the formation, growth, and dissipation of clouds and precipitation. It encompasses a broad range of phenomena ranging from water molecules to thunderstorms. It is particularly concerned with the processes by which cloud, rain, snow, and hail particles are produced. Clearly an instrument such as radar, particularly coherent radar, can make many observations crucial to the understanding of cloud physics.

In this chapter, a brief discussion is given of how radar has been used to observe the properties of clouds and precipitation. No attempt will be made to summarize all the important aspects of this subject or to give a comprehensive discussion of the processes of cloud and precipitation growth (for this purpose, the reader is referred to the excellent books by Mason 1971 or Fletcher 1962). Instead, by examining a selected group of investigations, one can illustrate how radar has been used in the past. It is hoped that such information will serve to stimulate new uses in the future. Certainly as Doppler-radar techniques advance, it should be possible to obtain those observations needed to adequately describe the distributions of air motion and precipitation-particle sizes in time and space.

10.1 Precipitation in Convective Clouds

An unsolved problem of fundamental importance is one dealing with the mechanisms for precipitation initiation in convective clouds. It is not known which of the two processes, the sublimation-coalescence (Bergeron-Findeisin) or the condensation-coalescence process, plays the dominant role in the growth of hydrometeors. In the former process it is assumed that ice crystals of the order of 100 μ grow by the direct deposition of water molecules and that the crystals enlarge rapidly by coalescence, melt while descending through the warm parts of the cloud, and fall to the ground as rain. The other process assumes that cloud droplets produced by condensation reach sizes large enough to continue growing by coalescence.

173

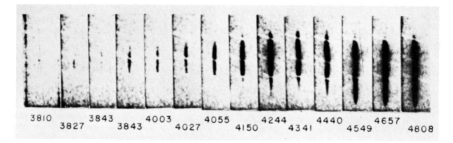

Fig. 10.1. Series of photographs of an RHI scope showing the growth of a convective echo. The light slanted lines are at 5,000-foot (1.52-km) intervals; times are in minutes and seconds. From Battan (1953*b*).

In order to learn more about these two mechanisms, visual observations have been made of growing convective clouds, and the temperatures at their summits have been noted at the time that rain was observed falling out of the base. In other investigations, airplanes have been used to observe the temperatures of convective clouds and to determine whether they contain precipitation. Both these schemes suffer the disadvantage that the rain is not observed until some time after its formation. One must assume that the precipitation-formation process probably begins from a few minutes to possibly 10 minutes prior to the time the rain is seen to fall through the cloud base. In the meantime, the cloud top may have ascended some thousands of feet and altered its structure significantly. When flying through a cloud, one samples only a very small part of it, and, since the initial precipitation does not always form in the same part of the cloud, one might expect that, on the average, the time of precipitation detection would lag behind the time of its formation. The advantage of radar rests on its ability to scan through many clouds and note when and where precipitation begins to form in any part of them.

A substantial quantity of data has been collected on the altitudes and temperatures of initial echoes in convective clouds (Jones 1950; Bowen 1951; Reynolds and Braham 1952; Battan 1953*b*; Braham 1958; Clark 1960; Battan 1963*c*; Browning and Atlas 1965). Such observations are easily obtained by means of a radar whose antenna can be scanned automatically in the vertical plane. It is desirable that the vertical scanning be done fairly rapidly while the antenna rotates slowly through any given azimuthal sector. The frequency with which any cloud is observed clearly depends on the scanning rates, the horizontal beam width, and the size of the sector being examined. Figure 10.1 shows an example of the type of data one obtains with such an arrangement.

Airborne radar sets with vertically scanning antennas or fixed vertically pointing antennas have also been used for noting the development

Fig. 10.2   Scope of a 3-cm airborne AN/APQ-13 with a vertically scanning antenna. The airplane was flying through a cloud at an altitude of 16,200 feet (4.93 km) just above a short bright band. A strong convective echo extending to about 23,000 feet (7.0 km) appears on the right.

and spread of precipitation. Figure 10.2 gives an example of a convective echo observed on an airborne radar whose antenna scanned the vertical plane perpendicular to the direction of flight.

It has been known for a long time that in the tropics convective clouds everywhere warmer than freezing often produce rain. Radar measurements taken over the midwestern United States and at other locations outside the tropics have shown that many initial echoes occur at temperatures exceeding 0° C. These data have led to the conclusion that the condensation-coalescence process may initiate precipitation in cumuli devoid of ice crystals.

Several investigators, starting with Braham, Reynolds, and Harrell (1951), have examined the relationships between cloud sizes (or temperature) and precipitation by conducting so-called cloud censuses. This entails the simultaneous observation of cloud-top altitude and the presence or absence of a precipitation echo. When observations are collected by means of an airplane equipped with a vertically scanning radar, the aircraft is flown at an arbitrary heading, and each cloud in its flight path is observed to see if it is producing a radar echo. At the same time, a measurement is made of the altitude of the cloud top, possibly by means of a second airplane flying just over the first. It should be noted that estimates of the vertical extents of clouds extending more than about 5,000 feet above an airplane are frequently in error by many thousands of feet. Usually the estimates are too small.

An aircraft equipped with a side-looking camera taking photographs at fixed, short-time intervals may supply stereographic pairs of photographs from which cloud-top heights may be calculated.

When a cloud census is taken with ground equipment, it is most convenient to use vertically scanning radar equipment for noting the presence of precipitation. Cloud-top observations can be made by means of a double theodolite system, but a better technique involves the use of a pair of carefully calibrated cloud cameras (Kassander and Sims 1957; Orville and Kassander 1961). From the photographs one can calculate the locations and the dimensions of clouds in the field of view.

Data collected during a cloud census are most easily interpreted if each cloud is examined only once. The probability of precipitation in a cumulus cloud increases as the cloud duration increases. Therefore, if precautions for taking only one observation per cloud are not adopted, the final conclusions will be biased in favor of precipitating clouds. One can overcome this difficulty by taking observations at intervals of time equal to or exceeding the normal lifetimes of the clouds involved. For convective clouds, a period of 30 minutes is adequate, if one employs the additional constraint that only clouds with well-defined upper limits will be included. This, of course, eliminates older clouds with diffuse anvil tops.

Cloud-census studies have clearly shown that, in tropical regions, precipitation is almost always initiated in the parts of the clouds warmer than freezing (Byers and Hall 1955). In large tropical cumulonimbus clouds, the ice process surely plays a role in rain production, but it has been positively established that ice crystals are not essential for the rain initiation in cumuli over the ocean.

When data obtained in the tropics and in the central and southwestern United States on the proportion of clouds whose echoes are a function of cloud-top temperature are plotted on the same abscissa, it is evident that there are large differences in different regions (fig. 10.3). It should be recognized, however, that the observed temperature distributions

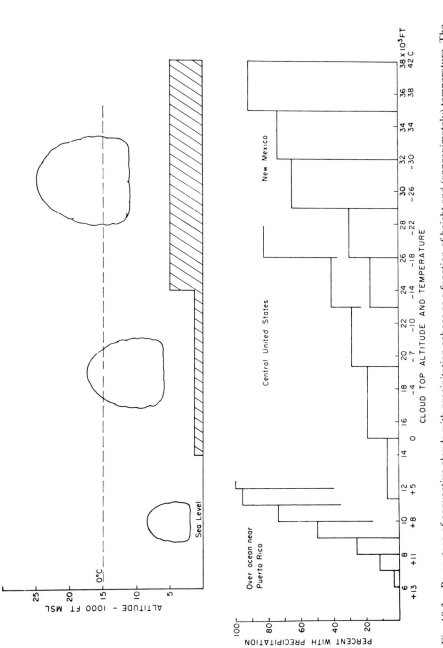

Fig. 10.3. Percentage of convective clouds with precipitation echoes as a function of height and (approximately) temperature. The upper part of the diagram shows schematic clouds with a 20 percent "likelihood" of containing precipitation echoes. Data from New Mexico from Braham et al. (1951). Illustration from Battan and Braham (1956).

could occur even if echo initiation came about because of the condensation-coalescence process. In the three regions represented in figure 10.3, the cloud bases were at different altitudes, but the altitudes of the 0°C isotherm was about the same in the three regions. From the available observations, it has been concluded that the condensation-coalescence process plays an important role in initiating precipitation in cumuli in warm, humid air outside the tropics.

Various authors have measured the rates of intensification of radar echoes from convective clouds and sought to explain them. Moore et al. (1962, 1964), by means of a vertically scanning 3-cm radar, measured echo-intensity increases as large as 40 dB/min. They ascribed them to very rapid growth of precipitation particles caused by electrical forces following a lightning discharge. The intensification of the precipitation echo following lightning is not inconsistent with the frequent observations of rainfall only minutes following the first lightning stroke from a storm. Such an event has been called a "rain gush."

Saunders (1965) employed an M-33 radar system consisting of a 10-cm radar having a PPI presentation and a 3-cm tracking radar to observe the development of shower clouds over the island of Barbadoes in the Caribbean Sea. He reported that, as the cloud tops ascended to their maximum altitudes at 3–5 km, radar reflectivities increased, reaching maxima not exceeding 3×10^5 mm^6/m^3. The maximum rate of echo intensification was 10 dB/min. The clouds were only weakly electrified, and the growth of precipitation was ascribed to gravitationally induced coalescence. Kessler (1966b) presented a theoretical analysis of the growth of raindrops in a convective cloud by means of coalescence. His calculations yielded a sudden rainfall initiation in some circumstances. Nevertheless, he noted that his analysis does not rule out the possibility that rain gushes might be initiated by electrical effects.

The role of lightning in precipitation formation can be unraveled by means of a Doppler-radar system allowing the observation of a developing thunderstorm in three dimensions. Battan (1964) used a single vertically pointing 3-cm radar to observe a thunderstorm which apparently produced only one lightning stroke. Although rain did reach the ground about two minutes after the lightning, the Doppler radar showed that the precipitation particles had started their downward trajectory before the lightning occurred. These results indicate the need for more Doppler-radar observations of the growth of precipitation in relation to lightning, preferably by means of a three-Doppler system.

Water contents and rainfall from several intense thunderstorms have been calculated by Geotis (1971) and Pell (1971). They measured 10-cm radar reflectivity and used equations such as those given in chapter 7 to calculate R and M. Earlier, Hamilton (1964) had calculated the vertical profile of rainfall intensity in convective clouds near Montreal, Canada, and found maxima aloft. On the other hand, in continuous rain, the rates increased downward, reaching a maximum at the base of the storm.

10.2 Vertical Extent of Convective Clouds

As noted in chapter 9, the side lobes of a radar set may cause large errors in cloud-top heights when the cloud's radar reflectivity is high. As a result, measurements of echo altitudes made with a vertically scanning radar must be treated with caution.

Before the middle forties, information about the vertical extent of thunderstorms was scarce. Visual observations showed that they sometimes extended to great altitudes, but the number of measurements (e.g., by means of two theodolites) was small. The first systematic series of observations by means of vertically scanning radar was made by the Thunderstorm Project (Byers and Braham 1949). In the summer of 1946 a 10-cm radar was used in Florida, and in 1947 a 3-cm AN/TPS-10 was employed in southern Ohio. The relatively crude data revealed, for the first time, that thunderstorms regularly extend to altitudes exceeding 10 km and occasionally penetrate into the stratosphere.

It can be shown from a consideration of the buoyancy of a rising parcel of air that, in order for it to penetrate far into the very stable stratosphere, the air must have high updraft velocities (see Vonnegut and Moore 1960 and Saunders 1962.) Notwithstanding this fact, early radar observations, by means of the AN/CPS-9, of tropopause penetrations of 3–5 km were reported in the literature and offered as a characteristic of thunderstorms producing violent weather (Donaldson, Chmela, and Shackford 1959). Jordan (1962) and others expressed serious doubts about the accuracy of many of the extreme echo heights which had been reported. Subsequent work by Probert-Jones (1963) and Donaldson (1964), noted in chapter 9, showed that radar measurements of the vertical extent of strong echoes may be greatly in error. There is no doubt, however, that large thunderstorms may reach the stratosphere.

In the USSR, considerable work has been done in the study of the relation of the height of echo summits to the character of the storm. For example, Kotov (1960) and Kotov and Zhui-Tszyun (1961) examined the height distribution of convective clouds producing only precipitation as opposed to the height distribution of those producing both rain and lightning and hence classified as thunderstorms. Wilson and Kessler (1963) also related the vertical extents of echoes and their intensities to the character of the precipitation.

Several research groups in the Soviet Union have developed empirical schemes based on radar data for discriminating between thunderstorms giving rain and those giving hail (Sulakvelidze, Bibilashvili, and Lapcheva 1965, 1968; Voronov and Gaivoronskii 1969; Salman, Gashina, and Divinskaya 1969; Antonov and Medaliev 1969). For the most part the presence of hail was related to such factors as echo intensity and vertical extent. Somewhat similar relations between echo-top height and hail were reported by Donaldson (1958), Cook (1958), Douglas and Hitschfeld (1958), Pell (1969), and others. More will be said about this subject in section 10.5.

10.3 Growth of Convective Clouds

From a small sample of 3-cm radar observations of growing cumulus clouds, Workman and Reynolds (1949) found that on the average the echo top ascended more rapidly than the cloud top. When the echo first appeared, it was below the actual cloud tops, but, by the time the cloud reached its maximum height, the echo top was very close to the cloud top. Saunders and Ronne (1962), who examined the relative heights of convective clouds and their radar echoes by means of a 10-cm WSR-57, found that in almost every case the visible cloud exceeded the "measured" echo tops, but usually by less than a kilometer. The measurements were corrected by subtracting a height increment equal to half the beam width times the range. The results of this analysis might indicate that the vertical velocity of the top of the radar echo of convective clouds as seen by the WSR-57 would give a good estimate of the vertical velocity of the cloud top.

Measured growth rates of convective echo tops, as expected, have been highly variable, ranging as high as about 20 m/sec (Battan 1953b) but usually less than 5 m/sec.

Woodward (1959) and Saunders (1962) concluded, on the basis of laboratory experiments on convective clouds, that the vertical motion in the core of a convective cloud is about twice the speed of the cap. Sulakvelidze, Bibilashvili, and Lapcheva (1965) concluded that maximum updraft velocities as high as 20–25 m/sec occur 1–2 km below the cloud top. They found cloud-top velocities averaging about 2 m/sec and average updraft maxima of about 12 m/sec. The decrease of upward speed from the core to the cap was found by Battan and Theiss (1966) in a series of 3-cm Doppler-radar observations made when the antenna was pointing vertically. The profiles of inferred updraft velocities shown in figure 10.4 were obtained by means of the scheme discussed in chapter 8 wherein 1 m/sec is added to the negative velocity tail of the Doppler spectrum. It can be seen that, during the building phase of this cloud, velocities at the echo top were perhaps half the maximum velocities lower in the cloud.

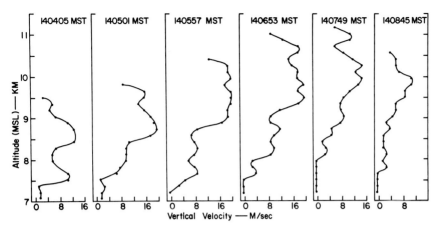

Fig. 10.4. Profiles of vertical velocities of the air in a thunderstorm inferred from a vertically pointing 3-cm pulsed-Doppler radar. From Battan and Theiss (1966).

Between the period 1405 and 1407 MST, the mean slope of the echo top versus the time curve was 12.6 m/sec, while the instantaneous Doppler vertical velocity was 12 m/sec; obviously they are in excellent agreement. Maximum speeds measured in the core of the updraft exceeded 19 m/sec, the highest speed which could be measured by the radar.

It has been observed by a number of writers (e.g., Byers and Braham 1949) that some large thunderstorms grow in a pulsating fashion. In some cases, succeeding echo "towers" extend to higher altitudes, with each sequence of growth taking 10–20 minutes.

On the other hand, certain large, hail-producing thunderstorms change slowly with time and sometimes have been referred to as being "steady" (e.g., Browning and Ludlam 1962; Browning 1963; 1965; Dennis et al. 1970).

As noted in chapter 8, a pulsed-Doppler radar may yield data on the distribution of updraft speed and other cloud properties. When a thunderstorm passes over a vertically pointing radar, one may obtain the data depicted in figure 10.5. They were taken from Battan and Theiss (1970*a*,*b*). The first three diagrams show the height-time distribution of updraft velocity (in meters per second), the logarithm of effective radar reflectivity (where Z_e is in millimeters to the sixth power per cubic meter), and the spread of the Doppler spectra (in meters per second). The last quantity can be related to the terminal velocity of the fastest-falling particles, providing turbulence spreading of the Doppler spectrum is negligibly small. Figure 10.5,*d* presents the pattern of depolarization in decibels. Some discussion of the interpretation of these data is given in chapter 5.

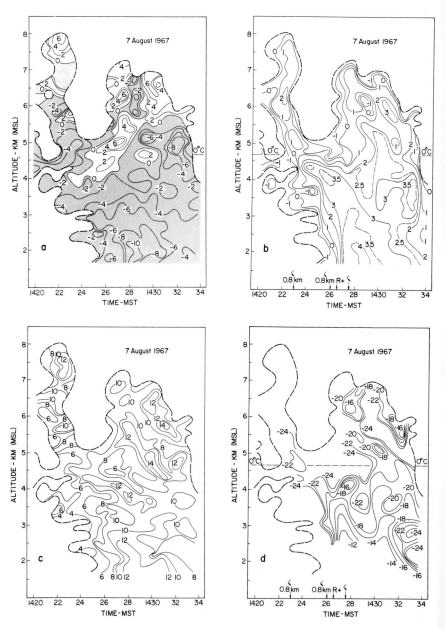

Fig. 10.5.   Vertical time sections of: *a*, updraft velocity in meters per second; *b*, radar reflectivity log *Z*; *c*, spread of the Doppler spectrum in meters per second; *d*, depolarization in decibels. Data were collected on 7 August 1967 in Arizona by Battan and Theiss (1970*a, b*).

Information such as that shown in figure 10.5 obviously tells a great deal about the physical properties of the storm. It is clear that the pattern of vertical air motions is quite turbulent, with important velocity changes over distances of 500-1,000 m. The "updraft" more nearly resembles an aggregate of buoyant, rising bubbles than it does a rising jet of air. As has been observed by other investigators (Probert-Jones and Harper 1961; Donaldson, Armstrong, and Atlas 1966; Easterbrook 1967), updrafts are mostly restricted to the upper part of the cloud, while downdrafts are mostly in the lower half.

From the spread of the Doppler spectrum, it can be inferred that in some regions (those with the higher velocities) the particles must have been ice particles, possibly small hailstones. Ice crystals, snowflakes, and raindrops cannot have terminal velocities exceeding about 12 m/sec even in the upper levels of the cloud (Foote and du Toit 1969). The cross-polarization measurements support the inference of the presence of ice particles and furthermore indicate that they must have been wet. They also lead to the speculations that the large hydrometeors were probably distorted into a form more nearly prolate than oblate.

The data in figure 10.5 came from a single zenith-pointing radar. It is not possible in this case to discriminate between time and space changes in the cloud. Furthermore, it is not possible to know how close the time section is to the center of the cloud. Such uncertainties mean that generalizations about thunderstorms on the basis of just a few cloud studies are somewhat risky. Nevertheless, the measurements shown here indicate the type which can be obtained by means of a pulsed-Doppler radar when it is used in conjunction with another cross-polarized antenna and receiver. A dual — or triple — Doppler-radar system could overcome many of the uncertainties inherent when a single radar is employed.

10.4 Duration of Convective Echoes

From PPI data, studies have been made of the duration of convective radar cells. If time-lapse photographs are examined, it is apparent that the rates of development and dissipation are quite rapid. Over a period of several minutes, the general appearance of the echo pattern may change significantly. If attention is focused on a particular echo, it is found that it becomes larger by two processes: (1) the outward expansion of the original echo, and (2) the growth of new "cells" immediately next to and merging with the original ones. The second process can proceed so fast that in a short time it is impossible to specify whether the original "cell" is still in existence. In studying the duration of convective echoes, it is important to define the types of echoes considered.

TABLE 10.1 Distribution of Duration of Radar Clouds for Different Sizes of Echoes

Duration (Min)	Maximum Horizontal Dimension of Echo (Km)								
	0–1.5	1.6–3.1	3.2–4.7	4.8–6.3	6.4–7.9	8.0–9.5	9.6–11.1	11.2–12.7	Total
0.0–4.9	. . . .	. . . .	. . . .	. . . .	. . . .	. . . .	. . . .	. . . .	. . . .
5.0–9.9	1	2	. . . .	. . . .	. . . .	. . . .	. . . .	. . . .	3
10.0–14.9	1	3	6	. . . .	. . . .	. . . .	. . . .	. . . .	10
15.0–19.9	1	9	5	. . . .	. . . .	. . . .	. . . .	. . . .	15
20.0–24.9	. . . .	7	6	4	1	. . . .	. . . .	. . . .	18
25.0–29.9	. . . .	2	5	1	. . . .	. . . .	. . . .	. . . .	8
30.0–34.9	. . . .	. . . .	5	. . . .	. . . .	. . . .	. . . .	. . . .	5
35.0–39.9	. . . .	. . . .	1	1	2	. . . .	. . . .	. . . .	4
40.0–44.9	. . . .	. . . .	1	. . . .	. . . .	. . . .	. . . .	1	2
45.0–49.9	. . . .	. . . .	. . . .	. . . .	. . . .	1	. . . .	. . . .	1
50.0–54.9	. . . .	. . . .	. . . .	. . . .	. . . .	1	. . . .	. . . .	1
Total	3	23	29	6	3	2	. . . .	1	67

SOURCE: Battan 1953a.

Battan (1953a) investigated the duration of individual radar "cells" which did not appear to merge with any other cells during their lifetimes. The data were taken from the PPI scope of a 10-cm radar scanning at a rate of 6 revolutions per minute. The results of this study are shown in table 10.1. The mean duration of the echoes was 23 minutes. Also, it was found that the average time for each echo to reach maximum diameter was 10.3 minutes. By means of 3-cm, RHI data, Battan (1953b) found that the average time required for individual convective echoes to attain maximum *height* was 9.5 minutes. These values are in agreement with the results of a study by Workman and Reynolds (1949) which showed that the average time taken by twelve New Mexico thunderstorm cells to reach maximum height was 11 minutes. Kotov and Zhui-Tszyun (1961) also reported that shower echoes had average durations between 10 and 20 minutes. It should be noted that all these durations apply to individual radar "cells."

Since some thunderstorms during their lifetimes may contain many such cells, the average duration of a thunderstorm can be several times the average of about 20 minutes found to be typical of convective clouds in midwestern and southwestern United States. A study of the duration of convective echoes by Blackmer (1955) yielded a mean value of about 42 minutes. Observations have shown that some of the large, so-called steady thunderstorms may last for many hours.

10.5 Hail in Convective Clouds

A number of studies have been made in attempts to ascertain how radar may be used to determine directly whether a thunderstorm contains hail. Harrison and Post (1954) reported that hail was noted in a high percentage of PPI echoes having fingerlike protrusions 1–5 miles in length and scallops or blunt protuberances 2–5 km from the edge of thunderstorm echoes (fig. 10.6). Most of their observations were made by means of 5-cm equipment and were collected on the eastern slopes of the Rocky Mountains in the vicinity of eastern Colorado. In parts of the country where hail frequency is high (such as the Great Plains) the high-intensity protuberance from an existing thunderstorm echo may be taken as evidence that hail is likely. In regions of low hail frequency, this criterion is less reliable.

As noted in section 10.2, many investigators have related the presence or absence of hail to the vertical extent of thunderstorm echoes. In the USSR, empirical expressions have been developed yielding the probability of hail to a number of radar-measured properties (see Battan 1970). The number of properties considered ranged from eight at the Georgian Academy of Sciences (Tbilisi) to three at the Main Geophysical Observatory (Leningrad), and in some cases only two were considered at the High Altitude Geophysical Institute (Nalchik). Quantities generally considered to be important are the height and temperature at the top of the echo, the maximum echo intensity (Z_m), and the temperature at the level of Z_m.

Ludlam (1960) also offered a table for inferring the presence of hail and lightning frequency on the basis of the vertical extent of the radar echo and Z_m. It was based in part on earlier data collected by Donaldson (1958, 1959), Shackford (1960), and others. Geotis (1963) reported

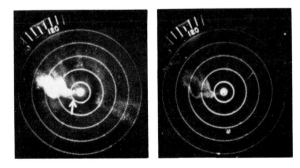

Fig. 10.6. Echo associated with hail as observed with an airborne 5.5-cm radar set with and without contour mapping. The arrow points to the finger considered as an indicator of the presence of hail. Courtesy of H. T. Harrison, United Air Lines, Inc.

that radar-reflectivity measurements by means of a 10-cm radar could be used to identify hailstorms and allow estimates of maximum stone sizes. Douglas (1963b) constructed a series of curves relating hail probability to maximum echo height. Changnon and Staggs (1970) studied the time variation of the vertical structure of the radar echoes from a limited number of thunderstorms and hailstorms. Dennis, Schock, and Koscielski (1970) summarized the radar characteristics of hailstorms over western South Dakota, giving particular attention to maximum echo height and equivalent reflectivity. It is evident that these echo characteristics are good indicators of the likelihood of hail.

It is important that an accurate technique for the direct observation of hail be developed. Various avenues of attack have been and continue to be examined. For the most part the analyses have examined those features of hailstones which discriminate them from rain and snow, namely, particle diameter, shape, and fall speed. They determine, respectively, backscattering cross section, depolarization, and Doppler shift frequency.

In the early sixties, theoretical and experimental work yielded a great deal of information about the backscattering cross section, σ, of ice spheres. This subject was discussed in chapters 4 and 5. With σ and the sphere concentration as functions of D, calculations have been made of Z_e, the equivalent reflectivity factor of hailstones. This type of analysis was first made by Atlas and Ludlam (1961). They assumed various size-distribution functions and calculated Z_e as a function of wavelength for wet- and dry-ice spheres. The curves in figure 10.7 apply to a shower of wet-ice spheres of a uniform size and in such a concentration that they have a liquid-water content of 1 g/cm³.

This diagram can be used to illustrate the technique of inferring hailstone sizes if they are assumed to be uniform in diameter. The values of Z_e are measured at the three wavelengths and compared with theoretical curves such as those in figure 10.7. That diameter which most closely yields calculated Z_e's matching those observed is assumed to be the diameter of the hailstones.

A diagram of Z_e versus D can be constructed for any type of ice sphere (e.g., one having a solid ice core covered with a layer of water). If the hailstones are distributed according to some assumed power law, the value of Z_e as a function of maximum diameter D_m can be calculated by integrating the contribution to Z_e by all hailstones. In such a case a measurement of Z_e is used to infer D_m.

A scheme similar to the one just outlined has been employed by Sulakvelidze, Bibilashvili, and Lapcheva (1965). One of their colleagues, Abshaev (1968), proposed that, by assuming a certain size distribution, the maximum hailstone diameter, D_m, can be obtained from a measurement of the ratios of the reflectivities at 3.2 and 10 cm.

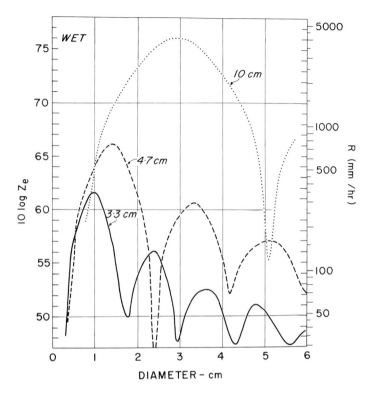

Fig. 10.7. Radar reflectivity as a function of the diameter of uniform, wet-ice spheres. The units of Z_e are millimeters to the sixth power per cubic meter, and the concentration of particles of diameter D was assumed to be the number yielding an average water content of 1 g/m³. The equivalent rainfall rate was calculated from the relation $Z = 486R^{1.37}$. From Atlas and Ludlam (1961).

Clearly, there are a number of difficulties with the hail-measurement procedures just reviewed. They hinge on uncertainties about particle shapes, compositions, and size-distribution functions, and on difficulties in precisely measuring Z_e, especially at attenuation wavelengths. Nevertheless, they deserve additional attention.

Recently Eccles and Atlas (1970) developed a new scheme for detecting hail. It employs two radar sets, operating at different wavelengths, which examine the range distribution of backscattered power. Measurements are made of the range derivative of the ratio of the average power measured by the two radars. If $\overline{P_{10}}$ and $\overline{P_3}$ are the average powers received by 10-cm and 3-cm radars, respectively, one can write

$$\overline{P_{10}} = \frac{C_{10} Z_{10}}{r^2}, \tag{10.1}$$

$$\overline{P_3} = \frac{C_3 Z_3}{r^2} \, 10^{-0.2 \int_{r_0}^{r} k \, dr}, \tag{10.2}$$

where k is the attenuation coefficient at $\lambda = 3$ cm, and attenuation is assumed to be zero at $\lambda = 10$ cm.

The quantity y is defined by the expression

$$y = 10 \log \frac{\overline{P_{10}} C_3}{P_3 C_{10}} = 10 \log \frac{Z_{10}}{Z_3} + 2 \int_{r_0}^{r} k \, dr \, ; \tag{10.3}$$

$$\frac{dy}{dr} = \frac{dF}{dr} + 2k, \tag{10.4}$$

where the quantity F is $10 \log (Z_{10}/Z_3)$.

The term y is essentially a measure of the ratio of reflectivities and is the quantity used in earlier work by Atlas and Ludlum (1961) and Sulakvelidze, Bibilashvili, and Lapcheva (1965) to arrive at conclusions about the presence of hail. Uncertainties about the attenuation lead to uncertainties about y and hence about the inferred hail sizes. Eccles and Atlas (1970) indicate that this difficulty can be overcome almost entirely by measuring dy/dr and using it to infer the presence of hail. At the time they offered their new technique, data on the attenuation by wet hail were not available. Relevant information cited in chapter 6 shows that attenuations at 3 and 10 cm, by wet-ice spheres and those coated by spongy ice, depend on the size and amount of water on the spheres.

In section 8.9 a discussion was given of how vertically pointing pulsed-Doppler radars may be employed to estimate the size spectra of hail. If a multiple Doppler-radar scheme is employed to measure the terminal speed of the backscattering particles, such a procedure makes it possible to detect the presence of hail.

Section 5.5 discusses how measurements of depolarization have been employed to identify hail. The work of Barge (1970, 1972), in particular, is promising.

10.6 Continuous Precipitation

"Continuous precipitation" is sometimes thought of as precipitation which falls over a very large area with only small changes in intensity over small distances. When viewing continuous precipitation on a PPI scope, one finds that it is seldom uniform in intensity—in fact, there generally are centers of heavier rain imbedded in large areas of lighter rain (fig. 10.8). The variable structure of widespread rain is most evident when the echoes are presented in vertical cross section (fig. 10.9). One of the most interesting features of figure 10.9 is the band of high echo intensity at about 6,000 feet (1.83 km).

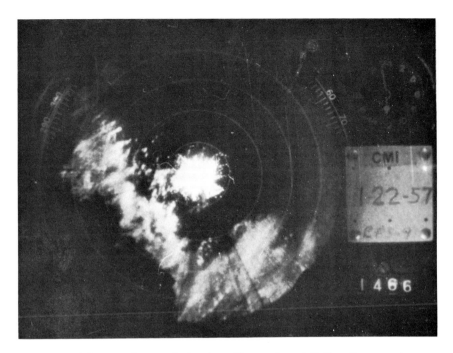

Fig. 10.8. PPI-scope photograph showing widespread precipitation. Range markers are at 25-mile (about 40-km) intervals. Courtesy of G. E. Stout, Illinois State Water Survey.

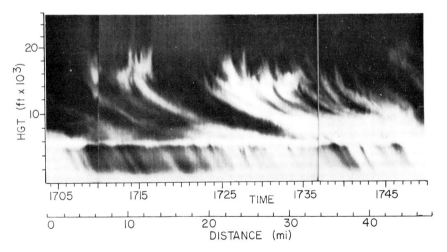

Fig. 10.9. Height-time record obtained with a vertically pointing radar. The wind at an altitude of 5.5 km (18,000 ft) (the assumed generating level) was about 27 m/sec (63 mi/hr). The distance scale was calculated on the assumption that the whole pattern moved at this speed. Courtesy of Stormy Weather Group, McGill University.

10.7 Bright Band

Observations by means of a vertically scanning radar sometimes reveal that just below the zero-degree isotherm there is an increase in echo intensity in a narrow altitude range (figs. 10.10 and 10.11). The nearly horizontal band of bright echo is called the "bright band." It usually is observed when precipitation is light (Ramana Murty, Roy, and Biswas 1965). The characteristics of the band can be explained in terms of several factors: (1) differences in radar reflectivity of ice and water particles, (2) differences in particle concentration above and below the 0°C isotherm caused by differences in the terminal velocity of snow and ice particles having essentially the same mass, (3) variations in growth rate of the falling particles, and (4) variations in reflectivity with changes in particle shape. Quantitative studies of the bright band have been made by a number of investigators who have extended the theory first presented by Ryde (1946).

In their analysis, Austin and Bemis (1950) assumed that the precipitation rate through a level above the bright band was the same as that through a level below the bright band. This assumption is not entirely valid because, as the snow melts and as the hydrometeors grow by accretion or condensation, the precipitation intensity increases. Austin and Bemis assumed uniform ice spheres above the melting level and made calculations of the heat transferred to each ice sphere by means of a suitable transfer equation. The sphere was maintained at a temperature of 0°C, and the rate of melting was computed. Knowing the ratio of water and ice and assuming that the mixture was homogeneous, they computed the index of refraction of the particle by means of equation (5.1). As noted in chapter 5, this expression is not considered to be valid when an absorbing medium such as water is involved in the mixture. The degree to which equation (5.1) yields incorrect results still is not known.

Austin and Bemis also assumed that, at the initial time, above the melting layer, the frozen spheres had diameters of 5 mm and a fall velocity of 1 m/sec. The completely melted particles were assumed to have diameters of 1 mm. With this information, it was possible to calculate the change in radar reflectivity caused by the melting of the particle and by the change in the terminal velocity of the particles. The effects of coalescence on particle size and reflectivity were estimated. The results are shown in figure 10.12. It is seen that, if the falling frozen precipitation had a reflectivity of 1.0 at the 0°C isotherm, its value would increase to about 20 at 300 m below the melting level and then decrease rapidly to 5 at about 360 m where the frozen particles would be melted completely.

Wexler (1955) also made estimates of the contributions of various factors, including the effects of particle shape, to the changes in echo

Fig. 10.10. Well-defined bright band on the RHI of a 10-cm radar in Boston on 21 January 1959. The bright band was at a height of about 8,000 ft (2.4 km). Two dark height markers are at altitudes of 5,000 and 10,000 ft (1.52 and 3.05 km) and the heavy range mark is at 40 km. Courtesy P. M. Austin, M.I.T.

intensity through the bright band. He assumed that the falling snow particles had spheroidal shapes and calculated the effective axial ratios from measured depolarization ratios of power scattered from the melting layer. The results of his analysis are shown in table 10.2. It is evident that the greatest contribution to the echo increase is made by the increase in the dielectric constant as the snow melts. Table 10.2 indicates that reflectivity changes attributed to particle growth by condensation are small. Wexler (1955) suggested that growth by coalescence above the melting region might cause an increase in echo intensity by several decibels. The major factor contributing to the decrease in intensity below the bright band is the increase in fall velocity, which acts to decrease the drop concentration.

Observations reveal that in most cases the center of the bright band is generally from about 100 to 400 m below the 0° C isotherm. Austin and

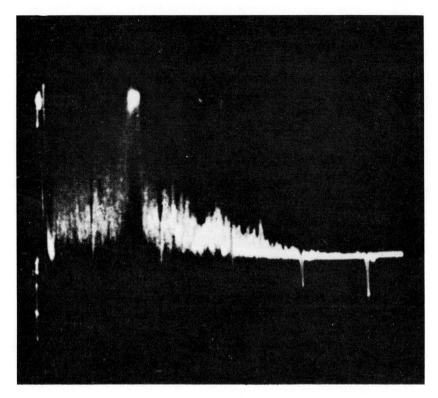

Fig. 10.11. Appearance of the bright band on the R-scope of a radar set with a vertically pointing antenna. From Foster (1953).

Bemis (1950) reported an average value of about 250 m; Hooper and Kippax (1950a) reported 100 m. Measured ratios of the radar reflectivity in the center of the bright band to the reflectivity in the snow perhaps 500 m above it have ranged as high as 100 in extreme cases but are most frequently between 15 and 30 (about 12–15 dB). The ratio of the radar reflectivity in the bright band to that in the rain below has been found to range between about 4 and 9 (about 6–10 dB).

Vertically pointing pulsed-Doppler radars have yielded new data on particle sizes and fall speeds in bright-band cases. An excellent example is shown in figure 8.3. In this instance it can be seen that above the bright band the particle-fall speeds were mostly between about zero and 2 m/sec. In the rain region, most of the backscattered power was coming from drops falling at speeds between about 2 and 6 m/sec. These results show that the assumptions on fall speeds made by Austin and Bemis

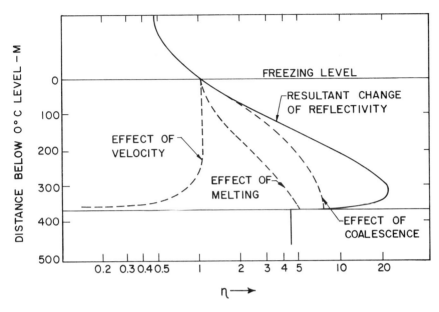

Fig. 10.12. Schematic drawing showing the effects of particle coalescence, melting, and changes in the terminal velocity on radar reflectivity through the bright band. From Austin and Bemis (1950).

(1950) were not unreasonable. Of course, it must be realized that there is a certain degree of variability from one case to the next.

Lhermitte and Atlas (1963) observed mean Doppler velocity and effective radar reflectivity, Z_e, by means of a vertically pointing X-band radar. The data in one case are shown in figure 10.13. Again it can be seen that particle velocities of between zero and 2 m/sec, and about 6 m/sec, were measured above and below the bright band, respectively. From their analyses of the factors considered to be relevant, Lhermitte and Atlas (1963) concluded that above the bright band (between levels 1 and 2 in

TABLE 10.2   Echo Intensity Changes in Decibels through Bright Band Attributed to Various Physical Processes

Layer	Melting (Dialectric Constant)	Fall Velocity	Shape	Growth (Condensation)	Total
Snow to bright-band level . . .	+6	−1	$+1\frac{1}{2}$	0	$+6\frac{1}{2}$
Bright-band level to rain	+1	−6	$-1\frac{1}{2}$	$+\frac{1}{2}$	−6

Source: Wexler 1955.

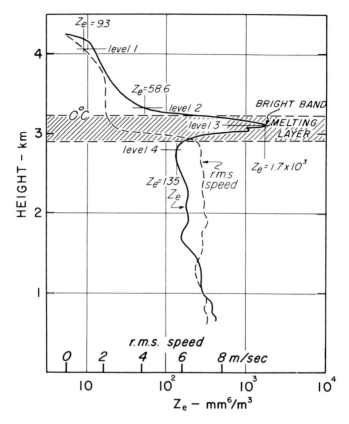

Fig. 10.13.   Simultaneous profiles of reflectivity factor Z and root-mean-square particle-fall speed in light (1 mm/hr), steady precipitation with a bright band. From Lhermitte and Atlas (1963).

fig. 10.13) ice-crystal aggregation took place with each flake at level 2 composed of between nine and twenty-seven of the ice particles at level 1, which was about 800 m higher. Since Z_e increased by a factor of 30.6 between the level just above the bright band (level 2) to the center of the bright band (level 3), it was concluded that there was a continuation of snowflake aggregation because melting alone could only increase Z_e by a factor of about 4.7. It was inferred that each particle at level 3 was composed of from five to seven of those at level 2.

The increase of fall speed in the rain could only account for about one-third of the observed decrease in reflectivity. Lhermitte and Atlas (1963) concluded that there must have been raindrop breakup, with each one divided into four to six drops. Earlier, Gunn and Marshall (1958) had proposed that in order to explain their observations there would have to "be considerable breakup of large particles when snow turns to rain at the melting level." Ekpenyong and Srivastava (1970), from a detailed theoretical analysis of the radar characteristics of the bright band, concluded that the aggregation and breakup of melting snowflakes is a distinct possibility. Uncertainties about particle shapes, composition, and size distributions make the quantitative aspects of the aggregation and breakup conclusions subject to question. Zwack and Anderson (1970), on the basis of observations of signal intensity, concluded that there was ice-particle aggregation above the bright band and raindrop breakup below it but no breakup in the melting layer. On the other hand, du Toit (1967), employing a Doppler radar, analyzed a bright-band case and concluded that aggregation of ice particles above the bright band and breakup of raindrops below were of minor consequence. This view was supported by Ohtake (1969), who made simultaneous observations of snow particles and raindrops on a mountain slope. He also noted, contrary to the conclusion of Gunn and Marshall (1958), that there was not a considerable increase of precipitation intensity from the top of the melting layer to the bottom. In earlier studies, Caton (1964, 1966) and Gorelik et al. (1967), who studied changes in raindrop spectra in the lowest 800 m of the atmosphere by means of Doppler radar, found little evidence of drop breakup.

The truth may be that the importance of coalescence and breakup may differ from one bright-band situation to the next.

The time variations of the Doppler velocities of the hydrometeors producing a bright band are illustrated in figure 10.14. An X-band radar was employed. The location of the bright band at 3,800 m is clearly delineated by the sharp gradient of vertical velocity. Above it, particle velocities are generally less than 2 m/sec; below it, they are generally from 5 to 6 m/sec. The diagram also illustrates the variable nature of a cloud system producing what might be called "continuous precipitation."

Incidentally, bright bands are sometimes observed in the dissipating stages of thunderstorms. Battan, Theiss, and Kassander (1964) observed a well-defined bright band even when lightning activity was still in progress. Such a situation is not common, but neither can it be said to be rare.

10.8 Precipitation-Generating Levels and Snow Trails

Observations taken with vertically pointing or scanning radar sets during the passage of regions of continuous precipitation have shown interesting echo patterns (fig. 10.9). It is seen that there are long, sloping echo "streamers" with a fairly concentrated cell at the top. The trails become more horizontal with decreasing altitude. Several investigators have

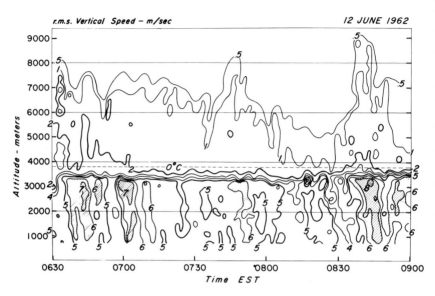

Fig. 10.14. Height-time contour chart of root-mean-square particle-fall speed recorded by vertically pointing Doppler radar at Sudbury, Massachusetts, in more or less steady rain on 12 June 1962. Contours are at intervals of 1 m/sec except for an interval of 0.5 m/sec for uppermost snow crystals. Note 0°C level at 3,800-m altitude. From Lhermitte and Atlas (1963).

given similar interpretations for these precipitation streaks (see Marshall 1953*b*; Gunn and Marshall 1955).

It is postulated that the cells at the top of the precipitation trails are the regions where the snow crystals are produced. These cells have been termed "generating cells or elements." At any time, the generating cells are found to be at approximately the same altitude, which is therefore called the "generating level." Gunn et al. (1954) reported that the cells frequently occur in stable air some hundreds of meters above frontal surfaces. The cells have been observed to have lifetimes of the order of several hours and diameters of a few kilometers. Sometimes they are oriented in lines. In general, the generating cells appear to move with the winds at the appropriate level (Langleben 1956; Wexler and Atlas 1959). Langleben (1956) reported that generating cells are not always cellular or well defined. Frequently, the echoes are in the form of diffuse patches. The changes in appearance of the generating-cell echoes have indicated the presence of vertical motions within them. The mechanism by which these elements are formed was studied by Douglas, Gunn, and Marshall (1957), Wexler and Atlas (1959), and others. It has been proposed that, once ice-crystal formation in the generating cell begins, it can be maintained by convection caused by the heat released during the deposition of vapor on the crystals.

The shape of the snow streaks depends on the fall velocity of the snow and the vertical distribution of the wind. The trajectory of any particle is given by

$$\frac{dx}{dz} = \frac{u(z)}{w_t(z)}, \tag{10.5}$$

where x is the horizontal distance taken in the plane of the streak; z is the vertical dimension, with the origins taken at the generating element so that z increases downward; and $w_t(z)$ and $u(z)$ are the terminal velocities of the particle and the wind in the x direction, respectively. From an integration one obtains the equation for the trajectory,

$$x - x_0 = \int_0^z \left(\frac{u}{w_t}\right) dz. \tag{10.6}$$

Marshall (1953b) compared computed streak shapes with those observed on an RHI scope. On one day, the wind increased linearly with height. By setting $u = az$ and $w_t = b$, one obtains

$$x - x_0 = \frac{a}{2b} z^2. \tag{10.7}$$

After substituting the appropriate a obtained from wind observations and selecting a value of $b = w_t = 1.2$ m/sec, it was found that the calculated and observed streaks corresponded closely. It was concluded that there was snow aggregation in the generating cell.

Sometimes only a small portion of any streak can be seen on an RHI scope, and the streaks may appear as nearly horizontal lines. Their vertical motions will depend on the slope of the line and the movement of the entire pattern relative to the ground. If the pattern in the plane of the streak moves with a known horizontal velocity, the motion of the streak relative to the ground at any point can be calculated.

Photographs of snow streaks show that sometimes the particles fall into supercooled clouds at lower elevations. The snowflakes and snow crystals in the streak can then continue growing by sublimation and riming. After passing out of the subfreezing part of the cloud, the frozen particles melt and in some cases may continue growing by coalescence.

10.9 Cloud-Seeding Tests

Radar has been used by various investigators to evaluate the effects of cloud-modification experiments. For the most part, it has served primarily to detect the presence or absence of precipitation particles, but in some instances radar has been used to make estimates of the quantity of rainfall from seeded and nonseeded clouds.

Vertically pointing or scanning airborne radar sets were employed by Smith (1950) and Braham, Battan, and Byers (1957) in studies of the results of seeding cumulus clouds. In particular, the investigations were concerned with whether one could induce the formation of precipitation in clouds which would not have rained naturally. The experimental procedures involved randomly selecting a cumulus cloud which did not contain a precipitation echo, seeding it, and then noting whether a precipitation echo subsequently developed. The major advantages of using radar for such an experiment are twofold. By proper calibration, one can assure that the droplet sizes needed for an echo at a particular range are reasonably constant. Thus the appearance of an echo represents an objective observation of the growth of cloud droplets to precipitation size. Furthermore, radar makes it possible to note whether precipitation has formed anywhere inside the cloud.

By means of properly designed tests involving the random seeding of half an appropriately selected sample of cumulus clouds and by using radar to ascertain whether precipitation has formed in the seeded and nonseeded clouds, it is possible to draw inferences regarding the effects of the seeding.

Ground radar obviously has useful applications in evaluating the results of seeding. In a program of seeding of orographic cumuli over a mountain range in southeastern Arizona, Battan (1967) made use of an X-band height-finding radar and a pair of carefully calibrated cloud cameras. In this investigation, a randomization scheme was adopted which involved seeding, with an airborne silver iodide generator, on one of two adjacent days on which suitable cumulus clouds were predicted. From photographs of the RHI scope, studies were made of the frequency of echo formation, the altitude of initial echo formation, rates of echo growth, and maximum echo altitudes. By combining radar and photogrammetric data, cloud censuses were conducted. The effects of seeding were studied by making similar measurements on seeded and nonseeded days and comparing the results.

Airborne and ground radar were used extensively by Simpson, Brier, and Simpson (1967) and Simpson (1967) in the conduct and evaluation of tests of the effects of heavy ice-nuclei seeding of convective clouds in the tropics. Weinstein and MacCready (1969) carried out somewhat similar studies of convective clouds near Flagstaff, Arizona. These investigations concluded, from a series of carefully documented experiments, that the seeding of certain convective clouds caused them to grow more than they would have grown without seeding. Radar was used to locate clouds eligible for seeding and to observe their behavior in terms of horizontal and vertical growth.

Woodley and Herndon (1970) used observations made by means of a 10-cm radar to measure precipitation from convective clouds involved in Simpson's seeding experiments. They used the expression $Z = 300R^{1.4}$, which was obtained by a slight modification of a Z-R expression derived by Sims, Mueller, and Stout (1963) from an analysis of raindrop observations in showers in Miami, Florida. Woodley and Herndon reported that radar estimates of point rainfall averaged within 30 percent of values yielded by rain gauges. Woodley (1970) concluded that the seeded clouds yielded more rainfall than comparable nonseeded clouds.

Dennis, Schock, and Koscielski (1970) described a modern procedure for employing radar in the evaluation of the effects of ice-nuclei seeding on convective clouds. As a test cloud moves, its properties are observed and recorded, with particular attention given to measurements of Z_e and the heights at which precipitation first appears.

Radar has been used extensively in weather-modification projects in the Soviet Union. In an earlier section, mention was made of the use of radar to discriminate between thunderstorms containing only rain and those containing hail. The techniques in the USSR were developed because of the practical needs of scientists concerned with the reduction of the damage done by hail. Radar is used to decide which clouds to seed and when and where to seed them. Sulakvelidze, Bibilashvili, and Lapcheva (1965) gave a detailed account of the various procedures employed.

At the Ukrainian Hydrometeorological Research Institute in Kiev, V. M. Muchnik used radar to evaluate the effects of Dry Ice seeding on precipitation (see Battan 1970). Radar could not measure rainfall with sufficient accuracy to detect the expected effects of seeding. On the other hand, 3-cm radar observations have dramatically shown the effects of seeding layers of supercooled stratus clouds. The experimental technique consisted of flying an airplane back and forth along a 20-km track across the wind while dispersing pellets of Dry Ice. Clouds not producing any precipitation were seeded. The results of such an experiment are shown in figure 10.15. The PPI scope shows a sawtooth-shaped echo about 20 km across which was reported to conform to the pattern of seeding.

Airborne-radar observations have been employed by various investigators to observe the properties of precipitation patterns before, during, and after the heavy ice-nuclei seeding of a hurricane in August 1969 (Black, Senn, and Courtright 1972; Fujita and Black 1970; Senn et al. 1970). The analyses were particularly concerned with the changes of the echo-free area in the eye of the storm, the shape of the echo patterns

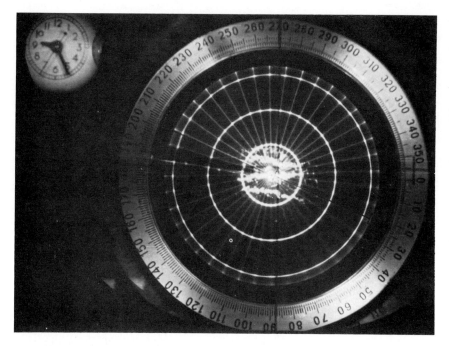

Fig. 10.15.   PPI scope of 3-cm radar showing the echoes produced by the seeding of a stratus cloud with pellets of Dry Ice. Courtesy of Ukrainian Hydrometeorological Research Institute, Kiev.

around the eye, and the character of the echo. It was found, for example, that the bright band was a widespread phenomenon throughout the storm.

The material in this section is not intended to be a complete review of how radar has been used in weather modification programs. Instead, an attempt has been made to note briefly procedures which have been used in the past in order that the reader may appreciate one of radar's important applications. It appears that radar still has not been used to its full potential by most weather-modification investigators. To do so, it is necessary to make careful quantitative measurements and employ them to calculate the relevant properties of the clouds and precipitation.

11 Radar Observations of Medium- and Large-Scale Systems

Since radar may observe the pattern of precipitation over a large region at essentially the same time, it has supplied a great deal of information about such phenomena as thunderstorms, squall lines, hurricanes, and, in some cases, extratropical cyclones. Except for hurricanes, the so-called synoptic-scale storm systems have not received the attention they deserve. A large fraction of the efforts of radar meteorologists has been devoted to the observation of mesoscale weather — thunderstorms, squall lines, and tornadoes.

11.1 Thunderstorms

Precipitation echoes from mature thunderstorms usually are easily distinguished from other echoes. On a PPI scope they are characterized by high echo intensities and sharp gradients of intensity (fig. 11.1). On an RHI scope, the echoes have large vertical extent and fairly high intensity through a relatively narrow vertical column (fig. 11.2). In this regard, the reader is reminded that RHI scopes often have height scales which are expanded; sometimes they are as much as five times greater than the range scale. On such scopes, as shown in figure 11.2 and 11.3, echoes are distorted. During the growth stages of convective storms, bright bands are almost never seen, but they sometimes are observed during the late stages of dissipation.

The vertical distributions of echo intensities in New England thunderstorms were reported by Donaldson (1958, 1961*a*). Figure 11.4, depicting the median profiles of echo intensity, shows maximum echo intensities increasing with the severity of the thunderstorm weather. Median values of Z_e approached 10^6 mm^6/m^3 in the most severe storms and generally occurred at altitudes of about 20,000 ft (6,100 m). Radar reflectivities of about 10^7 mm^6/m^3 have been observed in severe thunderstorms, but such intensities are rare, and when they occur they usually are found at altitudes above 6 km, according to Donaldson (1961*a*). Other measurements of the vertical distributions of echo intensities in thunderstorms, in general, have shown results similar to Donaldson's.

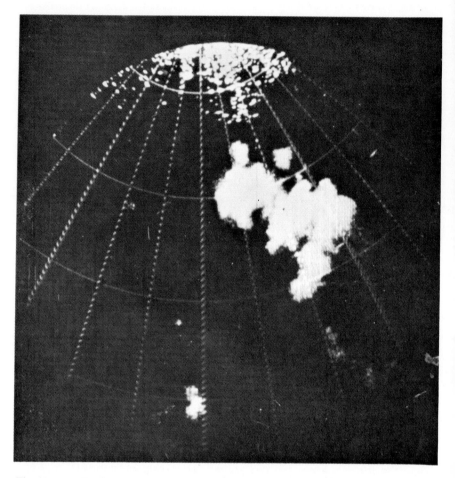

Fig. 11.1. *a*, Typical thunderstorm echoes on an off-center PPI of a 10-cm search-radar set. This is a PPI scope with the center of the presentation electronically moved off the center of the scope. Range markers are at 10-mile (16-km) intervals. *b*, A large thunderstorm echo on the PPI of the 10-cm WSR-57. Range markers are at intervals of 20 nautical miles (37 km). Isoecho contours are at about 10-dB intervals of Z_e with the outside gray scale equal to about 2×10^1 mm^6/m^3. Courtesy of National Severe Storms Laboratory, National Oceanic and Atmospheric Administration.

By definition, a convective cloud does not become a thunderstorm until thunder is heard or lightning is seen. Therefore, on the basis of echo intensities and distributions alone, one cannot be absolutely certain that a given convective echo is a thunderstorm. Nevertheless, it is usually safe to assume that an echo whose top has grown rapidly to over 9 or 10 km is, or will shortly become, a thunderstorm. Kotov (1960) and others in the USSR sought to discriminate between showers and

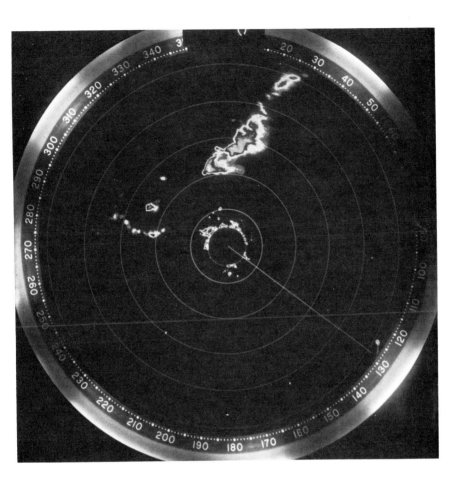

thunderstorms on the basis of cloud-top heights or temperatures. For example, it was concluded that, in the vicinity of Leningrad, echoes extending above the −22° C level could be considered to be thunderstorms.

In a later section it is shown that, in certain circumstances, lightning in thunderstorms can be detected by means of radar. Such observations have been infrequent, however, and at the present time one cannot plan on using radar lightning detection to determine whether a cloud is a thunderstorm.

Examination of certain thunderstorms in Ohio by means of vertically scanning radar has shown that they undergo shearing as a result of wind effects. From a study of the observations such as those shown in figure 11.3, Byers and Battan (1949) found that, in general, the radar cloud shear

Fig. 11-2.   A thunderstorm echo on the RHI of the 4.5-cm AN/MPS-4 radar. Range markers are at intervals of 10 nautical miles (18.5 km). Height markers are at intervals of 20,000 feet (about 6.1 km). The large thunderstorm extends to about 16 km. The isoecho contours are at 10-dB intervals, and the effective radar reflectivity of the outside edge is 2×10^2 mm^6/m^3. Courtesy of National Severe Storms Laboratory, National Oceanic and Atmospheric Administration.

in mature thunderstorms was about 50–75 percent of the wind shear. The theory for the shape of snow streamers (see chap. 10) cannot be applied readily to thunderstorms because strong and highly variable vertical air motions play an important role in determining the trajectories of the particles relative to the ground.

Malkus (1952) and C. W. Newton at the University of Chicago showed that the differences between thunderstorm shear and wind shear may be explained by assuming that the horizontal momentum of the cloud air is conserved as it is transported to higher or lower levels by thunderstorm updrafts and downdrafts. For example, consider a case in which the wind is constant in direction but increases with height (see Byers and Braham 1949). The updraft air reaching any altitude is assumed to have a horizontal momentum depending on the momentum of the air coming through the cloud base and of the air entrained through the sides of the cloud. As a result, the horizontal momentum of updraft air at any altitude would be smaller than that of the environment air at the same altitude, and the shear of the horizontal motion of the cloud air will be smaller than that of the environment.

Similar reasoning leads to the conclusion that, when the wind speed increases with height and a cloud contains a downdraft, the cloud air in low levels will have a greater horizontal momentum than the environmental air. As a result, the cloud will have a smaller vertical shear than the environmental wind shear.

The model of air motion in a thunderstorm just described apparently only applies to a fairly simple, relatively short-lived storm.

Detailed studies of the three-dimensional structure of some thunderstorms show them to be quite complicated. This is particularly the case when the storms are large, long-lived, and produce large hail or tornadoes. The environment of such storms commonly has a wind field which varies in speed and direction with height.

Although models of thunderstorms were proposed by many persons during the period 1884–1940, Newton (1950) made the first detailed analysis based on quantitative measurements of the three-dimensional structure of a line of severe thunderstorms. Over the intervening years, radar has been used extensively in Canada, England, the United States, and the USSR to observe severe thunderstorms and to develop physical models. The volume of *Meteorological Monographs* edited by Atlas (1963) contains detailed discussions of many aspects of the structure of severe thunderstorms.

Sulakvelidze, Bibilashvili, and Lapcheva (1965) reported the views of certain Soviet scientists on the properties of hail-producing thunderstorms. They visualized a quasi-stationary updraft increasing in speed with height up to a maximum at an altitude in the vicinity of the 0° C isotherm. It was further asserted that above the level of maximum updraft speed there is a so-called accumulation zone. It comes into being, in theory, because precipitation particles carried above the level of maximum updraft speed cannot fall to lower altitudes. The role of the updraft in increasing the liquid-water content aloft was studied earlier by Weickmann (1953) and Marshall (1961). According to calculations by the latter, concentrations of rain water up to 40 g/m^3 might be attained in certain circumstances.

The concept of an accumulation zone, examined by various investigators (Dennis, Schock, and Hartzell, 1969; Dennis, Schock, and Koscielski 1970), is also supported by the observations showing maximum echo reflectivities at the appropriate altitudes. Soviet scientists have proposed that most hailstone growth takes place in the accumulation

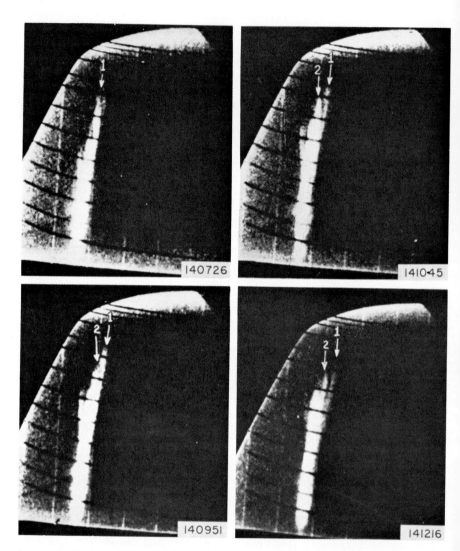

Fig. 11.3.   Shearing of the top of a thunderstorm which extended to about 14 km as observed by a 3-cm AN/TPS-10 height-finding radar set. The growth of several cloud turrets could be followed. On this scope, the dark horizontal lines are at 5,000-foot (1.52-km) intervals, and range markers, the bright vertical lines, are at 10-mile (16-km) intervals. Time to the nearest second is shown in the lower right-hand corner. From Byers and Battan (1949).

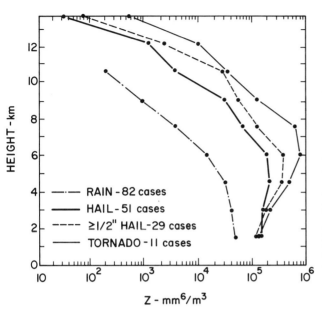

Fig. 11.4. Median profiles of core Z in 1957–58 New England thunderstorms, arranged by categories of severe weather. The 51 cases of hail include the 29 cases of large hail (diameter of 1/2 inch or larger) which are plotted separately. Also, the 11 tornado profiles are taken from the all-inclusive rain and hail categories. From Donaldson (1961a).

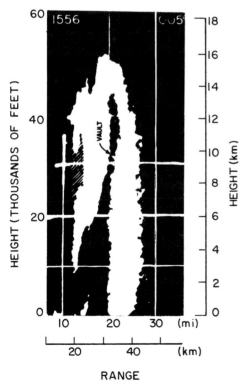

Fig. 11.5. Vertical section through a severe thunderstorm near Oklahoma City obtained with a 10-cm AN/FPS-6 radar. This is an original RHI photograph having an exaggerated vertical scale. The value of Z_e at 20-mile range was 10^4 mm^6/m^3. From Browning (1965).

zone, where very high concentrations of supercooled liquid water are assumed to be present. Hitschfeld and Douglas (1962) had proposed essentially the same mechanism.

The reportedly highly successful Soviet techniques of hail-damage suppression involves the introduction of ice nuclei directly into the accumulation zone. This procedure is designed to produce more (and smaller) hailstones capable of melting before they reach the ground.

On the other hand, the English scientists Browning and Ludlam (1962) offered a different view on the structure of a hailstorm. In some respects, their concept of air motion in a large thunderstorm resembles that put forward by Newton and Newton (1959). In a series of papers based on the careful evaluation of conventional radar data, Browning (1963, 1964, 1965) concluded that intense, traveling hailstorms are in a quasi-steady state. Browning and Donaldson (1963) showed that a distinctive feature of this model is that the updraft air enters the storm along its leading edge and follows a path which tilts into the wind as it goes to greater altitude. The strong updraft carries larger particles upward, leaving a so-called echo-free vault. Figure 11.5 shows an RHI photograph illustrating such a vault, and figure 11.6 is a drawing, to scale, of the same storm. Observations such as this one also were made by other investigators (e.g., Chisholm 1970; Marwitz and Berry 1971). More recently Marwitz (1972a,b,c) made detailed analyses of severe hailstorms by means of azimuthally and vertically scanning S-band radars. He also made observations around some of the storms by employing radar-tracked chaff and instrumental aircraft. These analyses encompassed

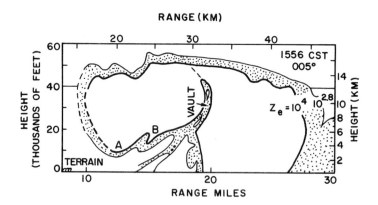

Fig. 11.6.   Vertical section from figure 11.5 drawn in true scale. Note the curtain of precipitation entering the section at 15-mile range and then being borne upward into the storm's vault. From Browning (1965).

two storms in Colorado and two storms in Alberta, Canada. He compared his observations with various features of the hailstorm models of Sulakvelidze, Bibilashvili and Lapcheva (1965) and Browning and Ludlam (1962).

A detailed analysis of the mesoscale wind field associated with Alberta hailstorms was made by Ragette (1971), who employed a network of pilot balloon stations. A point of interest is that in general he found a preponderance of downward air motion at low levels throughout the horizontal extent of the storm echo.

Wexler (1969) disagreed with Browning's interpretation of the causes of the echo-free vault and proposed that it is not a region of strong updrafts. Instead, Wexler suggested that it is a region of dry air with the active thunderstorms on one side and precipitation falling from aloft on the other side. More recently Marwitz et al. (1970) and Marwitz and Berry (1971) supported the view that the "echo-weak" vaults are places where updrafts prevail.

11.2 Thunderstorm Movement

Many studies have been made of the relation between the movement of thunderstorm echoes and the wind. The conclusions of the various studies, although differing in detail, have shown that, in general, the "translation" of a thunderstorm is highly correlated with the wind velocities at the altitudes at which the cloud is located. Before going into details of some of the findings, several terms should be defined.

The movement of the centroid of the area defined by a radar echo is sometimes found to follow a peculiar trajectory which has no obvious relation to the wind velocity. This occurs because thunderstorm echoes normally change rapidly as a cell grows and new cells develop adjacent to and merge with the original one. It has been found convenient to refer to that portion of the movement of the centroid that results from the growth of new echoes as the "propagation" of the echo. The motion of the echo centroid which is not a result of propagation can be called the "translation" of the echo. It can be directly related to the wind velocity; the propagation depends on the wind velocity only to the extent that the wind distribution may establish conditions favoring the development or dissipation of the echo. In general, under conditions of strong winds the translation effects predominate; when the winds are light, propagation can be the dominant factor, with the result that the centroid of the echo can have erratic movements.

One of the earliest studies of convective echo movements was made by Brooks (1946), who observed shower echoes by means of a 10-cm radar. He apparently did not try to differentiate translation from propagation and reported that small echoes moved with the winds at an altitude about 1.5 km and that the larger ones moved with the winds at about 3.4 km. It also was shown that the velocities of echoes from frontal precipitation are highly correlated with the wind at 700 mb (Ligda and Mayhew 1954).

The Thunderstorm Project made an investigation of the translation of individual radar cells by taking only those cells which were well defined and tracking them as long as they could be identified (Byers and Braham 1949). It was found that, when the mean wind speeds at altitudes between 0.6 and 6.0 km were greater than 4.5 m/sec, there was a good correlation between the echo movements and wind velocities in the layer 3.4–6.0 km (fig. 11.7). As can be seen, the correlation of echo and wind directions was particularly high. It also was found that the mean deviation between echo and wind direction was smallest when the winds at 3.0–3.7 km were used. In general, the echo speed was smaller than the wind speed at all altitudes.

When the mean wind between the surface and 6.0 km was less than 4.5 m/sec, the correlations between echo velocities and wind velocities were not as high as those shown in figure 11.7. There were large variations in the correlation coefficient from one level to the next. It is evident that, at these low speeds, propagation is very important in determining the movement of the echo centroid.

Since its introduction to meteorology, radar has been used extensively to observe the formation and movement of thunderstorms. Such information has been employed to predict the arrival of thunderstorms over a particular point, such as an airport. Kessler (1961) and Wilson and Kessler (1963) examined how radar data may assist the weather forecaster. Accurate predictions of the arrival of a severe thunderstorm, even if given less than an hour beforehand, can be extremely valuable because vulnerable airplanes and other equipment can be moved under cover or tied down. Such information is also of vital importance for controlling airplanes in the air and motor vehicles on busy highways.

It sometimes is possible to predict accurately the passage of a widespread squall line several hours in advance and the time of arrival of an individual thunderstorm up to perhaps 20 minutes in advance, but usually these times are practical upper limits (Wilson 1966b).

Barclay and Wilk (1970) described a scheme for using a digital computer to detect the motion of thunderstorm echoes with a view to predicting their positions for intervals of 1–30 minutes. The technique consisted of using digitized radar data with a spacial resolution of 1.8 km, for the identification, location, and tracking of thunderstorm echoes. Observations were obtained at intervals of 2–3 minutes, and storms having "core" intensities of 10^3–10^4 min^6/m^3 were tracked by this procedure.

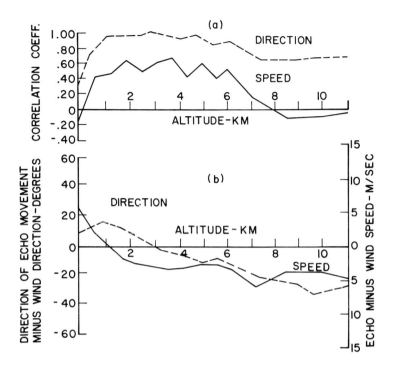

Fig. 11.7. Movement of 41 individual thunderstorm echoes over Ohio: *a*, correlations between echo and wind direction and speed as a function of altitude; *b*, mean deviations between echo and wind direction and speed as a function of altitude. From Byers and Braham (1949).

In the prediction of thunderstorm paths, one must always be alert to the possibility of the dissipation of existing storms or, more importantly, the development of new storms in the area ahead of existing storms.

11.3 Lines of Thunderstorms – Squall Lines

In general, squall conditions not associated with frontal passages usually are caused by organized lines or bands of active thunderstorms (see fig. 11.8). It has been common for many years to consider the term "squall line" to be synonymous with a line of thunderstorms.

Systematic studies of squall-line characteristics observed by means of a high-powered 10-cm radar set having a narrow horizontal beam and a wide vertical beam were made by the Thunderstorm Project. The observations were collected over southern Ohio during May–September 1947 (Byers and Braham 1949). During this period there were 56 days on which extensive radar data were obtained. On 32 days, lines of thunderstorms were noted: on 6 days the lines were along surface cold

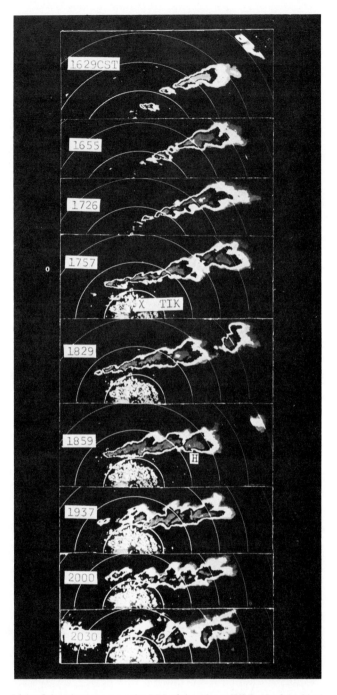

Fig. 11.8.   Line of thunderstorms on the PPI of the 10-cm WSR-57 of the National Severe Storms Laboratory in Norman, Oklahoma. Range markers are at intervals of 20 nautical miles (37 km). From Kessler (1970).

fronts; on 19 days the lines were ahead of cold fronts; and on 7 days the lines apparently had no association with surface cold fronts. In general, it was found that the squall lines far in advance of fronts were relatively short (25–150 km in length), were less well defined than the typical prefrontal lines, and tended to be parallel to the winds below the 700-mb level.

Austin and Blackmer (1956) studied bands of echoes in New England and reported that they were often aligned nearly in the direction of the wind at a steering level above 700 mb. De and Kundu (1966) observed premonsoon squall lines near Tripura, India, by means of a 3.2-cm radar. About 70 percent of them were more than 90 km long and were generally less than 20 km wide.

Most analyses of the properties of organized patterns of thunderstorms have consisted of the interpretation of photographs of PPI scopes. Kessler (1966*a*) presented a computer program for calculating the average lengths of echoes and the bandedness of the echo patterns.

Over the United States, widespread lines of severe thunderstorms are sometimes found just ahead of cold fronts. They are most often observed during the late spring and early summer, and sometimes they produce violent wind gusts, hail, and tornadoes. Such storm systems were discussed by Newton (1963) and Fujita (1963), who summarized their own outstanding analyses of standard meteorological and radar observations as well as earlier studies by Williams (1948), Stout and Hiser (1955), Tepper (1959), Newton and Newton (1959), and others.

Radar observations have shown that, in the area ahead of cold fronts, convection is sometimes concentrated within a zone rather than along a single line (see fig. 11.9). The squall line drawn on the weather map usually represents the position of this zone of activity rather than an individual line. The Thunderstorm Project found squall zones to be of the order of 300 km ahead of the surface front, of the order of 100–300 km wide, and nearly parallel to the cold front. Within the squall zone it was common to find several identifiable lines of thunderstorms. During the night and early morning hours the lines were more clearly defined. During the afternoon, convection sometimes became so active that it was difficult to delineate individual lines clearly.

To obtain information about the length of squall zones and extensive squall lines, it is necessary to have radar coverage over an area much larger than can be handled by one radar set. Observations by a network of radar sets of the Air Defense Command were combined first by Ligda (1957) and his colleague S. Bigler at Texas A & M University and showed that sometimes the lengths of the zones of convection extend for more than 1,500 km (fig. 11.10). Kessler (1968) and Wilk et al. (1967) showed

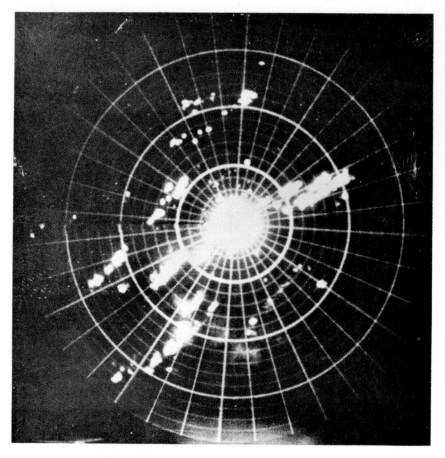

Fig. 11.9. Squall zone with lines of thunderstorm echoes on PPI of 10-cm search radar.
Heavy range markers are at 50-mile (about 80-km) intervals.

how modern data-processing techniques are employed to combine quantitative measurements of echo intensity and then to combine the observations from several radars (see fig. 7.5). The duration of the squall zone
can be long — 24 hours or more. Quite evidently, the space and time
scales of these squall zones exceed those conventionally considered
representative of mesoscale phenomena. Little is known about the relative frequency of such extensive zones of thunderstorms.

    Individual prefrontal squall lines observed in Ohio by the Thunder-
storm Project were frequently found to have durations of several hours,
although occasionally a severe and widespread one lasted more than 12
hours. Their maximum widths usually were less than about 70 km and
their lengths less than 300 km. As might be expected, the sizes and

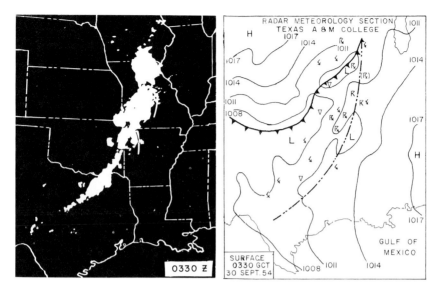

Fig. 11.10. Composite radar picture showing a large-scale squall line. The various radar photographs used in the composite picture were retouched and all nonweather echoes removed. A surface weather map for the same time as the radar data is shown on the right. From Ligda (1957).

intensities of the lines almost never reached an equilibrium, or a steady state, but rather were constantly in the process of change.

Prefrontal squall lines tend to be parallel to the associated cold fronts but sometimes exhibit large differences. At times such a line of thunderstorms extends over a warm front almost perpendicular to it.

The speed of movement of prefrontal squall lines has been reported at times to exceed the speed of the associated fronts. When a line of echoes is examined in detail, it is found that the individual echo elements which combine to form the line are constantly changing—old ones dissipate and new ones develop. The individual echoes can range in size from a few kilometers in diameter to several tens of kilometers, and the duration of each echo is small relative to that of the line itself.

It has been observed that the movements of the individual convective elements generally move in a direction which is clockwise from the axis of the squall line but usually by less than 90° (fig. 11.11). Thus the echoes usually have components of movement along the line and toward the left looking along the direction of squall-line movement.

The echo elements on various parts of squall lines sometimes move at different velocities. This results, at least in part, because wind variations over a distance of several hundred kilometers sometimes are fairly

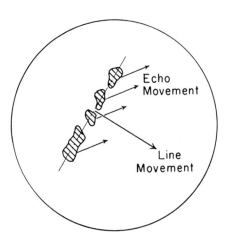

Fig. 11.11. Schematic drawing illustrating the movement of a squall line and the individual echoes in the line.

large. On some occasions the differences in echo velocity are large enough to cause the axis of the line to rotate and produce noticeable changes in the shape and length of a line of thunderstorms (e.g., see Bradbury and Fujita 1968).

Hitschfeld (1960) concluded that the motion of a system of well-developed thunderstorms was related to low-level wind velocities only in a general way. He found instances where the echo velocity differed substantially from the wind velocity at all heights. Newton and Fankhauser (1964) showed that, in a squall-line situation wherein the wind veered strongly with height, the individual storms moved in a direction as much as 60° to the right or 30° to the left of the mean wind in the cloud layer. The storms most often moved more slowly than the mean wind. Browning and Fujita (1965) found that most storms moved to the right of the wind, but at least one storm moved to the left. Hammond (1968) also reported a storm moving to the left of the wind direction.

Various types of mesoscale systems have been studied in detail by means of radar and other, more standard instruments. Arakawa et al. (1968) reported on the detailed structure of a subtropical mesoscale cyclone. Rinehart and Towery (1968) analyzed mesoscale cyclones near central Illinois. The use of radar to observe and track mesoscale precipitation systems was discussed by Matsumoto and Ninomiya (1968), Hamilton (1970), and Prosser (1970). Subramanian and Banerji (1964) and Kundu and De (1966) employed a 3-cm radar at Agartala, India, to observe mesoscale precipitation systems before and after the monsoon.

The distribution of showers over the Florida peninsula was examined by Frank, Moore, and Fishberg (1967), who employed digitized radar data. They found that the spatial and temporal variations of convective clouds were highly correlated with the behavior of the sea breeze.

The structure and movement of snow storms downwind of the Great Lakes were studied by Peace (1966), who employed a 10-cm radar.

11.4 Use of Chaff Winds to Study Thunderstorms

For certain purposes it is desirable to obtain a detailed picture of the wind structure around one or more thunderstorms. This can be done by tracking targets which move approximately with the wind.

One of the earliest schemes for carrying out such an operation was proposed by Warner and Bowen (1953). It consists of dropping bundles of radar-reflecting strips of metal foil (usually called "chaff," or "window") from an airplane, a balloon, or a rocket and tracking them with a radar set (fig. 11.12). To maximize the radar cross section, the strips of foil are half a wavelength long. Each dipole has a radar cross section of several square centimeters. From the distance traversed by an ensemble of reflectors in a given length of time, one can calculate its velocity. The horizontal component of motion gives the wind velocity. Anderson and Hoehne (1956) and others used chaff tracking to measure high-altitude winds.

By means of an appropriately spaced array of chaff bundles, it is possible to make measurements of the small and mesoscale structure of air

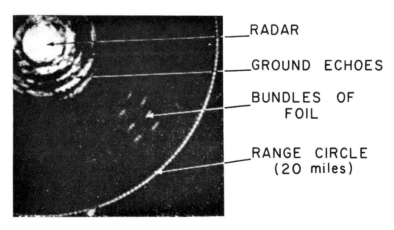

Fig. 11.12.   Chaff echoes. From Warner and Bowen (1953).

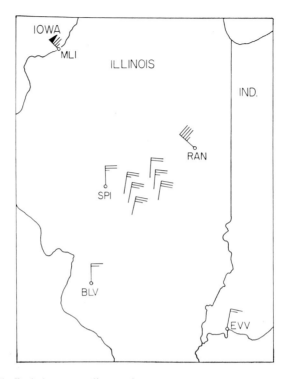

Fig. 11.13.   Chaff winds on a medium scale

movements and to measure horizontal divergences over fairly small
areas. The chief limitation on area size is that the spacing of the chaff
bundles must exceed the resolution distance of the radar. For the study
of small-scale motions, the interval between bundles can be separated
by a distance of about 1 km. The upper limit of chaff spacing is governed
by the detection capabilities of the radar sets. For the measurement of
winds it is desirable to have a narrow horizontal beam and fairly wide
vertical beam.

University of Chicago investigators carried out a series of tests to
evaluate the utility of the chaff technique (Battan 1958). The chaff used
in the experiments had a nominal falling speed of about 80 cm/sec. Some
types of chaff have a terminal speed below about 30 cm/sec. It should be
noted that in order for a series of chaff bundles to be at approximately
the same altitude the airplane making the releases must descend at the
fall rate of the chaff.

Examples of the types of measurements which can be made by means
of the chaff technique are given in figures 11.13 and 11.14. The wind data

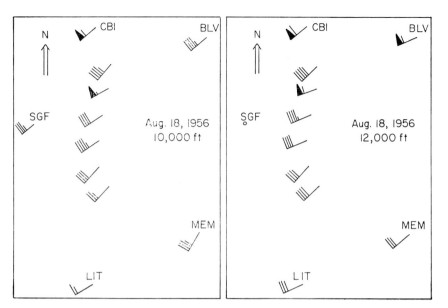

Fig. 11.14.   Chaff winds at two altitudes

plotted in central Illinois in figure 11.13 were obtained by flying two airplanes on parallel paths spaced about 40 km apart; each airplane dropped
chaff bundles at about 20-km intervals. The map also has pilot-balloon
winds plotted at the appropriate stations. From a measurement of the
time rate of change of the area defined by the chaff, a divergence of 4 ×
10^{-5} sec^{-1} was calculated. This appears to be a reasonable value, in view
of the cloudless sky at the time of the observations.

Figure 11.14 shows how the chaff technique can be used to make measurements of wind-speed gradients in regions of strong shear. A line of
chaff perpendicular to the stream lines yielded details of the wind profile.
Chaff was dropped at intervals of about 45 km over a line about 220 km
long. The initial drop was at about 12,000 feet (3.65 km). Since the fall
speed of the chaff was known, the vertical positions could be computed,
and winds were measured at 10,000 feet (3.05 km). Each wind vector
represents an average wind over a vertical distance of about 1,500 feet
(460 m). It can be seen that the "chaff winds" were consistent with the
pilot-balloon winds at both altitudes and gave a detailed picture of the
horizontal wind shear.

By means of a suitable vertically scanning radar, it is possible to make
observations of the pattern of vertical velocity by noting the changes in
altitude of the individual packets of chaff.

Fankhauser (1968), Jessup (1971) and Marwitz (1972*a*) made analyses of the mesoscale wind field around thunderstorms by tracking chaff dropped from airplanes. These data were combined with radar observations of the storms and other, more conventional observations.

If a suitable Doppler radar is available the velocity of the chaff can be observed in order to obtain essentially instantaneous wind velocities. The techniques involved were discussed by Jiusto (1961) and Pilié, Jiusto and Rogers (1963). Lhermitte (1969*a,b*), Chernikov et al. (1969), and Gorelik and Tolstykh (1970) observed chaff by means of X-band Doppler radars and measured turbulent air motions at low altitudes. Incidentally, as noted earlier in chapter 8, if there are detectable targets such as precipitation or, as will be seen in chapter 12, backscatterers such as insects, Doppler radar can supply very detailed wind observations in the free atmosphere (e.g., see fig. 8.16).

11.5 Observations of Lightning

It is known that lightning may occasionally produce images on the scope of a radar set. Under conditions to be discussed later, the ionized and heated channel of a lightning discharge has sufficient reflectivity to backscatter enough power to give a detectable echo. In some circumstances, the pulse of electromagnetic energy generated during the discharge contains adequate power at the radar frequency to give a detectable signal on a scope. Such a signal is called a "sferic."

When a lightning channel backscatters the incident radar pulse, the echo appears at a radar range corresponding to the distance and at the correct bearing of the channel. On the other hand, when a radar receiver detects a sferic, its indicated range will be independent of the actual range because the time of initiation of the sferic pulse is independent of the time that the scope trace starts at range zero. The sferic bearing on the scope will be correct in the sense that it will appear at the azimuth corresponding to the center of the antenna beam when it is pointing in such a direction that the lightning flash is within the volume illuminated by the beam.

The ability of a sferic receiver to observe the direction to a lightning flash was the basis for the sferic lightning detectors used extensively during World War II. Such systems consisted of three "sferic receivers" operating at frequencies of about 10 kHz, where lightning-generated power is nearly at its maximum. The three receivers simultaneously measured the bearing to the sferic sources, and, by triangulation, it was possible to locate them. Such schemes could observe thunderstorms at great distances—several thousand kilometers. This feature tended to compensate for their lack of spatial precision.

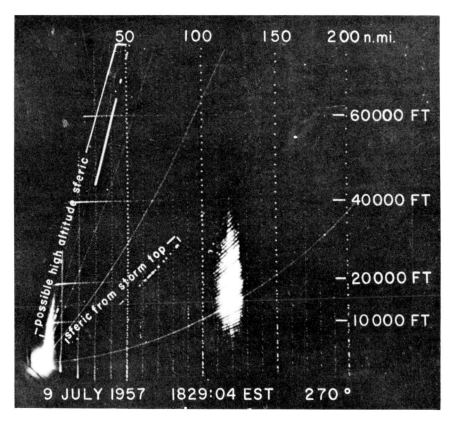

50   100   150   200 n.mi.

— 60000 FT

— 40000 FT

— 20000 FT

— 10 000 FT

Possible high altitude sferic

Sferic from storm top

9 JULY 1957   1829:04 EST   270°

Fig. 11.15. Photograph of microwave sferic on a 10-cm height-finding radar set. From Atlas (1958*a*).

The detections of microwave sferics by means of radar were reported by Hewitt (1953), Ligda (1956), and Atlas (1958*a,b*), who employed radars operating at wavelengths of 50, 23, and 10.7 cm respectively. Atlas's (1958*a*) observations (fig. 11.15) showed that at times lightning signals were composed of a number of pulses (average 10.5), whose average duration was about 27.5 μsec. The average spacing between pulses corresponded to about 20 μsec. Some of the pulses saturated the scope and were estimated to have a signal power of about 7×10^{-12} watts.

Atlas assumed that the lightning sferic was produced by the stepped leader in a lightning stroke and, following Watt and Maxwell (1957), assumed that the radiated field intensity (proportional to the square root of the power), normalized to a given range and receiver bandwidth, varied as f^{-1}. Those investigators terminated their curve at $f = 100$ kHz. Atlas daringly extrapolated to 10^4 MHz. More recent observations of radiation from lightning, which were summarized by Oetzel and Pierce (1968), showed that Atlas's extrapolation was not far off the mark. Their data yielded signal amplitudes (normalized to a 1-kHz bandwidth and a 10-km range) of about 60 and 4 μv/m at frequencies of about 2×10^2 and 1.1×10^4 MHz. Atlas's (1958b) observation on this coordinate system appears at a frequency of 2.8×10^3 MHz and a signal strength of about 25 μv/m. At the same frequency, the Oetzel and Pierce data give a signal strength of about 10 μv/m.

It is evident that a sensitive microwave receiver may detect lightning sferics when the antenna is pointing at the flash. With conventional radar receivers and the typical antenna scanning patterns, the likelihood of detecting very weak sferic signals is small.

Microwave radar has detected the signals backscattered by the lightning-stroke path (Ligda 1950, 1956; Browne 1951; Marshall 1953a; Miles 1952, 1953; Hewitt 1953, 1957; Jones 1954; Atlas 1958a. When a lightning discharge occurs, a narrow channel a few centimeters in diameter is highly ionized and its temperature is increased greatly in a matter of microseconds (see Uman 1969). Browne (1951) and Dawson (1972) showed that the radar backscattering from a lightning stroke cannot be explained in terms of the dielectric discontinuity caused by the hot channel. On the other hand, echoes from lightning channels can be accounted for as backscattering from regions of high free-electron densities. It is known that a radio wave incident on a region of free electrons causes them to oscillate. The oscillations, in turn, lead to an electromagnetic radiation which may be detected as a "reflected wave."

A satisfactory theory for lightning echoes must explain the observed echo duration. In order to measure this quantity, the radar antenna usually is pointed continuously at the region where the lightning stroke is expected to occur. Miles (1952, 1953) measured durations of the order 0.3 second by means of a clever observational technique. The radar antenna was pointed toward the zenith while it rotated around the beam axis. The antenna was always "looking" upward, but on a PPI scope the trace rotated in synchronism with the beam rotation. A fixed target at a fixed range appeared as a circular arc at that range. Miles's 10-cm radar antenna required 6 sec for a complete rotation. When a lightning channel occurred within the antenna beam, it produced an echo appearing as an arc at the appropriate radar range, and the echo duration was proportional to the length of the arc on the PPI.

Atlas (1958a) estimated lightning-echo durations of 0.5 second. Ligda's (1950) records showed that the signal intensity reached a maximum in a fraction of a second and then decreased exponentially to the noise level of the radar in a period of 1–5 seconds. These observations were obtained with 10-cm radar equipment.

The duration of lightning echoes is attributed to the rapid recombination of electrons and ions. If the concentration of free electrons is given by n, and a_e is the recombination coefficient, the decrease of n with time is given by

$$\frac{dn}{dt} = -a_e n^2. \tag{11.1}$$

Integrating this expression yields

$$\frac{1}{n} - \frac{1}{n_0} = a_e t, \tag{11.2}$$

where n_0 is the concentration at time zero. Atlas (1958a) assumed values of a_e and calculated the time required for electron concentrations to decrease from a particular initial value. He found that, for a_e equal to 0.9×10^{-6} and 0.9×10^{-7} cm^3/sec, the electron concentration in one second would fall to about 10^7 and 10^8 cm^{-3}, respectively. Atlas argued that this result supported the view that electron concentrations between 10^6 and 10^9 cm^{-3} could account for the lightning echoes he detected by means of the 10.7-cm AN/FPS-6 radar. These electron concentrations are far below those calculated for *critical reflections* by Ligda (1956) and shown in table 11.1.

Uman and Orville (1964) inferred that in a lightning stroke n_0 may exceed 10^{17} cm^{-3}. From equation (11.2) it can be shown that n will decrease to 10^{10} cm^{-3} in periods of about 10^{-2} second or less. Therefore, it follows that, if critical reflection were required, the probability of lightning detection by means of 3- or 10-cm radar would be quite small.

Atlas (1958a) calculated the concentration of free electrons needed to explain the observed radar-echo intensities. He employed a theory for ionized meteor trails and assumed that the discharge channel was a vertical cylinder with a diameter between 10 and 100 m. He further assumed that, at the time of echo detection, the external electric field was essentially zero. These conditions yielded electron densities of 10^6–10^9 cm^{-3}. Atlas's assumed channel diameters obviously were much

TABLE 11.1   Concentration of Free Electrons Required for Critical
                    Reflection of Electromagnetic Wave

Wavelength (Cm)	Electron Concentration (Cm^{-3})	Wavelength (Cm)	Electron Concentration (Cm^{-3})
3	1×10^{11}	23	1×10^9
10	1×10^{10}	50	3×10^8

SOURCE: Ligda 1956.

larger than those of observed visible lightning channels. He argued that
the low electron concentrations ($\leq 10^9$ cm^{-3}) could exist without producing a visible glow. In this way he accounted for his own and earlier
observations (e.g., Marshall 1953a; Jones 1954) that most lightning
echoes extended upward from thunderstorm tops (fig. 11.16) even though
few lightning discharges are seen to go from cloud tops to clear air.

Another analysis of the electron concentration in a radar reflective
lightning channel was made by Hewitt (1957). He assumed that the
channel was 2 cm in diameter and had a twisted shape and that the external electric field was 3×10^4 v/cm. This model yielded an electron
concentration of about 10^{12} cm^{-3}. The quantitative differences of electron density found by Hewitt (1957) and Atlas (1958a) are largely a
result of their differing assumptions.

Recently Dawson (1972) calculated the radar cross sections of a cloud-
to-ground lightning stroke for two limiting cases of overdense and
underdense plasmas. He used realistic models of lightning-channel

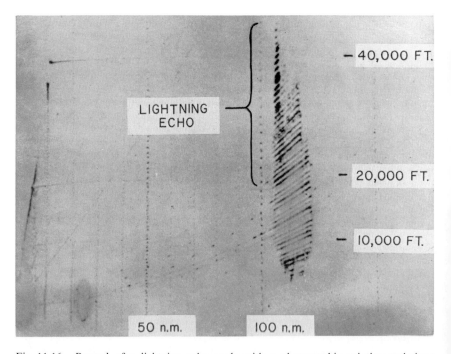

Fig. 11.16. Record of a lightning echo made with a photographic printing technique
proposed by Ligda (1956). This illustration was obtained by superimposing a positive
transparency of the photographic frame showing the lightning and precipitation and a
negative of a slightly earlier frame showing only the precipitation. The precipitation echoes
tend to cancel each other. From Atlas (1958a).

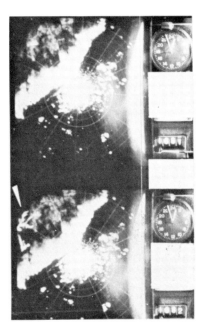

Fig. 11.17. Photographs of a PPI scope showing lightning echoes. The arrows in the lower photographs (about 50-km long) point to the lightning echoes. The top photographs, taken less than 1 minute earlier, do not show the lightning echoes. Courtesy of M. G. H. Ligda.

dimensions and electron densities and obtained cross sections at radar wavelengths of 3.2, 10, 23, and 150 cm. He concluded that radars operating at wavelengths 10 cm or greater should detect a typical lightning channel for periods up to about 100 msec after initial stroke occurrence. Dawson also found that the cross sections vary little over the wavelength interval 10–150 cm.

On the other hand, at wavelengths of 3 cm or less, the backscattering cross section decreases very rapidly as the electron concentration in the channel decreases. A lightning channel is likely to be detectable at 3 cm for no more than about 5 msec. The wavelength dependence explains why lightning echoes seldom are detected on 3-cm radars even though they are used widely.

Ligda (1956) presented a number of spectacular examples of lightning echoes observed by means of 23-cm. radar equipment. The PPI photographs show long, branching echo streamers extending for many tens of kilometers (fig. 11.17). These echoes apparently were produced by cloud-to-cloud lightning discharges. Ligda pointed out that the echoes

exhibited a large variety of shapes, and he proposed a tentative classification system. It included four basic echo types according to the location
of the charge centers and the discharge mechanism.

Additional investigation of lightning echoes should lead to a better
understanding of the processes of thunderstorm electrification. A knowledge of the time and location of lightning occurrence as a function of the
age and temperature of a convective cloud is also pertinent to the questions of the mechanism of precipitation.

11.6 Tornadoes

It long has been recognized that the tornado, the most violent of meteorological phenomena, is usually associated with thunderstorms. Because
of the lack of suitable observational techniques, it has been difficult to
learn a great deal about tornadoes. As is well known, they are quite small,
sometimes having diameters of less than a few hundred meters, and of
short duration, usually less than a few minutes. From visual observations
alone, it is almost impossible to delineate accurately the size and distribution of thunderstorms at the time of tornado occurrence. With radar
it has been possible to make accurate observations of the distribution of
thunderstorm precipitation over a large area and to obtain photographic
records at very short time intervals. By means of radar data, some interesting facts have been learned about tornadoes.

The earliest known series of radar observations of a tornado-producing
thunderstorm was obtained by the Illinois State Water Survey (Stout
and Huff 1953). Some of their photographs are shown in figure 11.18.
This was a particularly valuable series of observations because it was
started before tornadoes occurred and continued for a substantial period
as the tornado system traveled for tens of kilometers. The tornadoes occurred on the southwest or rear right side of the existing thunderstorm, or
"mother cloud," as it is sometimes called. The entire echo had a generally
eastward movement. Other radar observations of tornadoes also revealed
that the tornadoes developed on the rear right side of the mother cloud
(Penn, Pierce, and McGuire 1955); however, there are reports of tornado occurrences on other edges of the thunderstorms (Hoecker 1957;
Freund 1966; Bradbury and Fujita 1966; and others).

The most interesting feature of figure 11.18 is the narrow southward
protuberance from the echo and its rapid whirl from a straight echo to
a "six shape" to a closed ring. When the film taken during the development of this echo is projected at a speed higher than actual speed, the
change in the echo is quite clear. It should be noted that the radius of the
ring of echo is of the order of 5 km, while the tornadoes had a diameter

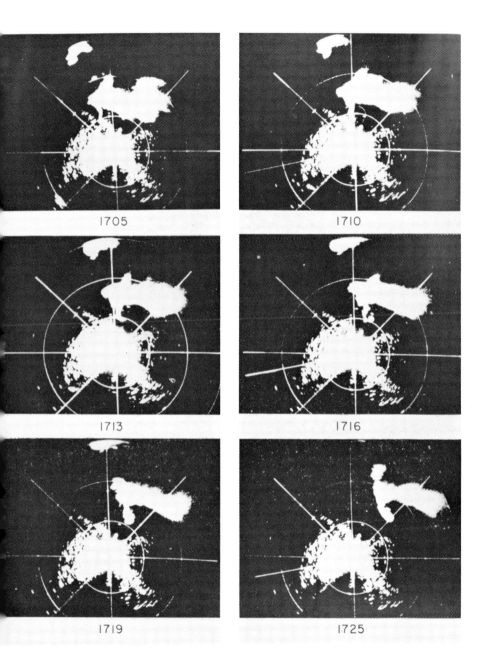

Fig. 11.18.   Series of scope photographs showing the formation of a tornado echo. The range markers are at 10-mile (about 16-km) intervals. The time of each photograph is noted. The radar was a 3-cm AN/APS-15 with characteristics similar to those of the AN/APQ–13. From Stout and Huff (1953).

of perhaps a tenth this size. Fujita (1958) made a detailed analysis of
this case. He showed that the tornado funnels occurred in a circulatory
system which was small but still many times the size of the tornado
funnel. This system was called a "tornado cyclone" by Brooks (1959),
who found it from a careful study of surface observations of pressure.

Over the years Fujita (1963, 1970) and his associates (e.g., Fujita,
Bradbury, and Van Thullenar 1970; Browning and Fujita 1965) made
detailed analyses of radar and other observations of tornado situations.
They found, for example, that a severe thunderstorm may lead to a
tornado cyclone perhaps 15–30 km in diameter. Individual tornado funnels are spawned, usually 2–5 km to the right of the path of the tornado
cyclones. The funnels often move in the same direction, toward and
across the path followed by the center of the tornado cyclone. As a
tornado cyclone, which is sometimes identified by the hook-shaped radar
echo, travels, a series of tornado funnels can be produced at intervals
of some tens of minutes.

A detailed analysis of the famous Palm Sunday (11 April 1965) tornadoes was published by Fujita, Bradbury, and Van Thullenar (1970).
Meticulous studies were made of the damage patterns and of radar,
satellite, and other meteorological data. At least thirty-seven separate
tornadoes were identified as the storm system passed from Iowa to Ohio
leaving a toll of 258 dead and 3,148 injured. Radar was used to observe
the growth, movement, and dissipation of the thunderstorms associated
with the funnels. The scope photographs from a number of radar sets
were used to construct "a composite picture of the echo patterns in relation to the advancing dry cold front and to study the direction and rate
of motion of the echoes with respect to the midtropospheric winds." In
this storm the tornadoes were moving abnormally fast, over 25 m/sec.
Incidentally, the maximum tangential wind speeds in the tornadoes were
estimated at about 80 m/sec.

A few vertical cross sections through echoes associated with tornadoes
were reported (Bull and Harper 1955; Schuetz and Stout 1957). Bigler
(1958) summarized the earlier observations and stated that a well-
developed tornado cyclone may extend to about 9 km. The limited, RHI
sections through the "six-shaped" type of echo showed that a region devoid of echo extended vertically from the ground to altitudes between
about 2.5 and 10 km and was surmounted by a ridge of echo.

Hook-shaped appendages such as the one shown in figure 11.18 are
fairly small and change rapidly, and, as a result, they have been found
only at short ranges where the radar resolution is high. The use of low-
powered radar equipment or the operation of a radar receiver at reduced
gain settings also favors the detection of echo details. When a radar set
has excessive detection capabilities or poor range and azimuth resolution, the hook may be lost inside a larger echo. Partly as a result of these

restrictions, there are few records giving the development of the characteristic echoes shown in figure 11.18.

An interesting hook-shaped echo associated with a mesoscale thunderstorm system yielding very heavy rainfall was reported by Arakawa (1967). The echo was shaped like a comma but was not attached to a parent thunderstorm. It was about five times larger than the hook echoes associated with tornado-producing systems.

Radar observers in regions where tornadoes occur with high frequency have reported that tornadoes are associated with thunderstorm echoes having protruding fingers; V-shaped notches; or doughnut shapes (so-called dry holes, i.e., small nonecho areas within fairly intense echoes). One might speculate that these echo features are also found in figure 11.18. For example, the dry-hole, or doughnut, shape is similar to the pattern seen when the whirling echo has made a complete cycle. If the various echo shapes were, in fact, indicative of the presence of tornadoes or severe thunderstorms, one would have some cornerstones on which to base forecasting rules. Unfortunately, it has not been established that only tornado echoes have these shapes. On the contrary, it has been found that tornadoes frequently occur in association with echoes which do not have the peculiar shapes discussed in preceding paragraphs, but, rather, have the oval or irregular shapes commonly observed with shower-type precipitation (Bigler 1955; Popov 1955).

Some observers have reported tornadoes occurring with extremely intense echoes. Many of these reports are based on qualitative observations taken with radar sets operating at maximum, or at least high, receiver-gain settings. Under these conditions, scope saturation is reached by most heavy rain. It is difficult to interpret such qualitative reports. However, quantitative measurements by Donaldson (1961a) in New England revealed that tornado-producing thunderstorms exhibited higher reflectivities than other thunderstorms. As a rule of thumb, it can be said that a $Z_e \geq 10^5$ mm^6/m^3 at an altitude of 10 km in New England storms, when observed by means of a 3-cm radar, indicates a good chance that the thunderstorm will produce a tornado. On the other hand, it is possible to have tornadoes when smaller values of Z_e occur.

In summary, it should be noted that the identification of a tornado by means of a conventional radar is not easy. One can conclude, on the basis of available data, that if tornadoes have been predicted in a certain area the sudden appearance of an appendage from an existing thunderstorm echo which then develops into the "hook" or "six shape" can be taken as a sign that a tornado has probably formed. Pending further research, the rapid development of intense thunderstorm echoes with the extension of echo protuberances and the occurrence of "dry holes" should be taken as evidence that severe thunderstorms may be developing, and efforts should be made to obtain visual observations in the vicinity of the storms. If the thunderstorm echo does have a tornado ac-companying it, the storm can be tracked with the radar set. Some tornado systems maintain themselves for many hours and may travel for more than 100 km. Communities in the path of such a system sometimes can be forewarned in sufficient time to permit the saving of life and property.

There is some evidence that another means of obtaining corroboration of the presence of a tornado is the use of sferics equipment, a system for noting the occurrence of lightning and its bearing from the station. This scheme was first proposed by Jones (1951). It was reported that the frequency of sferics reaches a pronounced maximum prior to the forma-tion of severe thunderstorms or tornadoes (Dickson 1956). By means of a network of sferics receivers or one receiver in connection with a radar set, one can determine the location of the source of high sferics activity. The technique of employing sferic signals for tornado identification is getting increasing attention.

As noted in section 8.13, a number of investigators have expressed the view that a Doppler radar would be a suitable device for tornado identification and location. It appears that a pulsed-Doppler radar for tornado detection could be built with existing technology if sufficient funds were available. In view of the loss of life and injuries by tornadoes, it appears essential that a prototype Doppler radar for tornado detection be developed, if possible. Once that has been done, questions about its practicality for day-to-day operations can be resolved.

11.7 Hurricanes

Before the introduction of radar, meteorologists were aware of certain important features of the pattern of precipitation around a hurricane. It was known that the heaviest precipitation occurred in the right-forward quadrant of the cyclone and that the rain area was composed of series of squalls. Details of the rain distribution could only be speculated upon from studies of the time variations at widely scattered rain gauges. By means of radar, it has been possible to obtain observations of the rain pattern at a particular time and to examine its evolution as the hurricane moves and ages.

The earliest radar observations of hurricanes by Maynard (1945) and H. Wexler (1947) revealed that the precipitation associated with hurricanes generally was oriented in circular or spiral bands, which con-verged near the center of the storm. Figure 11.19 shows hurricane Donna on 6 September 1960. The spiral echo patterns in some hurricanes are quite obvious and can be identified for long periods of time. In other

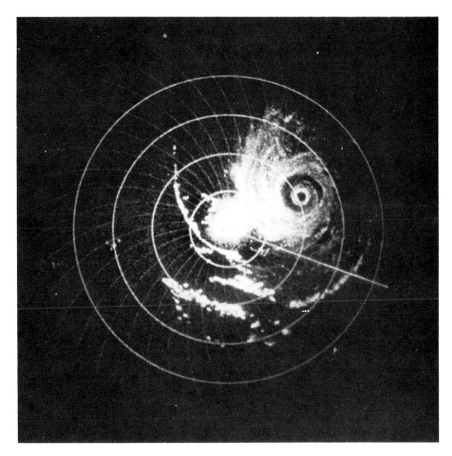

Fig. 11.19. Hurricane Donna on 6 September 1960 observed by means of an airborne 10.7-cm radar. Range markers are at intervals of 50 nautical miles (about 92 km). From Jordan, Schatzle and Cronise (1961).

hurricanes the rain distribution is rather confused, especially after the storm has had an overland trajectory.

Many analyses of the cloud and precipitation distributions in hurricanes have been made. Kessler (1957, 1958), Kessler and Atlas (1956), and Hardy, Atlas, and Browning (1964) employed radars equipped with PPI and RHI scopes to examine the three-dimensional structure of two hurricanes passing near Cape Cod, Massachusetts.

Outstanding radar observations of hurricanes have been obtained by means of airborne radar installed on U.S. Navy reconnaissance airplanes. The AN/APS-20, a 10.4-cm radar employing a PPI, and the AN/APS-45, a 3.2-cm radar yielding RHI data, were used by Schatzle

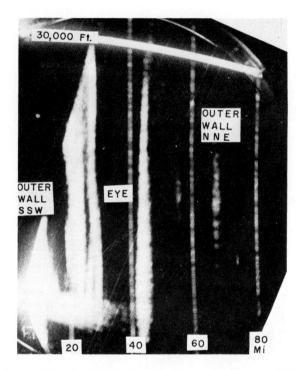

Fig. 11.20.   Cross section through hurricane Donna on 6 September 1960. Observation
by means of airborne 3.2-cm radar. From Jordan, Schatzle and Cronise (1961).

and Cronise (1960); Jordan, Schatzle, and Cronise (1961); and Jordan,
Hurt, and Lowrey (1960). Excellent observations have been made of
vertical cross sections taken through the eyes of some hurricanes. Figure
11.20 depicts a vertical section through hurricane Donna. The eye-wall
echoes were narrow, extended to an altitude of about 10 km, and were
close to vertical. This observation was quite different from the report
of Bigler and Hexter (1960), who, on the basis of a series of constant-
height PPI displays, concluded that the eye of hurricane Debra had a
slope of about 45°. Tatehira and Itakura (1966) concluded, from RHI
data, that the eye of a typhoon they studied in detail was vertical.

Otani (1964) collected CAPPI radar observations of a hurricane. He
employed a 5.7-cm radar at Nagoya, Japan, to observe typhoon Thelma.
His system yielded echo-intensity distributions at five levels between
2 and 6 km and at zero-degree elevation angle. In addition he obtained
vertical cross sections through the storm.

Many investigators have reported that, although the eye-wall cloud
shows strong convective features with intense echoes extending to great

altitudes, large echo regions in hurricanes display a bright band indicating the fall of frozen precipitation. Senn (1966*b*) stated, "The bright band was found in almost all parts of the storm with precipitation heights appreciably exceeding the melting level, especially in and around the eye wall and inner spiral band region where it was considerably higher than in the outer precipitation areas."

Early observations of the change of the eye in a hurricane were reported by Rockney (1956). Imai (1963) observed the changes in eye structure and size of six typhoons approaching Japan. He reported that, in general, the typhoon eye began to shrink a couple of hours before it reached the coastline. Complete "filling" occurred within an hour or so after the eye passed over land. It was concluded that the shrinking starts at low altitude and proceeds upward. Tatehira and Itakura (1966) presented a series of PPI observations of typhoon Lucy showing its eye decreasing in diameter as it approached Japan (fig. 11.21). They concluded that this change "seems to be related with the proximity of the land mass and with the cold water mass near the coast."

A number of authors observed hurricanes having "double-eye structures" (Jordan and Schatzle 1962; Fortner 1958). Well-documented measurements of such an event were reported by Hoose and Colon (1970), who had hurricane Beulah under radar surveillance throughout the period when two "eyes" developed. Figure 11.22 presents a sequence of photographs of the scope of a 23-cm radar set located at San Juan, Puerto Rico. During the period of observation, the hurricane followed a track toward the northwest and at one point passed within about 80 km of the coastline. The photographs clearly show a ring of echoes enclosing the inner eye of the hurricane surrounded by another concentric eye-wall cloud.

The radar observations were confirmed by an Air Force reconnaissance airplane which penetrated the eye at 2352 GMT on 9 September 1967. It was reported that the inner eye had an average diameter of about 13 km and the outer eye a diameter of about 46 km. The maximum wind speed of 54 m/sec at flight level (2,600 m) was found at a radius of about 22 km, i.e., just inside the outer wall cloud.

Hoose and Colon noted that, as in earlier cases of double-eye hurricanes, the second eye appeared shortly before the storm reached maximum intensity. The transition from one eye to two eyes and back again took about 13 hours. During this period the region of maximum wind shifted from the inner eye wall to the clear area between the wall clouds and finally to the outer eye wall.

From an examination of a number of hurricanes in the vicinity of Miami, Senn and Hiser (1957, 1959) verified that the characteristic bands of precipitation are, in fact, spiral in shape. They found that 500–600 km ahead of the system of spiral bands there usually exist narrow,

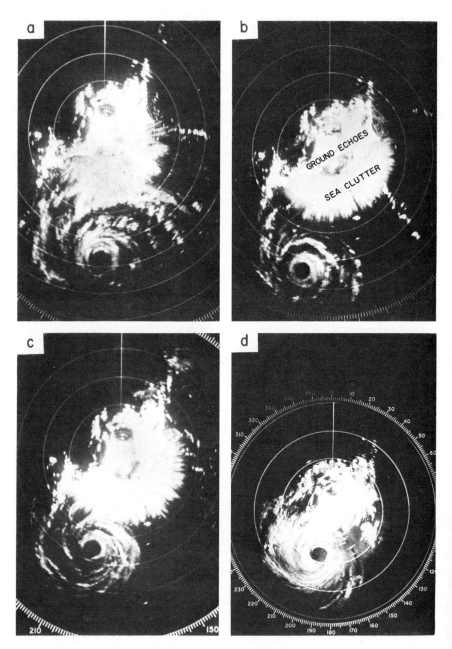

Fig. 11.21. PPI pictures of typhoon Lucy taken with 10.4-cm Mt. Fuji radar. Range markers are at 100-km intervals. *a*, 03 JST, 21 August 1965, elevation −1.7°; *b*, 16 JST, 21 August 1965, elevation −1.7°; *c*, 01 JST, 22 August 1965, elevation −1.7°; *d*, 14 JST, 22 August 1965, elevation −0.5°. From Tatehira and Itakura (1966).

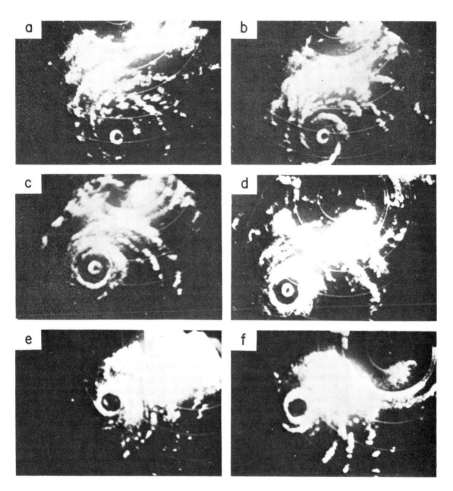

Fig. 11.22.   Photographs of PPI of radar at San Juan, P.R., showing formation of double eye in hurricane Beulah. Range markers are at intervals of 20 nautical miles (about 37 km). *a*, 1430 GMT, 9 September 1967; *b*, 1630 GMT, 9 September 1967; *c*, 1930 GMT, 9 September 1967; *d*, 2130 GMT, 9 September 1967; *e*, 0230 GMT, 10 September 1967; *f*, 0330 GMT, 10 September 1967. From Hoose and Colon (1970).

well-defined lines of echoes moving in the same direction as the hurricane. On some occasions, other squall lines up to 400 km long were observed "to move through a storm across the spiral band circulation." They found that an equation of a logarithmic spiral described the typical spiral band relative to the storm center:

$$\log_e r = A + B\theta, \qquad (11.3)$$

where r is the radial distance from the center of the storm, θ is the angle between the radius and an assumed axis, and A and B are constants.

The constant A was determined empirically, and B is given by

$$B = \tan \alpha, \qquad (11.4)$$

where α is the crossing angle between a band and any intersecting circle having the same center as the spiral. Figure 11.23 gives an example of a spiral of $\alpha = 15°$ fitted to an actual hurricane band.

A number of spiral overlays were made with different values of α. By means of the fairly objective technique of fitting the appropriate overlay over the radarscope display, it is possible to find the "center of the storm." Senn and Hiser (1957) asserted that, with this scheme, one can normally locate the storm center to within 13 km when the mean radius of the precipitation band is less than 80 km and to within about 16 km when the mean radius is greater than 80 km.

Jordan (1963) made an independent evaluation of the use of the spiral-overlay technique for locating hurricane centers. He compared center locations obtained by means of that technique with the center positions read from official storm tracks prepared "on a postanalysis basis" by the U.S. Weather Bureau National Hurricane Center and published each year in the *Monthly Weather Review*. Jordan found discrepancies in the center position which were substantially greater than the position errors cited by Senn and Hiser (1957). Jordan reported that in about half the cases the discrepancies were less than 40 km. In evaluating this result it must be borne in mind that the "official track positions" are not necessarily correct. In fact, considering the nature of the information used to construct them, one can be certain that the tracks are subject to position errors.

Following a suggestion by Jordan (1963), Siravamakrishnan and Selvam (1966) tested the spiral-overlay technique of hurricane-center location when used in conjunction with cloud photographs obtained by the TIROS weather satellite. The locations of, and changes of intensity of, a number of typical cyclones in the Indian Ocean were obtained successfully. It was concluded that the spiral-overlay scheme "is very useful in locating the storm center from TIROS photographs especially in sparse data regions."

Once a hurricane is located by means of either weather-satellite cameras or a radar, it is important to predict its motion and future positions. Standard weather observations for the construction of upper-level wind maps normally are taken every 12 hours. In many instances, the hurricane tracks change over time periods even smaller than an hour. Jordan and Stowell (1955) and Senn (1961) used radar data and examined fluctuations of the motions of the eyes of a few hurricanes. Senn concluded that, "significantly large and sometimes systematic variations in both the speed and direction of the radar eye exist" when they are observed on either a 5-minute or a 30-minute time base.

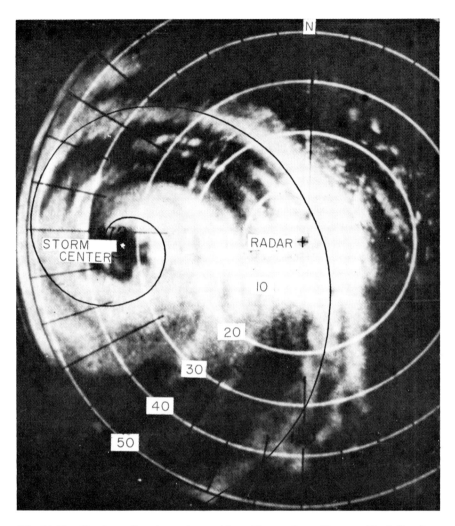

Fig. 11.23. Hurricane Connie as observed by a 10-cm radar at Hatteras, North Carolina, 12 August 1955. The precipitation band is fitted with a spiral of $\alpha = 15°$. Range markers are at 10-mile (about 16-km) intervals. From Senn and Hiser (1957).

Attempts were made by Senn (1966a) and Sadowski (1964) to find certain features of the radar picture of a hurricane which would indicate the future movement. Such factors as the following are thought to be of some help in predicting storm movement: the orientation of the prehurricane squall lines, the change in the eye-wall configuration, the location in the eye wall of maximum echo intensity. It appears that, to date, sufficient evidence has not been accumulated to formulate reliable rules for short-range forecasts of hurricane movement based only on radar observations.

In an earlier section of this chapter, a discussion was given of the correlation between echo and wind velocity. Various investigators have tracked radar echoes in hurricanes to obtain the pattern of wind velocities (Senn and Hiser 1960; Jordan 1960; Watanabe 1963). Senn (1966*b*) examined the vertical shear of the horizontal wind by means of radar data. Fujita et al. (1967) used radar and satellite cloud data to obtain the air-velocity field in a typhoon. From kinematic analyses they derived a picture of the three-dimensional structure of the storm. In addition, they devised a mathematical model of a tropical cyclone.

11.8 Observations of Cyclonic and Frontal Precipitation

During the late 1960s radar meteorologists began giving increasing attention to the properties of large-scale weather systems. In earlier years there had been some analyses of cyclonic weather systems, but the efforts, for the most part, were quite modest. One of the exceptions to this generalization was the research activities of Boucher (1957, 1958), who proposed a classification of the echo patterns associated with cyclones. It was based on observations collected near Boston by means of a vertically pointing 1.25-cm radar. This wavelength is seldom used now, but similar echo characteristics should be observed on the HIT displays of K-band radars.

Boucher (1957) classified the echoes into four basic types (fig. 11.24), according to the following definitions:

1. Closely-spaced but distinct cells or elements emanating from essentially a single level — the cell generating level being most commonly found at temperatures $-10°$ and $-15°C$ but ranging from $+4°$ to $-20°C$ and extending vertically from about 1 to 5 km.
2. Closely-spaced cells or elements originating from diverse levels, and consequently having a broader range of temperatures at the generating level, between $-5°$ and $-25°C$.
3. Uniform echoes with or without widely-spaced embedded streamers most frequently originating within a temperature range $-15°$ to $-30°C$.
4. Irregular (unstable) cells, with tops at different levels most frequently reaching temperatures below $-15°C$.

The synoptic weather patterns were divided into three classes:

Class A consisted of prewarm front or precyclonic patterns. In these cases, radar observations were taken with a surface low-pressure area

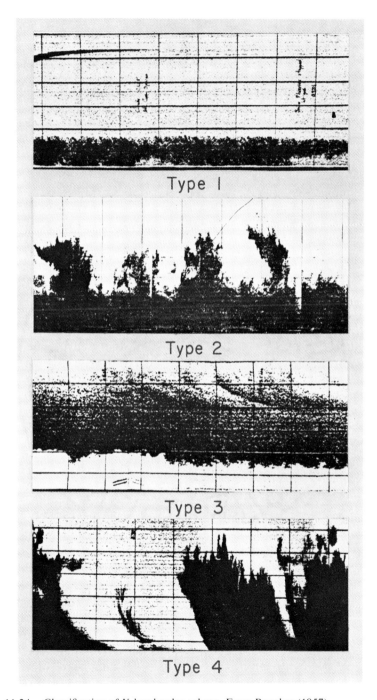

Fig. 11.24.   Classification of K-band radar echoes. From Boucher (1957).

west, southwest, south, or southeast of the station. This class was most frequent and occurred in 74 of the 170 situations studied.

Class B included cases in which a cyclone or trough, usually with a cold front, was approaching, passing, or moving away from the station. The center of low pressure was situated to the northwest, north, or northeast. This class occurred 37 times.

Class C included cases in which the center of low pressure was northeast or east of the station, with no fronts approaching the station. This class was observed 33 times.

Twenty-six of the surface maps could not be classified into any of these three categories.

Type 1 echoes were found most frequently with synoptic class C, i.e., in the rear of cyclones, and were associated with "either altocumulus or stratocumulus precipitans, often capped by a temperature inversion or a sharp moisture discontinuity which gives it its characteristic uniform top." Sometimes type 1 echoes were found with other synoptic classes, but in those situations the echoes originated in altocumulus clouds and hence at a higher altitude.

Type 2 echoes were usually associated with synoptic class A, generally close to the cyclone centers not far in advance of the surface warm fronts. Also, these echoes frequently were found within and behind surface troughs.

Type 3 echoes were almost always found with synoptic class A, well in advance of the surface warm front. The long, sloping streamers are of the type discussed in chapter 10.

Type 4 echoes were characteristic of convective clouds generally found in the summer season. It is evident that these echoes differ significantly from the essentially layer echoes in types 1–3. The clouds giving type 4 echoes were cumulus congestus and cumulonimbus, with vertical and horizontal dimensions of the same order of magnitude.

A generalized cyclone model was prepared by Boucher to show the distribution of echo types around a typical cyclone. As a cyclone approaches, the cloud forms are of a stable type, with cirrus streamers having smooth trajectories as ice particles fall into lower decks of altostratus. The appearance of the echo indicates little, if any, turbulence. Near the center of the cyclone, the cloud forms show more turbulent conditions. The clouds of the layer type—altostratus and nimbostratus clouds—have cumuliform protuberances from their tops. On the rear side of the cyclone, conditions again become stabilized, and the fairly uniform decks of altocumulus or stratocumulus precipitans predominate. Several case studies were made of cyclones passing over the radar station. Sometimes the change in echo type was quite abrupt. In one case the pattern changed from the smoothness of type 3 to the raggedness of type 2 in a few minutes, which suggests a sudden variation in the stability of the atmosphere.

Boucher also examined the rate of precipitation and concluded that the upper limit of the hourly rate of precipitation appeared to be a function of the depth of the precipitation echo.

Boucher (1958) carried out case studies of a number of New England cyclones. From PPI and RHI photographs he drew inferences about the precipitation processes involved and the patterns of vertical motion. Of particular interest was the observation that "the moderate to heavy rates of cyclonic precipitation, such as occur within 200 mi of a major cyclone of the northeaster type, are accompanied by the development of a precipitation system characterized by closely-spaced localized updrafts of the order of a few miles in diameter within the general cyclonic systems of rising motion." He also observed that in one storm the intensification of the cyclone was accompanied by an increase in the vertical extent of the echoes on the RHI and intensification of the echoes on the PPI. This work indicated how observations from a noncoherent radar can be used to study the behavior of cyclonic systems.

An interesting aspect of echoes of type 3 in figure 11.24 is the appearance of the nearly vertical protuberances extending downward from the base of the echo. Various names have been given to these extensions— "precipitans," "danglers," and "virga." In a talk at the Massachusetts Institute of Technology in 1955, R. H. Douglas and J. S. Marshall first applied the name "stalactites," and it was generally accepted. The origin of precipitation stalactites has been considered by various investigators. Atlas (1955) maintained that cooling by evaporating precipitation just below the cloud base leads to destabilization and convection through a narrow layer. He visualized that the overturning could cause a reduction in the vertical wind shear throughout the region. In addition, the upward motion could support particles until they grew large enough to fall. Their descent would be essentially vertical until they reached a lower layer of dry air, where they again would be subject to evaporation, and the entire process would be repeated. In stepwise fashion the lower boundary of precipitation would advance downward through the dry layer until it reached the ground. On the other hand, Marshall and Gordon (1957) expressed the opinion that the stalactites "can be attributed to downdrafts, resulting from evaporative sublimation."

Small-scale variations in radar reflectivity, air motions and precipitation in cyclone-scale weather systems have been examined by a number of authors. Tatehira (1966) employed a 10-cm radar on Mt. Fuji to study large rainbands. Foote (1968) analyzed the time and space perturbations of vertical particle velocities in "continuous" precipitation and found significant variations over distances of 2–3 km and 350–800 m.

Austin and Houze (1970) observed that practically all cyclonic storms in New England exhibited regions of precipitation covering areas of 10^2–10^3 km^2.

Doppler radar has begun to yield interesting details of the structures of medium and large-scale weather systems. Boucher et al. (1965) used data from a C-band pulsed-Doppler radar and the VAD technique to measure the wind pattern in precipitation on the forward side of an advancing cyclone in New England. Their observations, taken every 12 minutes for 7 hours, revealed marked changes in air motion over distances of about 5 km. In a later investigation employing the same radar, Boucher and Ottersten (1971) observed snow at altitudes below a kilometer and detected undulations in the wind velocity which they believed to be orographically generated wave phenomena.

In 1963 Tatehira and Fukatsu employed conventional weather data and noncoherent radar data to make a mesoscale analysis of a cold front. Subsequently, Browning and Harrold (1970) studied the three-dimensional airflow at a cold front by means of an X-band pulsed-Doppler radar. They made alternate series of observations parallel to and perpendicular to the front. The data indicated intense horizontal convergence (10^{-2} sec^{-1} averaged over 500 m vertically and horizontally), which was associated with updrafts up to 8 m/sec. This strongly ascending air was the source of convective clouds and precipitation (see fig. 11.25). Harrold and Browning (1969), by means of the same 3.2-cm Doppler radar, observed the time and space fluctuations of the horizontal wind in the lowest 1,500 m of the atmosphere during widespread precipitation. In a subsequent paper in 1969, they used the same equipment to examine small- and medium-scale air motions and precipitation patterns in a traveling wave. They used a scheme proposed by Caton (1963), a variation of the VAD technique, to measure divergence. Harrold and Browning (1969) reported maximum divergence values of about 2×10^{-4} sec^{-1}, a quantity of the same order as was found earlier by Caton (1963) and Harrold (1966). Wexler (1968), Wexler, Chmela, and Armstrong (1967), and Wexler (1970) used a 5.4-cm Doppler radar and VAD procedures to measure the patterns of radar reflectivity, wind velocity, and divergence in various weather systems. In the second paper Wexler, Chmela, and Armstrong observed a New England snowstorm for 6 hours during the passage of short wave troughs. They measured maximum divergence of about 2×10^{-4} sec^{-1}. Similar measurements were described by Wexler (1970) in a later paper.

Observations of widespread frontal precipitation in England obtained by the 3.2-cm Doppler radar used by Harrold and Browning (1967) were analyzed by Atlas et al. (1969). They noted medium- and small-scale perturbations in the wind filed in and near the melting level. The

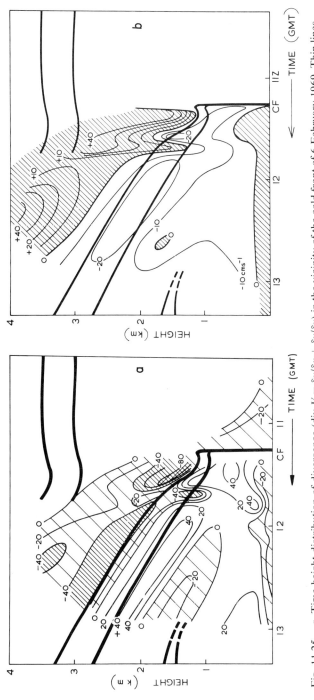

Fig. 11.25. *a*, Time-height distribution of divergence (div $V = \delta u/\delta x + \delta v/\delta y$) in the vicinity of the cold front of 6 February 1969. Thin lines are isopleths of div V at intervals of 20×10^{-5} sec^{-1}. Regions with div V negative are hatched; the hatching is widely spaced where div V is between zero and -40×10^{-5} sec^{-1} and closely spaced where div V is less than -40×10^{-5} sec^{-1}. *b*, Time-height distribution of w in the vicinity of the cold front of 6 February 1969, computed from (*a*). Thin lines are isotachs at intervals of 10 cm/sec. Regions of ascent are hatched. From Browning and Harrold (1970).

mesoscale perturbations of the wind were ascribed to pressure perturbations produced by horizontal variations of temperature resulting from variations of cooling by melting snow. The wind perturbations were reported to move with the velocity of the precipitation generators and to have amplitudes which increased as the precipitation rate increased. This explanation is similar to the earlier explanation for precipitation stalactites given by Atlas (1955).

In the 1969 study, Atlas and his colleagues also found that the wind velocity in the melting region exhibited marked perturbations over a scale of a few kilometers. This observation confirmed earlier reports by Harrold and Browning (1967), who found also that these small-scale features moved with the winds in the melting layer. Atlas et al. did not find this to be the case and proposed that the perturbations represented wave motions initiated by large-scale cooling.

The recent studies of the kinematic properties of weather systems by means of pulsed-Doppler radar are supplying the information which should help theoreticians to derive realistic mathematical models of frontal and cyclonic structures. A still greater understanding of the influence of cloud and precipitation processes on storm behavior should come from the use of satellite and radar data.

Nagle and Serebreny (1962) compared the observations made by a ground-based radar with cloud photographs from a satellite and showed that only a small fraction of the cloudy area yielded precipitation. Salman et al. (1969) also investigated how satellite cloud data and ground-based radar observations can be combined to analyze the characteristics of medium- and small-scale cloud systems.

It would be of interest to use observations from a satellite and from a network of Doppler radars to study the complete history of a cyclone. Released latent heat plays a vital role in cyclone development. With suitable observations, it should be possible to make estimates of the rate of formation and the fall of precipitation and estimates of released latent heat as a function of time. This information could then be compared with the deepening or filling of cyclonic systems. It should be possible to make fairly accurate calculations of energy exchanges in the storm. A better description of the evolution of the storm should lead to improved theoretical models. It is hoped that they will assist the weather forecaster and make it possible to assess the likelihood that cyclones can be beneficially modified.

12   Clear-Air Echoes

On many occasions, radars detect echoes from regions in the atmosphere which are devoid of clouds or contain clouds composed of particles too small to be detected. Some of the earliest observations of this type were reported by Friend (1939, 1940, 1949). He ascribed them to sharp gradients of temperature and humidity which could not be measured by the slowly responding sensing elements in a radiosonde. Friend speculated that radar could be used for the meteorological sounding of the atmosphere.

As the detection sensitivities of radar have increased, the number of observations of clear-air echoes also has increased. The absence of a target readily detectable by visual means inspired early observers to employ names such as "ghost echoes" or "phantom echoes," but for many years it has been general to refer to them as "angel echoes."

In recent years speculation about the origin of angel echoes has been replaced with a widespread acceptance that they are caused primarily by insects, birds, or regions of the atmosphere where there are strong refractive-index gradients. Each of these targets produces characteristic echoes which can be identified when appropriate radars are used to make the observations. Since the observations are consistent with theory, it generally is believed that clear-air echoes can be explained satisfactorily. Since the middle 1960s there have been substantial efforts to employ radar observations of clear-air echoes to observe air motions. Particular attention is being given to such phenomena as convection, wave motions, and clear-air turbulence.

12.1 Types of Angel Echoes

Clear-air echoes have been observed on radars operating in a variety of modes, either with fixed antenna beams or with beams scanning in azimuth or elevation. As noted in an excellent review by Hardy and Katz (1969), a wide variety of echo shapes has been observed, and as will be seen below they have been given distinctive names. Nevertheless, it

now appears reasonable to classify angel echoes into two broad categories: (1) dot angels (or point angels), and (2) angels having substantial
lateral or vertical extents. The first category is ascribed to the backscattering by discrete, single targets such as birds and insects. The second
category of angels is usually caused by inhomogeneities of refractive
index but may also be produced by large numbers of birds or insects
dispersed in such a fashion that their spacings are generally less than the
resolution distance of the radar.

12.2 Dot Angels

Dot, or point, angels appear on a scope as small echoes whose dimensions are essentially determined by the pulse length and beam width of
the radar. The dimensions of the target are small with respect to the
resolution distances of the radar.

Dot angels have been observed often by means of vertically pointing
radar sets (fig. 12.1). Some of the early studies employed K-band radar,
but the echoes are readily detected on longer wave radars. Dot angels
also have been detected when the radar antenna was scanning in azimuth
or elevation and have been followed by means of automatic-tracking
radar equipment (e.g., Roelofs 1963).

One of the earliest comprehensive studies of angel echoes was made
by Plank (1956), who also presented a historical survey of earlier observations. He employed a 1.25-cm radar and observed angel echoes
on 57 days over a period of 15 months. He calculated the backscattering
cross sections of insects and birds and found that his radar set could
detect them in some circumstances. Plank stated, "It seems justifiable
to conclude that insects and birds are valid angel sources which contribute importantly to angel activity." Some years earlier, this view was
expressed in even stronger terms by Crawford (1949), who observed insects in the beam of a searchlight and at the same time detected them on
radars operating at 1.25 and 3.2 cm. He concluded that possibly the only
source of dot-angel echoes was flying insects and birds.

From a consideration of the habits of insects and birds likely to be
present in the Boston area, however, Plank (1956) concluded that "it
does not appear possible to explain *all* angel activity using the insect-bird
hypothesis." On the other hand, on almost all days it was possible for
large gradients of refractive index to exist.

During the 1960s many investigators, operating equipment at various
wavelengths, measured the radar cross sections, σ, of angel echoes. The
data are shown in figure 12.2. Also depicted are the cross sections of
typical insects and birds. Over the years most observations of dot angels
were obtained by means of radars operating at 3 cm or less. The reason

(a)

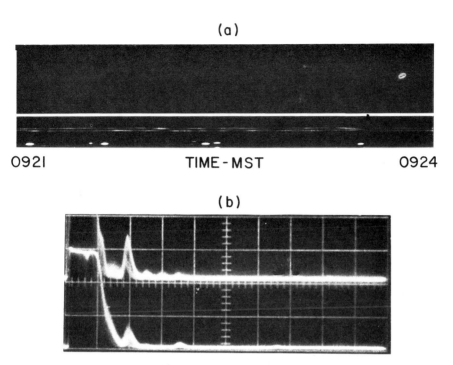

0921   TIME - MST   0924

(b)

Fig. 12.1. Angel echoes obtained by means of a vertically pointing 3-cm radar near Tucson, Arizona: *a,* Dot angels near the ground with a layer of angel echoes about 1.6 km above the ground on 10 October 1962. The solid line is a calibration signal. See Battan (1963*b*). *b,* Dot angel on A-scope on 7 August 1967. Lower trace shows signal in plane perpendicular to plane of polarization of radar. Height markers are at intervals of 1,000 feet (about 305 m). See Lofgren and Battan (1969).

for this is found in the sensitivity of the equipment and the wavelength dependence of σ. As noted by Hardy and Katz (1969), the 0.86-cm AN/TPQ-11 radar can easily detect a single mosquito at a range greater than 2 km.

Before the development of very sensitive equipment, dot-angel detection at wavelengths of 10 cm and larger was rare because of the small backscattering cross sections of individual targets at these wavelengths. In the case of insects, Rayleigh backscattering would prevail, and hence the backscattering cross section would be proportional to λ^{-4}.

When atmospheric scientists at the Air Force Cambridge Research Laboratories began using the ultrasensitive 10- and 71.5-cm radar sets at Wallops Island, Virginia, angel echoes were observed commonly at these long wavelengths (Atlas, Hardy, and Konrad 1966; Hardy, Atlas, and Glover 1966; Glover et al. 1966). Simultaneous observations at these wavelengths and at 3.2 cm for the first time made possible an

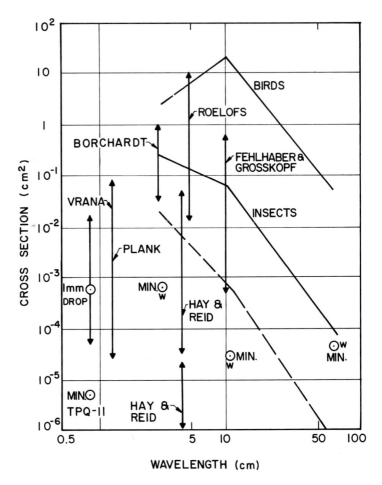

Fig. 12.2. Cross sections of dot angels, insects, and birds as a function of wavelength. The insect and bird cross sections are illustrated schematically. The minimum detectable cross sections for the AN/TPQ-11 radar and the Wallops Island radars are indicated by MIN. TPQ–11 and MIN. *W* respectively. From Hardy and Katz (1969).

adequate analysis of the wavelength dependence of the backscattering cross section of angel echoes.

Hardy, Atlas, and Glover (1966) concluded that there are two kinds of angel echoes. Type I echoes appear as incoherent echoes at long ranges (r) or at wide beam widths (θ), but when observed at high resolution, namely, small r or θ, the echoes are coherent. Furthermore, at wavelengths between 3 and 10, σ varies between λ^{-1}, and λ^{-2}; at λ between 70 and 71, σ varies between λ^{-3} and λ^{-4}. They concluded that such targets are large insects or birds. Type II echoes, to be discussed later, are incoherent at all ranges, show little wavelength dependence, and generally are weak or not detected at 3 cm. They are ascribed to backscattering by refractive-index fluctuations in the atmosphere.

Deam and LaGrone (1965) observed dot angels at 3.3 cm and 9.1 cm and suggested, as considered earlier by LaGrone, Deam, and Walker (1964), that insects were the source of dot angels. They were convinced that the targets were particulate matter.

The data in figure 12.2 show many measurements made by various investigators. In the K-band region, Vrana (1961) and Plank (1956) found backscattering cross sections between about 2×10^{-5} and 8×10^{-2} cm². At wavelengths between 3 and 10 cm Hay and Reid (1962), Borchardt (1962), Roelofs (1963), and Fehlhaber and Grosskopf (1964) reported cross sections between 10^{-6} and 10 cm².

The generalized curve for birds is an approximation because of the large variation of sizes and the dependence of σ on the shape and orientation. These data were collected by Konrad and Hicks (1966) and Glover and Hardy (1966). Hardy and Katz (1969) speculated that the peak in the bird curve at 10 cm could be ascribed to "the complicated wavelength dependence exhibited by Mie-type scatterers."

The curves for insects were assembled from data collected by means of the Wallops Island radars (characteristics given in the Appendix) by Glover et al. (1966). Live insects were dropped from an airplane and tracked as they descended toward the ground. Simultaneous measurements of their cross sections were made at wavelengths 3.2, 10.7, and 71.5 cm. The two curves in figure 12.2 show the probable range of values for fairly large insects. In their tests Glover et al. tracked such insects as the hawkmoth (*manduca sexta*) and the worker honey bee (*apis mellifera*).

Laboratory measurements of the scattering cross sections of ten insect types were made by Hajovsky, Deam, and LaGrone (1966), who used a 3.2-cm microwave test facility. The insects ranged in length from 5 to 20 mm and in diameter from 1 to 6 mm. Longitudinal (σ_L) and transverse backscattering cross sections (σ_T) were measured. The values of σ_L ranged from 0.02 to 1.22 cm² except for the longest insect (a blue-winged locust), which had $\sigma_L = 9.6$ cm². The values of σ_T ranged from 0.01 to 0.12 cm², again with one exception, the same blue-winged locust, with $\sigma_T = 0.96$ cm². It is evident that for the most part the measurements by Hajovsky, Deam, and LaGrone are in agreement with those shown in figure 12.2, but their largest ones extend substantially above the Hardy and Katz (1969) insect curve. This can be attributed to the fact that the largest insects used by Hajovsky, Deam, and LaGrone were larger than those observed by Glover et al. (1966).

Measurements of the depolarization of X-band radar signals by dot angels were made by Chernikov (1966), Chernikov and Shupiatskii

(1967), and Lofgren and Battan (1969). The investigations employed
bistatic vertically pointing X-band radar systems and obtained similar
results. Figure 12.3 shows the frequency distribution of depolarization
caused by dot angels over the Arizona desert. The angels had cross
sections ranging from 8×10^{-5} to 1.3×10^{-1} cm². A mean depolarization
of -10.3 dB was calculated under the assumption that all the angels were
present simultaneously. It was assumed, further, that the targets were
randomly oriented, and it was found that the mean depolarization could
have been produced by uniform prolate water scatterers with an axial
ratio of 2.8, according to the calculations of Atlas, Kerker, and Hitschfeld (1953). The axial ratios of those insects listed by Hajovsky, Deam,
and LaGrone (1966), which also are common in Arizona, are 2.2, 2.2,
3.0, 3.5, and 9.3. The cross-polarization analyses support the conclusion
that most dot angels can be insects.

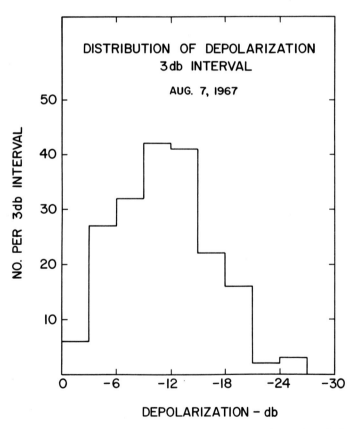

Fig. 12.3.   The distribution of the depolarization of dot-angel echoes. From Lofgren and
Battan (1969).

Measurements of the vertical velocities of angel targets were made by
Battan (1963*b*) and Lofgren and Battan (1969) by means of a vertically
pointing pulsed-Doppler radar. For the most part the targets had vertical
speeds between −3 and +3 m/sec. Figure 12.4 shows the frequency of
angel-echo observations as a function of altitude and vertical velocity
on 10 October 1962. This is the same day on which figure 12.1, *a*, was
obtained. The dot angels at altitudes below 1.4 km were ascending at
0.5–1 m/sec. On 7 August 1967 there were alternate periods, 10–20
minutes long, when the movement of the dot-angel echoes was mostly
downward at 0.5–1.0 m/sec, then upward at the same speeds, then downward again. These results are not inconsistent with the notion that insects were being transported by convective currents. It is interesting
to note in figure 12.4 that the vertical velocites in the layer of angel
echoes, a part of which is shown in figure 12.1, *a*, move both upward
and downward, with the upward movement occurring at a somewhat
higher frequency.

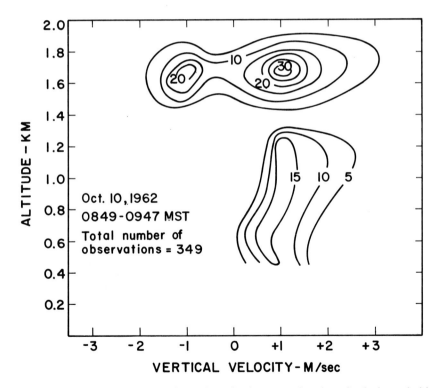

Fig. 12.4.   Frequency of observations of angel echoes as a function of velocity and altitude observed on 10 October 1962 in Arizona by means of a vertically pointing X-band
pulsed Doppler radar. From Battan (1963*b*).

There is little doubt that almost all dot angels are attributable to individual, widely spaced insects or, in some instances, birds. One such
target in a volume defined by the pulse length and the beam width is
adequate to give an echo at the ranges and altitudes of most dot angels,
below about 2 km. For this reason, it is not surprising that the sources
of dot angels are seldom seen.

During the period 1960–65 there was a series of articles which offered
an explanation of dot angels based on specular reflection from regions
of the atmosphere having high refractive-index gradients (see Atlas 1964
for a discussion). Apparently excessively large gradients of refractive
index are needed to explain the observed cross sections unless unreasonable assumptions about the shape and character of the reflecting surface are made. Furthermore, the multiwavelength observations at Wallops
Island show wavelength dependence which is not consistent with the
theory of specular reflection from curved surfaces. It now generally is
held that dot angels cannot be explained as specular reflections from sharp
refractive-index gradients.

Once it is accepted that dot-angel echoes are caused by slow-flying
insects, the insects may be used as tracers, and Doppler radars can map
the wind field. In such operations it is essential to recognize uncertainties caused by the flight characteristics of the insects. These uncertainties
can be large in some cases because, as shown by Fowler and LaGrone
(1969), some insects can fly at substantial speeds. For example, *Apis*
worker honeybees have been found to have average flight speeds from
2.5 to 7.2 m/sec and maximum speeds up to 8 m/sec. Incidentally, birds
have flight speeds of about 10–20 m/sec (Eastwood 1967) and hence are
not good air tracers.

Lhermitte (1966a) made unique detailed measurements of the low-
level jet stream over Oklahoma (fig. 8.16). He speculated that the minute
targets, whose large number allowed him to use the VAD technique, were
particulate matter or insects. Insects the size of a housefly (with σ about
10^{-2} cm^3) would have been large enough to account for the observed
reflectivities. Other studies of the horizontal wind field by means of the
VAD observations of dot angels were made by Lhermitte and Dooley
(1966) and Browning and Atlas (1966).

Atlas, Harris, and Richter (1970) used a sensitive, high-resolution
FM-CW radar to measure the horizontal speed of dot angels. Their
technique requires accurate measurements of target range, variation with
time of relative signal intensity, and a knowledge of the beam width of
the radar. They reported that the echoes, assumed to be insects, had
cross sections of 10^{-5}–10^{-3} cm^2 at a wavelength of 10 cm, vertical speeds
from -0.86 to $+0.75$ m/sec, and horizontal speeds between 0.9 and
5.0 m/sec. These results are consistent with the data given by Fowler
and LaGrone (1969).

Various authors, particularly Ottersten (1970*a*) and, much earlier, Plank (1956) and Atlas (1959a), examined the variation with time of day and season and altitude of angel echoes.

12.3 Angels in Layers

Some of the earliest observations of angel echoes showed them to be structured in the form of horizontal layers. They were found to correspond in height to regions of large refractive-index gradients. Figure 12.5, from Lane and Meadows (1963), is an example of a layer of angel echoes from clear sky observed by means of a vertically pointing 10-cm radar. The vertical profile of refractive index in *N* units was measured with a Birnbaum 3-cm refractometer mounted on an airplane.

Layer echoes have also been obtained by means of vertically scanning antennas. Among the most striking are those collected by the sensitive radar sets at Wallops Island, Virginia. Figure 12.6 shows a sharp echo layer, about 1 km above the ground, as it appeared on a 10.7-cm radar. As Hardy and Glover (1966) noted, it coincided in height with a pronounced temperature inversion. Atlas, Hardy, and Konrad (1966) and Atlas et al. (1966) detected the tropopause layer by means of ultrasensitive 10.7-cm and 71.5-cm radars.

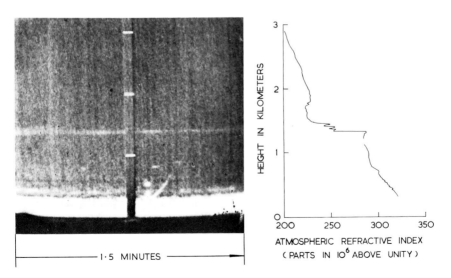

Fig. 12.5.   Simultaneous radar and refractometer soundings at 1755 GMT on 29 August 1961. From Lane and Meadows (1963). Reproduced by permission of the Radio and Space Research Station of the U.K. Science Research Council.

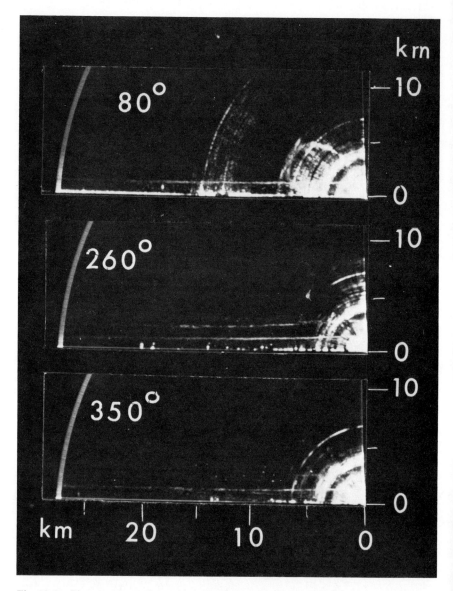

Fig. 12.6.   Photographs at three azimuths of the range-height indicators at a wavelength of 10.7 cm at Wallops Island, Va., 0530 EST, 4 September 1965. The sky was perfectly clear at the time of the observation. The layer near 1 km is coincident with a very pronounced inversion. The circumferential arcs at short ranges are ground echoes seen by the side lobes. From Hardy and Glover (1966).

Although the association of angel-echo layers and layers of strong refractive index has been recognized since the early observations of Friend in about 1940, there has been considerable uncertainty about the reflection mechanisms. Early theoretical studies by Gordon (1949), Swingle (1953), and Bauer (1956) yielded expressions for calculating the refractive-index gradients which would be required to yield the observed power-reflection coefficients. In these treatments it was assumed that the reflection was specular. The disturbing feature of these analyses is that excessively large gradients were found to be necessary. For example, Plank, Cunningham, and Campen (1957) found from Swingle's equation that, to account for observed angel echoes, gradients of 20, 6.2, and 2 N units per centimeter would be needed at wavelengths of 1.25, 3.2, and 10 cm, respectively.

In a series of papers which he summarized in a later survey article, Atlas (1964) attempted to overcome the difficulty of the extreme gradients of N by assuming partial reflections from surfaces concave to the radar. It is evident that smooth layers of high refractive-index gradients approaching a hemispherical shape would have greatly enhanced back-scattering cross sections. Under real conditions in the atmosphere, however, the constraints required in the theory are not likely to apply. It is now generally held by most investigators that specular reflections seldom, if ever, can produce layer angels. Instead it has been convincingly shown that they can be explained as backscattering from regions of refractive-index inhomogeneities. Booker and Gordon (1950) developed a theory to show how such inhomogeneities could explain the forward scattering of radio waves beyond the horizon.

Various investigators analyzed the backscattering of electromagnetic waves by a turbulent medium. Notable among them is Tatarski (1961), whose work has been used by a number of scientists to explain layer angels in the atmosphere (Smith and Rogers 1963; Atlas, Hardy, and Naito 1966; Atlas, Hardy, and Konrad 1966; Hardy, Atlas, and Glover 1966; Ottersten 1969, 1970a).

As shown in chapter 3, the refractive index, n, in the atmosphere depends on the vapor pressure, temperature, and pressure. In the lower atmosphere, water vapor differences are most important in accounting for differences in n, but at higher altitudes where vapor pressures are low, changes in n are mostly a result of changes in temperature. In the discussion of the propagation of a radar beam through the atmosphere, it was assumed that n varied smoothly with height and was spherically stratified. For many purposes such an assumption is valid. On the other hand, if through a region of the atmosphere where the spatial gradient of n is high there is also a considerable amount of turbulence, the irregular, small-scale fluctuations of n can lead to appreciable scattering of the incident microwaves.

Tatarski (1961) showed that the reflectivity in the backscattered direction is given by

$$\eta = \frac{\pi^2}{2} k^4 F_n^*(k),$$ (12.1)

where k is the wave number and $k = 4\pi/\lambda$ and F_n^* is called the space spectrum, or the "spatial power-spectral density, and is a three-dimensional representation of the refractive index field and is obtained by a Fourier transform of the three-dimensional refractive index convariance function" (Ottersten 1970a).

The spectrum $F_n^*(k)$ extends over a wide range of scales, but only the Fourier mode with a wavelength of $\lambda/2$ contributes significantly to the backscattering. Over the inertial subrange limited by wave numbers k_0 and k_m, one can write $F_n^*(k)$ in terms of $F_n(k)$, the so-called normalized one-dimensional spectrum of refractivity. Turbulence is assumed to be homogeneous and isotropic over this range of wave numbers. Wave number k_0 is associated with macroscale eddies of scale L_0 and is the scale beyond which turbulence is no longer isotropic. Eddies with wave numbers beyond k_m lose energy rapidly by viscosity. The turbulent eddies in the inertial subrange do not lose much energy as a result of viscosity. Instead, there is a transfer of energy from eddies of scale greater than L_0, through the inertial subrange to the smaller-scale eddies.

Batchelor (1955) and Silverman (1956) showed that

$$F_n(k) = \frac{2}{3} k_0^2 \, k^{-5/3}.$$ (12.2)

From Obukhov (1949), Hardy, Atlas, and Glover (1966) obtained

$$F_n^*(k) = 0.033 \, C_n^2 k^{-11/3},$$ (12.3)

which is valid in the inertial subrange. The quantity C_n^2 is a measure of the mean-square fluctuations of the refractive index as a function of distance $(\overline{\Delta n^2})$ and is given by

$$C_n^2 = 1.56 \, (\overline{\Delta n^2}) \, k_0^{2/3} = 5.26 \, (\overline{\Delta n^2}) \, L_0^{-2/3},$$ (12.4)

where $k_0 = \dfrac{2\pi}{L_0}$.

By substitution, it is found that the reflectivity

$$\eta = 0.39 \, C_n^2 \, \lambda^{-1/3}$$ (12.5)

and hence that

$$\eta = 0.61 \, (\overline{\Delta n^2}) \, k_0^{2/3} \, \lambda^{-1/3}.$$ (12.6)

Saxton et al. (1964), who used the same theory described by Tatarski (1961), also derived an expression for η in terms of the one-dimensional normalized spectral density of the mean-square fluctuations of refractive index.

The validity of this theory has been tested by comparing the reflectivity of angel echoes at several wavelengths. Atlas et al. (1966) showed that the reflectivity of the tropopause decreased by a factor of between 2 and 4 as λ went from 10.7 to 71.5 cm, while theory predicted a decrease of 1.84. The discrepancy was regarded to be within experimental error. The same investigators found a 10.7-cm value of $\eta = 7.7 \times 10^{-17}$ cm^{-1}. Substituting this quantity in equation (12.4) yielded $C_n^2 = 4.4 \times 10^{-16}$ cm$^{-2/3}$. This falls within the range of C_n^2 of 10^{-16}–10^{-14} cm$^{-2/3}$ estimated theoretically by Atlas, Hardy, and Naito (1966).

Lane (1967) employed a balloon-borne refractometer to measure the refractivity structure in the vicinity of elevated, stable angel-echo layers which were being detected by a vertically pointing 10-cm radar. He performed power-spectrum analyses on twenty records to obtain the mean-square fluctuation in refractivity and calculated the quantities η and C_n^2 at $\lambda = 10$ cm. Reflectivities ranged from about 10^{-15} to 5×10^{-14} cm^{-1} while C_n^2 was between about 10^{-14} and 5×10^{-13} cm$^{-2/3}$. In Sweden, Ottersten (1964) reported that at 10 cm the strongest reflectivities from layer angels were about 10^{-14} cm^{-1}.

Kropfli et al. (1968) carried out an experimental test of the theory of backscattering by refractivity fluctuations. They made measurements of radar reflectivity and at the same time used a microwave refractometer to measure the spatial variations of refractive index. The refractometer was suspended about 25 m below a helicopter which was flown along an inbound radial course over a range interval of 28 km–7.5 km. The helicopter was automatically tracked by the 10.7-cm radar at Wallops Island while it simultaneously measured the radar-signal strength at a fixed-range increment ahead of the refractometer.

In this investigation, Kropli et al. calculated the backscatter of microwaves by homogeneous, isotropic refractivity fluctuations by means of an expression ascribed to Saxton et al. (1964),

$$\eta = \frac{\pi}{8} k^2 \, (\overline{\Delta n^2}) \, F_n \, (k), \qquad (12.7)$$

where, as noted above, $F_n(k)$ is the normalized, one-dimensional wavenumber spectrum of refractive index along the direction of propagation evaluated at wave number $k \; (= 4\pi/\lambda)$.

From the refractometer measurements, Kropfli et al. (1968) evaluated $(\overline{\Delta n^2}) F_n(k)$. The available data sample did not yield a value at the appropriate wave number k, and hence it was necessary to extrapolate it by using the $-5/3$ law (eq. [12.2]). Measured 10.7-cm radar reflectivity was then plotted against the extrapolated value. It was found that the observed values of η were within 3 dB of the predicted values in almost all cases. The agreement was striking, considering the need for extrapolation and other uncertainties. For example, the radar sampled a much larger volume than the refractometer. The results strongly support the validity of the theory. In this test the maximum measured C_n^2 was about 2×10^{-14} cm$^{-2/3}$.

The excellent results obtained by Kropfli et al. (1968) serve to confirm the validity of the $-5/3$ law expressed in equation (12.2). Further confirmation is found in the work of Chernikov et al. (1969), who calculated the spectral-power density of turbulence as a function of wave number. They made simultaneous measurements by means of aircraft and a Doppler radar observing chaff dispersed continuously for 40–50 minutes from a captive balloon.

Hardy and Katz (1969) asserted that layer-angel echoes produced by regions of refractive-index inhomogeneities usually have C_n^2 between 10^{-15} and 10^{-13}, but in extreme cases C_n^2 may be as high as 10^{-12} cm$^{-2/3}$ (see fig. 12.7).

12.4 Lines of Echoes on Conventional Radars

It now is evident that angel echoes can be explained either as backscattering from discrete targets, such as insects or birds, or as reflections from regions having highly perturbed fields of refractive index. In the light of this knowledge, it is possible to explain observations of angel echoes found to be of particular interest or of those with curious structures.

Several investigators reported ring-shaped angel echoes which expanded with time (Elder 1957; Ligda 1958; Harper 1959; Eastwood, Bell and Phelps 1959; Eastwood, Isted and Rider, 1962). They are illustrated in figure 12.8. Elder (1957) observed that on the 23.4-cm AN/FPS-3 they appeared to start at a point and to form a ring which expanded rapidly. After one ring had grown to a diameter of several kilometers, a second ring sometimes formed. The rings attained diameters of tens of kilometers. As many as four rings were observed to originate at nearly the same point within an interval of 3–5 minutes. The average radial velocity of the ring segments was about 22 m/sec.

Eastwood, Isted and Rider (1962) made a very detailed analysis of ring angels. They observed them often on a 23-cm radar. In one incident there were 18 rings which formed at intervals of 2.5 minutes and expanded to a maximum diameter of about 30 km. Simultaneous radar and visual observations convincingly showed that the rings were composed of waves of starlings (*Sturnus vulgaris*) flying away from roosting

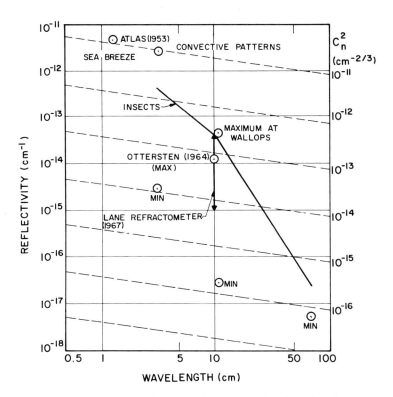

Fig. 12.7. Radar reflectivity as a function of wavelength for clear-air radar echoes. The values of the three-dimensional fluctuations in refractive index, $C_n{}^2$, as derived from theory, are shown on the scale at the right. The reflectivity varies approximately as wavelength to the power of $-1/3$ for scattering from refractive-index fluctuations and as wavelength to the power of -4 for scattering from insects. Values of reflectivity derived from direct measurements of refractivity spectra are consistent with the reflectivities observed with radar. The points labeled MIN correspond to the minimum detectable cross sections (fig. 12.2) for the 3.2, 10.7, and 71.5-cm radars at Wallops Island (see Appendix). After Hardy and Katz (1969).

areas at about sunrise. The average flight speed was about 21 m/sec. Harper (1959) had reported earlier that echoes in the forms of expanding arcs also were caused by bands of starlings.

Ligda (1958) concluded that the ring angels he observed in Texas were caused by red-winged blackbirds (*Agelaeus pheoniceus*) flying from a common roosting ground.

There is little doubt that the occurrence of "ring angels" can be associated with diverging rings of widely spaced birds.

Atlas (1960) used a 1.25-cm radar set near the shoreline in the vicinity of New Bedford, Massachusetts, and pointed the beam toward the sea on a day when a sea breeze was expected. A series of waves of echoes was observed moving toward the shore. They first appeared at a distance

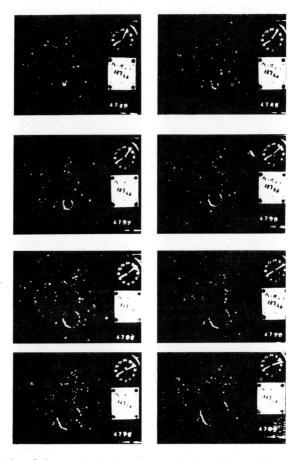

Fig. 12.8.   Series of phtographs showing ring-angel echoes observed with an L-band radar set. From Elder (1957).

of about 3.2 km out to sea (4 km from the radar set). The echoes had the incoherent characteristics of precipitation echoes but were occurring in clear air. Almost immediately after the echoes reached the vicinity of the radar, the temperature started falling rapidly, the wind shifted, the relative humidity increased, and microwave refractometer readings increased rapidly. Over a period of 45 minutes, the index of refraction increased by 30 N units, while the temperature dropped 3.4° C and the vapor pressure rose 1.02 mb. Substitution of these changes of temperature and vapor pressure in equation (3.11) yields a change of only about 9 N units. The discrepancy was probably a result of differences in the response times of the instruments involved.

Radar observations of the sea-breeze discontinuity were obtained by pointing the radar beam either horizontally or vertically and recording the echoes on a range-time facsimile recorder (fig. 12.9). The approaching sea-breeze echoes are plainly evident. From the slope of the echo, one can calculate that the speed of advance of the sea-breeze front was about 4 m/sec. This value is in close agreement with the observed wind component. The echoes observed when the beam was pointing vertically, unlike those obtained when it was pointing horizontally, were steady for periods of many seconds.

Newell (1958*b*) observed the "sea breeze front" by means of 3.21- and 10.7-cm radars. He measured the reflectivities, η, at both wavelengths and calculated the quantity κ defined by

$$\frac{\eta_3}{\eta_{10}} = \left(\frac{\lambda_3}{\lambda_{10}}\right)^{\kappa}. \tag{12.8}$$

The coefficients κ in the sea-breeze observations were +0.9, +1.5 and −1.8. In Rayleigh scattering, $\kappa = -4$. These results suggested that the sea-breeze echoes were not caused by insects, which were small with respect to the wavelength. On the other hand, if backscattering were caused by fluctuations in the refractive index, κ would have been −0.33, according to equation (12.6).

Goetis (1964) used the same radar equipment employed by Newell and examined six sea breezes. He found values of κ ranging from −4 to +2, and, because the refractive-index gradients needed for specular reflection would have been excessive, Goetis (1964) concluded that a more satisfactory explanation was that the sea-breeze echoes were caused by insects and birds. Goetis (1964) reported reflectivities at 10.7 cm ranging from 10^{-9} to 10^{-10} cm^{-1} and at 3.21 cm ranging from

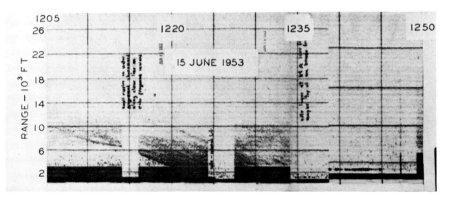

Fig. 12.9.   A range-time record of sea-breeze echoes observed with a horizontally pointing 1.25-cm radar set. During three brief periods at 1215, 1225, and 1235, the radar beam was pointing vertically. From Atlas (1960).

10^{-10} to 10^{-11} cm^{-1}. Such high reflectivities were unlikely to be produced by refractive-index fluctuations, according to Hardy and Katz (1969). They, too, proposed that for this reason the sea-breeze echoes probably were caused by insects in sufficient concentrations that there were a number of them within each sampling volume.

A land-breeze front was observed by means of the ultrasensitive 10.7-cm radar at Wallops Island, Virginia (Meyer 1971). Echoes were recorded on PPI and RHI.

Various investigators have reported long, thin lines of angel echoes on the PPI scopes of radars operating at wavelengths between 3 and 72 cm (fig. 12.10). The lines are sometimes seen to be associated with the

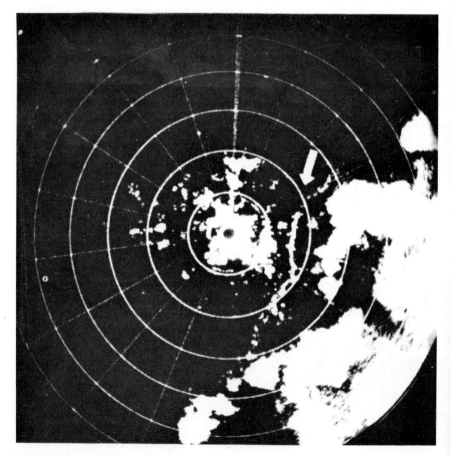

Fig. 12.10.   Example of a thin line of angel echoes (*arrow*) in the vicinity of strong thunderstorm echoes. From Harper (1960), Crown copyright reproduced by permission of the Controller, Her Majesty's Stationery Office.

boundary between the cool air flowing outward from the base of a group of thunderstorms and the surrounding warmer air. At the boundary, there may be a sharp gradient of average refractive index, a turbulent environment, and, one would expect, an upward motion of warm air over the boundary. As noted by Atlas (1964), most observers attributed such angel echoes to backscattering caused by the strong gradients of refractive index at the boundary (e.g., Leach 1957; Luckenback 1958; Brown 1960). On the other hand, Harper (1958, 1960) and others concluded that the lines of echoes could be caused by birds. In one instance, when a well-defined line echo moved over the radar station, Harper employed a telescope and saw many swifts darting in and out of the field of view. He concluded that the echoes indicated the presence of thermals causing the lifting of insects. Certain types of birds, e.g., the swift, feed on these insects. In general, they are restricted to altitudes below 30 m but on occasion may reach several hundred meters.

Harper's observations certainly showed that, on at least some occasions, there are enough birds and insects to account for line echoes. For reasons noted earlier, it is not likely that they could be produced by specular reflections from regions of large gradients of refractive index. It is likely, however, as concluded by Berson and Simpson (1971), that in some cases turbulent air motions across the boundaries between cool and warm air may produce spectra of refractivity eddies capable of backscattering detectable power.

The lines of angels associated with thunderstorms sometimes are irregular in shape and intensity. Straighter, more uniform lines of angel echoes have been observed along cloud-free cold fronts (Ligda and Bigler 1958; Fujita 1970; and others). The one observed on the scope of a 3.2-cm AN/CPS-9 by Ligda and Bigler (1958) lasted for more than 2 hours. For a better understanding of the backscattering in this type of case, quantitative measurements need to be made of the structure of the refractive-index field in the reflecting zones. In view of the persistent nature of some of these lines, this does not appear to be an impractical task. At the same time, observations could be made of the insect population in the echo zone.

12.5 Study of Convection in Clear Air

As early as 1957, Harper, Ludlam, and Saunders observed 10-cm echoes which appeared in the form of a mantle when viewed in vertical cross section. The echoes corresponded in position to the edges and tops of cumulus clouds, but Harper, Ludlam and Saunders (1957) expressed the opinion that the echoes were associated with strong refractive-index gradients normally found near the surfaces of rapidly building cumulus. Atlas (1959*b*), who observed mantle echoes on the powerful 10-cm AN/FPS-6 radar, concurred in that opinion.

Since the ultrasensitive radar sets at Wallops Island, Virginia, have become available for use by meteorologists, it has become possible to obtain striking observations of convective currents in the clear sky. Hardy and Ottersten (1969) reported that during cloudless summer days convective echo patterns are observed consistently on the scopes of the 10.7-cm radar. As shown in figure 12.11, the echoes appear in the lower atmosphere and have a wavelike appearance. The target reflectivities increase with wavelength, which indicates that backscattering is not produced by small scatterers.

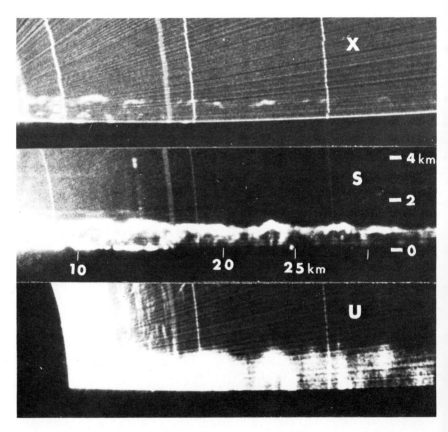

Fig. 12.11. Simultaneous photographs of range-height indicators at wavelengths of 3.2 cm (X-band), 10.7 cm (S-band), and 71.5 cm (UHF) taken while the sky was clear, 0850 EST, 10 May 1966, at Wallops Island, Virginia; azimuth 250°. The definite wavelike perturbations are the boundaries of convective cells which have the doughnut shape in figure 12.12. From Hardy and Ottersten (1969).

The horizontal structure of the convective echoes is indicated on the PPI photograph in figure 12.12. The irregular circles of echo about 1–3 km in diameter and several hundred meters in height observed by Atlas and Hardy (1966), Hardy and Ottersten (1969), and others are associated with rising thermals. The echoes persist for periods as long as 20–30 minutes. The schematic cross section in figure 12.13 was constructed from the analysis of RHI observations and PPI observations taken at various elevation angles. These data show that the echo-free regions in the nearly circular echoes decrease in size at higher altitudes. Also, the overall diameter of the echo decreases. This feature was clearly illustrated by Konrad (1970), who employed an instrumented airplane to show that the so-called doughnut-shaped echoes were associated with the edges of convective cells. He found that the convective cells were cool and moist relative to the environment.

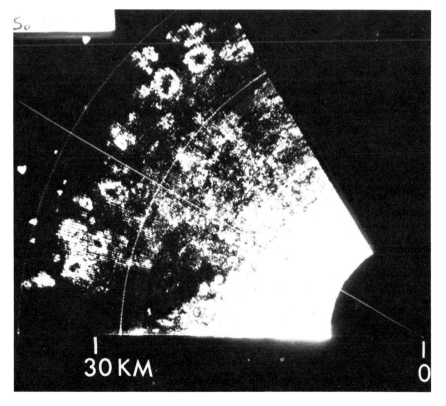

Fig. 12.12.   Sector PPI photo at 3-degree elevation angle taken at 1052 EST, 15 August 1967, with the 10.7-cm radar at Wallops Island. The strobe line indicates the 300-degree azimuth. Echoes in horizontal section at the appropriate altitude and range display the characteristic doughnut shape. From Hardy and Ottersten (1969).

In the schematic diagram in figure 12.13 the strongest gradient of refractive index, n, would be expected at the summit of the convective cell. The gradients would decrease around the periphery of the cell and would be quite small at the interior.

Harrold and Browning (1971) showed that, on some days, a high-power, high-gain 10.7-cm radar in England detects almost continuous layers of clear-air echoes associated with convection. They suggested that, by identifying areas of deep convection in clear air, it might be possible to predict the location of shower formation more precisely than is possible at present.

On rare occasions 3-cm radar sets scanning the clear sky have observed PPI echo patterns with a strong resemblance to Bénard-cell convection (Atlas 1959a; Hardy and Ottersten 1969). The last authors reported that the individual convection cells are 5–10 km in diameter and 1–2 km in height. Also, they noted that the echo reflectivities were as high as 3.2×10^{-12} cm^{-1}, a value which cannot be reasonably expected as a result of backscattering by refractive-index inhomogeneities. Their calculations revealed that the high echo intensities could be produced by small insects. If their backscattering cross sections were equivalent to water spheres with diameters of 2.5 mm, three insects per 10^3 m^3 could be enough to account for the estimated backscattered signals. It seems likely that the Bénard-cell type of echo pattern corresponds to the pattern of air motion traced out by widely separated insects carried by the air currents.

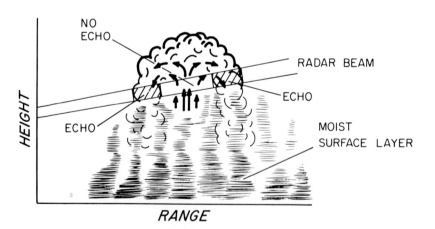

Fig. 12.13.   Sketch of vertical section of the cell structure. The radar outlines the boundary of the cell, where the refractive-index fluctuations are largest; when the radar is scanned in azimuth, a doughnut-shaped echo results. The air flow within the cell, indicated by the arrows, has been deduced from detailed studies of the cell evolution by examining three-dimensional radar patterns of individual cells. From Hardy and Ottersten (1969).

12.6 Clear-Air Turbulence (CAT)

The realization that layers of angel echoes can be produced by inhomo-geneities of refractive index, coupled with the well-known fact that the echoes often coincide with layers through which the average value of n changes markedly, makes it reasonable to expect that layers of angel echoes are regions where clear-air turbulence would be expected. Read-ers interested in the theory of clear-air turbulence are referred to a detailed review prepared by Dutton (1971).

The term "clear-air turbulence," or CAT, commonly refers to the effect of air motions on an airplane. If a typical airplane length is taken to be 10–100 m, it can be inferred that variations in air motion over this scale are the most common cause of airplane turbulence. On the other hand, the theory of the radar reflectivity of regions of refractive-index fluctuations shows that changes of n over a scale distance of $\lambda/2$ are mostly responsible for the backscattering.

In the atmosphere, under the influence of wind shear, there is a broad spectrum of turbulence which, as noted earlier, varies in intensity accord-ing to $k^{-5/3}$ when k is the wave number. Presumably, at least much of the time, when the energy at the wave number corresponding to half the radar wavelength is high, the energy at the much longer wavelengths would also be high.

Atlas et al. (1966), employing the sensitive 3.2-, 10.7-, and 71.5-cm radars at Wallops Island, Virginia, first reported the detection of the tropopause and related the clear-air echoes at high altitudes to clear-air turbulence. Subsequently Hicks et al. (1967) used the same radar equip-ment and simultaneously probed the echo layers with an instrumented F-106 airplane. Four flights were made, and there was excellent agree-ment between the altitudes (between 6 and 11 km) of the angel-echo layers and the altitudes of clear-air turbulences. Similar results were reported by Glover et al. (1969) and Boucher (1970), who employed the same equipment as Hicks et al., and Crane (1970), who used the very sensitive 23.2-cm radar at Millstone Hill. The last author probed clear-air echoes and turbulence in the lower stratosphere. Kropfli (1971), citing the work of earlier investigators, examined how radar measure-ments of clear-air reflectivity could be used to estimate turbulence intensity.

Clear-air turbulence can be caused by various mechanisms in the atmo-sphere. At high altitudes, turbulence is common when there is strong wind shear across a thermally stable layer. In such a circumstance, irregu-larities in the mean wind field can lead to the transfer of energy from the mean field into turbulent kinetic energy. As noted by Glover et al. (1969), the strong wind shears needed to bring about clear-air turbulence are most likely when there is marked thermal stability and hence a large gradient of potential temperature, θ. The shear-generated mechanical turbulence in a layer through which there is a large gradient of the mean temperature will lead to turbulent variations of refractive index. Since these inhomogeneities are responsible for the radar backscatter, it has been proposed that the strength of the backscattered signal from clear-air layers should give a rough estimate of turbulence intensity.

Glover et al. (1969) and Browning and Watkins (1970) considered the occurrence of CAT in terms of the Richardson number,

$$Ri = \frac{g}{\theta} \left(\frac{\Delta\theta}{\Delta z}\right) \left(\frac{\Delta V}{\Delta z}\right)^{-2}, \tag{12.8}$$

where $\Delta V/\Delta z$ is the vector wind change over the height interval Δz, θ is potential temperature and g is the acceleration of gravity. Turbulence is associated with Ri below about 0.5. Note that Ri is a ratio of two gradients and that a small Ri can occur when $\Delta\theta/\Delta z$ is small if the wind shear is small and $\Delta V/\Delta z$ is large. Experimental data collected at Wallops Island (Glover et al. 1969) and in England (Browning and Watkins 1970) showed that clear-air echoes and CAT are associated with atmospheric layers having small, positive Richardson numbers.

12.7 Wave Motions and Turbulence

There is little doubt that, by means of ultrasensitive radar equipment at wavelengths of 10 cm and longer, it is possible to detect layers of angel echoes associated with strong shear and turbulent zones in the atmosphere. More information is needed about radar reflectivities as a function of energy in turbulence scales of the order of 10–100 m. Further, it is essential that more be learned about the mechanisms leading to the turbulent air motion.

Observations collected since the middle 1960s by means of sensitive radars not only reveal that often a layer of echoes coincides with a layer of clear-air turbulence, but they also show some interesting details about echo structure. Hicks and Angell (1968) observed a clear-air echo layer located at an altitude of about 3.5 km and having the appearance of a braided rope (fig. 12.14). They observed similar echoes on eleven occasions during a 6-week period in May and June 1966. The echoes tended to be aligned in the direction of the wind shear and occurred in regions of relatively stable temperature-lapse rates or inversions. These conditions favor the formation of gravity waves. Hicks and Angell (1968) offered the explanation that the braided echoes were produced by refractive index inhomogeneities associated with breaking gravity waves.

Studies of the detailed turbulence structure of the clear-air echo layers

Fig. 12.14.   S-band RHI scope photograph taken on 1 June at 1932 GMT showing braided-appearing phenomena at 3.5 km in a visually clear atmosphere. The range markers are at intervals of 5 nautical miles (about 9.2 km). From Hicks and Angell (1968).

have been reported by Hicks (1968), Ottersten (1969, 1970*a,b*), Browning and Watkins (1970), Starr and Browning (1972), and Mather and Hardy (1970), who used sensitive conventional radars having narrow beam widths. Generally, the antennas were scanned in the vertical plane and echo patterns were presented on range-height indicators.

Extremely fine details of the wave structure of low-level, wave-induced, clear-air echoes have been reported by Gossard and Richter (1970), Gossard, Richter, and Atlas (1970), and Atlas, Harris, and Richter (1970) (see figs. 12.15 to 12.17). They employed the vertically pointing, 10-cm, frequency-modulated, continuous-wave (FM-CW) radar at the Naval Electronics Laboratory Center at San Diego, California. The radar system developed by Richter (1969) had a height resolution of 1–2 m and was extremely sensitive. It had a minimum detectable radar cross section of a point target of 3.7×10^{-6} cm^2 at 1 km. For distributed targets, the minimum detectable reflectivity was 4.2×10^{-15} cm^{-1}. The

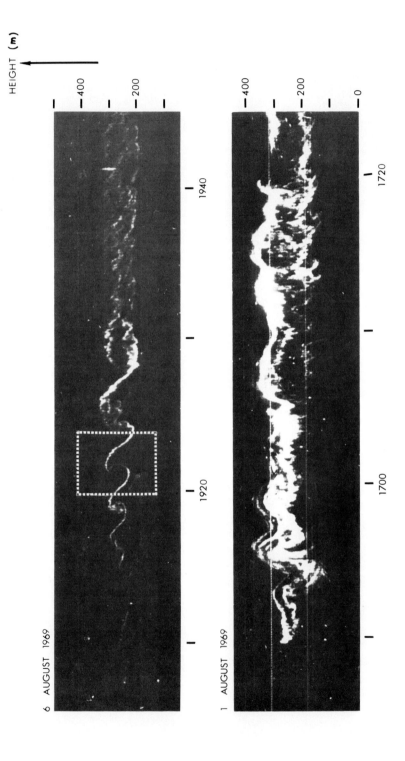

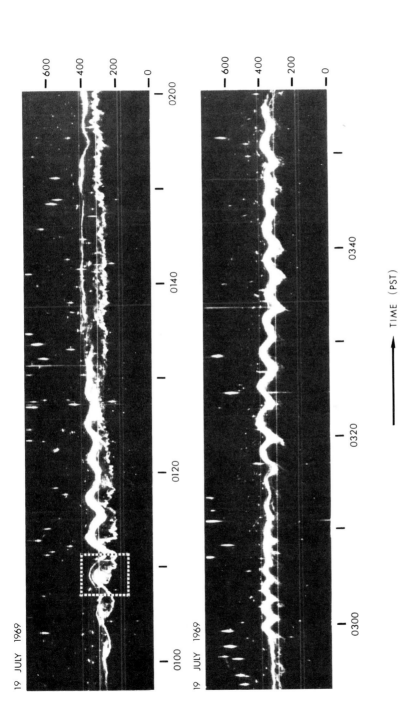

Fig. 12.15. Wave patterns in the clear sky over San Diego, California, detected by means of vertically pointing, S-band FM–CW radar. The dot-angel echoes are ascribed to insects. Courtesy of J. H. Richter and E. E. Gossard.

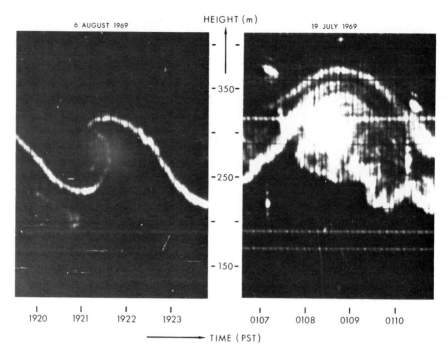

Fig. 12.16. Enlarged photograph of the waves shown inside the dotted boxes in figure 12.13. Courtesy of J. H. Richter and E. E. Gossard.

radar was capable of detecting an individual insect whose cross section was about 10^{-3} cm² at a distance up to 4 km. Stratmann et al. (1971) described how this radar could be calibrated by firing 0.44-cm copper spheres up to heights of about 140 m within the radar beam.

It has been surmised that the braided echoes noted earlier represent wave motions in the atmosphere. As the waves increase in amplitude they may cause the turbulent motion experienced by aircraft. It has been further speculated that when the waves "break" turbulence may become serious and, in rare instances, cause structural damage to aircraft.

The evidence presented by Atlas et al. (1970), Gossard, Jensen, and Richter (1971), and others indicates that clear-air echoes can be associated with long-period gravity waves (fig. 12.17) and shorter-period (1–5 minutes), unstable, breaking Kelvin-Helmholtz (K-H) waves (fig. 12.15). Atlas et al. (1970), Browning and Watkins (1970), and Browning (1971) analyzed the sequence of events leading to the growth of K-H waves and concluded that the waves begin to form when the Richardson number is slightly positive. The FM–CW radar showed the initiation of

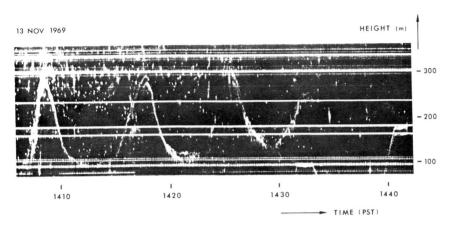

Fig. 12.17.   Internal gravity wave over San Diego observed by means of vertically pointing, S-band FM–CW radar. From Gossard and Richter (1970).

the K-H waves at the base of an inversion, their amplification with time, the development of roll vortices, and then the breaking of the waves and the resulting turbulence.

Atlas et al. (1970) observed that the K-H waves initiated stable waves in the dynamically stable layer immediately above an unstable one. They found that, in clear-air echo strata only a few meters thick, radar reflectivities were typically 10 times and occasionally 300 times greater than the previously recorded maximum clear-air reflectivities. The differences between these and earlier observations were accounted for largely on the grounds that the latter were averages over a much larger volume. It was proposed that the high reflectivities were caused by "major centimetric scale perturbations in refractivity," but the origin of such perturbations in layers only a few meters thick with large dynamic stability was called "a mystery deserving attention."

Browning's (1971) observations revealed that each of seventeen occurrences of K-H waves occurred in association with a minimum value of the Richardson number embedded within a strongly sheared stable layer. As noted above, Atlas et al. (1970) reported that the K-H waves occurred in the dynamically stable layer immediately above an unstable one.

It has become evident that ultrasensitive, high-resolution radar can furnish many details about the structure of the atmosphere. Just a few years ago angel echoes were regarded as interesting, but not of particularly great significance. Now most of them can be explained, and they are a source of valuable information. The capability to detect insects and birds and, in some instances, the ability to discriminate between them has given ornithologists (see Eastwood 1967) and entomologists the means for observing the movements and behavior of these creatures.

The value of radar for the detection of wave motions in the clear atmosphere and for the measurement of the turbulent behavior of the atmosphere is just becoming realized. Inevitably there will be more and better observations of the fields of refractivity and of air motion. Such information is of crucial importance to problems involving the transfer in the atmosphere of energy, mass, and momentum. In 1940, Friend visualized that radar might be used as an instrument for sounding the atmosphere. Some three decades later, it appears that this vision has become almost a reality.

Appendix

The Characteristics of Various Radar Sets Used for Meteorological Observations

Radar Set and Source of Data	Characteristic								
	λ (cm)	P_t (kw)	PRF (Hz)	τ (μsec)	Ant. Dia (m)	Ant. Gain (dB)	ϕ (Vert.) (Deg.)	θ (Hor.) (Deg.)	P_{min} (dBm)
AN/TPQ-11 (Speed 1965)	0.86	140	1,000	0.5	2.14	56	0.25	0.25	−99
AN/TPQ-6 (Donaldson 1955b)	0.86	12.5	492;* 2,460	1.0; 0.2	2.14	54	0.29	0.29	−87
MRL-1† (USSR) (Atlas 1965)	0.86	100	600*	0.5	3*	58	0.23	0.23	−85*
AN/APS-34 (Modified) (Atlas 1960)	1.25	10.8	800;* 1,600	0.5; 0.25	2.44	54	0.37	0.37	−88
MRL-1† (USSR) (Atlas 1965)	3.2	300	300; 600	2; 1	3*	46	0.7	0.7	−98*
AN/CPS-9 (Speed 1965)	3.2	250	186; 931	5; 0.5; 0.5	2.36	42	1.0	1.0	−104
ARS-3 (USSR) (Borovikov et al. 1967)	3.2	230		0.5	3*	46‡	0.95	0.85	−93
AN/APQ-13 (Modified) (Battan 1959)	3.2	40	1,000	1.0	0.76	33‡	4	4	−83
JAFNA "X" (Wallops Is.) (Glover et al. 1966)	3.2	900	320*	2.0	10.4	58	0.21	0.21	−101
VGI (USSR) (Sulakvelidze, Bibilashvili, and Lapcheva 1965)	3.2	50	1,250*	0.5	0.75	36‡	3	3	−90*

	Wavelength								
MRU-Doppler (England) (Boyenval 1960; Browning et al. 1968)	Fixed 3.2	10	2,426	0.8	1.52*	39	1.5	1.5	−105*
	Mobile 3.2	10	10,000	0.5	1.22*	38	2	2	−108*
AN/APS-45 (Senn 1966b)	3.2	450	450*	1.8	0.70×2.14*	40[‡]	1.0	3.1*	−103
NOAA (Dual Doppler) (Lhermitte 1970)	3.22	20	1,953	0.3	2.44*	46[‡]	0.9	0.9	−103*
CAL Doppler (Rogers and Jiusto 1966)	3.22	2	5,000	0.5	2.44	46[‡]	0.9	0.9	−95*
Arizona Doppler (Theiss and Kassander 1963)	3.25	40	4,000	0.25	1.83	42.5	1.3	1.3	−105
University of Texas[§] (Deam and LaGrone 1965)	3.3	250	1,000*	0.25	1.38*	40[‡]	1.25	1.25	−100
AN/TPS-10 (Battan 1959)	3.3	65	1,000	1	0.9×3.12*	44[‡]	0.7	2.0	−83
AN/MPS-4 (Hiser, Senn, and Courtright 1970)	4.5	120	300	1.3	0.92×4.27*	40	0.8	3.8*	−103
AN/FPS-77 (Speed 1965)	5.3	300	324	2	2.44	41	1.6	1.6	−107
AFCRL Porcupine Doppler (Wexler, Chmela, and Armstrong 1967)	5.45	17	917;* 1,834 3,300	8.0; 8.0; 0.5	4.9*	45[‡]	1	1	−115

The Characteristics of Various Radar Sets Used for Meteorological Observations (continued)

Radar Set and Source of Data	λ (cm)	P_t (kw)	PRF (Hz)	τ (μsec)	Ant. Dia (m)	Ant. Gain (dB)	ϕ (Vert.) (Deg.)	θ (Hor.) (Deg.)	P_{min} (dBm)
University of Texas§ (Deam and LaGrone 1965)	9.1	1,000	1,000*	1.3	5.2	40	1.25	1.25	−100
NCAR Coherent Radar (Nat. Ctr. Atmos. Res. 1970)	9.3	1,000	750, 2,000	1	3.05	34	3	3	−110
UM/10 (Hiser, Senn, and Courtright 1970)	9.9	500	300	2	3.66*	39‡	1.9	2.1	−110
Navy FM – CW (Richter 1969)	10	0.15#	–	–	3*	35	2.3	2.3	−150
Radar in Sweden (Ottersten 1964)	10	500	500*	0.6	4	40	1.8	1.8	−100
Radar in S. Africa (Miles 1953)	10	500	500	1.9	3	36‡	3	3	
VGI Radar (USSR) (Sulakvelidze, Bibilashvili, and Lapcheva 1965)	10	250	1,250*	0.8	1.5	33‡	4	4	−90*
WSR-57 (Wilk et al. 1967)	10.0	450	164	4	3.36*	38.5	2	2	−110
Mt. Fuji Radar (Japan) (Tatehira 1966)	10.4	1,500	160	4*	5	42‡	1.5	1.5	−112

Characteristic

Radar									
Radar (Canada) (Chisholm 1970)									
WDS-67** (Sirmans 1970)	10.5	400	1,500	0.7	9.15	46	0.8	0.8	−105
NSSL Doppler (Brown et al. 1971)	10.6	500	1,300	1.0	9.1	46‡	0.8	0.8	−105*
SCR-615 (Austin and Williams 1951)	10.7	600	400*	1.5	2.44	35	3	3	−93
AN/FPS-6 (Atlas 1958a)	10.7	5,000	300–400 (variable)*	2.0	2.28×9*	41‡	0.85*	3.2*	−105
RRE (England) (Browning and Watkins 1970)	10.7	1,000	800	1.3	25	53*	0.33	0.33	−111
JAFNA "S" Band (Wallops Is.) (Glover et al. 1966)	10.7	3,000	320; 960*	0.1 – 1.3	18.4	51	0.48	0.48	−110
ARSR-1 (Belesky 1971)	22.2– 23.4	5,000	360	2	7×14	34	3.75	1.2	
Millstone Hill L-Band (Crane 1970)	23.2	4,000	20	10	25.6	47.1	0.6	0.6	−125*
AN/FPS-3 (Elder 1957)	23.4	750	400	3	5.5×16	39‡	3	1.28	−109
JAFNA "UHF" Band (Wallops Is.) (Glover et al. 1966)	71.5	6,000	320; 960*	0.2 – 3.0	18.4	35	2.9	2.9	−105

*These data were calculated or obtained from sources other than the cited reference.

† The MRL-1 is a dual wavelength radar.

‡ Calculated from $G = \pi^2/\theta\phi$.

§ Part of a modified M-33 radar.

∥ The frequency actually scans from 2.8 to 3.1 GHz (10.7–9.7 cm).

This is a CW radar with average power output of 150 w.

** A modified AN/CPN-18.

References

Abshaev, M. T. 1968. Radiolokatzionnye metody izmerenniia miko-strukturnykh kharakteristtik oblakov [Radar methods for measuring the microstructural characteristics of clouds]. *Proc. Third All-Union Conf. Radar Meteor.*, pp. 72–86. Moscow: Hydrometeor. Service.

Abshaev, M. T., and Rozenberg, V. I. 1969. Rasseianie i oslablenie radioizlucheniia santimetrovogo diapazona gradom [Scattering and attenuation of radio emission in the centimeter range by hail]. *Izvest. Akad. Nauk SSSR, Fiz. Atmos. i Okeana, Moscow* 5:803–9.

Aden, A. L., and Kerker, M. 1951. Scattering of electromagnetic waves by two concentric spheres. *J. Appl. Phys.* 22:1242–46.

Anderson, A. D., and Hoehne, W. E. 1956. Experiments using window to measure high altitude winds. *Bull. Amer. Meteor. Soc.* 37:454–57.

Antonov, V. S., and Medaliev, Kh. Kh. 1969. Zavisimost mezhdu kompleksom radiolokatzionnikh kharakteristikh oblakov i atmosfery i vidom vypadaiyshchikh na zemliy osadkov [The relationship between the complex of radar characteristics of clouds and the atmosphere and the form of precipitation falling to the ground]. *Meteor. i Gidrol., Moscow*, no. 4, pp. 84–85.

Aoyagi, J. 1963. The quantitative estimation of the heights of radar echo tops. *Proc. Tenth Wea. Radar Conf.*, pp. 123–33. Boston: Amer. Meteor. Soc.

———. 1964. Areal rainfall amounts obtained in a 3.2-cm radar and a raingage network. *Proc. Eleventh Wea. Radar Conf.*, pp. 116–19. Boston: Amer. Meteor. Soc.

———. 1969. Mean Doppler velocities of precipitation near the ground. *Proc. Thirteenth Radar Meteor. Conf.*, pp. 22–25. Boston: Amer. Meteor. Soc.

Appleton, E. 1946. The influence of tropospheric conditions on ultra-short-wave propagation. *Meteorological factors in radio wave propagation*, pp. 1–17. London: Physical Society.

Arakawa, H. 1967. A hook-shaped echo accompanied by a mesocyclone associated with the catastrophic rainstorm of 25 July 1957 in Kyashu, Japan. *J. Appl. Meteor.* 6:439–41.

Arakawa, H.; Watanabe, K.; Tsuchiya, K.; and Fujita, T. T. 1968. *A mesometeorological study of a subtropical mesocyclone.* SMRP Research Paper no. 68. Chicago: Dept. of Geophysical Sciences, Univ. of Chicago.

Armijo, L. 1969. A theory for the determination of wind and precipitation velocities with Doppler radars. *J. Atmos. Sci.* 26:570–73.

Armstrong, G. M., and Donaldson, R. J., Jr. 1969. Plan shear indicator for real-time Doppler radar identification of hazardous storm winds. *J. Appl. Meteor.* 8:376–83.

Atlas, D. 1947. *Preliminary report on new techniques in quantitative radar analysis of rainstorms.* Rept. AMNW 7-4, pt. I. Dayton, Ohio: AMC, Wright-Patterson AFB.

———. 1948. *Some experimental results of quantitative radar analysis of rainstorms.* Rept. AMNW 7-4, pt. II. Dayton, Ohio: AMC, Wright-Patterson AFB.

———. 1953. Optical extinction by rainfall. *J. Meteor.* 10:486–88.

———. 1954. The estimation of cloud parameters by radar. *J. Meteor.* 11:309–17.

———. 1955. The origin of "stalactites" in precipitation echoes. *Proc. Fifth Wea. Radar Conf.,* pp. 321–28. Boston: Amer. Meteor. Soc.

———. 1958a. Radar lightning echoes and atmospherics in vertical cross-section. In *Recent advances in atmospheric electricity,* pp. 441–59. New York: Pergamon Press.

———. 1958b. Radar as a sferics detector. *Proc. Seventh Wea. Radar Conf.,* pp. C1–C8. Boston: Amer. Meteor. Soc.

———. 1959a. Radar studies of meteorological "angel" echoes. *J. Atmos. Terrest. Phys.* 15:262–87.

———. 1959b. Meteorological angel echoes. *J. Meteor.* 16:6–11.

———. 1960. Radar detection of the sea breeze. *J. Meteor.* 17:244–58.

———. 1963. Radar analysis of severe storms. In *Severe local storms,* edited by D. Atlas. *Meteor. Monographs* 5(27):177–220.

———. 1964. Advances in radar meteorology. In *Advances in geophysics,* 10:318–478. New York: Academic Press.

———. 1965. Activities in radar meteorology, cloud physics, and weather modification in the Soviet Union (June 1965). *Bull. Amer. Meteor. Soc.* 11:696–706.

———. 1966. The balance level in convective storms. *J. Atmos. Sci.* 23:635–51.

Atlas, D., ed. 1969. *Atmospheric exploration by remote probes.* Vol. 2, Washington, D.C.: Nat. Acad. Sci.

Atlas, D., and Banks, H. C. 1951. The interpretation of microwave reflections from rainfall. *J. Meteor.* 8:271–82.

Atlas, D.; Browning, K. A.; Donaldson, R. J., Jr.; and Sweeney, H. J. 1963. Automatic digital radar reflectivity analysis of a tornadic storm. *J. Appl. Meteor.* 2:574–81.

Atlas, D., and Chmela, A. C. 1957. Physical-synoptic variations of drop-size parameters. *Proc. Sixth Wea. Radar Conf.*, pp. 21–30. Boston: Amer. Meteor. Soc.

Atlas, D., and Hardy, K. R. 1966. Radar analysis of the clear atmosphere: Angels. *Proc. XV General Assembly of URSI* (Munich, 5–15 Sept.) pp. 401–69.

Atlas, D.; Hardy, K. R.; Glover, K. M.; Katz, I.; and Konrad, T. G. 1966. Tropopause detected by radar. *Science* 153:1110–12.

Atlas, D.; Hardy, K. R.; and Joss, J. 1964. Radar reflectivities of storms containing spongy hail. *J. Geophys. Res.* 69:1955–61.

Atlas, D.; Hardy, K. R. and Konrad, T. G. 1966. Radar detection of the tropopause and clear air turbulence. *Proc. Twelfth Wea. Radar Conf.*, pp. 279–84. Boston: Amer. Meteor. Soc.

Atlas, D.; Hardy, K. R.; and Naito, K. 1966. Optimizing the radar detection of clear-air turbulence. *J. Appl. Meteor.* 5:450–60.

Atlas, D.; Harper, W. G.; Ludlam, F. H.; and Macklin, W. C. 1960. Radar scatter by large hail. *Quart. J. Roy. Meteor. Soc.* 86:468–82.

Atlas, D.; Harris, F. I.; and Richter, J. H. 1970. Measurement of point target speeds with incoherent non-tracking radar: Insect speeds in an atmospheric wave. *J. Geophys. Res.* 75:7588–96.

Atlas, D.; Kerker, M.; and Hitschfeld, W. 1953. Scattering and attenuation by non-spherical atmospheric particles. *J. Atmos. Terrest. Phys.* 3:108–19.

Atlas, D., and Ludlam, F. H. 1961. Multi-wavelength radar reflectivity of hailstorms. *Quart. J. Roy. Meteor. Soc.* 87:523–34.

Atlas, D.; Metcalf, J. I.; Richter, J. H.; and Gossard, E. E. 1970. The birth of "CAT" and microscale turbulence. *J. Atmos. Sci.* 27:903–13.

Atlas, D., and Mossop, S. C. 1960. Calibration of a weather radar by using a standard target. *Bull. Amer. Meteor. Soc.* 41:377–82.

Atlas, D., and Srivastava, R. C. 1971. A method of radar turbulence detection. *IEEE Trans. Aero. and Elect. Systems* AES-7:179–87.

Atlas, D.; Srivastava, R. C.; and Sloss, P. W. 1969. Wind shear and reflectivity gradient effects on Doppler spectra. II. *J. Appl. Meteor.* 8:384–88.

Atlas, D.; Tatehira, R.; Srivastava, R. C.; Marker, W.; and Carbone, R. E. 1969. Precipitation induced mesoscale wind perturbations in the melting layer. *Quart. J. Roy. Meteor. Soc.* 95:544–60.

Atlas, D., and Wexler, R. 1963. Backscatter by oblate ice spheroids. *J. Atmos. Sci.* 20:48–61.

Austin, J. M., and Blackmer, Jr. R. H. 1956. The variability of cold-front precipitation. *Bull. Amer. Meteor. Soc.* 37:447–53.

Austin, P. M., and Bemis, A. C. 1950. A quantitative study of the "bright band" in radar precipitation echoes. *J. Meteor.* 7:145–51.

Austin, P. M., and Houze, Jr., R. A. 1970. Analysis of precipitation areas. Preprint vol. Fourteenth Radar Meteor. Conf., pp. 329–34. Boston: Amer. Meteor. Soc.

Austin, P. M., and Richardson, C. 1952. A method of measuring rainfall over an area by radar. *Proc. Third Radar Wea. Conf.,* pp. D13–D20. Montreal: McGill Univ.

Austin, P. M., and Williams, E. L. 1951. Comparison of radar signal intensity with precipitation rate. Weather Res. Tech. Rept. no. 14. Cambridge, Mass.: Dept. of Meteor., M.I.T.

Barclay, P. A., and Wilk, K. E. 1970. Severe thunderstorm radar echo motion and related weather events hazardous to aviation operations. Tech. Memo. ERLTM-NSSL 46. Norman, Okla.: ESSA, National Severe Storms Lab.

Barge, B. L. 1970. Polarization observations in Alberta. Preprint vol. Fourteenth Radar Meteor. Conf., pp. 221–24. Boston: Amer. Meteor. Soc.

——— . 1972. Hail detection with a polarization diversity radar. Sci. Rept. MW-71. Montreal Stormy Weather Group, McGill Univ.

Bartnoff, S., and Atlas, D. 1951. Microwave determination of particle-size distribution. *J. Meteor.* 8:130–31.

Bartnoff, S.; Paulsen, W. H.; and Atlas, D. 1952. Experimental Statistics in cloud and rain echoes. *Proc. Third Radar Wea. Conf.,* pp. G1–G8. Montreal: McGill Univ.

Batchelor, G. K. 1955. The scattering of radio waves in the atmosphere by turbulent fluctuations in refractive index. Tech. Rept. no. 26. Ithaca, N.Y.: School of Electrical Engineering, Cornell Univ.

Battan, L. J. 1953a. Duration of convective radar cloud units. *Bull. Amer. Meteor. Soc.* 34:227–28.

——— . 1953b. Observations on the formation and spread of precipitation in convective clouds. *J. Meteor.* 10:311–24.

——— . 1958. Use of chaff for wind measurements. *Bull. Amer. Meteor. Soc.* 39:258–60.

——— . 1959. *Radar meteorology.* Chicago: Univ. of Chicago Press.

——— . 1963a. Some observations of vertical velocities and precipitation sizes in a thunderstorm. *Proc. Tenth Wea. Radar Conf.,* pp. 303–8. Boston: Amer. Meteor. Soc.

——— . 1963b. The vertical velocities of angel echoes. *Proc. Tenth Wea. Radar Conf.,* pp. 309–15. Boston: Amer. Meteor. Soc.

——— . 1963c. Relationship between cloud base and initial radar echo. *J. Appl. Meteor.* 2:333–36.

———. 1964. Some observations of vertical velocities and precipitation sizes in a thunderstorm. *J. Appl. Meteor.* 3:415–20.

———. 1967. Silver iodide seeding and precipitation initiation in convective clouds. *J. Appl. Meteor.* 6:317–22.

———. 1970. Weather modification in the U.S.S.R.—1969. *Bull. Amer. Meteor. Soc.* 50:924–45.

———. 1971. Radar attenuation by wet ice spheres. *J. Appl. Meteor.* 10:247–52.

Battan, L. J., and Braham, R. R., Jr. 1956. A study of convective precipitation based on cloud and radar observations. *J. Meteor.* 13:587–91.

Battan, L. J.; Browning, S. R.; and Herman, B. M. 1970*a*. Tables of the radar cross sections of dry and wet ice spheres. Tech. Rept. no. 21. Tucson: Inst. Atmos. Physics, Univ. of Arizona.

———. 1970*b*. Attenuation of microwaves by wet ice spheres. *J. Appl. Meteor.* 9:832–34.

Battan, L. J., and Herman, B. M. 1962. The radar cross sections of "spongy" ice spheres. *J. Geophys. Res.* 67:5139–45.

Battan, L. J., and Theiss, J. B. 1966. Observations of vertical motions and particle sizes in a thunderstorm. *J. Atmos. Sci.* 23:78–87.

———. 1968. Detection of hail by means of Doppler radar. Tucson: Sci. Rept. no. 24. Inst. Atmos. Phys., Univ. of Ariz.

———. 1970*a*. Measurements of vertical velocities in convective clouds by means of pulsed-Doppler radar. *J. Atmos. Sci.* 27:293–98.

———. 1970*b*. Depolarization of microwaves by hydrometeors in a thunderstorm. *J. Atmos. Sci.* 27:974–77.

———. 1971*a*. Observed Doppler spectra of hail. Sci. Rept. no. 25. Tucson: Inst. Atmos. Phys., Univ. of Ariz.

———. 1971*b*. Wind gradients and variance of Doppler spectra. Sci. Rept. no. 26. Tucson: Inst. Atmos. Phys., Univ. of Ariz.

Battan, L. J.; Theiss, J. B.; and Kassander, A. R., Jr. 1964. Some Doppler radar observations of a decaying thunderstorm. *Proc. Eleventh Wea. Radar Conf.*, pp. 362–65. Boston: Amer. Meteor. Soc.

Bauer, J. R. 1956. The suggested role of stratified elevated layers in trans-horizontal short-wave radio propagation. Tech. Rept. no. 124. Cambridge, Mass.: Lincoln Lab., M.I.T.

Bean, B. R., and Dutton, E. J. 1968. *Radio meteorology.* New York: Dover.

Bechtel, M. E., and Prinsen, H. W. 1967. Errors in R-meter measurement of the velocity spread of meteorological targets resulting from radar frequency instabilities. *J. Appl. Meteor.* 6:57–60.

Belesky, R. K. 1971. Precipitation detection probabilities by Salt Lake City ARTC radars. *J. Appl. Meteor.* 10:1355–60.

Beran, D. W., and Clifford, S. F. 1972. Acoustic Doppler measurements of the total wind vector. *Proc. Second Symposium on Meteor.*

Observations and Instrumentation, pp. 100–109. Boston: Amer. Meteor. Soc.

Beran, D. W.; Little, C. G.; and Willmarth, B. C. 1971. Acoustic Doppler measurements of vertical velocities in the atmosphere. *Nature* 230:160–62.

Beriuliev, G. P.; Beznis, L. I.; Borovikov, A. M.; Chernikov, A. A.; Kostarev, V. V.; Mazin, I. P.; Potyomkin, I. G.; Shapiro, B. C.; and Smirnov, V. I. 1966. The results of radar measurements of areal rainfall. *Proc. Twelfth Conf. Radar Meteor.*, pp. 220–21. Boston: Amer. Meteor. Soc.

Berson, F. A., and Simpson, K. G. 1971. Radar line echoes and bird movements. *Weather* 26:23–32.

Bigler, S. G. 1955. An analysis of tornado and severe weather echoes. *Proc. Fifth Wea. Radar Conf.*, pp. 167–75. Boston: Amer. Meteor. Soc.

———. 1958. Observations of a tornado using the AN/CPS-9 radar. *Proc. Seventh Wea. Radar Conf.*, pp. K1–K5. Boston: Amer. Meteor. Soc.

Bigler, S. G., and Hexter, P. L., Jr. 1960. Radar analysis of hurricane Debra. *Proc. Eighth Wea. Radar Conf.*, pp. 25–32. Boston: Amer. Meteor. Soc.

Black, P. G.; Senn, H. V.; and Courtright, C. L., 1972. Airborne radar observations of eye configuration changes, bright band distribution, and precipitation tilt during the 1969 multiple seeding experiments in hurricane Debbie. *Mon. Wea. Rev.* 100:208–17.

Blackman, R. B., and Tukey, J. W. 1958. *The measurement of power spectra.* New York: Dover.

Blackmer, R. H. 1955. The lifetime of small precipitation echoes. *Proc. Fifth Wea. Radar Conf.*, pp. 103–8. Fort Monmouth, N.J.: Signal Corps, Engineering Lab.

Blanchard, D. C. 1953. Raindrop size distribution in Hawaiian rains. *J. Meteor.* 10:457–73.

Booker, H. G., and Gordon, W. E. 1950. Theory of radio scattering in the troposphere. *Proc. I.R.E.* 38:401–12.

Borchardt, H. 1962. Wolkenbeobachtungen mit einem doppelwelligen Radargerat [Cloud observations with a Doppler radar]. *Beit. Physik Atmosphare* 35:43–68.

Born, M., and Wolf, E. 1959. *Principles of optics.* London: Pergamon Press.

Borovikov, A. M.; Kostarev, V. V.; Maziu, I. P.; Smirnov, V. I.; and Chernikov, A. A. 1967. *Radiolokatsionnye izmereniya osadkov* [Radar measurement of precipitation rate]. Leningrad: Gidrometeor.

Izdatel'stvo. (Translated in 1970. Available in English from Clearinghouse for Federal Scientific and Technical Information, U.S. Dept. of Commerce, Washington, D.C.)

Børresen, J. A. 1971. Doppler radar study of shear zones and turbulence in a snowstorm. *J. Appl. Meteor.* 10:433–42.

Boston, R. C. 1970. Radar attenuation and reflectivity due to size-distributed hydrometeors. *J. Appl. Meteor.* 9:188–91.

Boston, R. C., and Rogers, R. R. 1969. Hail detection by Doppler radar. *J. Appl. Meteor.* 8:837–40.

Boucher, R. J. 1951. Results of measurements of raindrop size. *Proc. Conf. on Water Resources,* pp. 293–97. Bull. 41. Urbana: Illinois State Water Survey.

———. 1957. Synoptic-dynamic implications of 1.25 cm vertical beam radar echoes. *Proc. Sixth Wea. Radar Conf.,* pp. 179–88. Boston: Amer. Meteor. Soc.

———. 1958. *The development and growth of precipitation in three New England coastal cyclones: A radar-synoptic analysis.* Meteor. Radar Studies, no. 9. Cambridge, Mass.: Blue Hill Meteor. Obs. Harvard Univ.

———. 1970. *Mesoscale meteorological structure during radar CAT detection.* Preprint vol. Fourteenth Radar Meteor. Conf., pp. 107–10. Boston: Amer. Meteor. Soc.

Boucher, R. J., and Ottersten, H. 1971. Doppler radar observation of wind structure in snow. *J. Appl. Meteor.* 10:228–33.

Boucher, R. J.; Wexler, R.; Atlas, D.; and Lhermitte, R. M. 1965. Mesoscale wind structure revealed by Doppler radar. *J. Appl. Meteor.* 4:590–97.

Bowen, E. G. 1951. Radar observations of rain and their relation to mechanism of rain formation. *J. Atmos. Terrest. Phys.* 1:125–40.

Boyenval, E. H. 1960. Echoes from precipitation using pulsed Doppler radar. *Proc. Eighth Wea. Radar Conf.,* pp. 57–64. Boston: Amer. Meteor. Soc.

Bradbury, D. L., and Fujita, T. 1966. Features and motions of radar echoes on Palm Sunday 1965. *Proc. Twelfth Conf. Radar Meteor.,* pp. 319–24. Boston: Amer. Meteor. Soc.

Bradley, J.; Farnese, A.; Hexter, P.; and Lukashchewsky, B. 1964. An engineering evaluation of STRADAP. *Proc. Eleventh Wea. Radar Conf.,* pp. 282–85. Boston: Amer. Meteor. Soc.

Braham, R. R. Jr. 1958. Cumulus cloud precipitation as revealed by radar—Arizona, 1955. *J. Meteor.* 15:75–83.

Braham, R. R. Jr.; Battan, L. J.; and Byers, H. R. 1957. Artificial nucleation of cumulus clouds. *Meteor. Monographs.* 2:47–85.

Braham, R. R. Jr.; Reynolds, S. E.; and Harrell, J. H. 1951. Possibilities for cloud seeding as determined by a study of cloud height versus precipitation. *J. Meteor.* 8:416–18.

Brantley, J. Q., and Barczys, D. A. 1957. Some weather observations with continuous wave Doppler radar. *Proc. Sixth Wea. Radar Conf.,* pp. 297–306. Boston: Amer. Meteor. Soc.

Brooks, E. M. 1959. The tornado cyclone. *Weatherwise* 2:32–33.

Brooks, H. R. 1946. A summary of some radar thunderstorm observations. *Bull. Amer. Meteor. Soc.* 27:557–63.

Brown, H. A. 1960. Report on radar thin lines. *Proc. Eighth Wea. Radar Conf.,* pp. 65–72. Boston: Amer. Meteor. Soc.

Brown, E. N., and Braham, R. R., Jr. 1963. Precipitation particle measurements in cumulus congestus. *J. Atmos. Sci.* 20:23–28.

Brown, R. A., and Peace, R. L., Jr. 1968. Mesoanalysis of convective storms utilizing observations from two Doppler radars. *Proc. Thirteenth Radar Wea. Conf.,* pp. 188–91. Boston: Amer. Meteor. Soc.

Brown, R. A.; Baumgarner, W. C.; Crawford, K. C.; and Sirmans, D. 1971. Preliminary Doppler velocity measurements in a developing radar hook echo. *Bull. Amer. Meteor. Soc.* 52:1186–88.

Browne, I. C. 1951. A radar echo from lightning. *Nature* 167:438.

Browne, I. C., and Robinson, N. P. 1952. Cross-polarization of the radar melting band. *Nature* 170:1078–79.

Browning, K. A. 1963. The growth of hail within a steady updraft. *Quart. J. Roy. Meteor. Soc.* 89:490–506.

———. 1964. Interaction of two severe local storms. *Proc. Eleventh Wea. Radar Conf.,* pp. 366–71. Boston: Amer. Meteor. Soc.

———. 1965. Some inferences about the updraft within a severe local storm. *J. Atmos. Sci.* 22:669–77.

———. 1971. Structure of the atmosphere in the vicinity of large amplitude Kelvin-Helmholtz billows. *Quart. J. Roy. Meteor. Soc.* 97:283–99.

Browning, K. A., and Atlas, D. 1965. Initiation of precipitation in vigorous convective clouds. *J. Atmos. Sci.* 22:678–83.

———. 1966. Velocity characteristics of some clear air dot angels. *J. Atmos. Sci.* 23:592–604.

Browning, K. A., and Donaldson, R. J. 1963. Airflow and structure of a tornadic storm. *J. Atmos. Sci.* 20:533–45.

Browning, K. A., and Fujita, T. 1965. A family outbreak of severe local storms: A comprehensive study of the storms in Oklahoma on 26 May 1963. Special Rept. no. 32, pt. I. Bedford, Mass.: Air Force Cambridge Res. Labs.

Browning, K. A., and Harrold, T. W. 1969. Air motion and precipitation growth in a wave depression. *Quart. J. Roy. Meteor. Soc.* 95:288–309.

———. 1970. Air motion and precipitation growth at a cold front. *Quart. J. Roy. Meteor. Soc.* 96:369–89.

Browning, K. A.; Harrold, T. W.; Whyman, A. J.; and Beimers, J. G. D. 1968. Horizontal and vertical air motion and precipitation growth within a shower. *Quart. J. Roy. Meteor. Soc.* 94:498–509.

Browning, K. A., and Ludlam, F. H. 1962. Airflow in convective storms. *Quart. J. Roy. Meteor. Soc.* 88:117–35.

Browning, K. A., and Watkins, C. D. 1970. Observations of clear air turbulence by high power radar. *Nature* 227:260–63.

Browning, K. A., and Wexler, R. 1968. A determination of kinematic properties of a wind field using Doppler radar. *J. Appl. Meteor.* 7:105–13.

Bull, G. A., and Harper, W. G. 1955. West London tornado, December 8, 1954. *Meteor. Mag.* 84:320–22.

Bunting, D. C., and Latour, M. H. 1951. Radar-rainfall studies in Ohio. *Bull. Amer. Meteor. Soc.* 32:289–94.

Byers, H. R., and Battan, L. J. 1949. Some effects of vertical wind shear on thunderstorm structure. *Bull. Amer. Meteor. Soc.* 30:168–75.

Byers, H. R., and Braham, R. R. Jr. 1949. *The thunderstorm*. Washington, D.C.: Government Printing Office.

Byers, H. R., and Collaborators. 1948. The use of radar in determining the amount of rain falling over a small area. *Trans. Amer. Geophys. Union.* 29:187–96.

Byers, H. R., and Hall, R. K. 1955. A census of cumulus-cloud height versus precipitation in the vicinity of Puerto Rico during the winter and spring of 1953–54. *J. Meteor.* 12:176–78.

Carlson, P, E., and Marshall, J. S. 1972. Measurement of snowfall by radar. *J. Appl. Meteor.* 11:494–500.

Cartmill, R. H. 1963. Rainfall rate measurement using two radar sets of different wavelengths: Theory. *Proc. Tenth Wea. Radar Conf.,* pp. 265–70. Boston: Amer. Meteor. Soc.

Cataneo, R. A. 1969. A method for estimating rainfall rate–radar reflectivity relationships. *J. Appl. Meteor.* 8:815–19.

Cataneo, R. and Stout, G. E. 1968. Raindrop-size distributions in humid continental climatic and associated rainfall rate–radar reflectivity relationships. *J. Appl. Meteor.* 7:901–7.

Caton, P. G. F. 1963. The measurement of wind and convergence by Doppler radar. *Proc. Tenth Wea. Radar Conf.,* pp. 290–96. Boston: Amer. Meteor. Soc.

———. 1964. A study of raindrop size distributions in the free atmosphere. *Proc. Eleventh Wea. Radar Conf.,* pp. 136–41. Boston:

Amer. Meteor. Soc.

————. 1966. Raindrop-size distributions in the free atmosphere. *Quart. J. Roy. Meteor. Soc.* 92:15–30.

Changnon, S. A., and Staggs, D. W. 1970. *RHI radar-hail relations for weather modification experiments.* Urbana: Illinois State Water Survey.

Chernikov, A. A. 1966. Some new Soviet investigations of angel echoes. *Proc. Twelfth Wea. Radar Conf.,* pp. 291–92. Boston: Amer. Meteor. Soc.

Chernikov, A. A.; Mel'nichuk, Yu. V.; Pinus, N. Z.; Shmeter, S. M.; and Vinnichenko, N. K. 1969. Investigations of the turbulence in convective atmosphere using radar and aircraft. *Radio Science* 4:1257–59.

Chernikov, A. A., and Shupiatskii, A. B. 1967. Poliarizatsionnye kharakteristiki radiolokatsionnykh otrazhenii ot "iasnogo" neba [The polarization characteristics of radar "angel" echoes]. *Izvest. Akad. Nauk SSSR., Fiz. Atmos. i Okeana, Moscow* 3:136–43.

Chimera, A. J. 1960. *Meteorological radar echo study.* Final Report (Appendix C), Contract no. AF 33(616)-6352. Buffalo, N.Y.: Cornell Aero Labs.

Chisholm, A. J. 1970. The radar and airflow structure of Alberta hailstorms. Preprint vol. Fourteenth Radar Meteor. Conf., pp. 35–42. Boston: Amer. Meteor. Soc.

Clark, R. A. 1960. A study of convective precipitation as revealed by radar observations, Texas, 1958–1959. *J. Meteor.* 17:415–25.

Collis, R. T. H. 1963. A radar rainfall integrator. *Proc. Tenth Wea. Radar Conf.,* pp. 389–96. Boston: Amer. Meteor. Soc.

————. 1964. Radar precipitation measurements. *Proc. Eleventh Wea. Radar Conf.,* pp. 142–46. Boston: Amer. Meteor. Soc.

————. 1969. Lidar. In *Advances in geophysics,* 13:113–40. New York: Academic Press.

Cook, B. 1958. Hail determination by radar analysis. *Monthly Wea. Rev.* 86:435–38.

Cooley, J. W., and Tukey, J. 1965. An algorithm for the machine calculation of complex Fourier series. *Mathematics of Computation* 19:297–301.

Coons, R. D. 1947. Guided propagation of radar in thunderstorm conditions. *Bull. Amer. Meteor. Soc.* 28:324–29.

Crain, C. M. 1950. Apparatus for recording fluctuations in the refractive index of the atmosphere at 3.2 centimeters wavelength. *Rev. Sci. Inst.* 21:164–76.

Crane, R. F. 1970. Measurements of clear air turbulence in the lower stratosphere using the Millstone Hill L-band radar. Preprint vol.

Fourteenth Radar Meteor. Conf., pp. 101–6. Boston: Amer. Meteor. Soc.

Crawford, A. B. 1949. Radar reflections in the lower atmosphere. *Proc. Inst. Radio Eng.* 37:404–5.

Cumming, W. A. 1952. The dielectric properties of ice and snow at 3.2 cm. *J. Appl. Physics* 23:768.

Dawson, G. A. 1972. Radar as a diagnostic tool for lightning. *J. Geophys. Res.* 77:4518–28.

De, A. C., and Kundu, M. M. 1966. Movement of premonsoon squall lines observed by radar at Agartala Airport. *Proc. Twelfth Conf. Radar Meteor.*, pp. 330–33. Boston: Amer. Meteor. Soc.

Deam, A. P., and LaGrone, A. H. 1965. Quantitative observations of dot angel echoes at two frequencies. *Radio Science* 1:537–43.

Debye, P. 1929. *Polar molecules.* New York: Chemical Catalogue Co.

Dennis, A. A.; Koscielski, A.; Boardman, J. H.; and Peterson, G. A. P. 1970. Use of moving target areas and an on-line computer in experimental seeding of convective clouds. Preprint vol. Second National Conf. on Wea. Mod., pp. 190–92. Boston: Amer. Meteor. Soc.

Dennis, A. S.; Schock, C. A.; and Hartzell, C. L. 1969. *Accumulation zones in a South Dakota hailstorm.* Preprint vol. Sixth Conf. on Severe Local Storms, pp. 286–89. Boston: Amer. Meteor. Soc.

Dennis, A. S.; Schock, C. A.; and Koscielski, A. 1970. Characteristics of hailstorms of western South Dakota. *J. Appl. Meteor.* 9:127–35.

Dickson, E. G. 1956. Detection of developing tornadic activity. *Bull. Amer. Meteor. Soc.* 37:517–18.

Diem, M. 1966. Rains in the Arctic, Temperate, and Tropical Zones. Sci. Rept. Karlsruhe: Meteorologisches Institut Technische Hochschule.

Doherty, L. H. 1963. The scattering coefficient of rain from forward scatter measurements. *Proc. Tenth Wea. Radar Conf.*, pp. 171–75. Boston: Amer. Meteor. Soc.

Donaldson, R. J., Jr. 1955a. Drop-size distribution, liquid water content, optical transmission, and radar reflectivity in fog and drizzle. *Proc. Fifth Wea. Radar Conf.*, pp. 275–80. Boston: Amer. Meteor. Soc.

———. 1955b. The measurement of cloud liquid-water content by radar. *J. Meteor.* 12:238–44.

———. 1958. Analysis of severe convective storms observed by radar. *J. Meteor.* 15:44–50.

———. 1959. Analysis of severe convective storms observed by radar. II. *J. Meteor.* 16:281–87.

———. 1961a. Radar reflectivity profiles in thunderstorms. *J. Meteor.* 18:292–305.

——— . 1961*b*. Range distortion of thunderstorm reflectivity structure. *Proc. Ninth Wea. Radar Conf.*, pp. 165–74. Boston: Amer. Meteor. Soc.

——— . 1964. A demonstration of antenna beam errors in radar reflectivity patterns. *J. Appl. Meteor.* 3:611–23.

——— . 1965. Resolution of a radar antenna for distributed targets. *J. Appl. Meteor.* 4:727–40.

——— . 1967. A preliminary report on Doppler radar observation of turbulence in a thunderstorm. Env. Res. Papers, no. 255. Bedford, Mass.: Air Force Cambridge Res. Labs.

——— . 1970*a*. Vortex signature recognition by a Doppler radar. *J. Appl. Meteor.* 9:661–70.

——— . 1970*b*. Mapping a thunderstorm anvil flow by Doppler radar. *J. Appl. Meteor.* 9:911–15.

Donaldson, R. J., Jr.; Armstrong, G. M.; and Atlas, D. 1966. Doppler measurements of horizontal and vertical motions in a paired instability line. *Proc. Twelfth Conf. Radar Meteor.*, pp. 392–97. Boston: Amer. Meteor. Soc.

Donaldson, R. J., Jr.; Chmela, A. C.; and Shackford, C. R. 1959. Some behavior patterns of New England hailstorms. In *Physics of Precipitation*. pp. 354–69. Washington, D.C.: Amer. Geophys. Union.

Donaldson, R. J., Jr., and Tear, R. T. 1963. Distortions in reflectivity patterns by antenna side lobes. *Proc. Tenth Wea. Radar Conf.*, pp. 108–15. Boston: Amer. Meteor. Soc.

Donaldson, R. J., Jr., and Wexler, R. 1968. Notes on thunderstorm observation by fixed-beam Doppler radar. *J. Atmos. Sci.* 25:139–44.

——— . 1969. Flight hazards in thunderstorms determined by Doppler velocity variance. *J. Appl. Meteor.* 8:128–33.

Douglas, R. H. 1963*a*. Size distribution of Alberta hail samples. Sci. Rept. MW-36, pp. 55–71. Montreal: Stormy Weather Group, McGill Univ. (also presented at National Conference on the Physics and Dynamics of Clouds, Chicago, 24–26 March 1964).

——— . 1963*b*. Recent hail research: A review. *Meteor. Monographs* 5:157–67.

——— . 1964. Hail size distribution. *Proc. Eleventh Radar Wea. Conf.*, pp. 146–49. Boston: Amer. Meteor. Soc. (Same material as in Sci. Rept. MW-42, pp. 45–47. Montreal: Stormy Weather Group, McGill Univ.)

Douglas, R. H.; Gunn, K. L. S.; and Marshall, J. S. 1957. Pattern in the vertical of snow generation. *J. Meteor.* 14:95–114.

Douglas, R. H., and Hitschfeld, W. 1958. Studies of Alberta hailstorms. Sci. Rept. MW-27. Montreal: Stormy Weather Group, McGill Univ.

Dumoulin, G., and Cogombles, A. 1966. A comparison of radar values of precipitation intensities and rainfall rate from a raingage. *Proc. Twelfth Conf. on Radar Meteor.*, pp. 190–97. Boston: Amer. Meteor. Soc.

du Toit, P. S. 1967. Doppler radar observations of drop sizes in continuous rain. *J. Appl. Meteor.* 6:1082–87.

Dutton, J. A. 1971. Clear-air turbulence, aviation, and atmospheric science. *Reviews of Geophys. and Space Physics* 9:613–58.

East, T. W. R., and Dore, B. V. 1957. An electronic constant altitude display. *Proc. Sixth Wea. Radar Conf.*, pp. 325–30. Boston: Amer. Meteor. Soc.

Easterbrook, C. C. 1967. Some Doppler radar measurements of circulation patterns in convective storms. *J. Appl. Meteor.* 6:882–88.

Eastwood, E. 1967. *Radar ornithology.* London: Methuen.

Eastwood, E.; Bell, J. D.; and Phelps, N. R. 1959. Ring angels over southeast England. *Nature* 183:1759.

Eastwood, E.; Isted, G. A.; and Rider, G. C. 1962. Radar ring angels and the roosting behavior of starlings. *Proc. Roy. Soc.* B156:242–67.

Eccles, P. J., and Atlas, D. 1970. A dual wavelength radar hail detector. Tech. Rept. no. 14. Chicago: Lab. for Atmos. Probing, Univ. of Chicago.

Eccles, P. J., and Mueller, E. A. 1971. X-band attenuation and liquid water content estimation by dual-wavelength radar. *J. Appl. Meteor.* 10:1252–59.

Ekpenyong, B. E., and Srivastava, R. C. 1970. Radar characteristics of the melting layer: A theoretical study. Tech. Rept. no. 16. Chicago: Lab. for Atmos. Probing, Univ. of Chicago.

Elder, F. C. 1957. Some persistent "ring" angels on high powered radar. *Proc. Sixth Wea. Radar Conf.*, pp. 281–90. Boston: Amer. Meteor. Soc.

Fankhauser, S. C. 1968. Thunderstorm-environment interactions revealed by chaff trajectories in the mid-troposphere. *Proc. Thirteenth Radar Meteor. Conf.*, pp. 180–87. Boston: Amer. Meteor. Soc.

Farnsworth, G. W., and Mueller, E. A. 1953. Radar rainfall area integrator. *Proc. Conf. on Radio Meteorology*, art. IX-3. Austin: Univ. of Texas.

Fehlhaber, L., and Grosskopf, J. 1964. Untersuchung der Struktur der Trophosphare mit einem Vertikalradar [Investigation of the structure of the troposphere by means of vertically pointing radar]. *Machrichtentechnische Zeitschrift* 17:503–7.

Fleisher, A. 1953. The radar as a turbulence sensing probe. *Proc. Conf. Radio Meteor.*, art. XI-7. Austin: Univ. of Texas.

Fletcher, N. H. 1962. *The Physics of rainclouds.* London: Cambridge Univ. Press.

Foote, G. B. 1966. A *Z-R* relation for mountain thunderstorms. *J. Appl. Meteor.* 2:229–31.

——. 1968. Variance spectrum analysis of Doppler radar observations in continuous precipitation. *J. Appl. Meteor.* 7:459–64.

Foote, G. B., and du Toit, P. S. 1969. Terminal velocity of raindrops aloft. *J. Appl. Meteor.* 8:249–53.

Fortner, L. E., Jr. 1958. Typhoon Sarah, 1956. *Bull. Amer. Meteor Soc.* 39:633–39.

Foster, H. 1953. The use of radar in weather forecasting with particular reference to radar set AN/CPS-9. Tech. Rept. no. 20, Cambridge, Mass.: Dcpt. Meteor., M.I.T.

Fowler, M. S., and LaGrone, A. H. 1969. Comparison of insect's flight characteristics with observed characteristics of radar dot angels. *J. Appl. Meteor.* 8:122–27.

Frank, N. L.; Moore, P. L.; and Fishberg, G. E. 1967. On the use of digitized radar data for the Florida Peninsula. *J. Appl. Meteor.* 6:309–16.

Freund, R. F. 1966. Radar echo signature of tornadoes and funnel clouds aloft. *Proc. Twelfth Conf. on Radar Meteor.,* pp. 362–65. Boston: Amer. Meteor. Soc.

Friend, A. W. 1939. Continuous determination of air-mass boundaries by radio. *Bull. Amer. Meteor. Soc.* 20:202–5.

——. 1940. Developments in meteorological soundings by radio waves. *J. Aeronaut. Sci.* 7:347–52.

——. 1949. Theory and practice of tropospheric sounding by radar. *Proc. Inst. Radio Eng.* 37:116–38.

Fujita, T. 1958. Mesoanalysis of the Illinois tornadoes of 9 April 1953. *J. Meteor.* 15:288–96.

——. 1963. Analytical mesometeorology: A review. *Meteor. Monographs* 5:77–125.

Fujita, T. T. 1970. The Lubbock tornadoes: A study of suction spots. *Weatherwise* 23:160–73.

Fujita, T., and Black, P. G. 1970. In- and outflow fields of hurricane Debbie as revealed by echo and cloud velocities from airborne radar and ATS-III pictures. Preprint vol. Fourteenth Radar Meteor. Conf., pp. 353–58. Boston: Amer. Meteor. Soc.

Fujita, T. T.; Bradbury, D. L.; and Van Thullenar, C. F. 1970. Palm Sunday tornadoes of April 11, 1965. *Mon. Wea. Rev.* 98:29–69.

Fujita, T.; Izawa, T.; Watanabe, K.; and Imai, I. 1967. A model of typhoons accompanied by inner and outer rainbands. *J. Appl. Meteor.* 6:3–19.

Fujiwara, M. 1965. Raindrop-size distribution from individual storms.

J. Atmos. Sci. 22:585–91.

Gans, R. 1912. Über die Form ultramikroskopischer Goldteilchen [On the form of ultra-microscopic gold particles]. *Ann. Phys.* 37:881–900.

Geotis, S. G. 1963. Some radar measurements of hailstorms. *J. Appl. Meteor.* 2:270–75.

―――. 1964. On sea breeze "angels." *Proc. Eleventh Wea. Radar Conf.*, pp. 6–9. Boston: Amer. Meteor. Soc.

―――. 1968. Drop-size distribution in eastern Massachusetts. *Proc. Thirteenth Radar Meteor. Conf.*, pp. 154–57. Boston: Amer. Meteor. Soc.

―――. 1971. Thunderstorm water contents and rain fluxes deduced from radar. *J. Appl. Meteor.* 10:1233–37.

Gerhardt, J. R.; Tolbert, C. W.; Brunstein, S. A.; and Bahn, W. W. 1961. Experimental determination of the back-scattering cross sections of water drops and of wet and dry ice spheres at 3.2 cm. *J. Meteor.* 18:340–47.

Glover, K. M.; Boucher, R. J.; Ottersten, H.; and Hardy, K. R. 1969. Simultaneous radar, aircraft, and meteorological investigations of clear air turbulence. *J. Appl. Meteor.* 8:634–40.

Glover, K. M., and Hardy, K. R. 1966. Dot angels: Insects and birds. *Proc. Twelfth Wea. Radar Conf.*, pp. 264–68. Boston: Amer. Meteor. Soc.

Glover, K. M.; Hardy, K. R.; Konrad, T. G.; Sullivan, W. N., and Michaels, A. S. 1966. Radar observations of insects in free flight. *Science* 154:967–72.

Gordon, W. E. 1949. A theory of radar reflections from the lower atmosphere. *Proc. Inst. Radio Eng.* 37:41–43.

Gorelik, A. G. 1965. Odnovremennye izmereniia lagranzheva i eilerova masshtabov turbulentnosti v osadkakh v vide snega [Simultaneous measurements of Langrangian and Eulerian turbulence in snow precipitation]. *Izvest. Akad. Nauk SSSR, Fiz. Atmos. i Okeana, Moscow* 1:989–91.

―――. 1968. Wind structure investigations of boundary layer by radar "clear air" returns. *Proc. Thirteenth Radar Meteor. Conf.*, pp. 248–51. Boston: Amer. Meteor. Soc.

Gorelik, A. G.; Gritskiv, I. V.; Penyaz', L. A.; and Tsykunov, V. V. 1967. Rezultaty sovmestnykh radiolokatsionnykh i nazemnykh izmerenii mikrostruktury osadkov [Results of simultaneous radar and ground measurements of the microstructure of precipitation]. *Izvest. Akad. Nauk SSSR, Fiz. Atmos i Okeana, Moscow* 3:961–66.

Gorelik, A. G.; Kostarev, V. V.; and Chernikov, A. A. 1958. Radiolokatzionnoe izmerenie turbulentnykh dvizhenii v oblakakh [Turbulence measurements in clouds with radar]. *Meteor. i Gidrol., Moscow,* no. 5, pp. 12–19.

————. 1962. Novye vozmozhnosti radiolokatzionnogo izmereniia vetra [A possible new radar wind technique]. *Meteor. i Gidrol., Moscow,* no. 7, pp. 34–39.

Gorelik, A. G., and Logunov, V. F. 1968. Determination of vertical air motion velocity in rainfall by Doppler radar. *Proc. Thirteenth Radar Meteor. Conf.,* pp. 18–21. Boston: Amer. Meteor. Soc.

Gorelik, A. G., and Mel'nichuk, V. 1966. Radar measurements of turbulent parameters in clouds and precipitation. Abstract. *Proc. Twelfth Wea. Radar Conf.,* p. 104. Boston: Amer. Meteor. Soc.

Gorelik, A. G., and Smirnova, G. A. 1961. Sviaz fluktvatzii radioekho s mikostrukturoii osadkov [The relationship between the fluctuations of radio echoes and the microstructure of precipitation]. *Doklady Akad. Nauk SSSR, Moscow* 139:1098–1100.

Gorelik, A. G., and Tolstykh, V. G. 1970. Opredelenie koeffitzienta turbulentnoi diffuzii v svobodnoi atmosfere pri pomoshchi dipolnykh otrazhatelei [Determination of the turbulent diffusion coefficient in the free atmosphere with the aid of dipole reflectors]. *Izvest. Akad. Nauk SSSR, Fiz. Atmos. i Okeana, Moscow* 6:635–38.

Gossard, E. E.; Jensen, D. R.; and Richter, J. H. 1971. An analytical study of tropospheric structure as seen by high-resolution radar. *J. Atmos. Sci.* 28:794–807.

Gossard, E. E., and Richter, J. H. 1970. The shape of internal waves of finite amplitude from high resolution radar sounding of the lower atmosphere. *J. Atmos. Sci.* 27:971–73.

Gossard, E. E.; Richter, J. H.; and Atlas, D. 1970. Internal waves in the atmosphere from high-resolution radar measurements. *J. Geophys. Res.* 75:3523–36.

Groginsky, H. L. 1965. The coherent memory filter. *Electron Prog.* (Raytheon Co.) 9(3):7–13.

————. 1966. Digital processing of the spectra of pulse Doppler radar precipitation echoes. *Proc. Twelfth Wea. Radar Conf.,* pp. 34–43. Boston: Amer. Meteor. Soc.

Gunn, K. L. S., and East, T. W. R. 1954. The microwave properties of precipitation particles. *Quart. J. Roy. Meteor. Soc.* 80:522–45.

Gunn, K. L. S.; Langleben, M. P.; Dennis, A. S.; and Power, B. A. 1954. Radar evidence of a generating level for snow. *J. Meteor.* 11:20–26.

Gunn, K. L. S., and Marshall, J. S. 1955. Effect of wind shear on falling precipitation. *J. Meteor.* 12:339–49.

————. 1958. The distribution with size of aggregate snowflakes. *J. Meteor.* 15:452–66.

Gunn, R. and Kinzer, G. D. 1949. The terminal velocity of fall for water droplets in stagnant air. *J. Meteor.* 6:243–48.

Haddock, F. T. 1948. Scattering and attenuation of microwave radiation through rain. Washington, D.C.: U.S. Naval Res. Lab.

Hajovsky, R. G.; Deam, A. P.; and LaGrone, A. H. 1966. Radar reflections from insects in the lower atmosphere. *IEEE Trans. on Antennas and Propagation* 14:224–27.

Hamilton, P. M. 1964. Precipitation profiles for the total radar coverage. Sci. Rept. MW-37 Montreal, Stormy Weather Group, McGill University.

————. 1970. Use of detailed intensity radar data in mesoscale surface analysis of the 4 July 1969 storm in Ohio. Preprint vol. Fourteenth Radar Meteor. Conf., pp. 339–42. Boston: Amer. Meteor. Soc.

Hammond, G. R. 1968. A study of a left-moving thunderstorm of 23 April 1964. *Proc. Twelfth Radar Meteor. Conf.*, pp. 325–29. Boston: Amer. Meteor. Soc.

Hardy, K. R.; Atlas, D.; and Browning, K. 1964. The structure of hurricane spiral bands. *Proc. Eleventh Wea. Radar Conf.*, pp. 342–45. Boston: Amer. Meteor. Soc.

Hardy, K. R.; Atlas, D.; and Glover, K. M. 1966. Multiwavelength backscatter from the clear atmosphere. *J. Geophys. Res.* 71:1537–52.

Hardy, K. R., and Glover, K. M. 1966. 24-hour history of radar angel activity at three wavelengths. *Proc. Twelfth Wea. Radar Conf.*, pp. 269–74. Boston: Amer. Meteor. Soc.

Hardy, K. R., and Katz, I. 1969. Probing the atmosphere with high power, high resolution radars. *Atmospheric exploration by remote probes.* Vol. 2, pp. 217–43. Washington, D.C.: Nat. Acad. Sci. (Also see *Proc. I.E.E.E.* 57:468–80.)

Hardy, K. R., and Ottersten, H. 1969. Radar investigations of convective patterns in the clear atmosphere. *J. Atmos. Sci.* 26:666–72.

Harper, W. G. 1958. Detection of bird migration by centimetric radar: A cause of radar angels. *Proc. Roy. Soc.* B149:484–502.

————. 1959. Roosting movements of birds and migration departures from roosts as seen by radar. *Ibis.* 101:201–8.

————. 1960. An unusual indicator of convection. *Marine Observer* 30:36–40.

————. 1962. Radar backscattering from oblate spheroids. *Nubila* 5, no. 1:60–72.

Harper, W. G.; Ludlam, F. H.; and Saunders, P. M. 1957. Radar echoes from cumulus clouds. *Proc. Sixth Wea. Conf.*, pp. 267–73. Boston:

Amer. Meteor. Soc.

Harrison, H. T., and Post, E. A. 1954. *Evaluation of C-band (5.5 cm) airborne weather radar*. Denver, Colo.: United Air lines, Inc.

Harrold, T. W. 1966. Measurement of horizontal convergence in precipitation using a Doppler radar: A case study. *Quart. J. Roy. Meteor. Soc.* 92:31–40.

Harrold, T. W., and Browning, K. A. 1967. Mesoscale wind fluctuations below 1,500 meters. *Meteor. Magazine* 96:367–76.

——— . 1971. Identification of preferred areas of shower development by means of high powered radar. *Quart. J. Roy. Meteor. Soc.* 97:330–339.

Hartree, D. R.; Michel, J. G. L.; and Nicolson, P. 1946. Practical methods for the solution of the equations of tropospheric refraction. *Meteorological Factors in Radio Wave Propagation*, pp. 127–68. London: Physical Society.

Hay, D. R., and Reid, W. M. 1962. Radar angels in the lower troposphere. *Can. J. Phys.* 40:128–38.

Herman, B. M., and Battan, L. J. 1961*a*. Calculations of Mie backscattering of microwaves from ice spheres. *Quart. J. Roy. Meteor. Soc.* 87:223–30.

——— . 1961*b*. Calculations of Mie backscattering from melting ice spheres. *J. Meteor.* 18:468–78.

——— . 1961*c*. Calculations of the total attenuation and angular scatter of ice spheres. *Proc. Ninth Wea. Radar Conf.*, pp. 259–65. Boston: Amer. Meteor. Soc.

——— . 1963. Calculations of the total attenuation and angular scatter of ice spheres. *Proc. Int. Conf. on Electromagnetic Scattering*, pp. 251–59. New York: Pergamon Press.

Herman, B. M.; Browning, S. R.; and Battan, L. J. 1961. Tables of the radar cross sections of water spheres. Tech. Rept. no. 9. Tucson: Inst. Atmos. Phys., Univ. of Ariz.

Hewitt, F. J., 1953. The study of lightning streamers with 50-cm radar. *Proc. Phys. Soc. London, B* 66:895–97.

——— . 1957. Radar echoes from inter-stroke processes in lightning. *Proc. Phys. Soc. London, B* 70:961–79.

Hicks, J. J. 1968. Radar observations of gravitational waves in the clear atmosphere. *Proc. Thirteenth Radar Meteor. Conf.*, pp. 258–61. Boston: Amer. Meteor. Soc.

Hicks, J. J., and Angell, J. K. 1968. Radar observations of breaking gravitational waves in the visually clear atmosphere. *J. Appl. Meteor.* 7:114–21.

Hicks, J. J.; Katz, I.; Landry, C. R.; and Hardy, K. R. 1967. Simultaneous radar and aircraft observations of clear-air turbulence. *Science*

157:808–9.

Higgs, A. J. 1952. The measurement of precipitation by radar. *Proc. Third Radar Wea. Conf.*, pp. D49–D50. Montreal: McGill Univ.

Hiser, H. W.; Senn, H. V.; and Conover, L. F. 1958. Rainfall measurement by radar using photographic integration techniques. *Trans. Amer. Geophys. Union* 39:1043–47.

Hiser, H. W.; Senn, H. V.; and Courtright, L. F. 1970. Identification of damaging surface winds in tropical thunderstorms utilizing incoherent weather radar and meteorological observations. Coral Gables. Fla: Radar Meteor. Lab., School of Marine and Atmos. Sci., Univ. of Miami.

Hitschfeld, W. 1960. The motion and erosion of convective storms in severe vertical shear. *J. Meteor.* 17:270–82.

Hitschfeld, W., and Bordan, J. 1954. Errors inherent in the radar measurement of rainfall at attenuating wavelengths. *J. Meteor.* 11:58–67.

Hitschfeld, W., and Dennis, A. S. 1956. *Turbulence in snow generating cells*. Sci. Rept. MW-23. Montreal: Stormy Weather Group, McGill Univ.

Hitschfeld, W., and Douglas, R. H. 1962. A theory of hail growth: Alberta hail studies, 1961. Sci. Rept. MW-35, pp. 19–29. Montreal: Stormy Weather Group, McGill Univ.

Hoecker, W. H. 1957. Abilene, Texas, area tornadoes and associated radar echoes of May 27, 1956. *Proc. Sixth Radar Wea. Conf.*, pp. 143–50. Amer. Meteor. Soc.

Hood, A. D. 1950. Quantitative measurements at 3 and 10 cm of radar echo intensity from precipitation. Rept. no. 2155. Toronto: Nat. Res. Council of Canada.

Hooke, W. H.; Young, J. M.; and Beran, D. W. 1972. Atmospheric waves observed in the planetary boundary layer using an acoustic sounder and a microbarograph array. *Boundary Layer Meteor.* 2:371–80.

Hooper, J. E. N., and Kippax, A. A. 1950*a*. The bright band: A phenomenon associated with radar echoes from falling rain. *Quart. J. Roy. Meteor. Soc.* 76:125–31.

———. 1950*b*. Radar echoes from meteorological precipitation. *Proc. Inst. Elect. Engineers*, Pt. 1, 97:89–97.

Hoose, J. M., and Colon, J. A. 1970. Some aspects of the radar structure of hurricane Beulah on September 9, 1967. *Mon. Wea. Rev.* 98:529–33.

Hunter, I. M. 1954. Polarization of radar echoes from meteorological precipitation. *Nature* 173:165–66.

Imai, I. 1960. Raindrop size-distributions and *Z-R* relationships. *Proc.*

Eighth Wea. Radar Conf., pp. 211–18. Boston: Amer. Meteor. Soc.

———. 1963. Filling of typhoon eye by landing. *Proc. Tenth Wea. Radar Conf.,* pp. 214–21. Boston: Amer. Meteor. Soc.

Imai, I.; Fujiwara, M.; Ichimura, I.; and Toyama, Y. 1955. Radar reflectivity of falling Snow. *Papers in Meteor. Geophys. Tokyo* 6:130–39.

Jessup, E. A. 1971. Pilot chaff project at NSSL. NOAA Tech. Memorandum. TM ERL NSSL-56, Norman, Oklahoma: NOAA, National Severe Storms Lab.

Jiusto, J. E. 1961. Project wind shear. Progress Rept. no. 1. Buffalo, N.Y.: Cornell Aero. Lab., Inc.

Jones, D. M. A. 1955. 3 cm and 10 cm wavelength radiation backscatter from rain. *Proc. Fifth Wea. Radar Conf.,* pp. 281–85. Boston: Amer. Meteor. Soc.

———. 1956. Rainfall drop-size distribution and radar reflectivity. Res. Rept. no. 6. Urbana: Meteor. Lab., Illinois State Water Survey.

Jones, H. L. 1951. A sferic method of tornado identification and tracking. *Bull. Amer. Meteor. Soc.* 32:380–85.

Jones, R. F. 1950. The temperatures at the top of radar echoes associated with various cloud systems. *Quart. J. Roy. Meteor. Soc.* 76:312–29.

———. 1954. Radar echoes from lightning. *Quart. J. Roy. Meteor. Soc.* 80:579–82.

———. 1960. Size-distribution of ice crystals in cumulonimbus clouds. *Quart. J. Roy. Meteor. Soc.* 86:187–94.

Jordan, C. L. 1960. Spawinds for the eyewall of hurricane Daisy of 1958. *Proc. Eighth Radar Wea. Conf.,* pp. 219–26. Boston: Amer. Meteor. Soc.

———. 1962. On the maximum vertical extent of convective clouds. Sci. Rept. Tallahassee: Dept. of Meteor., Florida State Univ.

———. 1963. The accuracy of center positions of hurricanes as determined by the spiral-overlay technique. *Proc. Tenth Wea. Conf.,* pp. 202–7. Boston: Amer. Meteor. Soc.

Jordan, C. L.; Hurt, D. A.; and Lowrey, C. A. 1960. On the structure of hurricane Daisy on 27 August 1958. *J. Meteor.* 17:337–48.

Jordan, C. L., and Schatzle, F. J. 1962. The "double-eye" of hurricane Donna. Rept. no. 50, pp. 368–72. Washington, D.C.: Nat. Hurricane Res. Lab., U.S. Weather Bureau.

Jordan, C. L.; Schatzle, F. J.; and Cronise, W. C. 1961. Some interesting features of hurricane Donna. *Proc. Ninth Wea. Radar Conf.,* pp. 6–11. Boston: Amer. Meteor. Soc.

Jordan, E. C., and Balmain, K. G. 1968. *Electromagnetic waves and radiating systems.* Englewood Cliffs, N.J.: Prentice-Hall.

Jordan, H. M., and Stowell, D. J. 1955. Some small-scale features of the track of hurricane Ione. *Mon. Wea. Rev.* 83:210–15.

Joss, J., and List, R. 1963. Backscattering cross sections of mixtures of ice and water. *Z. angew. Math. Phys.* 14:376–80.

Joss, J., and Waldvogel, A. 1969. Raindrop size distribution and sampling size errors. *J. Atmos. Sci.* 26:566–69.

———. 1970. Raindrop size distributions and Doppler velocities. Preprint vol. Fourteenth Radar Meteor. Conf., pp. 153–56. Boston: Amer. Meteor. Soc.

Joss, J.; Schram, K.; Thams, J. C.; and Waldvogel, A. 1970. *On the quantitative determination of precipitation by radar.* Wissenschaftliche Mitteilung Nr. 63. Zurich: Eidgenössische kommission zum studium der Hagelbildung und der Hagelabwehr.

Juillerat, R., and Godard, S. 1963. Etude de la corrélation entre l'attenuation atmospherique d'une onde E. M. et l'intensité de pluie [Study of the correlation between the atmospheric attenuation of E. M. waves and the intensity of rain]. Internal company report, 17 April 1963. Paris: Lignes Télégraphiques et Téléphoniques.

Kassander, A. R., Jr., and Sims, L. L. 1957. Cloud photogrammetry with ground-located K-17 aerial cameras. *J. Meteor.* 14:43–49.

Kerker, M.; Langleben, M. P.; and Gunn, K. L. S. 1951. Scattering of microwaves by a melting, spherical ice particle. *J. Meteor.* 8:424.

Kerr, D. E. 1951. *Propagation of short radio waves.* New York: McGraw-Hill.

Kessler, E., III. 1957. Outer precipitation bands of hurricanes Edna and Ione. *Bull. Amer. Meteor. Soc.* 38:335–46.

———. 1958. Eye region of hurricane Edna, 1954. *J. Meteor.* 15:264–70.

———. 1961. An appraisal of the use of radar in observation and forecasting. *Proc. 9th Wea. Radar Conf.,* pp. 13–36. Boston: Amer. Meteor. Soc.

———. 1966a. Computer program for calculating average lengths of weather radar echoes and pattern bandedness. *J. Atmos. Sci.* 23:569–74.

———. 1966b. Lightning discharge and precipitation. *Quart. J. Roy. Meteor. Soc.* 92:308–10.

———. 1968. Radar measurements for the assessment of area rainfall review and outlook. *Radar Measurement of Precipitation for Hydrological Purposes,* pp. 1–29. Rept. no. 5. Geneva: World Meteorological Organization.

———. 1970. Thunderstorms over Oklahoma—22 June 1969. *Weatherwise* 23:56–69.

Kessler, E. III, and Atlas, D. 1956. *Radar synoptic analysis of hurricane Edna, 1954.* Geophysical Research Papers, no. 50. Bedford, Mass.: Air Force Cambridge Res. Labs.

Kessler, E., III, and Russo, J. A., Jr. 1963. A program for the assembly and display of radar-echo distributions. *J. Appl. Meteor.* 2:582–93.

Kodaira, N. 1960. The characteristics of the averaged echo intensity received by the logarithmic I.F. amplifier. *Proc. Eighth Wea. Radar Conf.,* pp. 255–61. Boston: Amer. Meteor. Soc.

——— . 1961. Radar areal-rainfall measurements. *Proc. Ninth Wea. Radar Conf.,* pp. 121–25. Boston: Amer. Meteor. Soc.

——— . 1963. Some use of a storage tube for weather radar. *Proc. Tenth Wea. Radar Conf.,* pp. 397–402. Boston: Amer. Meteor. Soc.

Konrad, T. G. 1970. The dynamics of the convective process in the clear air as seen by radar. *J. Atmos. Sci.* 27:1138–47.

Konrad, T. G., and Hicks, J. 1966. Tracking of known bird species by radar. *Proc. Twelfth Wea. Radar Conf.,* pp. 259–63. Boston: Amer. Meteor. Soc.

Kotov, N. V. 1960. Radiolakatzionnye kharakteristiki livnei i groz [Radar characteristics of rainstorms and thunderstorms]. *Trudy Glavnoi Geofiz. Obs., Leningrad,* no. 102, pp. 63–93.

Kotov, N. V., and Khe, Zhui-Tszyun, 1961. Nekotorye rezultaty radio-lokatsionnogo issledovaniia kharaktera dvizheniia ochagov livnei i groz [Some results of radar studies of the motions of rainstorms and thunderstorm cells]. *Trudy Glavnoi Geofiz. Obs., Leningrad,* no. 120, pp. 45–51.

Kraus, M. J. 1970. Doppler radar investigation of flow patterns within severe thunderstorms. Preprint vol. Fourteenth Radar Meteor. Conf., pp. 127–32. Boston: Amer. Meteor. Soc.

Kropfli, R. A. 1971. Simultaneous radar and instrumented aircraft observations in a clear air turbulent layer. *J. Appl. Meteor.* 10:796–802.

Kropfli, R. A., Katz, I.; Konrad, T. G.; and Dobson, E. B. 1968. Simultaneous radar reflectivity measurements and refractive index spectra in the clear atmosphere. *Radio Science* 3:991–94.

Kundu, M. M., and De, A. C. 1966. Radar study of a post monsoon depression. *Proc. Twelfth Radar Meteor. Conf.,* pp. 461–66. Boston: Amer. Meteor. Soc.

Labrum, N. R. 1952. The scattering of radio waves by meteorological particles. *J. Appl. Phys.* 23:1324–30.

LaGrone, A. H.; Deam, A. P.; and Walker, G. B. 1964. Angels, insects, and weather. *Radio Science J. Res.* (Nat. Bur. Standards, Washington, D.C.) 68D:895–901.

Lane, J. A. 1967. Radar echoes from tropospheric layers by incoherent back-scatter. *Electronics Letters* 3:173–74.

Lane, J. A., and Meadows, R. W. 1963. Simultaneous radar and refractometer soundings of the troposphere. *Nature* 197:35–36.

Langille, R. C., and Thain, R. S. 1951. Some quantitative measurements of 3 cm radar echoes from falling snow. *Canadian J. Phys.* 29:482.

Langleben, M. P. 1956. The plan pattern of snow echoes at the generating level. *J. Meteor.* 13:554–60.

Langleben, M. P. and Gunn, K. L. S. 1952. Scattering and absorption of microwaves by a melting ice sphere. Sci. Rept. MW-5. Montreal: Stormy Weather Group, McGill Univ.

Laws, J. O. 1941. Measurements of the fall-velocity of water drops and raindrops. *Trans. Amer. Geophys. Union.* 22:709–21.

Laws, J. O., and Parsons, D. A. 1943. The relation of raindrop size to intensity. *Trans. Amer. Geophys. Union.* 24:432–60.

Leach, W. 1957. Observed characteristics of convective cell bands. *Proc. Sixth Wea. Radar Conf.*, pp. 151–56. Boston: Amer. Meteor. Soc.

Leber, G. W.; Merritt, C. J.; and Robertson, J. P. 1961. WSR-57 analysis of heavy rains. *Proc. Ninth Wea. Radar Conf.*, pp. 102–5. Boston: Amer. Meteor. Soc.

Lemon, L. 1970. The formation of an anticyclonic eddy within a severe thunderstorm as revealed by radar and surface data. Preprint vol. Fourteenth Radar Meteor. Conf., pp. 323–28. Boston: Amer. Meteor. Soc.

Lhermitte, R. M. 1960*a*. New developments of the echo fluctuation theory and measurements. *Proc. Eighth Wea. Radar Conf.*, pp. 263–68. Boston: Amer. Meteor. Soc.

———. 1960*b*. The use of special "pulsed Doppler radar" in measurements of particle fall velocities. *Proc. Eighth Wea. Radar Conf.*, pp. 269–75. Boston: Amer. Meteor. Soc.

———. 1960*c*. Variations de la vitesse de chute des particules d'une précipitation étendue, a différents niveaux [Variations in the fall speed of particles in widespread precipitation at different levels]. *Comptes Rendus des Séances de l'Académie des Sciences* 250:899–901.

———. 1962. Note on wind variability with Doppler radar. *J. Atmos. Sci.* 19:343–46.

———. 1963*a*. Weather echoes in Doppler and conventional radars. *Proc. Tenth Wea. Radar Conf.*, pp. 323–29. Boston: Amer. Meteor. Soc.

———. 1963*b*. Motions of scatterers and the variances of the mean intensity of weather radar signals. Sudbury, Mass.: Sperry Rand Res. Ctr.

———. 1964. Doppler radars as severe storm sensors. *Bull. Amer. Meteor. Soc.* 45:587–96.

———. 1966*a*. Probing air motion by Doppler analysis of radar clear air returns. *J. Atmos. Sci.* 23:575–91.

———. 1966*b*. Application of pulse Doppler radar technique to meteorology. *Bull. Amer. Meteor. Soc.* 47:703–11.

———. 1966*c*. Doppler observation of particle velocities in a snowstorm. *Proc. Twelfth Wea. Radar Conf.*, pp. 117–24. Boston: Amer. Meteor. Soc.

———. 1968*a*. New developments in Doppler radar methods. *Proc. Thirteenth Radar Meteor. Conf.*, pp. 14–17. Boston: Amer. Meteor. Soc.

———. 1968*b*. Turbulent air motion as observed by Doppler radar. *Proc. Thirteenth Radar Meteor. Conf.*, pp. 498–503. Boston: Amer. Meteor. Soc.

———. 1969*a*. Atmospheric probing by Doppler radar. In *Atmospheric Exploration by Remote Probes*. Vol. 2, pp. 253–85. Washington, D.C.: Nat. Acad. Sci.

———. 1969*b*. Note on the observation of small-scale atmospheric turbulence by Doppler radar techniques. *Radio Science* 4:1241–46.

———. 1970. Dual-Doppler radar observations of convective storm circulation. Preprint Vol. Fourteenth Radar Meteor. Conf., pp. 139–44. Boston: Amer. Meteor. Soc.

———. 1971. Probing of atmospheric motions by airborne pulse Doppler radar techniques. *J. Appl. Meteor.* 10:234–46.

Lhermitte, R. M., and Atlas, D. 1961. Precipitation motion by pulse Doppler radar. *Proc. Ninth Wea. Radar Conf.*, pp. 218–23. Boston: Amer. Meteor. Soc.

———. 1963. Doppler fall speed and particle growth in stratiform precipitation. *Proc. Tenth Wea. Radar Conf.*, pp. 297–302. Boston: Amer. Meteor. Soc.

Lhermitte, R. M., and Dooley, J. 1966. Study of the motion of clear air targets. *Proc. Twelfth Wea. Radar Conf.*, pp. 293–99. Boston: Amer. Meteor. Soc.

Lhermitte, R. M., and Kessler, E., III. 1964. An experimental pulse Doppler radar for severe storm investigations. *Proc. Eleventh Wea. Radar Conf.*, pp. 304–9. Boston: Amer. Meteor. Soc.

———. 1965. A weather radar signal integrator. Tech. Memo. no. 2. Norman, Okla.: ESSA, Nat. Severe Storms Labs.

Ligda, M. G. H. 1950. Lightning detection by radar. *Bull. Amer. Meteor. Soc.* 31:279–83.

———. 1956. The radar observation of lightning. *J. Atmos. Terrest. Phys.* 9:329–46.

———. 1957. Middle latitude precipitation patterns as observed by radar. College Station, Tex.: Dept. of Oceanography and Meteor., A & M College of Texas.

———. 1958. Radar observations of blackbird flights. *Texas J. Sci.* 10:255–65.

Ligda, M. G. H., and Bigler, S. G. 1958. Radar echoes from a cloudless cold front. *J. Meteor.* 15:494–501.

Ligda, M. G. H., and Mayhew, W. A. 1954. On the relationship between the velocities of small precipitation areas and geostrophic winds. *J. Meteor.* 11:421–23.

List, R. 1959. Wachstum von Eis-Wassergemischen im Hagelversuchskanal [Growth of an ice-water mixture in a hail tunnel]. *Helv. Phys. Acta.* 32:293–96.

Litvinov, I. V. 1956. Funktsii raspredeleniia chastits zhidkikh osadkov [Distribution function of liquid precipitation particles]. *Izvest. Akad. Nauk SSSR, Ser Geofiz., Moscow*, no. 12, pp. 1474–83.

Lob, W. H. 1968. R-meter correction for boxcar-ing and receiver noise in incoherent weather radars. *J. Appl. Meteor.* 7:1018–25.

Lofgren, G. R., and Battan, L. J. 1969. Polarization and vertical velocities of dot angel echoes. *J. Appl. Meteor.* 8:948–51.

Lowan, A. N. 1949. *Tables of scattering functions for spherical particles.* Nat. Bur. Standards Appl. Math. Ser. 4, Washington, D.C.: Govt. Printing Office.

Luckenback, G. 1958. Two examples of non-precipitating echoes as observed on AN/CPS-9 radar. *Proc. Seventh Wea. Radar Conf.*, pp. D41–D47. Boston: Amer. Meteor. Soc.

Ludlam, F. H. 1960. The role of radar in rainstorm forecasting. Tech. Note no. 3, Contract no. AF 61(052)-254. London: Dept. of Meteor., Imperial College.

———. 1963. Severe local storms. *Meteor Monographs* 5:1–30.

McCallister, J.; Teaque, J. L.; and Vicroy, C. E. 1966. Operational radar rainfall measurements. *Proc. Twelfth Conf. on Radar Meteor.*, pp. 208–15. Boston: Amer. Meteor. Soc.

Macklin, W. C., and Ludlam, F. H. 1961. The fallspeeds of hailstones. *Quart. J. Roy. Meteor. Soc.* 87:78–81.

McCormick, K. S. 1970. Reflectivity and attenuation observations of hail and radar bright band. Preprint vol. Fourteenth Radar Meteor. Conf., pp. 19–24. Boston: Amer. Meteor. Soc.

Magono, C. 1957. On snowflakes. *Proc. Sixth Wea. Radar Conf.*, pp. 31–36. Boston: Amer. Meteor. Soc.

Malkus, J. S. 1952. Recent advances in the study of convective clouds and their interaction with the environment. *Tellus* 4:71–87.

Marshall, J. S. 1953a. Frontal precipitation and lightning observed by radar. *Canadian J. Phys.* 31:194–203.

————. 1953*b*. Precipitation trajectories and patterns. *J. Meteor.* 10: 25–29.

————. 1957. The constant-altitude presentation of radar weather patterns. *Proc. Sixth Wea. Radar Conf.*, pp. 321–24. Boston: Amer. Meteor. Soc.

————. 1961. Inter-relation of the fall speed of rain and the updraft rates in hail formation. *Nubila* 4:59–62.

————. 1969. Power-law relations in radar meteorology. *J. Appl. Meteor.* 8:171–72.

————. 1971. Peak reading and thresholding in processing radar weather data. *J. Appl. Meteor.* 10:1213–23.

Marshall, J. S., and Gordon, W. E. 1957. Radiometeorology. *Meteor. Monographs.* 3:73–113.

Marshall, J. S., and Hitschfeld, W. 1953. Interpretation of the *fluctuating* echo from randomly distributed scatterers. Pt. I. *Canadian J. Physics* 31:962–94.

Marshall, J. S.; Hitschfeld, W.; and Gunn, K. L. S. 1955. Advances in radar weather. *Advances in geophysics,* 2:1–56. New York: Academic Press.

Marshall, J. S.; Langille, R. C.; and Palmer, W. M. K. 1947. Measurement of rainfall by radar. *J. Meteor.* 4:186–92.

Marshall, J. S., and Palmer, W. M. K. 1948. The distribution of raindrops with size. *J. Meteor.* 5:165–66.

Marwitz, J. D. 1972*a*. The Structure and Motion of Severe Hailstorms. Part I: Supercell Storms. *J. Appl. Meteor.* 11:166–179.

————. 1972*b*. The Structure and Motion of Severe Hailstorms. Part II. Multi-Cell Storms. *J. Appl. Meteor.* 11:180–188.

————. 1972*c*. The Structure and Motion of Severe Hailstorms. Part III. Severely Sheared Storms. *J. Appl. Meteor.* 11:189–201.

Marwitz, J. D., and Berry, E. X. 1971. The airflow within the weak echo region of an Alberta hailstorm. *J. Appl. Meteor.* 10:487–92.

Marwitz, J. D.; Middleton, J. R.; Auer, A. H., Jr.; and Veal, D. L. 1970. The dynamics of updraft vaults in hailstorms as inferred from the entraining jet model. *J. Atmos. Sci.* 27:1099–1102.

Mason, B. J. 1971. *The physics of clouds.* Oxford: Clarendon Press.

Mather, G. K., and Hardy, K. R. 1970. Instrumented aircraft measurements in the vicinity of clear air radar structures. Preprint vol. Fourteenth Radar Meteor. Conf., pp. 49–52. Boston: Amer. Meteor. Soc.

Matsumoto, S., and Ninomiya, K. 1968. Some characteristic echo distributions related to the mesoscale convergence field. *Proc. Thirteenth Radar Meteor. Conf.*, pp. 202–5. Boston: Amer. Meteor. Soc.

Maynard, R. H. 1945. Radar and weather. *J. Meteor.* 2:214–26.

Medhurst, R. G. 1965. Rainfall attenuation of centimeter waves: Comparison of theory and measurement. *IEEE Trans. on Antennas and Propagation* AP-13:550–64.

Meyer, J. H. 1971. Radar observations of land breeze fronts. *J. Appl. Meteor.* 10:1224–32.

Mie. G. 1908. Beiträge zur Optik trüber Medien, speziell kolloidaler Metallösungen [Contribution to the optics of suspended media, specifically colloidal metal suspensions]. *Ann. Phys.* 25:377–445.

Miles, V. G. 1952. Radar echoes and lightning. *Nature* 170:365–66.

———. 1953. Radar echoes associated with lightning. *J. Atmos. Terrest. Phys.* 3:258–62.

Moore, C. B.; Vonnegut, B.; Machado, J. A.; and Survilas, H. J. 1962. Radar observations of rain gushes following overhead lightning strokes. *J. Geophys. Res.* 67:207–20.

Moore, C. B.; Vonnegut, B.; Vrablik, E. A.; and McCaig, D. A. 1964. Gushes of rain and hail after lightning. *J. Atmos. Sci.* 21:646–65.

Muchnik, V. M. 1961. O tochnosti izmereniya intensivnosti dozhdei radiolokatsionnymi metodami [The accuracy of radar rain-intensity measurements]. *Meteor. i Gidrol., Moscow,* no. 2, pp. 44–47.

Muchnik, V. M.; Markovich, M. L.; and Volynetz, L. M. 1966. On the evaluation of accuracy of the radar method of measuring the areal rainfall quantity. *Proc. Twelfth Conf. on Radar Meteor.,* pp. 216–19. Boston: Amer. Meteor. Soc.

Mueller, E. A., and Jones, D. M. A. 1960. Drop size distributions in Florida. *Proc. Eighth Wea. Radar Conf.,* pp. 299–305. Boston: Amer. Meteor. Soc.

Mueller, E. A., and Sims, A. L. 1966. Investigation of the quantitative determination of point and areal precipitation by radar echo measurements. Final Rept., Contract DA 28-043 AMC 00032(E). Urbana: Illinois State Water Survey.

Nagle, R. E., and Serebreny, S. M. 1962. Radar precipitation echo and satellite cloud observations of a maritime cyclone. *J. Appl. Meteor.* 1:279–95.

National Center for Atmospheric Research. 1970. Coherent cloud physics radar. In *Facilities for atmospheric research,* No. 13, pp. 26–28. Boulder, Colo.: Nat. Ctr. Atmos. Res.

Newell, R. E. 1958a. A comparison of solid hydrometeor shapes at wavelengths of 3 cm and 5,000 A. *Proc. Seventh Wea. Radar Conf.,* pp. B1–B7. Boston: Amer. Meteor. Soc.

———. 1958b. Intensity measurements on angels at 3 and 10 cm. *Proc. Seventh Wea. Radar Conf.,* pp. E50–E56. Boston: Amer. Meteor. Soc.

Newell, R. E.; Geotis, S. G.; Stone, M. L.; and Fleisher, A. 1955. How round are raindrops? *Proc. Fifth Wea. Radar Conf.*, pp. 261–68. Boston: Amer. Meteor. Soc.

Newton, C. W. 1950. Structure and mechanism of prefrontal squall line. *J. Meteor.* 7:210–22.

———. 1963. Dynamics of severe convective storms. *Meteor. Monographs* 5(27):33–58.

Newton, C. W. and Fankhauser, J. C. 1964. On the movements of convective storms, with emphasis on size discrimination in relation to water budget requirements. *J. Appl. Meteor.* 3:651–68.

Newton, C. W., and Newton, H. R. 1959. Dynamical interactions between large convective clouds and environment with vertical shear. *J. Meteor.* 16:483–96.

Obukhov, A. M. 1949. Struktura temperaturnogo polia v turbulentnom potoke [Structure of the temperature field in a turbulent current]. *Izvest Akad. Nauk SSSR, Ser. Geogr. i Geofiz., Moscow* 13:58–69.

Oetzel, G. N., and Pierce, E. T. 1968. The radio emissions from close lightning. In *Planetary electrodynamics,* 1:543–69. New York: Gordon & Breach.

Ohtake, T. 1968. Change of size distribution of hydrometeors through a melting layer. *Proc. Thirteenth Radar Meteor. Conf.*, pp. 148–53. Boston: Amer. Meteor. Soc.

———. 1969. Observations of size distribution of hydrometeors through the melting layer. *J. Atmos. Sci.* 26:545–57.

Orville, H. D., and Kassander, A. R., Jr. 1961. Terrestrial photogrammetry of clouds. *J. Meteor.* 18:682–87.

Otani, K. 1964. CAPPI analysis of typhoon Thelma. *Proc. Eleventh Wea. Radar Conf.*, pp. 350–53. Boston: Amer. Meteor. Soc.

Ottersten, H. 1964. Occurrence and characteristics of radar angels observed with a vertically-pointing pulse radar. *Proc. Eleventh Wea. Radar Conf.*, pp. 22–27. Boston: Amer. Meteor. Soc.

———. 1969. Atmospheric structure and radar backscattering in clear air. *Radio Science* 4:1179–93.

———. 1970a. Radar angels and their relationships to meteorological factors. *Forsvarets Forskningsanstalt* (Res. Inst. of Nat. Defense, Stockholm) 4, no. 2:1–33.

———. 1970b. Radar observations of the turbulent structure in shear zones in the clear atmosphere. Preprint vol. Fourteenth Radar Meteor. Conf., pp. 111–16. Boston: Amer. Meteor. Soc.

Peace, R. L. 1966. Radar characteristics of lake effect storms. *Proc. Twelfth Radar Meteor. Conf.*, pp. 454–60. Boston: Amer. Meteor. Soc.

Peace, R. L., Jr., and Brown, R. A. 1968. Comparison of single and double Doppler radar velocity measurements in convective storms.

Proc. Thirteenth Radar Meteor. Conf., pp. 464–70. Boston: Amer. Meteor. Soc.

Peace, R. L., Jr.; Brown, R. A.; and Camnitz, H. G. 1969. Horizontal motion field observations with a single pulse Doppler radar. *J. Atmos. Sci.* 26:1096–1103.

Pell, J. 1969. Differences between Alberta hail and non-hail storms as observed by radar. Preprint vol. Sixth Conf. on Severe Local Storms, pp. 296–301. Boston: Amer. Meteor. Soc.

————. 1971. The use of broad-beam radar for quantitative analysis of severe storms. *J. Appl. Meteor.* 10:1238–51.

Penn, S.; Pierce, C.; and McGuire, J. K. 1955. The squall line and Massachusetts tornadoes of June 9, 1953. *Bull. Amer. Meteor. Soc.* 36:109–22.

Petrushevskii, V. A.; Persin, S. M.; Shevela, G. F.; Sal'man, E. M.; and Vakenburg, S. I. 1968. Kompleks apparatury dlia avtomaticheskogo polycheniia i obrabotki radiolokatzionnykh meteorologicheskikh dannykh [Complex apparatus for the automatic collection and processing of radar meteorological data]. *Proc. Third All Union Conf. Radar Meteor.,* pp. 196–209. Moscow: Hydromet. Publ. House.

Pilié, R. J.; Jiusto, J. E.; and Rogers, R. R., 1963. Wind velocity measurements with Doppler radar. *Proc. Tenth Wea. Radar Conf.,* pp. 329a–1, Boston: Amer. Meteor. Soc.

Plank, V. G. 1956. A meteorological study of radar angels. Geophys. Res. Paper no. 52. Bedford, Mass.: Air Force Cambridge Res. Labs.

Plank, V. G.; Cunningham, R. M.; and Campen, C. F. 1957. The refractive index structure of a cumulus boundary and implications concerning radio wave reflections. *Proc. Sixth Wea. Radar Conf.,* pp. 273–80. Boston: Amer. Meteor. Soc.

Popov, N. I. 1955. Smerchi na Poberezhe Chernogo Moria [Tornadoes on the coast of the Black Sea]. *Meteor. i Gidrol., Moscow,* no. 5, pp. 35–37.

Probert-Jones, J. R. 1960. The analysis of Doppler radar echoes from precipitation. *Proc. Eighth Wea. Radar Conf.,* pp. 377–85. Boston: Amer. Meteor. Soc.

————. 1962. The radar equation in meteorology. *Quart. J. Roy. Meteor. Soc.* 88:485–95.

————. 1963. The distortion of cumulonimbus precipitation observed by radar. Tech. Rept. no. 13. London: Dept. of Meteor., Imperial College.

Probert-Jones, J. R., and Harper, W. G. 1961. Vertical air motion in showers as revealed by Doppler radar. *Proc. Ninth Wea. Radar Conf.,* pp. 225–32. Boston: Amer. Meteor. Soc.

Prosser, N. E. 1970. Mesoscale surface analysis techniques utilizing radar data. Preprint vol. Fourteenth Radar Meteor. Conf., pp. 343–46. Boston: Amer. Meteor. Soc.

Ragette, G. 1971. The low level mesoscale wind field of Alberta hailstorms. Sci. Rept. MW-69. Montreal: Stormy Weather Group, McGill Univ.

Ramana Murty, Bh. V., and Gupta, S. C. 1959. Precipitation characteristics based on raindrop size measurements at Delhi and Khandala during southwest monsoon. *J. Sci. Industrial Res.,* New Delhi, 18A: 352–71.

Ramana Murty, Bh. V.; Roy, A. K.; and Biswas, K. R. 1965. Radar echo intensity below bright band. *J. Atmos. Sci.* 22:91–94.

Reynolds, S. E., and Braham, R. R. 1952. Significance of the initial radar echo. *Bull. Amer. Meteor. Soc.* 33:123.

Richter, J. H. 1969. High resolution tropospheric radar sounder. *Radio Science* 4:1261–68.

Richter, J. H., and Gossard, E. E. 1970. *Lower tropospheric structure as seen by a high-resolution radar.* Rept. NELC/TR 1718. San Diego, Calif.: Naval Electronics Lab. Ctr.

Rinehart, R. E., and Towery, N. G. 1968. Radar observations of mesoscale cyclones. *Proc. Thirteenth Radar Meteor. Conf.,* pp. 176–79. Boston: Amer. Meteor. Soc.

Robbiani, R. L. 1965. High performance weather radar. *I.E.E.E. Trans. on Aerospace and Elect. Systems* AES-1:185–92.

Roberts, D. E. 1959. Melting bands and precipitation rates. Report RL 1902. London: Radar Res. Lab., Decca Radar.

Rockney, V. D. 1954. Radar rainfall by photographic integration. Master's Thesis, Dept. of Meteor., M.I.T.

———. 1956. Hurricane detection by radar and other means. *Proc. Tropical Cyclone Symposium,* pp. 179–97. Brisbane.

Roelofs, T. H. 1963. Characteristics of trackable radar angels. Res. Rept. no. 137. Ithaca, N.Y.: Ctr. for Radiophysics and Space Res. Cornell Univ.

Rogers, R. R. 1957. Radar measurements of gustiness. *Proc. Sixth Wea. Radar Conf.,* pp. 99–106. Boston: Amer. Meteor. Soc.

———. 1963. Radar measurements of velocities of meteorological scatterers. *J. Atmos. Sci.* 20:170–74.

———. 1964. An extension of the *Z-R* Relationship for Doppler radar. *Proc. Eleventh Wea. Radar Conf.,* pp. 158–60. Boston: Amer. Meteor. Soc.

Rogers, R. R., and Camnitz, H. G. 1962. Doppler radar: A probe for atmospheric turbulence. Mimeographed. Buffalo, N.Y.: Cornell Aero. Lab.

Rogers, R. R., and Chimera, A. J. 1960. Doppler spectra from meteorological radar targets. *Proc. Eighth Wea. Radar Conf.,* pp. 377–85. Boston: Amer. Meteor. Soc.

Rogers, R. R., and Jiusto, J. E. 1966. An investigation of rain on the Island of Hawaii. CAL Rept. VC-2049-P-1. Buffalo, N.Y.: Cornell Aero. Lab.

Rogers, R. R., and Pilié, R. J. 1962. Radar measurements of drop size distribution. *J. Atmos. Sci.* 19:503–6.

Rogers, R. R., and Tripp, B. R. 1964. Some radar measurements of turbulence in snow. *J. Appl. Meteor.* 3:603–10.

Rogers, C. W. C., and Wexler, R. 1963. Rainfall determination from 0.86 and 1.82 cm radar measurements. *Proc. Tenth Wea. Radar Conf.*, pp. 260–70. Boston: Amer. Meteor. Soc.

Rozenberg, V. I., 1970. Rasseianie mikroradiovln sloistoi gradinoi [Scattering of microwaves by flaky hailstones]. *Izvest. Akad. Nauk SSSR, Fiz. Atmos. i Okeana, Moscow* 6:168–77.

Rutkowski, W., and Fleisher, A. 1955. The R-meter: An instrument for measuring gustiness. *Proc. Fifth Wea. Radar Conf.*, pp. 255–60. Fort Monmouth, N.J.: Signal Corps Engineering Lab.

Ryde, J. W. 1946. The attenuation and radar echoes produced at centimeter wavelengths by various meteorological phenomena. *Meteorological Factors in Radio Wave Propagation*, pp. 169–88. London: Physical Society.

Sadowski, A. 1964. Evolution of hurricane Ginny as seen on WSR-57 radar at Charleston, S.C. *Proc. Eleventh Wea. Radar Conf.*, pp. 354–57. Boston: Amer. Meteor. Soc.

Sal'man, E. M. 1957. Radiolokatzionnye issledovaniia livnei i groz [Radar investigations of showers and thunderstorms]. *Trudy Glavnoi Geofiz. Obs., Leningrad*, no. 72, pp. 46–65.

Sal'man, E. M.; Brylev, G. B.; Zotov, V. K.; Divinskaya, B. Sh.; and Fedorov, A. A. 1969. Compleksnoe ispolzovanie radiolokatzionnykh i sputnikovykh nabliydenii pri analize meso- i makromasshtabnykh oblachnnykh sistem [Complex use of radar and satellite observations while analyzing meso- and macroscale cloud systems]. *Meteor. i Gidrol., Moscow*, no. 2, pp. 44–49.

Sal'man, E. M.; Gashina, S. B.; and Divinskaya, B. Sh. 1969. Radiolokatzionnye kriterii razdeleniia grozovoi i livnevoi deiatelnosti [Radar criteria for dividing thunderstorm and hail activity]. *Meteor. i Gidrol., Moscow*, no. 4, pp. 79–83.

Sal'man, E. M.; Petrushevskii, V. A.; Vaksenburg, S. I.; and Shevela, G. F. 1968. Apparatura i metod operativnogo polucheniia radiolokatzionnoi meteorologicheskoi informatzii ob oblakakh, oblachnykh sistemakh i opasnykh iavleniiakh [Apparatus and a method for the operational radar acquisition of meteorological data on clouds, cloud systems, and dangerous phenomena]. *Proc. Third All-Union Conf. Radar Meteor.*, pp. 181–95. Moscow: Hydromet. Publ. House.

Saunders, P. M. 1962. Penetrative convection in stably stratified fluids. *Tellus* 16:177–94.

—— . 1965. Some characteristics of tropical marine showers. *J. Atmos. Sci.* 22:167–75.

Saunders, P. M., and Ronne, F. C. 1962. A comparison between the height of cumulus clouds and the height of radar echoes secured from them. *J. Appl. Meteor.* 1:296–302.

Saxton, J. A.; Lane, J. A.; Meadows, R. W.; and Mathews, P. A. 1964. Layer structure of the troposphere: Simultaneous radar and microwave refractometer investigations. *Proc. Inst. Elect. Engineers 111*: 275–83.

Schaffner, M. 1963. A process for weather radar data. *Proc. Tenth Wea. Radar Conf.*, pp. 384–88. Boston: Amer. Meteor. Soc.

Schatzle, F. J., and Cronise, W. G. 1960. A synoptic and radar photographic presentation on the life cycle of hurricane Gracie (1959). *Proc. Eighth Wea. Radar Conf.*, pp. 403–17. Boston: Amer. Meteor. Soc.

Schuetz, J., and Stout, G. E. 1957. RHI radar observations of a tornado. *Bull. Amer. Meteor. Soc.* 38:591–95.

Sekhon, R. S., and Srivastava, R. C. 1970. Snow size spectra and radar reflectivity. *J. Atmos. Sci.* 27:299–307.

—— . 1971. Doppler radar observations of drop-size distribution in a thunderstorm. *J. Atmos. Sci.* 28:983–94.

Senn, H. V. 1961. Hurricane eye motion as seen by radar. *Proc. Ninth Wea. Radar Conf.*, pp. 1–5. Boston: Amer. Meteor. Soc.

—— . 1966a. Radar hurricane precipitation patterns as track indicators. *Proc. Twelfth Conf. on Radar Meteor.*, pp. 436–39. Boston: Amer. Meteor. Soc.

—— . 1966b. Precipitation shear and bright band observations on hurricane Betsy, 1965. *Proc. Twelfth Conf. on Radar Meteor.*, pp. 447–53. Boston: Amer. Meteor. Soc.

Senn, H. V.; Courtright, C. L.; Black, P. G.; and Willoughby, H. E. 1970. Precipitation shear and bright band observations in hurricane Debbie on 18 and 20 August 1969. Preprint vol. Fourteenth Radar Meteor. Conf., pp. 363–66. Boston: Amer. Meteor. Soc.

Senn, H. V., and Hiser, H. W. 1957. Tracking hurricanes with radar. *Proc. Sixth Wea. Radar Conf.*, pp. 167–70. Boston: Amer. Meteor. Soc.

—— . 1959. On the origin of hurricane spiral rain bands. *J. Meteor.* 16:419–26.

—— . 1960. The mean motion of radar echoes in the complete hurricane. *Proc. Eighth Wea. Radar Conf.*, pp. 427–34. Boston: Amer. Meteor. Soc.

Shackford, C. R. 1960. Radar indications of a precipitation-lightning relationship in New England thunderstorms. *J. Meteor.* 17:15–19.

Shifrin, K. A. and Cherniak, M. M. 1967*a*. Rasseianie i oslablenie santimetrovogo izlucheniia kapliami vody [Scattering and attenuation of centimeter waves by water drops]. *Trudy Glavnoi Geofiz. Obs., Leningrad,* no. 203, pp. 109–22.

————. 1967*b*. Indikatrisy rasseinaiia santimetrovoi radiatsii kapliami vody [Scattering indices of centimeter radiation by water drops]. *Trudy Glavnoi Geofiz. Obs., Leningrad,* no. 203, pp. 123–37.

Shupiatskii, A. B. 1957. Radiolokatsionnoe izmerenie osadkov po metodu etalonnoi tseli [Radar measurement of precipitation by means of a reference target]. *Trudy Tsentral. Aero Obs., Moscow,* no. 22.

————. 1959. Radiolokatzionnoe rasseianie nesfericheskimi chastitsami [Radar scattering by non-sperhical particles]. *Trudy Tsentral. Aero. Obs., Moscow,* no. 30, pp. 39–52.

Shupiatskii, A. B., and Morgunov, S. P. 1963. Irimenie poliarizatsionnykh metodov v radiolokatsionnykh issledovanniakh oblakov i osadkov [The application of polarization methods to radar studies of clouds and precipitation]. *Trudy Vsesoiuznoe Nauch. Meteor. Sovesh.* Leningrad, pp. 295–305.

Silver, S. 1951. *Microwave antenna theory and design.* New York: McGraw-Hill.

Silverman, R. A. 1956. Turbulent mixing theory applied to radio scattering. *J. Appl. Phys.* 27:690–705.

Simpson, J. 1967. Photographic and radar study of the Stormfury 5 August 1965 seeded cloud. *J. Appl. Meteor.* 6:82–87.

Simpson, J.; Brier, G. W.; and Simpson, R. H. 1967. Stormfury cumulus seeding experiment 1965: Statistical analysis and main results. *J. Atmos. Sci.* 24:508–21.

Sims, A. L.; Mueller, E. A.; and Stout, G. E. 1963. Investigation of quantitative determination of point and areal precipitation by radar echo measurements, 8th Quart. Tech. Rept., 1 July 1963–30 Sept. 1963. Urbana: Meteor. Lab., Illinois State Water Survey.

Sinclair, P. C. 1968. Vertical motion and temperature structure of severe convective storms. Rept. of Sixth Conf. Severe Local Storms, pp. 346–50. Boston: Amer. Meteor. Soc.

Sirmans, D. 1970. The R-meter. Rept. FA-68-WA1-148. Norman, Okla.: Nat. Severe Storms Lab.

Sirmans, D.; Watts, W. L.; and Horwedel, J. H. 1970. Weather radar signal processing and recording at the national severe storms laboratory. *I.E.E.E. Trans. on Geoscience Electronics* GE-8:88–94.

Sivaramakrishnan, M. V. 1961. Studies of raindrop size characteristics in different types of tropical rain using a simple raindrop recorder.

Indian J. Meteor. Geophys. 12:189–217.

Sivaramakrishnan, M. V., and Selvam, M. 1966. On the use of the spiral-overlay technique for estimating the center positions of tropical cyclones from satellite photographs taken over the Indian Region. *Proc. Twelfth Conf. on Radar Meteor.*, pp. 440–46. Boston: Amer. Meteor. Soc.

Skolnik, M. I. 1962. *Introduction to radar systems.* New York: McGraw-Hill.

Sloss, Peter W., and Atlas, D. 1968. Wind shear and reflectivity gradient effects on Doppler radar spectra. *J. Atmos. Sci.* 25:1080–89.

Smith, E. J. 1950. Observations of precipitation with an airborne radar. *Australian J. Sci. Res., Ser. A. Phys. Sci.* 3:214–23.

Smith, P. L., and Rogers, R. R. 1963. On the possibility of radar detection of clear-air turbulence. *Proc. Tenth Wea. Radar Conf.,* Boston, pp. 316–21. Amer. Meteor. Soc.

Smith, R. L., and Holmes, D. W. 1961. Use of Doppler radar in meteorological observations. *Mon. Wea. Rev.* 89:1–7.

Speed, D. K. 1965. General application of meteorological radar sets. Tech. Rept. 184. Scott AFB, Ill.: Air Weather Service, USAF.

Spilhaus, A. F. 1948. Drop size intensity and radar echo of rain. *J. Meteor.* 5:161–64.

Starr, J. R., and Browning, K. A. 1972. Observations of Lee waves by high-power radar. *Quart. J. Roy. Meteor. Soc.* 98:73–85.

Statts, W. F., and Turrentine, C. M. 1956. Some observations and radar pictures of the Blackwell and Udall Tornadoes of May 25, 1955. *Bull. Amer. Meteor. Soc.* 37:495–505.

Stepanenko, V. D. 1966. *Radiolokatsiya v meteorologii* [Radar in meteorology]. Leningrad: Hydromet. Publ. House. (Partial translation available from Clearinghouse for Federal Scientific and Technical Information, Washington, D.C.)

Stephens, J. J. 1961. Radar cross sections for water and ice spheres. *J. Meteor.* 18:348–59.

———. 1964. On the applicability of Rayleigh scattering in radar meteorology. *J. Appl. Meteor.* 3:211–12.

Stevenson, A. F. 1953. Electromagnetic scattering by an ellipsoid in the third approximation. *J. Appl. Phys.* 24:1143–51.

Stone, M. L., and Fleisher, A. 1956. The measurement of weather noise. Rept. no. 26. Cambridge, Mass.: Dept. of Meteor., M.I.T.

Stout, G. E., and Huff, F. A. 1953. Radar records Illinois tornadogenesis. *Bull. Amer. Meteor. Soc.* 34:281–84.

Stout, G. E., and Hiser, H. 1955. Radar scope interpretation of wind, hail, and heavy rain storms between May 27 and June 8, 1954. *Bull. Amer. Meteor. Soc.* 36:519–27.

Stout, G. E., and Mueller, E. A. 1968. Survey of relationships between rainfall rate and radar reflectivity in the measurement of precipitation. *J. Appl. Meteor.* 7:465–74.

Stratmann, E.; Atlas, D.; Richter, J. H.; and Jensen, D. R. 1971. Sensitivity calibration of a dual-beam vertically pointing FM-CW radar. *J. Appl. Meteor.* 10:1260–65.

Stratton, J. A. 1930. The effects of rain and fog upon the propagation of very short radio waves. *Proc. Inst. Elect. Engineers*, 18:1064–75.

Subramanian, D. V. and Banerji, A. K. 1964. Premonsoon squall lines in northeast India and East Pakistan. *Proc. Eleventh Wea. Radar Conf.* Boston: Amer. Meteor. Soc. pp. 398–403.

Sulakvelidze, G. K. 1968. Raboty VGI po indikatzii gradovykh ochagov [The work of VGI on the detection of areas of hail formation]. *Proc. Third All-Union Conf. Radar Meteor.*, pp. 43–49. Moscow: Hydromet. Publ. House.

Sulakvelidze, G. K.; Bibilashvili, N. Sh.; and Lapcheva, V. F. 1965. *Obrazovanie osadkov i vozdeistvie na gradovye protsessy* [Formation of precipitation and modification of hail processes]. Leningrad: Hydromet. Publ. House. (Translated in 1967. Available in English from Clearinghouse for Federal Scientific and Technical Information, U.S. Dept. of Commerce, Washington, D.C.)

Sulakvelidze, G. K., and Dadali, Yu. A. 1968. Izmerenie intensivnosti osadkov mnogovolnovym radiolokatorom [The measurement of precipitation intensity with a multi-wavelength radar]. *Proc. Third All-Union Conf. Radar Meteor.*, pp. 31–42. Moscow: Hydrometeor. Service.

Sweeney, H. J. 1970. Turbulence in the lower atmosphere. Preprint vol. Fourteenth Radar Meteor. Conf., pp. 197–202. Boston: Amer. Meteor. Soc.

Swingle, D. W. 1953. Reflections of electromagnetic waves from media of continuously variable refractive index. *Proc. Conf. Radio Meteor.*, art. IV-2. Austin: University of Texas.

Tarble, R. D. 1960. The use of multiple exposure radar photographs in the Weather Bureau's Hydrologic Program. *Proc. Eighth Wea. Radar Conf.*, pp. 437–43. Boston: Amer. Meteor. Soc.

Tatarski, V. I. 1961. *Wave propagation in a turbulent medium.* New York: McGraw-Hill.

Tatehira, R. 1966. Some features of huge radar rainbands as observed by Mt. Fuji Radar. *Proc. Twelfth Conf. Radar Meteor.*, pp. 426–431. Boston: Amer. Meteor. Soc.

Tatehira, R., and Fukatsu, H. 1963. Radar and mesoscale analysis of a cold front. *Proc. Tenth Radar Meteor. Conf.*, pp. 188–96. Boston: Amer. Meteor. Soc.

Tatehira, R. and Itakura, H. 1966. Radar observations of typhoon Lucy by Mt. Fuji Radar. *Proc. Twelfth Conf. Radar Meteor.*, pp. 432–35. Boston: Amer. Meteor. Soc.

Tepper, M. 1959. Mesometeorology — the link between macroscale atmospheric motions and local weather. *Bull. Amer. Meteor. Soc.* 40:56–72.

Theiss, J. B. 1963. More target data with sideband coherent data. *Electronics* 36:40–43.

Theiss, J. B., and Kassander, A. R., Jr. 1963. A new pulsed-Doppler radar for cloud observations. *Proc. Tenth Radar Meteor. Conf.*, pp. 355–59. Boston: Amer. Meteor. Soc.

Uman, M. A. 1969. *Lightning.* New York: McGraw-Hill.

Uman, M. A., and Orville, R. E. 1964. Electron density measurement in lightning from stark broadening of $H\alpha$. *J. Geophys. Res.* 69:5151–54.

Van Vleck, J. H. 1947a. Absorption of microwaves by oxygen. *Phys. Rev.* 71:413–24.

————. 1947b. The absorption of microwaves by uncondensed water vapor. *Phys. Rev.* 71:425–33.

Vonnegut, B., and Moore, C. B. 1960. Giant electrical storms. In *Recent Advances in Atmospheric Electricity,* pp. 399–410. New York: Pergamon Press.

Voronov, G. S., and Gaivoronskii, I. I. 1969. Radar investigations of hail processes in Moldavia. *Meteor. i Gidrol., Moscow,* no. 4, pp. 48–53.

Vrana, N. 1961. Some characteristics of radar angel echoes. Res. Rept. no. 32. Cornell Univ. Ithaca, N.Y.: Ctr. for Radiophysics and Space Res.

Wallace, P. R. 1953. Interpretation of the fluctuating echo from randomly distributed scatterers. II. *Canadian J. Physics* 31:995–1009.

Warner, J., and Bowen, E. G. 1953. A new method of studying the fine structure of air movements in the free atmosphere. *Tellus* 5:36–41.

Watanabe, K. 1963. Vertical wind distribution and weather echo in the case of a typhoon situation. *Proc. Tenth Wea. Radar Conf.,* pp. 222–25. Boston: Amer. Meteor. Soc.

Watt, A. D., and Maxwell, E. L. 1957. Characteristics of atmospheric noise from 1 to 100 kc. *Proc. Inst. Radio Eng.* 45:787–94.

Weickmann, H. K. 1953. Observational data on the formation of precipitation in cumulonimbus clouds. In *Thunderstorm Electricity,* pp. 66–138. Chicago: Univ. of Chicago Press.

Wein, M., and Gunn, K. L. S. 1964. Operational CAPPI and facsimile: Twelve months of appraisal and development. *Proc. Eleventh Wea. Radar Conf.,* pp. 338–41. Boston: Amer. Meteor. Soc.

Weinstein, A. I., and MacCready, P. B., Jr. 1969. An isolated cumulus cloud modification project. *J. Appl. Meteor.* 8:936–47.

Wexler, H. 1947. Structure of hurricanes as determined by radar. *Ann. New York Acad. Sci.* 48:820–44.

Wexler, R. 1947. Radar detection of a frontal storm 18 June 1946. *J. Meteor.* 4:38–44.

———. 1948. Rain intensities by radar. *J. Meteor.* 5:171–73.

———. 1955. An evaluation of the physical effects in the melting layer. *Proc. Fifth Wea. Radar Conf.*, pp. 329–34. Fort Monmouth, N.J.: Engineering Lab., Signal Corps.

———. 1967. The mean fall speed and variance of hail as detected by Doppler radar. *Proc. Fifth Conf. on Severe Local Storms.* pp. 178–82. Boston: Amer. Meteor. Soc.

———. 1968. Doppler radar measurements in a rainstorm with a spiral band structure. *Proc. Thirteenth Radar Meteor Conf.*, pp. 192–95. Boston: Amer. Meteor. Soc.

———. 1969. *Comments on the echo free vault.* Preprint vol. Sixth Conf. on Severe Local Storms., pp. 13–15. Boston: Amer. Meteor. Soc.

———. 1970. Doppler radar studies of storm motion. Final Rept., Allied Res. Associates, Inc. Bedford, Mass.: Air Force Cambridge Res. Lab.

Wexler, R., and Atlas, D. 1959. Precipitation generation cells. *J. Meteor.* 16:327–32.

———. 1963. Radar reflectivity and attenuation of rain. *J. Appl. Meteor.* 2:276–80.

Wexler, R.; Chmela, A. C.; and Armstrong, G. M. 1967. Wind field observations by Doppler radar in a New England snowstorm. *Mon. Wea. Rev.* 95:929–35.

Wiley, R. L.; Browning, K. A.; Joss, J.; and Waldvogel, A. 1970. Measurement of drop size distribution and vertical air motion in widespread rain using pulsed Doppler radar and disdrometer. Preprint vol. Fourteenth Radar Meteor. Conf., pp. 167–70. Boston: Amer. Meteor. Soc.

Wilk, K. E., and Kessler, E. 1970. Quantitative radar measurements of precipitation. *Meteor. Monographs* 11:315–29.

Wilk, K. E.; Watts, W. L.; Sirmans, D.; Lhermitte, R. M.; Kessler, E.; and Gray, K. C. 1967. The weather radar data system at the National Severe Storms Laboratory. *Proc. Fifth Conf. on Severe Local Storms,* pp. 14–23. Boston: Amer. Meteor. Soc. (Also Rept. no. 5, pt. 2, World Meteor. Organization, 1968.)

Williams, D. T. 1948. A surface micro-study of squall-line thunderstorms. *Monthly Wea. Rev.* 76:239–46.

Wilson, D. A. 1963. Drop size distribution as recorded by pulsed Doppler radar. Master's Thesis, Univ. of Arizona.

———. 1970. Doppler radar studies of boundary layer wind profile and turbulence in snow conditions. Preprint vol. Fourteenth Radar Meteor. Conf., pp. 191–96. Boston: Amer. Meteor. Soc.

Wilson, J. W. 1964. Evolution of precipitation measurements with the WSR-57 radar. *J. Appl. Meteor.* 3:164–74.

———. 1966a. Storm-to-storm variability in the radar reflectivity rainfall rate relationship. *Proc. Twelfth Conf. Radar Meteor.*, pp. 229–33. Boston: Amer. Meteor. Soc.

———. 1966b. Movement and predictability of radar echoes. Tech. Memo. IERTM-NSSL-28. Norman, Okla.: Nat. Severe Storms Labs.

———. 1970. Integration of radar and rainfall data for improved rainfall measurement. *J. Appl. Meteor.* 9:489–97.

Wilson, J. W., and Kessler, E., III. 1963. Use of radar summary maps for weather analysis and forecasting. *J. Appl. Meteor.* 2:1–11.

Woodley, W. L. 1970. Precipitation results from a pyrotechnic cumulus seeding experiment. *J. Appl. Meteor.* 9:242–57.

Woodley, W., and Herndon, A. 1970. A raingage evaluation of the Miami reflectivity rainfall rate relation. *J. Appl. Meteor.* 9:258–64.

Woodward, E. W. 1959. The motion in and around isolated thermals. *Quart. J. Roy. Meteor. Soc.* 85:144–51.

Workman, E. J., and Reynolds, S. E. 1949. Electrical activity as related to thunderstorm cell growth. *Bull. Amer. Meteor. Soc.* 30:142–44.

Zawadzki, I. I., and Ballantyne, E. 1970. HARPI: A new weather radar display. *Quart. J. Roy. Meteor. Soc.* 96:144.

Zwack, P., and Anderson, C. 1970. 25 July 1969: Showers and continuous precipitation. Preprint vol. Fourteenth Radar Meteor. Conf., pp. 335–38. Boston: Amer. Meteor. Soc.

Index